YSEC Yearbook of Socio-Economic Constitutions

Volume 2024

The broad theme of the series revolves around the constitutional frameworks for economic activities and their interaction with the social sphere. It is this very interaction this Yearbook strives to focus on. At the same time, it is this focus which distinguishes it from other formats in the field. The reference to "constitutions" mirrors the Yearbook's ambition to contribute to a better understanding of those legal rules which provide the very foundations for our economic and social well-being within a community governed by a constitution, irrespective of whether on the local, national, regional, or global level. The Yearbook aims to, first and foremost, provide a forum for doctrinal legal treatment of the questions that various socio-economic constitutions are faced with in today's globalized context, while at the same time remain open to neighbouring disciplines to the extent that they inform the doctrinal treatment. For further information please visit https://www.ysec-yearbook.eu/.

Steffen Hindelang • Stefan Korte • Nils Schaks
Editors

YSEC Yearbook of Socio-Economic Constitutions 2024

What are Socio-Economic Constitutions?

Springer

Editors
Steffen Hindelang
Department of Law
Uppsala University
Uppsala, Sweden

Stefan Korte
German University of Administrative Sciences
Speyer, Germany

Nils Schaks
Faculty of Law
University of Basel
Basel, Switzerland

ISSN 2662-7124 ISSN 2662-7132 (electronic)
YSEC Yearbook of Socio-Economic Constitutions
ISBN 978-3-031-89153-3 ISBN 978-3-031-89154-0 (eBook)
https://doi.org/10.1007/978-3-031-89154-0

This Springer imprint is published by the registered company Springer Nature Switzerland AG
The registered company address is: Gewerbestrasse 11, 6330 Cham, Switzerland

Preface

The fifth volume of the Yearbook of Socio-Economic Constitutions (YSEC Yearbook) is dedicated to a comprehensive examination of the defining characteristics of socio-economic constitutions. The numerous shifts and upheavals in global economies in recent years, away from liberalism towards geo-economics, prompt a closer examination of the phenomenon of socio-economic constitutions, which lends its name to the YSEC Yearbook.

The concept of a socio-economic constitution is one that is susceptible to a multitude of interpretations. Similarly, there is considerable diversity of opinion regarding the continued relevance of socio-economic considerations, or even the legal requirements of a constitution. In German discourse, for instance, this pair of terms is most closely aligned with the concept of *Wirtschaftsverfassung*, which is inextricably linked to the system of the social market economy, as coined in the aftermath of the Second World War. The ideological foundation of this economic system is formed by the understanding that neither a purely market-based nor a purely planned system is ultimately convincing in socio-political terms. In light of this, a third way was put forth: while a fundamental societal consensus in favour of competition necessitates individual freedoms, the latter are to be "socially contained". Therefore, state intervention in market activities is not an end in itself; rather, it is committed to the implementation of socio-political standards within the aforementioned market activities.

However, this third way is not precisely defined and allows for flexibility in its application over time and in different contexts. The contributions from our authors in this yearbook reflect this. The YSEC Yearbook contains articles on various jurisdictions, including South Korea, South Africa, Switzerland, Belgium, Germany, Sweden, and France, as well as articles on topics such as investment and competition law and constitutional values.

The chapters are structured to facilitate a comprehensive and systematic understanding of the intricate interrelationship between socio-economic and constitutional principles. They commence with an examination of foundational theoretical frameworks, progress to an analysis of different national models, and culminate in an investigation of contemporary global challenges.

Kristjánsson's examination of the difficulties in reconciling incommensurable constitutional values establishes a theoretical foundation for comprehending the inherent tensions in socio-economic constitutional frameworks.

Among the various jurisdictions examined, South Africa's model of transformative constitutionalism, as presented by *Liebenberg*, is particularly noteworthy. It represents a pioneering example of socio-economic constitutionalism in practice, emphasising the state's obligations to redress historical inequities and establishing a foundation for the practical application of socio-economic rights.

The constitutional model of the Swedish welfare state, as discussed by *Wilske*, illustrates a constitutional model influenced by EU law, which embodies socio-economic justice within a deeply embedded welfare framework.

Grégoire's analysis of France, Germany, and Belgium provides further insight into the European context, where constitutional courts strive to maintain economic neutrality while limiting state intervention. This approach allows for the protection of market principles while facilitating the accommodation of certain social objectives.

The approach taken in Switzerland, as explored by *Baumann* and *Winistörfer*, is distinct from interventionist models. It involves balancing a market-driven constitution with a policy of neutrality, thereby addressing the role of constitutional principles in global trade contexts. However, as international pressures intensify (e.g., sanctions), Switzerland confronts the challenge of reconciling its neutrality with demands for heightened regulation. Similarly, *Chang*'s examination of South Korea illustrates the complexities of integrating international treaties into national economic law, underscoring the tension between global commitments and domestic interests.

The following two chapters on EU law illustrate the manner in which European regulation undergoes modification in response to the emergence of novel challenges. In their chapter, *Weiß* and *Furculita* extend the discussion by examining how the EU is increasingly aligning trade and investment with social and environmental objectives, marking a significant advancement in socio-economic constitutionalism. *Franck*'s analysis demonstrates the EU's evolving approach to incorporating climate concerns within merger control. This approach seeks to balance consumer welfare with sustainability in competition law. This field of law has traditionally focused on fair competition, rather than the protection of other common goods.

In conclusion, *Yuan*'s chapter addresses the contemporary challenge of foreign investment screening, where economic and national security concerns converge, reflecting the intricate interplay between global economic interdependence and national sovereignty.

This transition from theory to specific national and regional models and then to globalised challenges aims to provide readers with a coherent overview of the diverse nature of socio-economic constitutionalism in a globalised world.

Uppsala, Sweden — Steffen Hindelang
Speyer, Germany — Stefan Korte
Basel, Switzerland — Nils Schaks
November 2024

Contents

Incommensurability, Comparativism, and Value Hybridism in Constitutional Theory

Hafsteinn Dan Kristjánsson

Contents

H. D. Kristjánsson (✉)
Law Department, Reykjavik University, Reykjavik, Iceland

Balliol College, University of Oxford, Oxford, United Kingdom
e-mail: hafsteinnk@ru.is

S. Hindelang et al. (eds.), *YSEC Yearbook of Socio-Economic Constitutions 2024*, YSEC Yearbook of Socio-Economic Constitutions (2025) 2024: 1–36, https://doi.org/10.1007/16495_2024_70, Published online: 26 February 2025

Abstract Many constitutionally (and internationally) protected rights are premised on the assumption that different values can be balanced. A prominent theory along those lines is Robert Alexy's theory of constitutional rights. However, that is far from obvious if there are multiple basic values that are *incommensurable*. Maybe the solution is Ruth Chang's *comparativism*. There are, though, reasons to be wary of so-called 'covering values' in light of which, she claims, that options can be compared. Instead, it is suggested, that the path forward is *value hybridism*. According to that view, different basic values can be compared overall *to an extent* simply in virtue of sharing whatever makes them vales. Beyond that there is no common measurement to make *overall* qualitative value judgments of the specific evaluative characteristics of each basic value. Apart from sharing to an extent whatever makes them values, they are, after all, distinct values. Nevertheless, they can be compared in light of constructed standards, such as social roles we occupy, within the context of pursuing a coherent life plan (for individuals) and a coherent well-ordered society (for political communities). They are 'locally' comparable in that sense even though there is no covering value in the normative domain determining their relations at the most fundamental level. Value judgments should be mutually supportive and there is a back-and-forth relationship between them. These claims can vindicate the structure of constitutionally protected rights in part but also bring their limits to light. Norms on balancing different principles and deciding on their limits are constructed standards. The claims can also have consequences for doctrines of margins of appreciation.

1 Introduction

The structure of many constitutionally protected rights, as well as human rights in international treaties, and the corresponding methodology to determine whether they have been violated is premised on the assumption that *different values* can be *balanced*. For instance, in a defamation case, freedom of expression and the right to privacy must be balanced to decide which right *weighs* more in the circumstance. The right to property can be limited by law that is *necessary* to pursue public interests.[1] Proportionality tests in general involve, if not explicitly, then implicitly,

[1] Here I have in mind rights in and similar to those found in the European Convention on Human Rights (ECHR), see Articles 8 (right to privacy), 10 (freedom of expression), and 1 of Protocol

the act of balancing different values. Whether an act is proportionate, that is goes further than is necessary to achieve a legitimate aim, depends not only on the values pursued but also, at least implicitly, the values sacrificed. Categorical and absolute rights, too, tend to entail an implicit balancing exercise to determine their scope.[2] Only acts above a certain threshold of seriousness count, for example, as torture, inhumane, or degrading punishment or treatment.[3] This structure is deep. Our very image of Lady Justice has her holding *scales*, which represent a balancing exercise done with a single measurement. Robert Alexy's prominent theory of constitutional rights is an excellent example of this approach. He claims that principles, as he defines them, can be balanced and that certain balancing and collision 'laws' stem from the very structure of principles. And the principle of proportionality follows logically from that structure. Considering all of this, it is of the utmost importance whether different values, or principles that reflect values, can, indeed, be balanced in this way.

It is far from clear that values or principles can be balanced, especially if *value pluralism* is true. How should we, for example, balance property and public health? They appear to be (or engage with) different values. Naturally, the question arises *in virtue of what* should these judgments be made? As Joseph Raz and John Finnis, among others, have highlighted, sometimes values are *incommensurable* because there is no common yardstick to measure them.[4] If incommensurability of values is true, then it may seriously undermine the structure of constitutionally protected rights and the methodology for determining them appears to be a façade. The very exercise of balancing rights, in so far as it involves comparing different values, crumbles since values are, on this view, incommensurate. When all is said and done, the judge is simply *choosing* whichever result he prefers. Principles of proportionality do not *really* limit the government or judges. After all, assessing the proportionality of an act cannot be done if it involves different values that cannot be measured in light of a common yardstick. At the end of the day, the judge chooses to either favour freedom of expression or the right to privacy *or* emphasis either property rights or public interests. But in many cases, there is no correct answer. There are no (definitive or conclusive) reasons to favour one option over the other. The situation is *underdetermined*. Our image of Lady Justice is, on this view, wrong: often there are *no scales* to perform these judgments (and the very symbol of scales may also be misleading).[5]

No. 1 (peaceful enjoyment of property) as well as the Charter of Fundamental Rights of the European Union. Something similar applies to other rights than human rights, such as the *four freedoms* in European Union law, that is the free movement of goods (Article 34 and 35), services (Article 56), persons (Article 45 and 49), and capital (Article 63) of the Treaty on the Functioning of the European Union.

[2]For absolute rights, see e.g., Articles 2 (right to life) and 3 (right against torture) in the ECHR. For categorical rights, see e.g., the f1st Amendment of the U.S. Constituton on free speech.

[3]See in this contex Article 3 of the ECHR.

[4]See e.g., Raz (1999), p. 46, and Finnis (1987), pp. 373–376.

[5]Chang (2017), p. 11, discusses whether balancing on a scale is appropriate for values.

Curiously, we sometimes make value-judgments with ease despite lacking a common measurement. Sometimes the choice appears clear to us because one option has much more value than the other even if the values are different. Why is that?

One answer might be Ruth Chang's *comparativism*. According to her, values are not commensurate, since that is not how values in the normative domain work, but they are, nonetheless, *comparable*. We can compare them in light of a *covering value* that encompasses both of the values at stake. While this approach supports the structure and methodology of constitutionally protected rights, it can be doubted whether covering values commonly exist, especially at the level of human rights. Is there a covering value that encompasses freedom of expression and the right to privacy, property and public health, consumer interests, the welfare of children and animals, environmental protection, and everything else we value and treat as parts of the common good or the rights of others? If there are different *basic or fundamental* values, then there are no further values 'beyond' them. That is what makes them basic.[6] And if the basic values are multiple, then comparativism is limited in an important way; we can only compare when we do not engage with different *basic* values. Furthermore, there are reasons to think that some candidates for covering values are *composites* of different values, or *empty shells*, and as such, merely placeholders for however we make judgments in light of different values. And they might not even be 'real' values at all but that depends on what we consider values to be.

Since comparativism appears to be limited in this regard, we are confronted again with our original challenge of incommensurability. The chapter argues for a solution in the form of *value hybridism*. Values are comparable *to an extent* simply in light of whatever makes them values but beyond that there is no common measurement. Value-judgments are not made in light of a common yardstick (they are not commensurate) or compared in light of a covering value. Instead, thin or limited value-judgments are made in the following way: we can recognize whether an option is valuable (sense that it has a value) and whether it is greater or lesser. These are *valuableness judgments*, and we can compare options in this way even if they engage incommensurate values. We make the judgment with the very sense or capacity that allows us to sense or recognize their value in the first place.

However, once the valuableness of options is roughly similar, these kinds of judgments are of limited help to us. A more fine-grained judgment of the specific qualitative characteristics of each value matters. It no longer becomes a question of whether something matters *a lot* or *very little* for our health but that it matters for our *health* as opposed to, for instance, the beauty in our life. These are *qualitative value judgments*, that is judgments that depend on a further assessment of the specific evaluative characteristics of whatever value is engaged. The values have some quality or 'uniqueness', which makes it the case that they are incommensurate and, at least if they are basic, incomparable overall in light of a covering value.

---

[6] See e.g., Finnis (1980), p. 59 onwards.

In these situations, there is space to choose to emphasis some values over others by setting and pursuing some goals, which is done as a part of and within the context of a particular coherent life plan pursued (for individuals) or in the pursuit of a coherent well-ordered society (for political communities). While there is no hierarchy among the basic values, yardsticks, or covering values to settle the right course of action determined beforehand, that is by gleaning at the structure of values in the normative domain, there is a factual context here and now and we have an agency to help us make these judgments *for us.* We can choose to emphasis certain values in light of our image of who we are, how we should treat others, what sort of life we should lead, and in the context of the life we have led up until now. The same applies to political communities. This is where politics enters the picture.

These claims about value hybridism and the back-and-forth relationship between value judgments vindicate the structure of constitutionally protected rights in a political state and the corresponding methodology, in part, but they also bring its limits to light. As such the claims may cast a light on and have consequences for *doctrines of margins of appreciation*, that is when and how much discretion courts should grant the legislature and the government. They also help us to see the truth in and the limits of Alexy's theory.

We will begin by exploring the structure of constitutionally and internationally protected rights, chiefly human rights, and ask what sort of rights they could be from the perspective of different legal theories, namely, legal positivism and antipositivism. Robert Alexys' theory of constitutionally protected rights will, then, be discussed since it has much explanatory force for legal practice in many jurisdictions, such as the case law of the European Court of Human Rights, the European Court of Justice, and the Federal Constitutional Court of Germany, that all balance different human rights as well as decide on their limits in light of other interests or values through a proportionality analysis that largely or roughly maps onto Alexy's theory. Despite its explanatory force, it will be argued that Alexy's theory depends on his particular definition of principles that can be questioned. Moreover, it is based on assumptions regarding the relationship of principles or values that do not hold, at least not to large enough extent, if basic values are incommensurate. Referring to the intensity of the realization of the value in the circumstances does not solve the problem since there is not yardstick to compare them overall if they are incommensurate.

Since Alexy's theory of constitutional rights has certain limitations, a vindication of the structure and methodology of constitutionally protected rights in some jurisdictions must be sought, at least partly, elsewhere. To do that, we must embark upon a journey into the normative domain of values to seek answers, which can, then, by tied back to issues in constitutional law and theory at the end. Only the initial steps in developing value hybridism will be taken here but much work remains to be done for a fully worked out theory. Moreover, only the first moves in applying value hybridism to constitutionally protected rights will be made here.

2 Constitutional Rights and Principles

2.1 The Structure and Corresponding Methodology of Constitutional Rights

In many jurisdictions, especially European, constitutionally protected rights, as well as human rights protected in international treaties, have the following structure: Some interest or value is protected to some extent, i.e., the right has a protective scope. The starting point or the general rule is that an individual should enjoy that interest (to that extent). For instance, according to the opening line of paragraph 1 of Article 9 of the ECHR: 'Everyone has the right to freedom of thought, conscience and religion.' However, the rights are limitable or an interference with the right is justifiable if certain conditions are met. Often, they are (i) being based on law, (ii) they must pursue a *legitimate objective*, and (iii) they must not go beyond what is *necessary* (i.e., be *disproportionate*). Sometimes these conditions are laid down specifically for the right in question. Returning to Article 9 of the ECHR, paragraph 2 states:

> Freedom to manifest one's religion or beliefs shall be subject only to such limitations as are prescribed by law and are necessary in a democratic society in the interests of public safety, for the protection of public order, health or morals, or for the protection of the rights and freedoms of others.

Other times, there are general limitation clauses. Paragraph 1 of Article 52 of the Charter of Fundamental Rights of the European Union is an example, but it states:

> Any limitation on the exercise of the rights and freedoms recognized by this Charter must be provided for by law and respect the essence of those rights and freedoms. Subject to the principle of proportionality, limitations may be made only if they are necessary and genuinely meet objectives of general interest recognised by the Union or the need to protect the rights and freedoms of others.

To assess the proportionality of a limitation or an interreference, more precisely, necessity in the narrow sense, the right in question must be balanced against the legitimate objective pursued. For example, a limitation of or an interference with the freedom of religion must be balanced against, for example, public safety or the protection of public order. The underlying assumption of this legal structure is that the disparate interests, or values, can be balanced. Only an interference, which pursues, for instance, public order that outweighs the interest or value in practicing one's religion in the circumstances in question can it be justified.

Moreover, paragraph 2 of Article 9 of the ECHR refers to the rights and freedoms of others, but they include the other rights protected by the Convention. The same applies to, for example, Article 8 (right to privacy) and Article 10 (freedom of expression). This legal structure requires Convention rights to be balanced against each other. To assess whether a freedom of expression can be limited by someone else's right to privacy, the latter right must outweigh the former in the circumstances in question. The same applies to whether the right to privacy can be limited by someone else's freedom of expression.

The same legal structure is used for other types of rights, such as the *four freedoms* of European Union Law. As an example, Article 36 of the Treaty on the Functioning of the European Union lays down the conditions for limiting the freedom to import and export goods according to Articles 34 and 35 and refers to specific objectives in that regard, including public morality and the protection of health and life of humans. The legal structure assumes that the interests in importing and exporting goods to other Member States can be balanced against public morality and the protection of health and life of humans.

2.2 *Constitutional Rights and Legal Positivism*

To assess whether the balancing exercise required by constitutionally and internationally protected rights, as the ones mentioned above, is possible, we must have some inkling about the nature of law. According to the *social facts thesis* (the *strong sources thesis*), which is the foundation of the school of thought often called *exclusive or hard legal positivism* and is associated with scholars such as Joseph Raz, all law is source-based, i.e., the existence and content of the law is solely determined by social facts.[7] It follows that Article 9 of the ECHR, and provisions like that, do not and cannot incorporate or contain a (genuine) moral principle. Moral principles cannot be the law. There are, at least, two possible implications of this.

First, constitutional provisions do not lay down moral tests for law, even though they have *morally-sounding* terms. Rather, they have a special *legal* meaning ascertained by interpretation in accordance with the relevant rules of interpretation and that meaning is further fleshed out by precedents (more social facts), if they are identified as sources of law in the legal system in question.[8] If a constitutional provision that lays down a human right is 'merely' *homonymous* to some moral principle, but not itself a moral principle, it is far from obvious that the right contains any value or weight that already 'exists' in a way that a moral value does. Legal principles or values are constructed or artificial. Freedom of expression as a purely legal construct can have a different place and weight in different legal structures. For a textualist and an originalist, such as Antonin Scalia, solving questions of constitutional rights is, presumably, simply a matter of ascertaining the meaning of the text.[9] However, it is unclear how such an approach can accommodate the balancing exercise required by the legal structure of these rights without involving law-creation by the judges.

---

[7] See e.g., Raz (1979), pp. 37–45.

[8] Green (2012), pp. xl–xli.

[9] Scalia (2018), p. 23 and onwards.

Secondly, constitutional provisions like these could be understood as *reference clauses*, i.e., clauses that refer to considerations 'outside of' law, including morality (either conventional or critical). This does not mean, for the exclusive legal positivists, that moral considerations are a part of the law. Rather, law refers to morality (or directs the judge to apply morality). So, moral principles must be consulted in the *application* of the law.[10] On this view, genuine moral principles or values can have a role and their 'nature' matters for constitutional law and theory.

According to the school of thought sometimes called *inclusive or soft legal positivism* and associated with scholars such as H.L.A. Hart, moral principles can be among the criteria of legal validity if they are authorized or referred to by sources of law.[11] For example, a constitution (a social fact) can lay down a moral principle. Some human right provisions could be like that. On this picture, (genuine) moral principles or values can have a role as a part of the law.

2.3 Constitutional Rights and Antipositivism

Ronald Dworkin has, for example, argued that the original meaning of the Bill of Rights of the U.S. Constitution is laying down abstract principles rather than dated and concrete rules.[12] Seen in light of his larger theory, constitutional provisions must be interpreted as a whole in light of a scheme of genuine moral principles and the principle of integrity can be seen as the 'master' principle.[13] From this perspective, the so-called balancing exercise seems to be a part of 'interpretation' (in the wide sense Dworkin uses the term), where each part of the constitution is interpreted in light of all the other parts. On this view, it is easy to see the role of genuine moral principles and values for identifying constitutional rights.

2.4 Alexy's Theory of Constitutional Rights

The preceding sub-sections have only given a cursory view of the possible roles of moral principles or values according to some theorists associated with inclusive and exclusive legal positivism and antipositivism. Two points have emerged. Either constitutional rights are purely legal, i.e., non-moral, and it is unclear how the balancing exercise is possible, or moral principles or values have some role. If the latter holds true, then that requires us to understand them in more detail, but we'll

---

[10] Raz (2009), pp. 193–195.

[11] Hart (2012), e.g., p. 247.

[12] Dworkin (2018), p. 122.

[13] Dworkin (1986), e.g., p. 93.

dive into that in the next section. Before we do that, let us briefly discuss Robert Alexy's prominent theory of constitutional rights.

According to Alexy, principles are *optimization commands or requirements*; 'they are norms that command that something be realized to the highest degree that is actually and legally possible.'[14] Legal possibility refers to countervailing rules and principles.[15] Moreover, constitutional principles have equal status. When principles collide, they must balanced considering the circumstances. The principle which is outweighed is not invalid.[16] Contrariwise, rules apply in an all-or-nothing fashion. They are definitive commands.[17] When rules collide, there is either an exception to the rule or the rule that does not apply, for example, because of priority rules like *lex specialis* and *lex posterior*, is invalid. The distinction between principles and rules is not one of degree, as Raz claims, but of quality, according to Alexy.[18]

Moreover, according to Alexy, the structure of principles implies the principle of proportionality; it 'logically follows from the nature of principles'.[19] Not only that, certain balancing and collision laws flow from this structure as well.[20] Referring to a specific case concerning the Basic Law, Alexy claims that the question in the balancing process is 'which of the requirements having *equal status in the abstract* had the *greater weight* in the *concrete case*.'[21] Alexy beliefs that Carl Schmitt's 'tyranny of values' can be solved by 'factoring the intensity of realization into the values as well as their rank'.[22]

According to this, principles of equal status are weighed according to the *intensity of their realization* in the circumstances in question and two principles that collide are *optimised* (i.e., realized to the highest degree that is actually and legally possible) according to their weight in that circumstance. Alexy gives us a Law of Balancing:

> The greater the degree of non-satisfaction of, or detriment to, one principle, the greater must be the importance of satisfying the other.[23]

Principles have *relative* but not *absolute* weight, he says, they cannot be determined independently.[24]

While Alexy states that 'hard' ordering, i.e., being intersubjectively binding, does not exist, 'soft orderings', can be created in two ways. First, by *prima facie*

---

[14] Alexy (2000), pp. 294–295, and Alexy (2002), pp. 47 and 50–54.

[15] Alexy (2000), p. 295.

[16] Alexy (2002), pp. 50–54.

[17] Alexy (2000), pp. 295–297, and Alexy (2002), pp. 48 and 49–50.

[18] Alexy (2002), p. 48.

[19] Alexy (2002), p. 66.

[20] Alexy (2000), pp. 296–299, and Alexy (2002), pp. 50–54.

[21] Alexy (2002), p. 51.

[22] Alexy (2002), p. 98 for quote, and for discussion pp. 98–99.

[23] Alexy (2002), p. 102.

[24] Alexy (2002), p. 102.

preferences in favour of particular values and principles that establish burdens of arguments. Secondly, by a 'network of concrete preference decisions', which appears in, for example, case-law.[25]

Alexy states that the open-ended manner of the catalogue of rights in the Basic Law opens up the legal system to morality.[26] Moreover, 'the most important principles of modern natural law have been incorporated into the constitution and thus also into positive laws' and the 'constitution makers tried 'to realize the idea of justice in the Basic Law."[27] For Alexy, 'general practical argumentation is a necessary component of constitutional rights discourse.'[28]

Interestingly, Alexy says that a theory of constitutional rights in the Basic law is *doctrinal*, since it focuses on enacted law of a particular legal system.[29] Nonetheless, many of his arguments are *general*, i.e., they apply to the structure of principles and rules and logical inferences made from that structure. Moreover, he defines principles in a particular way. Therefore, they should apply to many other legal systems as well. His Law of Balancing, for instance, is not presented as a contingent, local methodological norm.

2.5 Some Observations

Several observation regarding Alexy's theory can be made. First, there are reasons to be wary of the fact that principles are *defined* in a way that accommodates and explains the balancing exercise. The Law of Balancing and the principle of proportionality 'logically' follow because Alexy has *stipulated* that principles operate in that way. We can, though, question whether principles, or values, should be realised to the 'highest degree' possible. Why should principles, or values, not simply be promoted, satisfied minimally or to large enough degree? Alexy is clear that principles and values are distinct; a system of values concerns the best but a system of principles what ought to be.[30] Nonetheless, an example concerning values may be helpful in this context.

Suppose I choose to play tennis over a museum trip repeatedly. I choose to emphasise the value of play over aesthetic beauty in a way that does not optimize them. Nonetheless, I have not done anything wrong by that alone. I should act in a way that promotes or fosters values and not demotes, degrades, or destroys them. And while I should have some balance of values in my life, it is far from clear that I should optimize them. The same applies to a collision of the freedom of expression

---

[25] Alexy (2002), p. 99.

[26] Alexy (2002), p. 4.

[27] Alexy (2002), p. 366.

[28] Alexy (2002), p. 387.

[29] Alexy (2002), p. 6.

[30] Alexy (2002), p. 92.

and the right to privacy. Balancing them in an optimising way is not a conceptual or logical necessity but a *contingent* methodological norm. Principles as expressions of or standards reflecting values need not necessarily be optimising standards.

And just because principles enjoy equal status, i.e., they both are protected by the constitution, it does not follow that they should be balanced in an optimizing way. It is perfectly conceivable that one principle is considered to be *lex generalis* and the other *lex specialis*, i.e., they are treated in a way that Alexy thinks only applies to rules.[31]

Secondly, principles, or values, cannot simply be compared in light of the intensity of the realization of them in the circumstances in question if they are *incommensurate*. Intensity alone does not do the trick. If the values are incommensurate, they cannot be compared overall since there is no measurement in virtue of which to make the judgment and there is nothing that makes it the case that we should choose the value most intensely engaged.

Let us take an example about values again. If I choose to become a lawyer because it pays slightly better, even if I would have an amazing and much richer intellectual life as poorer philosopher, I have not made a balancing mistake. If I am in Rome and choose to play soccer over seeing Michealangelo's Sistine Chapel, even though I played soccer earlier that day, I have not made a balancing mistake. Alexy's mistake is to belief that values (and by extension principles) are comparable overall simply in virtue of how intensely they are engaged in the circumstances and without being compared in light of some metric, measurement, or yardstick. If values are *plural* and *incommensurable*, then intensity of realization is insufficient.

The first two points can be brought together in the following way: principles should not necessarily be defined in exactly the way Alexy does, and balancing as optimising in light of the intensity of realization does not necessarily or logically follow from the structure of principles and their equal status. Rather, it is a contingent methodological norm, or as Alexy himself notes on the theory in general, *doctrinal*. Even though the arguments are *general*, they are *definitional* and involve *logical* inferences, and, therefore, have a wider scope, it is plausible that Alexy's view of principles and their balancing is based on the particular structure of principles in the Basic Law and their limitation clauses.

Thirdly, it can be doubted that the principle of proportionality 'logically follows' from the structure of principles. It is easy to think of a legal system with something we might call principles without the proportionality principle and without thinking that some logical or conceptual mistake has been made. And even if the principle would 'logically' follow, it is not obvious why that principle would be 'law' if it would not based on a source of law identified by a norm of recognition. In other

[31] While Alexy's theory could accommodate such a situation under the rubric of 'legal possibility', it does not fit well with his discussion of the contrast between rules and principles. Possibly, Alexy could argue that equal status means that neither can take precedence over the other unless they are outweighed.

words, the principle of proportionality is not a logical or conceptual necessity of principles but a contingent norm.

Fourthly, it can be rejected that inapplicable rules in conflicts are invalid. Now, there might be a norm of recognition of a particular legal system to that effect, but it is not a feature of legal validity across all legal systems. A rule can exist and be valid in the sense that it has a basis in a source of law identified by a norm of recognition of the legal system even if it does not have legal effects according to its content, for example, because it conflicts with a more special rule (*lex specialis*). Another example is a national law that conflicts with a law of the European Union and is disapplied because of the principle of primacy. The national law, even if inapplicable, is not invalid.[32] Contrariwise, a principle that ranks lower than and conflicts with a constitutional principle (*lex superior*) can be invalid in a legal system where such a conflict is regulated by norms of recognition. There are, hence, reasons to reject Alexy's view of the validity of rules and principles in conflict-situations.

Moreover, instead of focusing on the structural features of rules and principles, which Dworkin focused on too in the beginning, the true distinction between the phenomena discussed by Dworkin boils not down to their (formal) structure but, instead, the difference between positive laws (represented as rules) and morality or genuine values (represented as principles): morality has different features than positive law.[33]

The assumption will be made in what follows, for the sake of discussion, that moral principles or values can be relevant for constitutional rights. The goal is to explore the nature of values with an eye to identify if and how they can be balanced as the structure of constitutional rights assumes. And it will be taken as a given, considering the discussion above, that the balancing of principles (and values) does not *merely* flow from formal/structural features of principles but, rather, how values relate to each other in the normative domain. We now turn to that issue.

3 Incommensurability, Value Pluralism, and Value Monism

3.1 Value Monism

We seem to be able to make rational choices and evaluative judgments even when confronted with different values. This may suggest that *value monism* is correct, but, very crudely put, according to that kind of view, there is a single fundamental value or a single intrinsically valuable property.[34] What could the *super-value* be?[35]

[32] For more on this view, see e.g., Kristjánsson (2023).

[33] Dworkin (1978), pp. 14–45.

[34] See e.g., Blum (2023), p. 627–628.

[35] For a suggestion that the value property is richness, see Kelly (2014). On value monism and the super-value, see e.g., Mason (2023), s. 4.2.

Suggestions include pleasure (hedonism) and satisfaction of one's preferences (preferentialism).[36] Neither appears to be a convincing candidate. It is difficult to identify a single value that accounts for all the other values. What value or value property could tie together as diverse values as beauty, play, and autonomy?

Moreover, it is unclear whether our evaluative judgments merely involve assessing the *quantity* of the super-value or also *qualities* of sub-values. John Stuart Mill, for example, claimed that there are higher and lower pleasures.[37] If it involves the latter, it is unclear how there can be different qualities of sub-values which are, nonetheless, traced back to one and the same super-value.

Further, value monism faces the objection of *rational regret* even when the choice is justified.[38] A legislator may rationally regret having to limit the citizens' freedom to protect them against dangers to their life and health stemming from COVID-19. In some cases, there is a *moral remainder* (or residue) because a choice to emphasis one value (life and health) involves a loss of another value (liberty).[39] But how could that be if there is only one value or one value property at the most fundamental level?

Further still, value monism does not seem to fit well with our experiences that *moral choices can be complex*, and we *value many kinds of things* in the world.[40] We love our family and friends, enjoy a beautiful painting, care about the environment, appreciate good food and wine, and cherish our privacy and autonomy.

3.2 Value Pluralism

Value pluralism, on the other hand, can explain rational regret, a moral remainder, the complexity of moral choices, as well our experiences that there are many different values. That is the school of thought, very roughly speaking, that there are at least several non-reducible, intrinsic values that are equal.[41] At the fundamental level, there is not a single value but multiple ones. And these values may conflict. A common example given is the tension between liberty and equality.[42]

However, as has already been noted, we seem to be able to make evaluative judgments that engage different values. How are we able to do that if the values are different?[43] We are also faced with the uncomfortable question of what makes the

---

[36] Blum (2023), p. 628.

[37] See e.g., Mill (2002), p. 241, Chang (1997), p. 16, and Blum (2023), pp. 637–638.

[38] See Williams (1973), pp. 166–186, and Stocker (1990). See also Mason (2023), s. 2.

[39] Mason (2023), s. 2.2.

[40] Blum (2023), pp. 628–629.

[41] See e.g., Finnis (1980), p. 93, and Kelly (2014). For a good overview, see e.g., Mason (2023).

[42] For a discussion of how they do no conflict, see Dworkin (2011), pp. 2–4 and more generally pp. 351–379.

[43] Blum (2023), p. 629.

different values *values* at all. We are left wondering: is there something deeper that explains all the values?[44]

Value monism and pluralism are not simply about *how many* fundamental values there are but the *relations* among them, at least at the most fundamental level.

3.3 Incommensurability

Let us stick with value pluralism for the moment. If there are multiple basic values that can conflict, the question arises whether there is, nevertheless, a *common measurement* (scales) in virtue of which an evaluative judgment can be made. If the answer to the question is yes, then there is a risk that such a theory ultimately collapses into value monism, at least if the measurement turns out to be a single value at the fundamental level. However, if there is no shared unit of measurement or a single metric to balance the values, then they are *incommensurate*.[45] What does that mean?

Take the following example. You can choose between a burger or a salad for dinner. You think the burger is tastier, but the salad is healthier.[46] If you choose based on tastiness, then you grab the burger. It wins on that metric. But if you want to be healthy, you choose the salad. You can *either* choose on the bases of tastiness *or* healthiness. However, there does not seem to be any *yardstick* that covers both tasty and healthy in virtue of which you can *compare them overall*. Just as there does not seem to be any measurement that covers at once the shortest and the funniest novel.[47] The values are incommensurate because there is no overall metric to measure tasty or healthy *or* shortest and funniest. You can either go for tasty or healthy *or* shortest or funniest, but you cannot make an overall judgment.

Now we face a problem. If values are incommensurate, then it has consequences for our ability to make rational choices since we are *unable to compare options overall*.[48] The reasons that speak in favour of choosing the burger are not stronger than the reasons for choosing the salad and vice versa. If there are few basic values, then, perhaps, the scope of the problem is small but if there are many fundamental values, then it is a pervasive problem.

Incommensurability of values has consequences beyond our dinner choice. It matters for constitutional law and theory as well. To the extent that human rights and proportionality tests involve evaluative judgments with different and incommensurate basic values, we cannot make an overall judgment and there are no reasons to favour one option over the other. Alexy's reference to the intensity of realization in

---

[44] See e.g., Mason (2023) s. 3.3, and Kelly (2014).

[45] See e.g., Chang (1997), p. 1.

[46] Chang (2016), pp. 215.

[47] Finnis (1987), pp. 373–376.

[48] Chang (1997), pp. 1 and 3.

the comparison cannot overcome this problem. The legislature, the administrative authorities, or the judge simply must *choose* which option to pursue, that is to choose to favour one value over another. On this view, politics is about which values to favour and which to sacrifice without there being reasons to choose one over the other. The outlook appears to be bleak.

4 Comparativism

Maybe there is a light at the end of the tunnel. Ruth Chang has proposed an intriguing theory that, at the least, lessens the problem. Only a very rough and ready summary of some of the claims she makes follows.

According to Chang, we should not think of values in terms of *commensurability* since that indicates a unit of measurement more suitable for the physical world (the non-evaluative world), where we measure length, width, height, weight, and so on. We measure a bag of potatoes in kilograms and can weigh it against a bag of flower. Things are different in the normative domain. We should replace cardinal ranking for (rough) ordinary ranking.[49] Hence, we should replace the idea of commensurability (in this narrow sense) for *comparability*.

Options are comparable when there is a positive value relation between them in respect of some value.[50] For example, one option is *better*, *worse*, or *equal* to another. Chang argues, though, that we should reject the *Trichotomy Thesis*, according to which these three are the only positive value relations.[51] There is a fourth value relation, she claims, between options in the normative domain. They can be *on a par*.[52] Options are on a par when they are in the neighbourhood of some covering value in such a way we do not favour one over the other.[53] The *small improvements argument* suggests this. If the burger and the salad would have equal value, then we could tip the balance by making the burger tastier, for example, by adding cheese.[54] Curiously, making small improvements to the tastiness of the burger does not tip the balance. The same applies to a choice of carrier between becoming a lawyer, which pays better, or a philosopher, which allows for greater pursuit of knowledge. If the options would be equal, then we could tip the balance by increasing the lawyer's salary. The reason why the balance is not tipped is that the burger and the salad or being a lawyer and philosopher have different evaluative characteristics. Moreover, we do not think that we can simply swap the burger for the salad or that it does not matter whether we become a lawyer or a philosopher. This,

[49] Chang (1997), p. 2, Chang (2016), pp. 217–220, and Chang (2017), pp. 6 and 11–12.

[50] Chang (1997), p. 4.

[51] Chang (1997), p. 4.

[52] Chang (1997), pp. 4–5, and Chang (2017), pp. 11–12.

[53] Chang (2017), p. 14.

[54] Chang (1997), pp. 23–27, and Chang (2017), pp. 1–5.

too, indicates that the options are not equal but on a par. So, options can be better, worse, equal, or on a par.

Furthermore, Chang claims that *comparability* justifies rational choice.[55] Every justifying reason has its force in virtue of comparison of alternatives.[56] Every choice situation is governed by a value.[57] Options are incomparable when none of the four positive value relations hold between them with respect to a covering value.[58] If options are *non-comparable*, then we are not in a choice situation. There is no choice to be made between eating a salad or a pencil for dinner.[59] Options are often comparable in a nominal-notable way.[60] For example, we can compare the tastiness of a burger to insects. However, the question we are interested in here is whether we can compare options overall. Chang answers the question in the affirmative. Different values can be compared in light of a *covering value* that covers both of them.[61] How does that work? Let us work with Chang's example.

Imagine that a university chair in philosophy becomes vacant. Two candidates apply. One has greater sensitivity to the history of the discipline, but the other is more original. The two candidates can, despite their disparate strengths and weaknesses, be compared in light of the covering value of *philosophical talent*. The value covers both historical sensitivity and originality.[62] The choice between the candidates is *hard* when one option is better in one aspect, but the other option is better in another aspect.[63] Neither option appears better overall. However, if one candidate has virtually no originality but only a slightly greater historical knowledge than the other candidate, which far exceeds him in originality, then the latter candidate is better *overall* in light of the covering value of philosophical talent.

Is it plausible that there are such covering values, especially since philosophers seem to have overlooked them? Chang claims that there are more covering values than we think. The reason why we have overlooked them is that they are *nameless*. We can, though, sense them and, perhaps, one day we will name them. The existence of the values does not depend on the accidental or contingent event of naming them.[64] Their existence is plausible, she says, because there must be something beyond the values and circumstances that gives the values their relative weight.[65] It cannot be merely further circumstances and the values do not 'put themselves

[55] Chang (1997), pp. 6 and 13, Chang (2016), p. 213, and Chang (2017) p. 8.

[56] Chang (1997), p. 12.

[57] Chang (1997), p. 7.

[58] Chang (1997), p. 6, and Chang (2017), p. 7.

[59] Chang (1997), pp. 29 and 33.

[60] Chang (1997), pp. 14–16.

[61] Chang (2009), p. 119, and Chang (1997), p. 5.

[62] Chang (2009), pp. 125–126, and Chang (2004).

[63] Chang (2017),

[64] Chang (1997), p. 32. Chang (2004).

[65] Chang (2009), p. 119.

together'.[66] For example, *sexual harassment* is a disvalue that, according to Chang, was not named until later.[67] In this context, it can be noted that Chang has a wide view of what counts as value. Among them are rules, rights, duties, obligations, and disvalues[68] as well as standards of excellence.[69]

It should be noted that comparativism is based on a two-tier approach. First, we choose a well-informed choice situation and, then, we make a choice in that situation.[70]

Importantly, there is, according to Chang, no good *simpliciter*, that is good full stop. A book is not simply good or bad. These kinds of judgments are made in terms of something. There is only goodness in a way.[71]

Lastly, reasons are *external* or *objective*, according to Chang, that is they are reasons in the virtue of goodness of something or a normative fact like a value, but not *internal* or *subjective*, that is reasons in virtue of our desires and that sort of things.[72] External reasons are given reasons.[73] They depend on what the facts in the world are, including facts about us. When the external reasons *run out*, we can, though, *create new reasons* by committing to an option. We do that by stipulating that something is a reason for us.[74] Those reasons are will-based. Since we can create new reasons or change the weight of existing reasons by committing to an option, we are not merely *passive* agents, who identify and respond to reasons given to us, but *active* agents that can create and change the weight of reasons. In so doing we *shape our identity* as opposed to drift through life.[75] For instance, we can choose to be healthy individuals and stipulate that the fact that the salad is healthy is the weightier reason for us. Chang's view is a hybrid of externalism (given-reasons) and will-based reasons (created reasons).[76]

---

[66] Chang (2009), pp. 136–138.

[67] Chang (2009), pp. 144–145, and Chang (2004).

[68] Chang (2009), p. 120.

[69] Chang (2004).

[70] Chang (2016), pp. 221–225.

[71] Thompson (1999), e.g. pp. 19 and 41.

[72] Among promiment internalists/subjectivits about reasons are Bernard Williams, and probably HLA Hart and John Rawls. See e.g., Chang (2013), p. 167. For a quick overview of internal and external reasons, see e.g., Finlay and Schroeder (2020).

[73] Among prominent externalists/objectivists about reasons are Plato, Derik Parfit, Joseph Raz, Thomas Nagel, T.M. Scanlon, and David Enoch. See e.g., Chang (2013), p. 167.

[74] See also Chang (2020a), p. 292.

[75] Chang (2020b).

[76] Chang (2013), pp. 163–187, 163, and 176–180, and Chang (2017), p. 15.

5 Observations

No knockdown arguments will be given here against comparativism. Instead, a few observations will be made about Chang's claims, and they will be used as starting points to state or develop positions.

5.1 Commensurability Is Dead. Long Live the Trichotomy Thesis

We should follow Chang's suggestion of *abandoning commensurability*, in the narrow sense described above, in the normative domain.[77] Values are not measured in a similar way as the weight of potatoes. Values are not measured in *units* of this or that. We do not *quantify* beauty into units, for example, when we assess the aesthetic value of a painting. 'This painting has 3,5 units of beauty and is, therefore, more beautiful than the other painting that only has 1 unit of beauty.' Moreover, value judgments do not only concern the quantity of the values engaged but also their specific evaluative characteristics. A proper deliberation concerning what to do is not simply adding and subtracting quantities of values.

Nevertheless, Chang has not given us sufficient reasons to reject the *Trichotomy Thesis*. What she describes as *parity* is just another way to be *equal*. Once we free ourselves of the shackles of the idea of commensurability and cardinal ranking in the normative domain, this becomes apparent. Being equal should not be equated with having the same unit or quantity as something else according to some common (cardinal) yardstick. The reason why equal and parity seem to have different properties is not because they are different value relations but because *what is being compared is different*. Comparing values is different from comparing potatoes in terms of their weight. Both the quantity and the qualities of the values compared (or the options compared in light of them) matter. This is especially true when we consider *overall* judgments of options in light of multiple considerations, such as tastiness and healthiness. Whether options are equal depends on an *overall* judgment of the intensity of the values and evaluative characteristics of the options but not a single metric that can be broken down to units of this or that.

The small improvements argument only suggests otherwise because it has a lingering residue of the idea of commensurability in the normative domain. The reason why adding cheese to the burger, and, thereby, making it tastier, does not tip the balance between the burger and the salad is because that is not the only relevant consideration in light of the covering value. However, if we made the burger healthier, for example, by adding lettuce or swapping the meat for a vegan meat, that might tip the balance. Making small improvements in the *evaluative*

[77] Chang (1997), p. 1. Namely a single scale of unit of value.

characteristics of the options might tip the balance whereas increasing the quantity of one value in small amounts, of which the option already has more, will not. That suggest that the options are, indeed, equal although they are equal in a different way than bags of potatoes are in terms of their weight.

As long as we are sensitive to the facts that what is being compared is different and it depends on an overall judgment of both quantity and qualities, not units according to a single metric, little or nothing is gained by adding a fourth value relation of parity.

If we were to insist that there is a fourth value relation, however, then there are reasons to explore why there are not even more value relations. Why are they not six? One for better, worse, and equal understood along the lines of units of measurement and then superior, inferior, and parity depending on our overall judgment considering a covering value that includes or is exclusive made in light of their evaluative characteristics. After all, if options can be *equal* in more than one way, why cannot they be *better* or *worse* in more ways, too?

5.2 No Covering Values for Basic Values

Sometimes we compare values in light of a more comprehensive value. This is the situation when two values are *not basic* but sub-values or instrumental. I can compare my freedom to make a contract and my freedom to dispose of my property in light of my autonomy or liberty.

Some values are basic or fundamental, though. There are no values 'beyond' them. That is what makes them basic. So, if a covering value is meant to be *more fundamental* than the basic values it covers, they are not basic. But if they are, then there is no further fundamental covering value. Comparativism seems to be limited when we compare different *basic* values on the assumption that they are multiple.

5.3 No Super-Value for All Other Values

Now, if there tends to be a more fundamental covering value, like philosophical talent for originality and historical sensitivity, we might be tempted to think that there is an even more comprehensive covering value for that and athletic talent, linguistic talent, and so on. And we might be further tempted to think that there is a covering value for the different types of talents just mentioned and being courteous and nice. This exercise ends in postulating a *single super-value* covering all other values. Since Chang is a value pluralist, she cannot maintain, and, indeed, she does not, that there is a super-value, Frankensteinian monstrosity, that covers all other values.[78] There is no such value that covers beauty, autonomy, life, play, sociability, etc. Covering values are, hence, not supreme but *wider*. At best, comparativism works when there happen to be covering values.

5.4 Composite Values?

Maybe the covering values are not meant to be more fundamental but at a *lower-level* or at the *same level* as the values being compared.[79] It is not immediately obvious that would be the proper way to compare options or how that would even work.

Suppose the covering value is a *composite* value. It is composed of the values being compared. For example, *philosophical talent* does not only cover historical sensitivity to the discipline and originality but is somehow an amalgam of them. They both *contribute* to philosophical talent in some way. However, if the covering value is *merely* a composition of the other values, it does not do any normative work in the comparison. It does not add anything. It becomes a placeholder for however we make value judgments involving different values. It becomes another way to say 'all-things-considered', but Chang believes that is only a placeholder for a more comprehensive value.[80]

5.5 Structured Values?

Perhaps the covering value is meant to have some sort of *structure* or *internal balance* and that adds to the values being compared. After all, covering values determine how values relate to each other.[81] To have a philosophical talent requires having, at least, some originality and historical sensitivity. Having one but not the other will not suffice. And increasing the quantity of one will not make up for the lack of the other value unless their overall balance is good enough.

But where does this structure come from?[82] It is plausible that there is a general requirement of practical reason that we should seek a balance among the values we engage in our lives. If the structure is simply *this requirement*, then it is the requirement but not the covering value doing the normative work. If the balance or structure is somehow built in a *unique* way for philosophical talent, and every other covering value, it is quite mysterious why that is the case and why historical sensitivity and originality have a unique value relations; it seems perfectly plausible

---

[78] Chang (2009), p. 147.

[79] Blum (2023), p. 645.

[80] Chang (2004).

[81] See e.g., Chang (2004).

[82] Mason (2023) s. 4.2, asks how the covering values determine the weight of the values.

that philosophical talent allows for a great discretion or open-endedness in the combination of originality and historical sensitivity, it only requires that both are present presumably as a matter of some sort of definition or stipulation. Moreover, it becomes less plausible that there are great many nameless covering values all with their own (unique) structure or internal balance.

5.6 An Empty Shell?

The worry is that the covering values, whether named or nameless, are empty shells. Take philosophical talent again as an example. The merit rule, that is the government should hire 'the most qualified candidate', is a law in some jurisdictions, even when hiring philosophy professors at public universities. What counts as being the most qualified candidate depends on each job.[83] Accordingly, there is a legal practice in some jurisdictions for assessing the most qualified candidate for various kinds of jobs. Interestingly, it is seldomly stipulated in practice that there *already* are distinct covering values for 'accounting talent', 'cleaner talent', 'bus driver talent', etc.

Moreover, when the merit rule is applied in legal practice in these jurisdictions, it is up to the legislature or the government to decide what sort of requirements to set for the job in question. The candidate that the best fulfils those requirements counts as the most qualified one. It is noteworthy that the merit rule is not applied as if there is *already a distinct covering value for that job* and the task of the employer is simply to evaluate the candidates in light of the correct covering value. Instead, according to the legal rule, the legislature or the government could decide to emphasis originality over historical sensitivity and vice versa. It could also add other requirements, such as punctuality, being prolific, and an engaging lecturer. The covering value of philosophical talent does not cover the added considerations.

Perhaps Chang could maintain that there is an even wider covering value, for instance, a distinct 'philosophy professor talent' but, again, that seems to be an empty shell that depends on whatever requirements are set for that role. Now, she might maintain that legal practice in these jurisdictions is mistaken. That might be the case but then we might fall back on our intuition of whether and how plausible it is that there is a distinct covering value for *each type of job* and *activity* (and maybe even with unique structures of the values covered existing in the normative domain).

5.7 Social Roles

What emerges from this discussion above is that 'philosophical talent' is *not a value* but a *social construct*. It is a *social role* constructed by social norms, beliefs,

[83] See e.g., Kristjánsson (2014), p. 72 onwards.

attitudes, etc. and it may come with role obligations. The reason why originality and historical sensitivity are 'covered' by philosophical talent is that is how that role has been socially constructed. To the extent that there is a structure or internal balance, aside from the general requirement mentioned above, it, too, is socially constructed. If this is true, then we end up comparing the values of options in light of a standard that is not itself a distinct value, that is a covering value, but a socially constructed role.

But why, then, does it appear to us that social roles like 'philosophical talent' are good or desirable?

5.8 Being a Value Vs. Having a Value

Which brings us to what are values. Whether a lot of unknown or, at the least, unnamed values exist depends on whether there are great many values and what values are. Chang seems to have an extremely wide view of values. She says values include rights, duties, and rules and she gives the example of *sexual harassment* as a disvalue. However, sexual harassment is a *type of act,* not a value. It is a type of *bearer of (dis-)value*. The act of sexually harassing someone *has* disvalue but it *is not* a disvalue. Paying someone a compliment, too, is not a value but it has a value. It is *valuable*. Not everything that is *valuable* is a *value*. Values are the entities that make acts and types of acts valuable, that is give them value. The value behind or engaged with by the act of sexual harassment is something like sexual autonomy (or more generally autonomy) and/or bodily integrity. The act of sexual harassment *has* a disvalue because it degrades, damages, or destroys sexual autonomy and/or bodily integrity. Likewise, even if rights, duties, and rules are normative, they are not values.

From this point of view, neither philosophical talent nor sensitivity to the history of the discipline are values even though they can be valuable. On this narrower understanding of values, it becomes far less plausible that there are many unknown nameless values that can serve as covering values. However, 'philosophical talent' as a socially constructed standard can *have* a value in light of other values engaged. And it becomes far more plausible that there are many unrecognised or unnamed standards, i.e., unconstructed or fully identified standards, that will be or are being constructed to perform certain value judgments.

If we were to stick with the wide sense of value, then it seems plausible that it would not suffice to simply compare originality and historical sensitivity in light of philosophical talent. It is not a basic normative fact. To do that we would have to figure out *why* philosophical talent is *valuable* and that would, eventually, lead us to some *value* or values in the narrow sense. Otherwise, the comparison would be an 'incomplete thought', whether such incomplete value judgments can be (somewhat) practical in real life. After all, we are not merely seeking an explanation of how value judgments can be made practically but a theory of values and/or value judgments.

5.9 Are the Covering Values Relative?

Yet another question that arises is whether the covering values are *relative*. In our example, the university might compare the candidates in light of philosophical talent, but they might also compare them in light of 'teacher talent' (assuming such a distinct covering value exists). It is not obvious why the university should choose 'philosophical talent' over 'teacher talent' or in virtue of what that choice would be made (perhaps an even further covering value).

Moreover, if the covering value of 'philosophical talent' has a structure, it seems plausible that it might have different structures in different cultures and situations. Sometimes the university needs or wants to emphasis originality and sometimes historical sensitivity, perhaps in light of the combination of the faculty already there. The question becomes whether the internal structure of covering value changes, not just the circumstances to which it applies. It is not obvious that there is a uniquely correct answer across different situations. That, too, may indicate that 'philosophical talent' is a social construct that can be *valuable* but not a *value*.

5.10 Good Simpliciter

It can be accepted that there is no good *simpliciter*, meaning that something just is good or bad. Rather, something is good *in light of something*. A book is good because it is engaging, funny, romantic, or entertaining. The term 'good' is just a placeholder or a formal term to describe something which has value or is valuable.

Nevertheless, that does not mean that finding something 'good' requires a (real) comparison of options. It can merely be an assessment and statement of *having enough of some value*. 'The book was good because it was rather exciting.' No judgment about the booking being *more* exciting than other books needs to be reflected in that statement (except in a nominal-notable way). We can say that the burger is tasty without saying it is tastier than the salad or keeping in mind things that are less tasty than a burger. An infant that tastes banana mash for the first time can like it—think it is good—without comparing it to other options. So, there is no good *simpliciter* but that does not mean it requires a (serious) comparison of options in light of whatever value is engaged. That would turn 'good' into 'better-than'.

5.11 Creating Reasons by Commitment

The creation of new reasons or changing the weight of existing reasons can be explained on a model of external or objective reasons even if we accept that will-based judgments are relevant. A hybrid view of reasons is not required.

The *act* of committing is a *fact*. It is a fact whether we commit, even though it may be a *new fact* which occurs when we are faced with a hard choice. When I am faced with a choice between a burger and a salad that are 'equal' or, according to Chang, 'on a par', and I stipulate that the fact the salad is healthy is a weightier reason for me by committing to having the salad (or committing to a healthy lifestyle or being a healthy person (see below)) and, in so doing, shape my identity as a healthy person, I have *changed the factual circumstances*. I have changed the reasons that are relevant for me. I have made the value more valuable *for me*. In one sense it is a fact *given to us* by how things are in the world but, in another sense, it is 'will-based' because I created the fact by using my will. But how can I do that?

The *will* is not a source of reason as such, but it can be used to create new facts that are reasons for us. That capacity is *valuable*. There may some value, such as *autonomy* or some other value related to being the author of one's own life and living responsibly, that make such will-based judgments or setting and pursuing goals *valuable*. We create new reasons for us by changing the facts in a way that is valuable.

According to this, externalists or objectivists about reasons are not bound to view agents as *passive* (at least in this wider sense). They can be *active* and shape their normative domain, although the explanation is different from Chang's. An objectivist can explain *why* exercising the will (forming an intention for an act)[84] matters as opposed to mainly stating that it *is* normative because you put your agency behind a reason and that is just something you do.[85]

6 Value Hybridism

If values are incommensurate, then principles (or values) cannot be balanced in an optimising way simply according to their intensity of realization in the circumstances, as Alexy claims. And while Chang's comparativism gives us hope, it appears to be limited. We have reasons to be wary about covering values, at least according to some understandings of what values are. We are, therefore, confronted again with our original challenge of how we can make overall judgments in light of different basic values. It is suggested here that *value hybridism* is the path forward. Let us start with a birds-eye-view.

According to value hybridism, values are comparable *to an extent* simply in virtue of being values. Nonetheless, they can only be roughly compared in that way. This is the kernel of truth in value monism. Beyond that rough comparison, a more fine-grained comparison is needed to assess the distinct evaluative characteristics of each value. There is no single common measurement in virtue of which to assess different

[84] Raz (1999), p. 48.

[85] Chang (2020b).

evaluative characteristics of basic values beyond the rough comparison. This is the kernel of truth in value pluralism.

So, values are comparable to an extent simply because they *share being values* but beyond that there is no common metric. Value monism fails because it assumes values can be *completely* compared in light of a single entity. Similarly, value pluralism, at least the radical branch, is mistaken in the view that values cannot be compared *at all*. According to value hybridism, the truth lies somewhere in between.

The rough assessment can be called a *valuableness judgment*. It is a thin or a limited judgments that involves a rough comparison of valuableness of options in the circumstances. The fine-grained assessment can be called a *qualitative value judgment*. It is a further judgment of the specific evaluative characteristics of the values. These two judgments stand in certain relations to each other. Valuableness judgments frame and limit qualitative value judgments. The latter take place within the context of our rough sense of the valuableness of the options.

Even though there is no common yardstick for different basic values to make qualitative value judgments, they can be compared *in a way*. Not because there is a covering value in the normative domain but because we can and do *construct* standards in our pursuit of a coherent life plan and a coherent well-ordered society. The standards are constructed, just as 'philosophical talent' is, as has been argued above, a socially constructed role.

Let us explore these claims a bit further.

7 Valuableness Judgments

We grasp value by using our senses or capacities.[86] We do that, at least in part, by using our practical reasonableness (or wisdom) (l. *phronesis*).[87] We can sense or grasp that *play* is a value. It is a good thing for us to play games. It is good in itself; it has intrinsic value. We grasp (or can reason) that it is a basic value because it is not instrumental or a sub-value. The same applies to other basic values, that include, among others, life, sociability, knowledge, and our practical reasonableness.[88]

We can also use our practical reasonableness to make judgments about the value of acts or states of affairs. The very same capacity allows us to sense or grasp whether something has *a lot* of value or *a little*, i.e., the intensity of the engagement with the value. In other words, we can make *valuableness judgments*, that is judgments about the (rough) value of something. We grasp that a salad is good because it is healthy and that a salad is healthier than a grilled cheese sandwich.

[86] See in this context Finnis (1980), pp. 60–63, 64–69 and 73. No stance is taken here on whether they are self-evident.

[87] Others have suggsted that we can use this capacity to make comparisons, e.g., Nagel (2012), pp. 128–141.

[88] For *a* list of basic values, see e.g., Finnis (1980), pp. 86–90.

So far, so good. The claim made here goes further. These valuableness judgments can be made *overall*. We can grasp the valuableness of a salad for dinner in light of its healthiness, tastiness, and so forth. A tastier salad, which is still healthy, has more value for us than a healthy salad that has an awful taste. We can recognize whether an option has a greater or lesser overall value by using the very sense or capacity that allows us to grasp that it has value at all and recognize what values are.

And the very capacity and faculties to reason that allow us to grasp, sense or identify values indicate that we should pursue, promote or engage with values in our actions. The pursuit of value allows us to compare options in terms of their rough valuableness. To many of us it is apparent that a hermit choosing to spend his life exclusively praying in isolation in the desert at the cost of all other valuable things in life is missing out; he is not living a 'full' or a 'rich' life. A life that mixes prayer (for the religious person) with a life spent in the accompany of family and friends (sociability), enjoying art (aesthetic value) and sports (play) and the pursuit of knowledge is a more valuable life. The pursuit of value suggests that a person should choose the latter life over the former life because it is more valuable even if the values engaged are distinct and different.

The claim is not that there is a *single* value property that makes something a value. Perhaps values have a complex structure and perhaps they only share a family resemblance. Maybe they have contingent but overlapping features. The claim is, rather, that whatever makes values *values* is *shared to large enough extent* that we can grasp their valuableness in a rough way. We can compare them *to the extent* that they share that. The basic insight is that it would be odd if values did *not share anything* and *to no extent* despite all being of the same kind. And we can compare whatever they share to the extent they share it.

This, but not the existence of a covering value, is the reason why we can with ease make evaluative judgments when there is a huge discrepancy between options. A burger that is only slightly tastier than a salad but a lot unhealthier is less valuable to us than the salad.

Importantly, valuableness judgments are not limited to assessing *quantity*, but can also include assessing the *qualities* of the values. A salad that has been arranged in a visually pleasing manner has some aesthetic value, but it might, nonetheless, be less important to us than its taste and healthiness. The most beautifully arranged salad might not trump a tasty and a healthy one, even if that salad is presented in the most unattractive manner.

However, it must be stressed that we can only compare options like this in a thin or a limited way. Valuableness judgments are *rough. Whatever values share and however they share that in virtue of being values is only to an extent.* Beyond that they are *qualitatively different*. That is what makes them *distinct* values. A rough judgment of valuableness cannot distinguish between options that are close in their overall valuableness in this sense. When a burger is slightly tastier, but a salad is slightly healthier, a valuableness judgment does not distinguish between them. Valuableness judgments support Alexy's view concerning the intensity of realization of the values but only to an extent since they are limited. While Alexy acknowledges discretion, that will not solve the problem since the limits of valuableness judgments suggest a far greater discretion than legal practice and Alexy's discussion indicate.[89]

Valuableness judgments are the kernel of truth in value monism. Whatever makes a value *a value*, on which no stance is taken here, and whatever enables us to grasp values and the value of options, also enables us to make overall (rough) valuableness judgments.

8 Qualitative Value Judgments

When options are not clearly distinguished by a valuableness judgment, we require a more fine-grained judgment of the specific evaluative characteristics of the values engaged. Those are *qualitative value judgments*. We must further assess the specific characteristics of, for instance, play and knowledge, and how they are reflected in the options with which we are confronted. The different characteristics of the values are, at least part of the reason, why we experience rational regret, there is a moral remainder, and it matters whether we become lawyers or philosophers or even pick a burger or salad for dinner. When fundamental values are involved, there is no covering value (that exists in the normative domain) to make qualitative value judgments.

Importantly though, qualitative value judgments are limited by valuableness judgments. Our rough sense of the valuableness of the options (of whatever they share and to the extent they share it), assuming we have not gotten it wrong, frames and limits the scope of qualitative value judgments. A further judgment on the evaluative characteristics of the tastiness of a burger does not change the fact whether it is delicious or unsavoury. When a sip of red wine tastes horribly to us, we are unlikely to learn to appreciate it a lot more with a further sensitivity to its qualities. That is why we say: 'I don't know much about wine, but I know what I like.' That statement reflects a valuableness judgment. But if we recognize the red wine's rough valuableness, we can come to appreciate it more in light of our more fine-grained judgment of its specific evaluative characteristics. In that case, we do not merely say: 'It was good' but, perhaps: 'Notice how the flavours harmonize, the earthy tones, and there is a lingering sweet taste.' The same applies to artwork. We might think a painting is beautiful, at first glance. On further inspection of its details and reflection, as we learn more about it, we might come to appreciate it more, and describe it as 'heavenly' or 'magnificent' or 'deep'. Sometimes we describe people that have honed their skill and sense of the details of a phenomenon as, for example, food, wine, or art connoisseurs. They have sharpened their skills in making certain qualitative value judgments. Some people have honed their skill for deliberation in a similar fashion. A sharpened skill for deliberation is a virtue of judges.

[89] Alexy (2002), pp. 396–414.

The kernel of truth in value pluralism is that there is no common measurement or covering value to make these qualitative value judgments where different basic values are engaged. So, the question becomes whether we are still able to make *some* overall judgments in that regard, within the limits and the framework of our valuableness judgments.

9 The Authors of Our Own Lives: And Political Communities

9.1 We Are the Authors of Our Own Lives

Many situations are *underdetermined* by the applicable reasons on what we should do. The values engaged and the circumstances we find ourselves in do not fully determine our rational course of action.[90] To take an example, the choice between becoming a professional football player or a law professor is not already determined by values *beforehand* or *in the abstract*. Sometimes our circumstances determine the choice for us. Suppose I am a lousy footballer but have a knack for theoretical engagement. Those facts may be reasons for me to pursue an academic carrier. In many circumstances, though, it is *up to us* to *choose*. And we should do that in light of certain moral requirements.

Each of us should take our own lives seriously and make something of it. We should be the *authors of our own lives*.[91] We must decide what sort of life we want to lead. That involves the ongoing project of setting and pursuing a *coherent life plan* that reflects the objective value of our lives and makes it meaningful.[92] We must pursue, promote, foster, etc. the different values engaged and choose a balance between them *for us*. Nonetheless, we are not entirely free in how we engage with values in our life. There are some requirements that should be upheld. For example, we should not purposefully act to damage or destroy a value and we need a balance of values to live a fulfilled or a flourishing life.[93] While there should not be (at least too much of) a disbalance, there are many ways in which there can be *a* balance. A football player may place an emphasis on the value of play but a law professor on knowledge.[94] However, a footballer or a professor that *only* or *excessively* pursues play or knowledge at the expense and neglect of all other valuable things does not live a fulfilled or a flourishing life. Beyond these and other requirements for engaging with values as well as our circumstances, it falls us to set and pursue goals as a part of a coherent life plan. Many of the judgments we make will not only

[90] Chang (2009), p. 137.

[91] See e.g., Dworkin (2011), pp. 13–14 and 203–204.

[92] See e.g., Finnis (1980), pp. 103–105.

[93] Finnis (1980), pp. 118–119.

[94] Finnis (1980), p. 93.

be incommensurable but also involve qualitative value judgments that cannot be compared overall in light of a covering value.

9.2 Standards Are Constructed Through Our Live Decisions

When we weave a coherent life plan and shape an image of the person we want to be through our decisions and acts, we *construct* standards.[95] Assuming we have constructed valuable standards, they become a benchmark for making further qualitative value judgments 'down the line' or value judgments are made within context of the standards. There is a back-and-forth relationship between value judgments. The constructed standards can serve as more *comprehensive considerations* in virtue of which we can make evaluative judgments. They serve the same function as a 'covering value' in Chang's comparativism.

Suppose I have chosen to be a professional footballer and I am in middle of training season leading up to a big game. At dinner time, I am faced with a choice between a burger and a salad to eat and beer and water to drink. The options can be evaluated in light of my chosen carrier path as a professional footballer. That is a *social role* I have chosen to occupy. It becomes a standard to make the evaluative judgment in the concrete circumstance in which I find myself. *From the perspective of the constructed standard*, as it applies to my concrete circumstance, I should emphasis healthiness above taste and, therefore, choose the salad and the water. It is the rational course of action *for me in those circumstances in light of my other judgments* regarding and that make up my coherent life plan.

Suppose now that I have retired as a professional footballer to enjoy other things in my life. In that circumstance, I might choose the burger and the beer. Notice that the evaluative characteristics of the burger and the salad or the beer and the water are the same in terms of tastiness and healthiness. Presumably, if there are such things as covering values, their value relations should be the same. However, not only my circumstances but also my other value judgments, that a form a part of my coherent life plan, have changed. Now I evaluate the options in light of a *different constructed standard*—or put another way—in light of other value judgments I have made. Now, I occupy a different role and am in a different place in my life. The rationale course of action could, hence, be different.

9.3 The Constructed Standards Are Valuable

The constructed standards, the other value judgments I make, are not *merely* further circumstances in the sense that they are facts that matter for the values engaged for

[95] and/or goals. See in this context, Raz (1999), p. 64.

the choice at hand, namely tastiness and healthiness. Rather, they are *valuable* standards in light of some *other* values and made within the context of pursuing a coherent life plan as authors of our own lives, which is itself valuable. The constructed standards are, despite being certain kinds of facts but not values themselves, no less capable of doing the normative work than Chang's covering values. The social role of a footballer is similar to her covering value of philosophical talent. Since the constructed standards are valuable and serve the role of being a 'yardstick' to perform value judgments *in light of*, they are not merely further circumstances that engage the values or the values *apply to* them.

9.4 Mutually Supportive Value Judgments

Qualitative value judgments are 'locally' comparable in light of other value judgments concerning our coherent life plan; they are comparable in light of socially constructed standards. This reveals something important about value judgments. Options (burger versus salad) are not simply assessed in light of values (tastiness and healthiness) and, perhaps, in light of some further values (covering value). Rather, there is a kind of *back-and-forth* relationship among value judgments in our lives, between fresh value judgments and constructed standards (past or other value judgments). The constructed standard is chosen (or 'matched') with the choice situation in the context of a coherent life plan.

The value judgment on whether I should have a burger, or a salad is made in light of some other value judgment concerning, for example, the role I occupy as a footballer and together they are made in the wider context of setting and pursuing a coherent life plan. Maybe the choice of becoming a footballer was made in light of a youth spent playing the game and excelling at it. When the time came it 'felt' like the natural choice because of the life led up until that point. And playing the game as a youngster was a choice over, for example, practicing the violin or doing homework. These choices form a part of the life we have led and are woven together in the ongoing project of setting and pursuing a coherent life plan. Each significant value judgment is made in light of and becomes a part of that coherent life plan. We test our value judgments in light of other value judgments, and they should be, at least to an extent, mutually supportive.[96] After all, it is a *coherent* life plan. Nonetheless, we are not 'bound' by our past value judgments that have disvalue or are less valuable. We can change our situation by, for example, constructing a new standard. A lazy and unhealthy habit can be abandoned in light of a choice to become more productive and healthier henceforth, i.e., a choice to pursue a more valuable life.

Importantly though, qualitative value judgments, which are comparable in this way, ultimately depend on or can be traced back to qualitative value judgments that

[96] For an idea about justification as being mutually supportive as parts of all the rest but cocerning values directly and interpretive reasoning, see Dworkin (2011), e.g., pp. 117 and 154.

are not comparable overall. After all, qualitative value judgments are not compared in light of a covering value that determines the relations between the values in the normative domain but only locally in light of our other value judgments, that is constructed standards, within the context of a coherent life plan.

Pursuing a coherent life plan is itself valuable because it matters for being the authors of our own life and, thereby, respecting and taking seriously the objective values of our lives. A part of the explanation that a will-based judgment, for instance, committing, can create a new reason for us is because that is valuable for us to be able to do as authors of our own lives. We commit to, for example, being healthy and set it as a goal in our coherent life plan and in light of that role of being healthy we assess the choice between the burger and the salad.

9.5 The Authors of our Political Community

Something similar applies to political judgments made within a political community. We must decide *what sort of community to be* and, in so doing, we are involved in an ongoing project of pursuing some idea of a coherent well-ordered society. These judgments create *socially constructed standards*. Political judgments can be locally comparable according to constructed standards even though they are ultimately traced back to or depend on qualitative value judgments that are not comparable overall.

Politics is the business of forming an idea of a coherent well-ordered society and constructing social standards in that context. *Political authorities*, in a wide sense, make the value judgments and constructs social standards, which then become benchmarks for making further value judgments 'down-the-line'. Again, those judgments are, though, limited by valuableness judgments. Pursing a well-ordered society is valuable in light of basic values, such as sociability. We are the authors of our own political community, also when that authorship is pursued through political authorities on our behalf. In other words, there is some value in constructing standards and making local comparisons in light of them.

10 Upshots

Value hybridism has potentially great *explanatory force*. We can make overall judgments, some of them with ease, *to an extent* by assessing the rough valuableness of the options or values. That explains why there are some 'relations' between values; they share something to large enough extent in virtue of being values. However, no stance is taken here on what exactly that is. That does not mean that the values are not different or that there is a single entity (value or property) that unifies them. Value hybridism is not based on such a simplification.

Nonetheless, the rough judgments are limited and there is no covering value (when understood as values in the narrow sense) to make a more fine-grained judgment of the specific evaluative characteristics of each value. That explains, at least partly, why moral choices can be complex, why the different values with their different evaluative characteristics may lead to rational regret and a moral remainder. It also explains our experiences that there are many different valuable things in our lives.

As a hybrid view, it can explain the strength of value monism and pluralism and avoid some of their weaknesses. Nevertheless, as is often the case with the middle ground, it might turn out to be unstable and be open to challenges from both sides. Only the initial steps in the developing and defending the view have been taken here.

11 Consequences for Constitutional Law and Theory

For the sake of discussion, it was assumed that moral principles or values can be relevant for balancing constitutionally and internationally protected rights. Therefore, we need to know whether they can be balanced and how. It was argued that Alexy's theory of principles is based on certain assumptions that may not hold true if values are incommensurable, and Chang's comparativism appears to be limited. However, if value hybridism is correct, then it has some consequences for constitutional law and theory.

Firstly, value hybridism vindicates the structure of constitutionally protected rights in a political state and the corresponding methodology. It is possible to make valuableness judgments when we balance, for instance, freedom of expression and the right to privacy or property rights and public interests. Sometimes a proportionality assessment is easy because the options are obvious in terms of their overall value even when they are only 'roughly' assessed. Restricting the movements of a person with 'the plague' to come to large gatherings is a judgment that would seem obvious to most of us even though it involves the different values of liberty and public health.

Secondly, qualitative value judgments can also be made in light of socially constructed standards, for example, other laws and social rules and roles, that indicate what sort of well-ordered society to which the political community is committed. Oftentimes, that commitment is made by political authorities issuing directives (constructed social standards) based on value judgments. We often make assessments in law in light of other laws or commitments reflected by the legal system. A more fine-grained assessment can be made in light of such standards. That is why a court may emphasis the freedom of expression, which the community has committed to by constitutionally protecting the right, over animal rights, which are not enshrined in the constitution. The assessment may be 'locally' comparable in this way, but it need not map onto the relations among the values in the normative domain (i.e., in the abstract).

Valuableness judgments support Alexy's theory to an extent. Nevertheless, they are limited. That coupled with the fact that there is no overarching value to make qualitative value judgments when different basic values are engaged suggests that we cannot simply rely on the intensity of the realization of the values in the circumstances when principles or values are balanced. Rather, we need socially constructed standards to make local value judgments. One such constructed and contingent standard could be a methodological norm that requires that all the principles should be balanced in an optimising way *a la* Alexy. Even if such a standard exists in a jurisdiction, other constructed standards are needed since the *intensity of the realisation cannot be compared overall*, even if the principles are treated as having equal rank, to the extent that valuableness judgments do not solve the problem. Constructed standards are needed to make qualitative value judgments. Alexy's two ways of 'soft ordering', i.e., indicating preferences and case-law, can be seen as such socially constructed standards. The fact that the freedom of occupation has been constitutionally enshrined can be taken as an indication for why it outweighs environmental protection that does not enjoy the standard. And the fact that the freedom of expression has been treated as a more important right in the case law than some other constitutionally important rights, such as social and economic rights, can be taken as an indication for why it should continue to do so, even though such value judgments need not correspond to how the values relate to each other in the normative domain.

Thirdly, the claims also bring to light the limits of the structure of constitutionally protected rights. Valuableness judgments are rough. They only rule out 'obvious' options. Furthermore, socially constructed standards are not always available, sometimes they are vague, indetermined, or open-textured, and sometimes there are multiple conflicting standards. Moreover, the standards are ultimately traced back to or depend on judgments that are not comparable overall. As a result, *doctrines of margins of appreciation* can be used to reflect these inherent limitations of evaluative judgments. They can explain *when* there is such a margin and *to what extent*.

Fourthly, we should, though, keep in mind that doctrines of margins of appreciation are themselves socially constructed standards, which may reflect value judgments concerning, for instance, democracy, which are made in light of some other standards, such as the social role of the legislature in the society in question. There is a constant back-and-forth between our value judgments. They are parts of a web of judgments made in the pursuit of a coherent well-ordered society.

12 Concluding Remarks

At first blush, it is not obvious how the structure of constitutionally protected rights and the corresponding methodology, which is premised on the assumption that different values can be balanced, can be vindicated if there are different basic values that are incommensurate. Value hybridism suggests, however, that different values can be compared to an extent. Beyond that they can be compared in light of constructed standards and are, in that sense, locally comparable even though such further judgments ultimately depend on some other judgments that are not comparable overall. Doctrines of margins of appreciation can be constructed and applied with the aim to track these inherent limitations of value judgments.

References

Alexy R (2000) On the structure of legal principles. Ratio Juris 13(3):294–304

Alexy R (2002) A theory of constitutional rights. Oxford University Press, Oxford

Blum C (2023) Value pluralism versus value monism. Acta Anal 38:627–652

Chang R (1997) Introduction. In: Chang R (ed) Incommensurability, incomparability, and practical reason. Harvard University Press, Cambridge, pp 1–34

Chang R (2004) All things considered. Philos Perspect 18(1):1–22

Chang R (2009) Putting together morality and well-being. In: Baumann P, Betzler M (eds) Practical conflicts: new philosophical essays. Cambridge University Press, Cambridge, pp 118–158

Chang R (2013) Grounding practical normativity: going hybrid. Philos Stud 164(1):163–187

Chang R (2016) Comparativism: the ground of rational choice. In: Errol L, McGuire B (eds) Weighing reasons. Oxford University Press, Oxford, pp 213–214

Chang R (2017) Hard choices. J Am Philos Assoc 3(1):1–21

Chang R (2020a) Do we have normative powers? Aristotelian Soc 94:275–300

Chang R (2020b) What is it to be rational agent? In: Chang R, Sylvan K (eds) The Routledge handbook of practical reason. Routledge, New York, p 6

Dworkin R (1978) Taking rights seriously. Harvard University Press, Cambridge

Dworkin R (1986) Law's empire. Hart Publishing, Oxford

Dworkin R (2011) Justice for hedgehogs. Belknap. Harvard University Press, Cambridge

Dworkin R (2018) Comment. In: Reed AA (ed) A matter of interpretation: Federal Courts and the law, New edn. Princeton University Press

Finlay S, Schroeder M (2020) Reasons for action. Internal vs. External. The Stanford Encyclopaedia of Philosophy. <https://plato.stanford.edu/archives/sum2020/entries/reasons-internal-external/>

Finnis J (1980) Natural law and natural rights. Clarendon Law Series, Oxford

Finnis J (1987) On reason and authority in law's empire. Law Philos 6:357

Green L (2012) Introduction. In: The concept of law, 3rd edn. Oxford University Press, Oxford

Kelly C (2014) Value monism, richness, and environmental ethics. Les ateliers de l'éthicque / The EthicsForum 9(2):110–129

Kristjánsson HD (2014) Ráðningar í opinber störf. Stjórnmál og Stjórnsýsla 10:45–82

Kristjánsson HD (2023) Is the principle of primacy absolute or relative? Explaining primacy in interlocking legal systems. Europarättslig tidsskrift 2023(2):233–254

Mason, E (2023) Value pluralism. The Stanford Encyclopaedia of Philosophy. <https://plato.stanford.edu/archives/sum2023/entries/value-pluralism/>

Mill JM (2002) In: Schneewind JB, Miller DE (eds) The basic writings of John Stuart Mill. Random House, New York

Nagel T (2012) The fragmentation of value. In: Nagel T (ed) Mortal questions. Cambridge University Press, Cambridge, pp 128–141

Raz J (1979) The authority of law. Essays on law and morality. Oxford University Press, Oxford

Raz J (1999) Engaging reason. On the theory of value and action. Oxford University Press, Oxford

Raz J (2009) Between authority and interpretation. Oxford University Press, Oxford

Scalia A (2018) Common law courts in a civil law system: the role of United States Federal Courts in interpreting the constitution and laws. In: Reed AA (ed) A matter of interpretation: Federal Courts and the law, New edn. Princeton University Press

Stocker M (1990) Plural and conflicting values. Oxford University Press, Oxford
Thompson JJ (1999) Goodness and advice. Tanner lecturers. Part 1. goodness. Princeton University Press, Princeton
Williams B (1973) Ethical consistency. In: Williams B (ed) Problems of the self. Cambridge University Press, Cambridge, pp 166–186

The South African Model of Socio-Economic Constitutionalism: Features and Fault Lines

Sandra Liebenberg

Contents

Abstract This chapter examines the key features and fault lines of the South African model of socio-economic constitutionalism. The chapter commences by examining the interlinkages between the transformative nature of the 1996 South African Constitution and its socio-economic commitments. It proceeds to examine how the holistic and integrated model of rights protection in the Constitution shapes and influences the character of South Africa's democracy. Thereafter it explores how the adjudication of the obligations imposed by the socio-economic rights provisions in the Bill of Rights influences the nature of socio-economic constitutionalism in South Africa. The final substantive part examines the South African model of socio-economic constitutionalism through the prism of the State's social policies. It identifies both the key features of these social policies as well as their major fault lines. The chapter concludes by synthesising its key findings, and identifies the insights that can be drawn from the South African experience of justiciable socio-economic rights for the broader global project of

S. Liebenberg (✉)
University of Stellenbosch, Stellenbosch, South Africa

Department of Public Law, Faculty of Law, Stellenbosch, South Africa
e-mail: sliebenb@sun.ac.za

S. Hindelang et al. (eds.), *YSEC Yearbook of Socio-Economic Constitutions 2024,* YSEC Yearbook of Socio-Economic Constitutions (2025) 2024: 37–66, https://doi.org/10.1007/16495_2024_74, Published online: 28 January 2025

socio-economic constitutionalism. It argues that greater attention must be paid to the developmental vision, concrete strategies, and concomitant state capacity required for realising socio-economic rights. This is vital if a model of socio-economic constitutionalism based on the constitutional recognition of socio-economic rights is to make a meaningful contribution to the crises confronting many contemporary constitutional democracies.

1 Introduction

Many contemporary democracies are confronting multiple crises with some scholars raising the question constitutional democracy is itself in crisis.[1] These crises include extreme political fragmentation and conflict, anti-immigrant mobilisation, rising right-wing populism, and contested policy responses to the climate crisis and environmental breakdown. Several studies demonstrate how socio-economic insecurity and inequality are both fuelling and complicating efforts to redress these crises.[2] The time is thus ripe to deepen scholarly inquiry on the concept of socio-economic constitutionalism, and its potential contribution to redressing the social and economic insecurity and inequalities that are eroding the foundations of constitutional democracy.

This project requires interrogating the key features of socio-economic constitutionalism and its manifestations in a range of comparative constitutional law jurisdictions, including the Global South.[3] This chapter aims to contribute to this project by examining the distinctive history and features of the South African model of socio-economic constitutionalism. It also seeks to identify key fault lines or weaknesses in the South African model, and the implications for the broader objectives of socio-economic constitutionalism.

The chapter commences by examining the interlinkages between the transformative nature of the 1996 South African Constitution and its socio-economic commitments. It proceeds to examine how the holistic and integrated model of rights protection in the Constitution shapes and influences the character of South Africa's democracy. Thereafter it explores how the adjudication of the obligations imposed respectively on state institutions and private actors have influenced the nature of socio-economic constitutionalism in South Africa. The final substantive part examines the South African model of socio-economic constitutionalism through the prism of the State's social policies. It identifies both the key features of these social policies as well as the major fault-lines in the implementation of socio-economic constitutionalism in South Africa. The chapter concludes by

[1] Graber et al. (2018).

[2] Gabriel et al. (2022); Kaika et al. (2024); Stiglitz (2012); Boonstra and Söderberg (2024).

[3] On South American "social constitutionalism", see, for example: Gargarella (2018), pp. 180–181.

synthesising its key findings and arguments, and identifies the insights that can be drawn from the South African experience for the broader global project of socio-economic constitutionalism.

2 Transformative and Socio-Economic Constitutionalism: An Inextricable Bond

A defining characteristic of the 1996 South African Constitution[4] is that of a "transformative constitution".[5] Its fundamental purposes are twofold: (1) to remedy the legacies of the injustices of the colonial and apartheid period in South Africa; and (2) to facilitate a transition to a more just future society. These two purposes[6] are reflected in the preamble to the Constitution which proclaims that it was adopted to "[h]eal the divisions of the past and to establish a society based on democratic values, social justice and fundamental human rights." Its stated objectives include to "[i]mprove the quality of life of all citizens and free the potential of each person."

Both the remedial and forward-looking dimensions of transformative constitutionalism require an account of "the injustices of the past"[7] and the normative contours of the future society which the Constitution envisages and seeks to bring into being.[8] This account of the envisaged future society is informed, to a significant degree, by the past it seeks to transcend. The forward-looking dimension of

[4]Constitution of the Republic of South Africa, 1996 ("the Constitution").

[5]The initial seminal article describing South Africa's Constitution as transformative is Klare (1998). A large body of scholarship and jurisprudence on transformative constitutionalism exists in South Africa. Certain scholars also contest and criticise the validity of the concept: see, for example: Sibanda (2020). However, for the reasons elaborated in this part, I regard the concept of transformative constitutionalism as apt to encapsulate the several distinctive features of the South African Constitution, and its aspiration to serve as a legal framework facilitative of fundamental changes in unjust political, economic and social structures. Klare (1998) described transformative constitutionalism as follows:

> [A] long-term project of constitutional enactment, interpretation and enforcement committed (not in isolation, of course, but in a historical context of conducive political developments) to transforming a country's political and social institutions and power relationships in a democratic, participatory and egalitarian direction. Transformative constitutionalism connotes an enterprise of inducing large-scale social change through nonviolent political processes grounded in law. (p. 150)

See also: Albertyn and Goldblatt (1998), p. 248.

[6]See Ruti Teitel's characterisation of the "simultaneously backward- and forward-looking" nature of constitutions adopted during period of political transition: Teitel (2000), pp. 191 and 215.

[7]On the role of history in constitutional interpretation, see De Vos (2001). See also the concurring separate judgments of Froneman J and Cameron J in *Daniels v Scribante* [2017] ZACC 13; 2017 (4) SA 341 (CC) ("*Daniels*").

[8]Pieterse (2005), pp. 157–158.

transformative constitutionalism is thus integrally connected to and informed by its backward-looking dimension.

In the South African context, the denial of the right to vote and multiple civil and political rights of the black population were integral to the colonial and apartheid regimes. At the same time, indigenous black communities were systematically dispossessed of their traditional lands and means of livelihood, such as cattle wealth.[9] The colonial and apartheid regimes also instituted systemic legislative and policy discrimination in black people's access to a range of social goods and services, including housing, health care, social services and education. This system of dispossession and discrimination generated high levels of poverty, and deep inequalities in the distribution of income and wealth in South Africa.[10]

The struggle for political liberation in South Africa was integrally bound up with the struggle for social, economic, and cultural dignity and equality. This is evident in historical articulations of rights such as, for example, the African Claims document adopted in 1942 by the African National Congress, which in turn guided the ANC's constitutional proposals.[11] Ngcukaitobi argues that the ethos of the African Claims document is reflected in the Bill of Rights in the Constitution.[12] Similarly the 1955 Freedom Charter integrates political freedoms alongside rights relating to the redistribution of land and others resources, housing, health care, education and culture.[13] Within the pan-Africanist tradition the restoration of land to the dispossessed African population was a central motif.[14]

This integrated understanding of the civil, political and economic, social and cultural dimensions of past injustices and future aspirations was influential in the constitutional negotiations leading to the eventual adoption of the 1996 Constitution.[15] It resulted in the adoption of a holistic and integrated Bill of Rights incorporating a generous suite of civil and political rights alongside socio-economic, land and environmental rights.[16] Proposals to cordon off and recognise socio-economic rights only in the form of judicially unenforceable directive principles of state policy[17] did not find favour with the participants in the Constitutional Assembly.

---

[9]Ngcukaitobi (2021), pp. 13–57.

[10]For a comprehensive account, see Terreblanche (2002); Seekings and Nattrass (2005).

[11]For example, the ANC's *Constitutional Guidelines for a Democratic South Africa* 1988 (https://www.tandfonline.com/doi/abs/10.1080/02587203.1989.11827765) and see also ANC: *Ready to Govern: ANC Policy Guidelines for a Democratic South Africa*. Available online at: https://www.anc1912.org.za/policy-documents-1992-ready-to-govern-anc-policy-guidelines-for-a-democratic-south-africa/.

[12]Ngcukaitobi (2018), pp. 217–272.

[13]The Freedom Charter adopted by the Congress of the People, Kliptown, 26 June 1955.

[14]Political Foundations of the Pan Africanist Congress of Azania (1989). Available online: https://s3.eu-west-1.amazonaws.com/bishopsgate/CAAG_163-0699-0701.pdf?mtime=20230403153821.

[15]Liebenberg (2010), pp. 1–22.

[16]The Bill of Rights is contained chapter 2 of the Constitution.

[17]Liebenberg (2010), pp. 11–14.

Instead, all the rights in the Bill of Rights were made subject to judicial enforcement.[18]

The recognition of socio-economic rights in the Bill of Rights is arguably the primary indicator of the commitment to socio-economic constitutionalism. Other indicators of the commitment to socio-economic development and transformation are encountered throughout the Constitution.[19] The constitutional text does not expressly prescribe any particular economic system or model of development. It has been argued that the constitutional description of the primary object of the Central Bank, namely, "to protect the value of the currency in the interests of balanced and sustainable economic growth in the Republic"[20] in effect restricts the adoption by government of expansionary economic policies.[21] However, as an organ of state, the Central Bank would be bound by the Bill of Rights, including its provisions relating to the realisation of socio-economic rights, and the achievement of substantive equality.[22]

Given the centrality of the Bill of Rights as "a cornerstone of democracy"[23] to the "objective normative value system"[24] of the South African Constitution, this chapter focuses primarily on the Bill of Rights, and the socio-economic rights provisions therein. However, other provisions in the Bill of Rights that can be be regarded as integrally related to the Constitution's socio-economic and transformative character are highlighted here.

The equality and non-discrimination clause (section 9) is explicitly aimed at achieving "the full and equal enjoyment of all rights and freedoms."[25] As the Constitutional Court held in its judgment in *Minister of Finance v Van Heerden*:[26]

---

[18]The Constitution, s 38 read with s 172.

[19]Examples of provisions reflecting this aim in provisions of the Constitution beyond the Bill of Rights include the following: s 152(1)(b) and (c) (the constitutional objectives of local government include the provision of services to communities in a sustainable manner and the promotion of social and economic development); s 153 (a) (the "development duties" of municipalities include giving priority to the basic needs of the community and promoting its social and economic development through its administration, budgeting and planning processes); s 195(c) and (e) (amongst the basic values and principles governing the public administration is that it must be "development orientated", responsive to people's needs, and encourage the public to participate in policy-making); s 214 (among the factors to be taken into account in the equitable division of national revenue between the three spheres of government and are the "developmental needs" of the different spheres of government, and the "economic disparities" within and among provinces.

[20]The Constitution, s 224.

[21]Heywood (2021), pp. 354–355.

[22]Section 8(1) of the Constitution states that the "Bill of Rights applies to all law, and binds the legislature, the executive, the judiciary and all organs of state." The concept of an "organ of state" is broadly defined in s 239 of the Constitution.

[23]The Constitution, section 7(1).

[24]*Carmichele v Minister of Safety and Security* [2001] ZACC 22; 2001 (4) SA 938 (CC) ("*Carmichele*"), para 54.

[25]The Constitution, section 9(2). On a substantive approach to the adjudication of equality rights, see Albertyn (2007).

[26][2004] ZACC 3; 2004 (6) SA 121 (CC), para 27.

> This substantive notion of equality recognises that besides uneven race, class and gender attributes of our society, there are other levels and forms of social differentiation and systematic under-privilege, which still persist. The Constitution enjoins us to dismantle them and to prevent the creation of new patterns of disadvantage.

In furtherance of this substantive notion of equality, express provision is made in section 9(2) for the taking of affirmative legislative and other measures "to protect or advance persons, or categories of persons, disadvantaged by unfair discrimination."[27] The Constitutional Court has referred to such affirmative measures as remedial or restitutionary equality.[28] The equality clause further prohibits discrimination by both public and private actors, and contains a capacious, open list of prohibited grounds of unfair discrimination.[29] Subsidiary legislation enacted to give effect to section 9 has incorporated "socio-economic status" as a potential ground of prohibited discrimination.[30] The Constitutional Court has also recognised that discrimination can occur on an intersection of various grounds of discrimination. For example, it held that the exclusion of domestic workers from social security legislation constituted intersectional discrimination on the grounds of race, gender and social class.[31]

The imperatives of socio-economic redress and transformation also informed the drafting of the property clause in the Bill of Rights (section 25). The drafters sought to craft section 25 so as to prevent pre-constitutional property rights being wielded to undermine legislative and other measures adopted "to achieve land, water and related reform, in order to redress the results of past racial discrimination."[32] The property clause (s 25) protects property rights against "arbitrary deprivation" and stipulates under what conditions property may be expropriated.[33] Thus, property may be expropriated only for a "public purpose" or in the "public interest", and subject to the payment of compensation. The "public interest" is defined broadly to include "the nation's commitment to land reform, and to reforms to bring about equitable access to all South Africa's natural resources."[34] A contextual and multi-factor approach is adopted to the calculation of "just and equitable" compensation for the expropriation of property. This approach is aimed at ensuring that historical

[27] The Constitution, section 9(2).

[28] *National Coalition for Gay and Lesbian Equality v Minister of Justice* [1998] ZACC 15; 1991(1) SA 6 (CC), para 61; *Minister of Finance v Van Heerden* [2004] ZACC 3; 2004 (6) SA 121 (CC), paras 28–32.

[29] The Constitution, section 9(3) and (4).

[30] Promotion of Equality and Prevention of Unfair Discrimination Act 4 of 2000, s 34 read with the definition of socio-economic status in s 1. See Basson (2023).

[31] *Mahlangu v Minister of Labour* ("*Mahlangu*") [2020] ZACC 24; 2021 (2) SA 54 (CC), paras 90; 96 and 102.

[32] The Constitution, section 25(8). See Coggin (2021) particularly on the history of the drafting of section 25 at pp. 3–10.

[33] The Constitution, section 25(1)-(3).

[34] The Constitution, section 25(4).

and contextual factors relating to the acquisition and use of the relevant property are taken into account in calculating compensation so that the latter is not reduced to the single factor of the market value of the property.[35] Finally, the property clause also imposes positive obligations on the state to take legislative and other measures to advance equitable access to land,[36] to improve tenure security,[37] and achieve the restitution of property to persons or communities dispossessed as a result of past racially discriminatory laws or practices.[38] The constitutional property clause and its legacies are contested.[39] However, the formulation of section 25 is clearly indicative of its fundamental purpose to facilitate socio-economic redress and redistribution in the area of property relations in South Africa.[40]

The wide sphere of application of the Bill of Rights is also a key feature of the South African model of socio-economic constitutionalism. The rights in the Bill of Rights impose obligations not only on the State, but also, under certain circumstances, on private parties (the so-called direct horizontal application of the Bill of Rights).[41] This application of the Bill of Rights to private parties is attributable to the understanding that the apartheid system was not only instituted and maintained by state power, but also by powerful corporate actors.[42] The interpretation and development of the Roman-Dutch common law regulating relationships between private parties by the courts under apartheid also did little to challenge the racially skewed acquisition and distribution of property and exploitative employment relationships.[43] It is thus not surprising that, in addition to the aforementioned provisions on the direct horizontal application of the Bill of Rights, section 39(2) of the Bill of Rights requires courts to promote "the spirit, purport and objects" of the Bill of Rights when developing the common law or customary law.[44] In other words, the courts are enjoined to develop the common law to align with the values and purposes of the Bill of Rights.[45]

---

[35] The Constitution, section 25(3). Thus, market value is only one factor, amongst several other factors, that must be considered in calculating "just and equitable" compensation in the particular circumstances of a case: s 25(3)(c).

[36] The Constitution, section 25(5).

[37] The Constitution, section 25 (6). See Pienaar (2014).

[38] The Constitution, section 25(7).

[39] See, for example: Modiri (2018).

[40] Coggin (2021); For an analysis of the impact of s 25 of the Constitution on land reform measures, see Dugard (2019).

[41] The Constitution, section 8(2) read with 8(3).

[42] See, for example, Truth and Reconciliation Commission, Report, Volume 4, chapter 2, Business and Labour. Available online: https://sabctrc.saha.org.za/originals/finalreport/volume4/volume4.pdf.

[43] For an analysis of the role of the Roman Dutch common law in the context of apartheid-era evictions, see Van der Walt (2009), pp. 60–76.

[44] Section 39(2).

[45] For a critique of the courts' response to this constitutional injunction, see Davis and Klare (2010).

The holistic, integrated model of fundamental rights' protection, the commitment to socio-economic redress and redistribution reflected in provisions such as the equality and property clauses, and the application of fundamental rights to private actors and law are key features of the transformative character of the South African Constitution.[46] Cumulatively, they represent a fundamental departure from a classic liberal model of constitutionalism, which aims to maximise private liberties and minimise public regulation of private transactions.[47] This model is generally hostile to affirmative state duties to provide or facilitate people's access to social goods and services, and to the regulation of private entities and conduct to secure the protection of vulnerable and disadvantaged groups.[48]

The recognition of socio-economic, land and environmental rights in the South African Bill of Rights (alongside and on equal terms to classic civil and political rights) signifies a holistic commitment to human well-being and flourishing.[49] It connotes a rejection of hierarchies and schisms between different categories of rights. These hierarchies and schisms tend to render invisible the socio-economic dimensions of human dignity, equality and freedom—values that animate the concept of fundamental human rights.[50] As expressed by Scott and Maklem:

> A constitutional vision that includes only traditional civil liberties within its interpretative horizon fails to recognize the realities of life for certain members of society who cannot see themselves in the constitutional mirror. Instead, they will see the constitutional construction and legitimation of a legal self for whom social rights are either unimportant or taken for granted. With the passage of time and absent important countervailing factors, this normative vision will help to confirm the very reality that it posits.[51]

This part has sought to demonstrate that the redress of the socio-economic legacies of colonialism and apartheid are central to the transformative character of the South African Constitution. This fundamental commitment is reflected in the holistic, integrated nature of the Bill of Rights as well as other features such as a commitment to substantive equality, land restitution and reform, as well as the application of the Bill of Rights to private actors. Socio-economic rights were intended to play a central role in fulfilling this commitment to redress historical injustices and transform their present-day legacies. As the Constitutional Court held

---

[46] Pieterse (2005).

[47] On the presumptions of the classic liberal tradition in the US context, see Lindsay (2017). Klare argues that the South African Constitution is best characterised as a "postliberal" Constitution: Klare (1998), pp. 151–156.

[48] Scott and Macklem (1992), pp. 45–48.

[49] Although this chapter does not focus on the implications of the inclusion of environmental rights in the Bill of Rights, it is fundamental to the model of development which must ultimately secure both socio-economic rights and the integrity and health of the environmental. See in this regard: Murcott (2022).

[50] For example, all three values are references in the Preamble of the Universal Declaration of Human Rights, UN General Assembly Resolution 217 A (III), 10 December 1948.

[51] Scott and Macklem (1992), pp. 35–36.

in the context of the interpretation of the right of access to adequate housing in section 26 of the Constitution:

> ...[W]hen this Court determines the content and socio-economic rights, it must consider their primary purpose, which is to promote substantive equality and human dignity, and also to undo the racialised system of poverty inherited from *apartheid. The* right to adequate housing is one such right, which must therefore serve a purpose that is both remedial and transformative.[52]

The following section considers the implications of the recognition of socio-economic commitments of the Constitution for South Africa's model of constitutional democracy.

3 Democracy Under South Africa's Model of Socio-Economic Constitutionalism

According to section 7(1) of the Constitution, the Bill of Rights "is a cornerstone of democracy in South Africa." This suggests that it not only enshrines the fundamental rights of all people in South Africa, but also shapes the nature and character of South Africa's democracy. The integrated set of fundamental rights in the Bill of Rights connotes a substantive understanding of democracy and the entitlements associated with membership of the South African political community. As expressed by Karl Klare:

> The inclusion of socio-economic rights reflects an understanding that political democracy and social and economic democracy are inextricably linked and mutually constitutive.[53]

The notion that a commitment to some level of social rights protection is constitutive of democracy and political citizenship is not novel in political theory and constitutional scholarship.[54] However, the South African experience is arguably distinctive given the centrality of socio-economic rights to the transformative purposes of the Constitution. The imperative of achieving a more just distribution of economic resources and access to social services were central to negotiations on the constitutional dispensation that would regulate the transition to democracy in South Africa.[55]

Under the South African model of socio-economic constitutionalism, the courts have an explicit mandate to enforce all the rights in the Bill of Rights, including socio-economic rights. When rights are found to be violated the courts must craft "appropriate", "just and equitable" remedies.[56] This has implications for the traditional liberal model of separation of powers doctrine premised on a strict division of

---

[52] Thubakgale and Others v Ekurhuleni Metropolitan Municipality and Others [2021] ZACC 45; 2022 (8) BCLR 985 (CC) ("*Thubakgale*"), para 107.

[53] Klare (2015), p. 466.

[54] See, for example: Marshall (1950); Lister (2005); Rawls (1993), p. 166; Michelman (2015); Gargarella (2006).

[55] Liebenberg (2010), pp. 1–22.

[56] The Constitution, section 38 read with section 172.

functions between the legislature, executive and judiciary, and the limited role of courts in reviewing legislative and executive action. As Klare observes:

> The default in social provision or neglect of fundamental rights does more than harm the claimants' dignity and well-being. It unbalances the equilibrium in the constitutionally controlled relationship between the represented and the representatives. A court's declaration of an unconstitutional state of affairs under these circumstances is not an affront to democracy and does not undermine government by the will of the people. Such action vindicates democracy and self-governance as conceived in the South Africa Constitution.[57]

This unbalancing of the democratic equilibrium through violations of socio-economic rights has contributed to the development of a more flexible and dialogic conception of the separation of powers doctrine.[58] It has also arguably contributed to the courts' willingness to design relatively experimental and far-reaching remedies in socio-economic rights cases.[59]

Socio-economic constitutionalism has also contributed to justifying participatory democracy as an integral component of the South Africa's conception of democracy.[60] The Constitutional Court has interpreted the various constitutional provisions requiring national and provincial legislatures to facilitate public involvement in the legislative process[61] to require the relevant legislature to take reasonable measures to enable the public to participate in the adoption of legislation.[62] Failure to comply with this obligation results in the invalidity of the relevant legislation. In the foundational judgment in this context, *Doctors for Life International v Speaker of the National Assembly* ("*Doctors for Life*"),[63] the Court noted that participatory democracy "is of special importance to those who are relatively disempowered in a country like ours where great disparities of wealth and influence exist."[64]

One of the central purposes of participatory democracy is thus the creation of deliberative spaces for the voices of the poor and marginalised to be heard in

---

[57] Klare (2015), p. 468 (footnotes omitted).

[58] See the observations of the Constitutional Court in a seminal judgment relating to land reform: *Mwelase v Director-General, Dept of Rural Development and Land Reform* 2019 (11) BCLR 1358 (CC) ("*Mwelase*"), paras 46–53.

[59] These remedies include, for example, structural interdicts (or injunctions) with the appointment of intermediaries to assist the courts in supervising the implementation of a remedial plan and orders for state representations to engage meaningfully with stakeholders in designing a remedial programme. For a discussion of recent jurisprudence in this context, see: Taylor (2019); Liebenberg (2022).

[60] On participatory democracy as a vital element of the South African concept of democracy, see De Vos et al. (2021), pp. 92–94.

[61] The Constitution, ss 59, 72 and 118. On public participation in the local sphere of government, see 152(e) of the Constitution.

[62] For a recent synthesis and exposition of the standard of reasonableness in the obligation to facilitate public participation in legislative processes, see: *Mogale v Speaker of the National Assembly* [2023] ZACC 14; 2023 (6) SA 58 (CC) ("*Mogale*"), paras 34–38.

[63] [2006] ZACC 11; 2006 (6) SA 416 (CC).

[64] *Doctors for Life*, para 115. See also the observations of Justice Sachs in his concurring judgment at para 234.

legislation affecting their socio-economic rights and interests. This purpose is well-expressed by the Court in its recent judgment in *Mogale v Speaker of the National Assembly* ("*Mogale*"):

> This case is about the significance of participatory democracy for millions of South Africans who for the most part live away from centres of power, in rural areas and in some of the poorest parts of our country. These are people who have the least access to power, wealth and influence. This case is about their ability to participate in the making of law that governs virtually every aspect of their daily lives, including access to land, basic services, and rights to the benefits of the land upon which they live.[65]

As Henk Botha notes, participatory democracy "has an important role to play in promoting political equality and integrating the marginalised and poor into the democratic community."[66]

In the context of its socio-economic rights jurisprudence, the Constitutional Court has also deepened the participatory dimension of democracy through its meaningful engagement doctrine.[67] According to this doctrine, one of the criteria for assessing the reasonableness of conduct impacting on socio-economic rights is whether steps were taken by relevant organs of state to meaningfully engage with the rights holders.[68] I have previously argued that this doctrine creates spaces in which the voices of the poor can be heard in decisions that affect their access to or enjoyment of socio-economic rights.[69] In so doing, it deepens the participatory dimensions of democracy under South Africa's model of socio-economic constitutionalism.

The following part examines how the normative content of South Africa's model of socio-economic constitutionalism has been developed through the judicial interpretation of socio-economic rights.

4 Socio-Economic Constitutionalism Through the Prism of Socio-Economic Rights Adjudication

As I have sought to demonstrate, the South African model of socio-economic constitutionalism extends beyond the socio-economic rights provisions in the Bill of Rights. Nevertheless, as these rights are the most visible and explicit commitment to socio-economic constitutionalism in the South African context, this part focuses on how their interpretation by the judiciary has influenced the nature and character of the South African model of socio-economic constitutionalism.

---

[65] *Mogale*, para 46.

[66] Botha (2012), p. 53.

[67] For a comprehensive analysis of the meaningful engagement doctrine, see Ray (2016).

[68] See, for example: *Occupiers of 51 Olivia Road, Berea Township v City of Johannesburg* [2008] ZACC 1; 2008 (3) SA 208 (CC) ("*Occupiers of 51 Olivia Road*").

[69] Liebenberg (2019).

The analysis is confined for present purposes to the socio-economic rights in sections 26(1) and (2) and 27 (1) and (2) of the Constitution. These provisions entrench the rights of everyone to have access to adequate housing, health care services including reproductive health care, sufficient food and water, and social security, including, if they are unable to support themselves and their dependants, appropriate social assistance.[70] A second subsection imposes a positive obligation on the State "to take reasonable legislative and other measures, within its available resources, to achieve the progressive realisation" of each of these rights.[71] A more comprehensive examination of socio-economic constitutionalism would also have to consider other rights, including labour rights, environmental rights, land rights, children's socio-economic rights, and the rights to basic education the Bill of Rights.[72]

This part focuses first on the the judicial interpretation of the obligations imposed on organs of state, before turning to the obligations imposed on private actors.

4.1 State Obligations

4.1.1 The Model of Judicial Review

In its jurisprudence on the positive obligations imposed by sections 26 and 27, the Constitutional Court has rejected an interpretation that would impose an enforceable minimum core obligation on the State to provide basic levels of the relevant rights to everyone. Litigants and *amici curiae* sought to persuade the Court to interpret sections 26 and 27 to impose a minimum core obligation on the State, drawing primarily on the doctrine of the UN Committee on Economic, Social and Cultural Rights, the treaty body under the International Covenant on Economic, Social and Cultural Rights.[73]

Instead, the Court has adopted a model of reasonableness review in which it assesses the overall reasonableness of the legislation or policy challenged in socio-economic rights litigation.[74] In so doing, it has developed several substantive and

---

[70]The Constitution, sections 26(1), 27(1) (a), (b) and (c).

[71]The Constitution, sections 26(2) and 27(2). Both provisions also contain a third subsection: section 26(3) deals with evictions of people from their homes, and section 27(3) deals with the right not to be refused emergency medical treatment.

[72]The Constitution, sections 23, 24, 25 (5)-(7), 28(1)(c), (d), (e) and (f), and 29.

[73]See, for example, UN Committee on Economic, Social and Cultural Rights (1990), para 10. In the litigation and jurisprudence, there has been no attempt to refer to comparative law sources such as *Existenzminimum* doctrine in German constitutional law or the *mínimo vital* doctrine in Colombian constitutional law: see, for example, Leijten (2015); Winkler and Mahler (2013); Landau (2012), pp. 207–229.

[74]The cases which laid the foundations of the reasonableness review model are analysed in Liebenberg (2010), pp. 131–213.

procedural criteria that are indicative of reasonable State conduct in relation to socio-economic rights. Thus, the Court has held that a reasonable government programme must make short-term provision for those living in desperate socio-economic need;[75] it should not contain unreasonable limitations or exclusions of groups;[76] and the policy should be flexible and responsive to changing circumstances so as to advance the progressive realisation of the right.[77] The Court has also identified certain procedural criteria for assessing the reasonableness of government's conduct in the area of socio-economic rights. Thus, relevant policy must be made transparent to the public,[78] and involve meaningful engagement with those whose socio-economic rights are impacted by the policy.[79] The Constitutional Court has held that reasonableness review with its guiding substantive and procedural criteria must be applied when a court is called upon to evaluate whether an organ of state has failed to comply with the positive obligations imposed by the rights in sections 26 and 27.

Thus litigants may mount a legal challenge to social legislation, policies and programmes on the basis that they are not compliant with one or more of the criteria of reasonableness. Such a challenge could be based, for example, on the argument that the benefits provided by the relevant programme unreasonably exclude certain groups, that the programme is inconsistent with relevant factual or scientific evidence,[80] or that government has failed to continually review the programme.[81] As synthesised in the *Mazibuko* judgment:

> When challenged as to its policies relating to social and economic rights, the government agency must explain why the policy is reasonable. Government must disclose what it has done to formulate the policy: its investigation and research, the alternatives considered, and the reasons why the option underlying the policy was selected.[82]

The Court adopts a different model of review when it is alleged that state conduct violates the negative obligations imposed by socio-economic rights. Where legislation or other forms of state conduct has the effect of depriving people of their existing access to socio-economic rights, this constitutes a violation of the negative obligation imposed by sections 26(1) and 27(1).[83] In such cases, the burden then

---

[75] See, for example, *Government of the Republic of South Africa v Grootboom* [2000] ZACC 19; 2001 (1) SA 46 ("*Grootboom*"), paras 44, 68, 99.

[76] *Minister of Health v Treatment Action Campaign* [2002] ZACC 15; 2002 (5) SA 721 (CC) ("*TAC*"), paras 70, 95, 122.

[77] *TAC*, paras 80, 95: *Mazibuko v City of Johannesburg* [2009] ZACC 28; 2010 (4) SA 1 (CC) ("*Mazibuko*"), paras 67, 162, 168.

[78] *TAC*, para 123.

[79] *Occupiers of 51 Olivia Road, Berea*, paras 9–23.

[80] *TAC*, paras 57–66.

[81] *Mazibuko*, para 66.

[82] *Mazibuko*, para 161. For a critique of the Court's approach to reviewing the quantification of social benefits, see Williams (2010).

[83] *Jaftha v Schoeman, Van Rooyen v Stoltz* [2004] ZACC 25; 2005 (2) SA 140 (CC) ("*Jaftha*"), para 34.

shifts to the State to justify this deprivation according to the stringent proportionality test of the general limitations clause in the Bill of Rights.[84] In previous work, I have characterised this as a two-step model of review compared to the one-step model of reasonableness review applied to the positive obligations imposed by socio-economic rights.[85] The latter one-step model combines a simultaneous consideration of factors relevant to the realisation of the right and the State's justifications for its acts or omissions.

Academic criticism of the reasonableness model of review has focused on the Court's refusal to endorse the minimum core approach to the adjudication of socio-economic rights.[86] Reasonableness review has also been criticised for its vagueness and orientation towards identifying good governance standards rather than identifying the normative content of the relevant socio-economic rights.[87] As a consequence, it is argued, the jurisprudence provides insufficient guidance to organs of state regarding their substantive obligations to fulfil the socio-economic rights in sections 26 and 27. This contrasts with the development of more substantive normative standards in the context of the judicial interpretation of the right to basic education entrenched in section 29(1)(a) of the Constitution.[88] In contrast to the socio-economic rights in sections 26 and 27, this right is formulated in unqualified terms in the Bill of Rights (subject only to the general limitations clause).

The reasonableness model of review is designed to respect the primary legislative role of the legislature and executive in giving effect to socio-economic rights,[89] whilst holding them accountable for certain standards of conduct. Thus, the normative indeterminacy of reasonableness review owes much to the Court's perceptions of appropriate institutional constraints of the judicial role.[90]

4.1.2 Shaping the Normative Features of Socio-Economic Constitutionalism

Despite the shortcomings of reasonableness review, the jurisprudence provides several insights into how the South African courts interpret the the obligations imposed by socio-economic rights on the State Six aspects of the jurisprudence are highlighted here for their contribution to shaping for the normative features of the South African model of socio-economic constitutionalism.

---

[84] The Constitution, section 36.

[85] Liebenberg (2023).

[86] The leading work in this regard is: Bilchitz (2007).

[87] See, for example, Brand (2004), pp. 43–53; Pieterse (2004); Liebenberg (2010), pp. 179–183; Liebenberg (2023).

[88] On the interpretation of the right to basic education by the courts, see Veriava (2019).

[89] *Mazibuko*, para 66.

[90] *TAC*, paras 37–38.

First, the jurisprudence establishes that the State is obliged to act positively to enact legislation and adopt policies and programmes to give effect to socio-economic rights.[91] Thus, the South African model of socio-economic constitutionalism does not permit the State to remain passive in relation to the socio-economic needs of its population, for example, by relegating the fulfilment of these needs solely to the market. Instead, it envisages an active role for the State in adopting the social legislation, policies and programmes that will advance the progressive realisation of socio-economic rights.

Second, the relevant social programmes must provide relief to those people and groups whose needs are urgent and who are living in dire circumstances.[92] This aspect of the reasonableness review criteria is justified particularly with reference to the value of human dignity in the Constitution.[93] The Court is careful not to prescribe what this threshold of provision should be, preferring to leave the specification in the hands of the executive and legislative authorities. Thus, the State must at least provide some safety nets, such as an emergency housing programme, to protect people against the most severe forms of socio-economic deprivation.

The third aspect to highlight is the close interrelationship affirmed in the jurisprudence between socio-economic rights and the right to equality entrenched in section 9 of in the Constitution. Beth Goldblatt and I have characterised this interrelationship as "interpretative interdependence".[94] This interdependence manifests when the Court draws on the underlying purposes and values of one right to interpret another right. In the context of socio-economic rights jurisprudence, this interpretive interdependence has typically manifested in the interplay between the right against unfair discrimination in section 9(3) of the Constitution and the socio-economic rights in sections 26 and 27. Thus in cases in which groups have been excluded from socio-economic programmes on grounds such as, nationality, race, gender, or socio-economic status (or an intersection of grounds), the Court has concluded that both the right against unfair discrimination in section 9 of the Constitution and the relevant socio-economic right has been violated.[95] In these cases, the values and purposes of the right to equality and non-discrimination have played a critical role in the Court's interpretation of the reasonableness of the exclusion of the relevant group from the impugned social programme. This

---

[91] *Mazibuko*, para 67.

[92] As expressed in the *Grootboom* judgment, government programmes to give effect to the right of access to adequate housing in section 26 of the Constitution must include reasonable measures "to provide relief for people who have no access to land, no roof over their heads, and who are living in intolerable conditions or crisis situations." *Grootboom*, para 99(c).

[93] *Grootboom*, paras 44 and 83.

[94] Liebenberg and Goldblatt (2007), p. 339.

[95] Significant judgments in this regard are: *Khosa v Minister of Social Development; Mahlaule v Minister of Social Development* [2004] ZACC 1; 2004 (6) SA 505 (CC) ("*Khosa*") (exclusion of non-citizen permanent residents from non-contribution social assistance legislation); *Mahlangu v Minister of Labour* [2020] ZACC 24; 2021 (2) SA 54 (CC) ("*Mahlangu*") (exclusion of domestic workers from statutory compensation scheme for work-related diseases and injuries).

interpretive approach underscores the close interdependence between the values of egalitarianism and social justice in the South African model of socio-economic constitutionalism.[96] As the Constitutional Court noted in the *Khosa* judgment, "... decisions about the allocation of public benefits represent the extent to which poor people are treated as equal members of society."[97]

The fourth aspect concerns the significant role of meaningful engagement in the Court's socio-economic rights jurisprudence. Thus where the decisions of organs of State will impact on people's socio-economic rights, they are required to engage meaningfully with those affected by their decisions.[98] As noted previously, participatory democracy is a key feature of the South African model of socio-economic constitutionalism, and finds particular expression in contexts where people are marginalised by poverty and social exclusion.

Fifth, as noted above, State conduct which deprives people of their existing access to socio-economic rights will attract a more stringent proportionality-based scrutiny under the general limitations clause. This implies that state conduct should be aimed at preserving and improving access to socio-economic goods and services rather than removing or reducing access. Although the latter conduct is not absolutely prohibited, it will attract a high degree of proportionality scrutiny. There are also increasing signs that the courts may adopt the doctrine of non-retrogression as endorsed by the UN Committee on Economic, Social and Cultural Rights.[99] During the Covid-19 pandemic, the High Court[100] referred to this doctrine in holding that the suspension of the National School Nutrition Programme amounted to a violation of both the right to basic education,[101] and the right of every child to basic nutrition.[102] There has been increasing interest amongst South African civil society organisations in invoking the doctrine of non-retrogression to challenge economic austerity policies which result in reduced access to socio-economic rights due to budgetary cut-backs.[103] Thus the courts' evolving jurisprudence on negative obligations and the doctrine of non-retrogression signals that the State should sustain and improve people's access to socio-economic well-being over time. Decisions that

---

[96] Social justice is one of the stated goals of the adoption of the Constitution in its Preamble, and "the achievement of equality" is one of the Constitution's foundational values (see section 1(a)).

[97] *Khosa*, para 74.

[98] See *Occupiers of 51 Olivia Road* and the discussion of participatory democracy in Part 3 above.

[99] This was already signalled in *obiter dictum* remarks of the Constitutional Court in the *Grootboom* judgment in referring to the UN Committee's doctrine of retrogressive measures as a corollary of the obligation of progressive realisation. See *Grootboom*, para 45. On the UN Committee's doctrine of non-retrogression, see Warwick (2019). The Committee on the Rights of the Child, which supervises the UN Convention on the Rights of the Child, has a similar doctrine: see CRC General Comment No. 19 (2016), para 31.

[100] *Equal Education v Minister of Basic Education* 2021 (1) SA 198 (GP).

[101] The Constitution, section 29(1)(a).

[102] The Constitution, section 28(1)(c).

[103] These and related developments are analysed in: Liebenberg (2021).

result in a deprivation or diminishment in access to socio-economic rights trigger a burden on the state to justify their necessity and proportionality.

Sixth, the criteria of reasonableness review do not constitute a closed list. The courts may develop further substantive and procedural criteria as its jurisprudence evolves. For example, there are indications in the recent housing rights jurisprudence of the Constitutional Court that the location of alternative accommodation when people are evicted from their homes will become a relevant factor in assessing the reasonableness of state conduct.[104] This is particularly important in redressing the legacy of spatial injustice which is both a legacy of the apartheid era, but also aggravated by current housing market dynamics such as gentrification.[105]

In conclusion, the model of review developed by the courts for adjudicating the positive obligations imposed on the State by sections 26 and 27 of the Constitution illuminates several important normative features of the South Africa model of socio-economic constitutionalism. The following part considers the implications of the courts' interpretation of the obligations imposed by socio-economic rights on private actors.

4.2 Obligations Imposed on Private Actors

In South Africa's mixed economy, many people rely on the private sector for access to a range of social goods and services such as housing, electricity, health care, food, and social security. The ability of people to pay for these goods and services is a key driver of socio-economic inequalities, particularly in relation to the quality of goods and services.[106] As is elaborated in Part 5.2, South Africa is one of the most unequal countries in the world in respect of income and wealth distribution. These socio-economic inequalities also largely track the racial inequalities of the colonial and apartheid eras.[107] In this context, the extent to which private providers of goods and services are subject to obligations imposed by socio-economic rights is of critical importance to the transformative objectives of the Constitution.

As noted in Part 2, the Bill of Rights has a broad sphere of application, applying not only to organs of State, but also to private actors and the law governing

---

[104] See, for example, the observations of Majiedt J in his minority judgment in *Thubakgale*, paras 104–116.

[105] This phenomenon is well-illustrated in a recent judgment of the Constitutional Court in *Charnell Commando and Others v City of Cape Town and Another* [2024] ZACC 27.

[106] In the context of the unreliability of State generated electricity through the state-owned enterprise, Eskom, the wealthy and upper middle-classes have increasingly transitioned to alternative energy sources such as solar power. The poor have remained dependent on the dysfunctional and unreliable energy supply by Eskom, deepening pre-existing socio-economic inequalities. See Culwick Fatti and Khanyile (2023).

[107] South African Human Rights Commission (2018), pp. 17–23.

relationships between private parties.[108] In the context of socio-economic rights, the Constitutional Court has held that private parties are bound by a negative obligation not to interfere with or deprive people of their access to socio-economic rights.[109] Such interference or deprivation can only be justified in terms of the stringent purpose and proportionality criteria of the general limitations clause in the Bill of Rights (section 36). Thus any rule of law (whether derived from legislation, the common law or customary law) that has the effect of depriving people of their existing access to a socio-economic right (such as housing) must be capable of being justified in terms of the general limitations clause.[110]

The Constitutional Court has noted that the purpose of the horizontal application of rights "is not to obstruct private autonomy or to impose on a private party the duties of the state in protecting the Bill of Rights."[111] Nevertheless, it has not excluded the possibility that, in appropriate circumstances, socio-economic rights could impose positive obligations on private parties. Relevant considerations would include the history of the right, its purposes, the impact of private conduct on the right, and whether a failure to impose such an obligation would "negate the essential content of the right."[112] Thus in the case of *Daniels v Scribante,* the Court held that a farm owner could not unreasonably withhold consent for a farm dweller to make modest, improvements, at her own expense, to her dwelling to improve its habitability in line with the standard of human dignity.[113]

In addition to the direct horizontal application of constitutional rights, the Constitutional Court has also held that common law concepts and doctrines must be interpreted and developed to align with the values and purposes of the Bill of Rights.[114] This is significant in ensuring that the bodies of law regulating relationships between private parties such as the law of contract or delict ("tort law")

---

[108] The main constitutional provisions governing the so-called "horizontal application" of rights in the Bill of Rights are sections 8(2) read with (3) and section 39(2).

[109] *Grootboom*, para 34; *Governing Body of the Juma Musjid Primary School v Essay NO* [2011] ZACC 13; 2011 (8) BCLR 761 (CC), para 58; *AB v Pridwin Preparatory School* [202] ZACC 12; 2020 (5) SA 327 (CC) ("*Pridwin*"), paras 130; 183–184.

[110] See, for example: *Gundwana v Steko Development CC* [2011] ZACC 14; 2011 (3) SA 608 (CC), paras 40–54; *Maphango v Aengus Lifestyle Properties (Pty) Ltd* [2012] ZACC 2; 2012 (3) SA 531, paras 32–33.

[111] *Governing Body of the Juma Musjid Primary School v Essay NO* [2011] ZACC 13; 2011 (8) BCLR 761 (CC), para 58; *Jaftha*, para 31.

[112] *Daniels*, paras 39–49; *Pridwin*, para 180.

[113] *Daniels*, paras 51–54.

[114] In so doing it has relied on section 39(2) of the Constitution which reads as follows:

> When interpreting any legislation, and when developing the common law or customary law, every court, tribunal or forum must promote the spirit, purport and objects of the Bill of Rights.

develop in ways that are consonant with the normative value system of the Bill of Rights.[115]

The horizontal application of socio-economic rights has contributed to a nuanced approach to adjudication, particularly where socio-economic rights such as housing come into conflict with well-established private law rights such as the right to property. This issue has arisen particularly in the context of the eviction of occupiers of land or housing from private property. Important legislation has been adopted in this context.[116] The Constitutional Court has interpreted this legislation to require a context-sensitive balancing of both the property and housing rights at stake and have developed a set of equitable and procedural justice factors to guide the adjudication of such cases.[117] As the Constitutional Court noted in one of its early landmark judgments:

> The judicial function in these circumstances is not to establish a hierarchical arrangement between the different interests involved, privileging in an abstract and mechanical way the rights of ownership over the right not to be dispossessed of a home or vice versa. Rather, it is to balance out and reconcile the opposed claims in as just a manner as possible taking account of al the interests involved and the specific factors relevant in each particular case.[118]

The conduct of private actors and the body of law that regulates these relationships is thus not insulated from judicial scrutiny for their consistency with the rights in the Bill of Rights, including socio-economic rights. However, despite the advances made under the Constitution in holding private actors accountable for conduct impacting on socio-economic rights, the legal framework facilitating private ownership and market transactions has not been fundamentally altered.[119] In this context, the majority of impoverished and disadvantaged people in South Africa rely on State social programmes for their access to socio-economic rights. These programmes are shaped by the social policies of successive post-apartheid governments. It is thus apt to consider the broad contours of post-apartheid social policy and its shortcomings next.

---

[115] See, for example: *Carmichele*, para 56; *Barkhuizen v Napier* [2007] ZACC 51 2007 (5) SA 323 (CC), paras 60–63; *Beadica 231 (CC) v Trustees for the time being of the Oregon Trust* [2020] ZACC13; 2020 (5) SA 247 (CC), paras 72–78.

[116] Prevention of Illegal Eviction from and Unlawful Occupation of Land Act 19 of 1998; Extension of Security of Tenure Act 62 of 1997.

[117] Van Der Walt (2009), pp. 146–161. Wilson (2021), pp. 57–81.

[118] *Port-Elizabeth Municipality v Various Occupiers* [2004] ZACC 7; 2005 (1) SA 217 (CC), para 23.

[119] For a critique of the enduring public/private divide in the post-apartheid legal order and its impact on socio-economic transformation, see Liebenberg and Kolabhai (2022).

5 Socio-Economic Constitutionalism Through the Prism of State Policy

5.1 A "Social Floor"

The primary orientation of post-apartheid social policy has been to put in place a "social floor" of subsidised services and benefits, largely targeted at those living in poverty.[120] This contrasts with alternative models based on the universal provision of decommodified social services, that is, services provided to all outside the dynamics of the market.[121] Examples of this "social floor" orientation in South African social policy are briefly considered.

In response to the *Grootboom* judgment, the national government adopted an emergency housing programme that provides temporary assistance to people facing exceptional situations of housing need through the allocation of grants to municipalities.[122] This assistance includes temporary access to a basic form of shelter and basic municipal services. The main generator of more secure, long-term housing access for the poor has been a housing subsidy scheme which provides grant finance to beneficiaries within a low-income bracket to acquire or build a first-time house.[123] A basic quantum of free water supply, electricity and sanitation services is provided to residents by local authorities with the possibility of indigent residents applying for a means-tested top-up supply.[124]

In the context of the right of access to social security, South Africa has an extensive means-tested, non-contributory social assistance programme. This programme provides social grants to defined categories of vulnerable groups such as older persons, persons living with disabilities, or to primary care givers for the care of children.[125] Provision is also made for a temporary "social relief of distress grant".[126]

---

[120] National Development Plan (2012), pp. 357–358.

[121] For an analysis of different models or approaches to social policy implementing socio-economic rights, see: Landau and Dixon (2019).

[122] National Housing Code, Part 2, vol 4 enacted in terms of the National Housing Act 107 of 1997.

[123] For details of the scheme, see: https://www.nhfc.co.za/finance-solutions/first-home-finance/.

[124] For an analysis and critique of these programmes of free basic municipal services, see: Dugard (2014); Socio-Economic Rights Institute of South Africa (2013). The constitutionality of the free basic water services and the indigency policies of the City of Johannesburg were unsuccessfully challenged in the *Mazibuko* judgment referred to above.

[125] These grants are provided in terms of the Social Assistance Act 13 of 2004. In the financial year 2023–2024, there were 18.8 million recipients of these grants: SA Government News Agency, "Social grants set of increase in 2024", 21 February 2024 (available online at https://www.sanews.gov.za/south-africa/social-grants-increase-2024).

[126] For details, see: https://www.gov.za/services/services-residents/social-benefits/social-relief-distress.

This model of social assistance has been criticised as inadequate in light of the high levels of structural unemployment in South Africa,[127] resulting in a large cohort of unemployed, able-bodied adults being excluded from any access to social security benefits.[128] Various civil society organisations have campaigned for the introduction of a universal basic income scheme.[129] During the Covid-19 pandemic government expanded the social relief of distress grant into a temporary programme providing R350 per month[130] to all unemployed adults who were not receiving other social grants. This grant has been extended annually since the pandemic, and the amount of the grant was increased marginally during 2024.[131] It is unclear whether this grant will be converted into a universal basic income grant (UBIG),[132] or a targeted grant for unemployed adults as implied in the President's 2024 State of the Nation Address.[133] Thus even though the State is committed to providing a social floor, this analysis of the social assistance programme reveals that this goal is far from being realised.

Turning to the right to health, he public health care system provides free health care services to pregnant women and children under the age of six years as well as free primary health care. Beyond primary health care, partially subsidised health care services are provided in the public sector, and patients are charged according to a means-test.[134] The public health care system in South Africa experiences ongoing medical staffing and equipment shortages, and delivers a limited range of services, often of poor quality, particularly in rural areas.[135] Another feature of South Africa's health care system is the stark disparities that exist between the under-resourced public health sector serving approximately 85% of the population, and the well-resourced private health sector serving only 15% of the population. There is some

[127] The official unemployment rate in the 2nd quarter of 2024 was 33.5% representing 8.4 million unemployed persons. According to the expanded definition (which includes those discouraged from actively seeking employment) the unemployment rate was 42.6%. See Statistics South Africa, Media Release, Quarterly Labour Force Survey (QLFS) – Q4: 2023, 20 February 2024 (available online at: https://www.statssa.gov.za/publications/P0211/Media%20release%20QLFS%20Q2%202024.pdf).

[128] In its concluding observations on the initial report of South Africa, the UN Committee on Economic, Social and Cultural Rights criticised the gap in social assistance coverage for those between the ages of 18 and 59 years with little or no income: UN Committee on Economic, Social and Cultural Rights (2018), paras 47(c) and 48 (c).

[129] Goldblatt and Rosa (2014), pp. 266–271.

[130] The equivalent of 17, 16 euros per month as of the exchange rate of 29 March 2024.

[131] The amount of the grant was increased to R370 per month with effect from 1 April 1014. It is estimated that there are approximately 9–10 million recipients of the "Covid-19 Social Relief of Distress Grant": Patel (2023).

[132] For example, the Social Policy Institute (https://www.spi.net.za/basic-income-grant/); and the Institute for Economic Justice (https://www.iej.org.za/projects/universal-basic-income-guarantee/).

[133] President Cyril Ramaphosa (2024).

[134] The primary legislative framework governing the provision of public health care services at present is the National Health Act 61 of 2003.

[135] See UN Committee on Economic, Social and Cultural Rights (2018), paras 63–67.

regulation of the affordability of private health care services through legislation such as The Medical Schemes Act 131 of 1998 and the Medicines and Related Substances Control Act 90 of 1997. In the sphere of health, the State has undertaken major legislative reform to transition to a national health insurance scheme ("NHI") providing comprehensive health care, free of charge at accredited health facilities.[136] The NHI represents a major policy shift, aiming to reverse the stark disparities in access to health care services between the public and private sector, and to secure universal free health care services.

However, as with all the state programmes delivering socio-economic rights, the implementation of the NHI faces multiple challenges. Many vital socio-economic programmes are poorly implemented due to a combination of inadequate resources, limited capacity in the public sector, corruption and maladministration.[137] In addition, the commodification of service delivery through privatised delivery and cost-recovery models has impeded access to quality social services by many residents in impoverished communities.[138]

5.2 *Fault Lines*

This overview of state policy suggests several fault lines in the South African model of socio-economic constitutionalism. Government social programmes have undoubtedly alleviated poverty, and provided increased access to basic levels of housing, health care, water and social security to millions in South Africa.[139] However, poverty, unemployment and economic inequality levels remain extremely high in South Africa. According to World Bank statistics cited in President Ramaphosa's 2024 State of the Nation Address, 55.5% of the population live under South Africa's National Poverty Line.[140] Moreover as the World Bank observes:

> South Africa is one of the most unequal countries in the world with Gini index at 63 in 2014/2015. Inequality is high, persistent, and has increased since 1994. High levels of income polarization are manifested in very high levels of chronic poverty, a few high-income earners and a relatively small middle class.[141]

---

[136] National Health Insurance Act 20 of 2023. At the time of writing, the Act was subject to much political contestation and had not yet been brought into operation.

[137] On efforts to redress these structural governance dysfunctions through innovative judicial remedies, see Liebenberg (2022).

[138] Ledger (2021); Dugard (2014), pp. 282–285.

[139] Many of these achievements are highlighted in the 2024 State of the Nation Address by President Cyril Ramaposa.

[140] World Bank (2020).

[141] World Bank (2020).

These stark statistics are indicative of the fact that the model of South African socio-economic constitutionalism has not succeeded in transforming the underlying structural drivers of poverty and inequality. The state has constructed a rudimentary social floor providing means tested social grants and services for the poor. However, it has not developed an effective developmental strategy for achieving the sustained transition of communities out of poverty.[142] Until such a strategy is developed and effectively implemented, the transformative purposes of socio-economic constitutionalism discussed in part 2 will not be achieved.

Moreover, programmes crucial to the realisation of socio-economic rights are frequently under-resourced. This suggests that the obligations imposed by socio-economic rights are not fully understood and integrated into economic policy and budgetary decision-making.[143] The robust requirements of public participation and consultation that have developed in the context of legislative and administrative decision-making,[144] have not been replicated in the economic policy and budgetary decision-making processes.[145]

This under-resourcing of the public sector and of publicly provided social goods and services has aggravated the inequalities and disparities in South African society. As Mark Heywood observes:

> In the last three decades, in the absence of the maximum available resources being made available by the state in South Africa, the public goods that should be the stuff of socio-economic rights have increasingly been privatised and have become the basis for new post-apartheid inequalities. ... It is most evident in the food, health, and education systems in South Africa, each of which has seen growth in the private market and exclusion of those who cannot afford to purchase their human rights. Those wholly dependent on the state, still overwhelmingly black people, who were historically disadvantaged by apartheid, are then left at the mercy of failing public health systems and inadequate basic education, which can no longer protect – never mind fulfil – their fundamental rights.[146]

Finally, the weak administration of existing programmes[147] suggests that insufficient attention has been paid to the requirements of state capacity building in all spheres of government. Although South Africa's National Development Plan committed to

---

[142] As the UN Committee on Economic, Social and Cultural Rights noted in its concluding observations on the initial report of South Africa (2018), para 16:

> While the Committee is well aware of the historical roots of such inequalities and welcomes the efforts pursued since the ending of apartheid, the persistence of such inequalities signals that the model of economic development pursued by the State party remains insufficiently inclusive. (para 16).

[143] Heywood (2021).

[144] See the discussion in Part 3 above.

[145] Heywood (2021), pp. 356–360; Liebenberg (2021), pp. 202–203.

[146] Heywood (2021), pp. 375–376.

[147] The judiciary has had to repeatedly deal with cases concerning the maladministration of socio-economic legislation and programmes adopted by the Court: see, for example, the *Thubakgale* and *Mwelase judgments of the Constitutional Court.*

building "capable and developmental state",[148] this objective was undermined by the phenomenon of state capture which prevailed under the leadership of former President Jacob Zuma.[149] The major challenge facing South African constitutional democracy in the next decade is to build institutions of state that are capable of implementing socio-economic rights through processes aligned to the transformative values and objectives of the Constitution.[150]

6 Conclusion

This chapter has sought to demonstrate how the South Africa model of socio-economic constitutionalism is inextricably linked to the unjust past it seeks to transcend, and the socio-economic legacies it aims to transform. Fundamental to this model is a holistic and integrated Bill of Rights with a wide sphere of application to public and private actors. The explicit inclusion of justiciable economic and social rights in the Bill of Rights is the most prominent marker of a commitment to socio-economic constitutionalism. However, there are other constitutional provisions which undergird socio-economic constitutionalism. These include the equality clause embracing a substantive conception of equality rights as well as a property clause which is designed to facilitate, rather than frustrate, restitution and reforms aimed at advancing a more just distribution of land and other property in South Africa.

The chapter highlighted how the integration of socio-economic rights in the Constitution has contributed to a conception of constitutional democracy which incorporates access to socio-economic rights as amongst the entitlements of democratic citizenship. It was also argued that concerns related to the marginal influence of disadvantaged and impoverished communities in the institutions of representative democracy has contributed to the development of robust constitutional requirements for participatory democracy in legislative processes. Participatory democracy has also been affirmed in administrative and other decision-making processes impacting on socio-economic rights through the meaningful engagement jurisprudence of the Constitutional Court.

The chapter proceeded to examine how the adjudication of the obligations imposed by socio-economic rights has contributed to developing the normative features of the South African model of socio-economic constitutionalism. These

[148] National Development Plan (2012), chapter 13, pp. 407–443.

[149] This phenomenon and its far-reaching consequences are documented in the Reports of the Judicial Commission of Inquiry into Allegations of State Capture, Corruption and Fraud in the Public Sector Including Organs of State (2022) (available online at https://www.statecapture.org.za/site/information/reports). This Commission was chaired by the former Chief Justice of South Africa, Justice RMM Zondo.

[150] For an argument that South Africa requires a "democratic, developmental state" to implement socio-economic rights, see Rosa (2012).

include requiring the State to be proactive in adopting the necessary policies and programmes to give effect to socio-economic rights. Such policies and programmes must incorporate provision for urgent socio-economic needs and avoid unfairly excluding particular groups or communities. Organs of state should engage with those directly affected by their decisions, particularly when the relevant decisions affect people's access to socio-economic rights. State social policy should be designed and implemented so as to sustain and improve people's access to socio-economic rights over time. Legislation or policies that result in a deprivation or diminishment in access to social rights can be challenged in court and the State will be placed under a burden of justifying the reasonableness and proportionality of its decisions. Finally, the adjudicative criteria of reasonableness review are not a closed list. Additional substantive and procedural criteria for reasonable government conduct may be identified by the courts. Thus, the model of socio-economic constitutionalism in South Africa is constantly evolving as the facts of new cases illuminate situations which are inconsistent with the values and purposes underpinning socio-economic rights.

The obligations imposed by socio-economic rights on private actors were also analysed. It was observed that the jurisprudence imposes primarily negative obligations on private actors to refrain from conduct which deprives people of their existing access to socio-economic rights. However, the Constitutional Court has also affirmed that, in appropriate circumstances, positive obligations may also be imposed on private actors by the socio-economic rights provisions in the Bill of Rights. The application of socio-economic rights to private actors has resulted in a more nuanced and balanced framework for adjudicating disputes involving a conflict between private law rights and socio-economic rights. However, the basic structure of private law rights which undergirds property rights and market exchanges remains in place. Many wealthy and upper-middle class South Africans rely on goods and services purchased from private service providers in the absence of reliable and good quality public services. It was argued that this trend deepens inequalities in access to socio-economic rights. These socio-economic inequalities represent a major fault line in the South African model of socio-economic constitutionalism.

The final part of the chapter explored socio-economic constitutionalism through the prism of State social policy in South Africa. It traced the broad contours of the State's social policies in the spheres of housing, social security, and health care services. It noted that the overall orientation of state social policy is to provide a basic "social floor" of goods and services targeted primary as impoverished and disadvantaged goods. While this has improved access to socio-economic rights by millions of South Africans, a sustainable model of development that eradicates poverty and reduces the high levels of economic inequality in South Africa has proved elusive thus far. Moreover, the under-resourcing and weak implementation of many existing socio-economic programmes suggests that insufficient attention has been paid to aligning economic and fiscal policies and state institutional capacity to the normative commitments of socio-economic rights.

The South African experience suggests that the recognition of socio-economic rights as justiciable rights in a country's Constitution can make an important contribution to advancing the normative commitments of socio-economic constitutionalism. The elaboration of the normative obligations imposed by socio-economic rights can open up a variety of avenues through which social movements, civil society organisations and other social formations can seek accountability for socio-economic rights violations by powerful public and private actors.[151]

However, as this chapter demonstrated, there are several fault lines in South African model of socio-economic constitutionalism, the most significant being the failure to redress the deep structural legacies of poverty and inequality inherited from the country's colonial and apartheid past. These fault lines in the South African model contain important insights for the broader project of advancing socio-economic constitutionalism through recognising justiciable socio-economic rights in a country's Constitution. First, the normative commitments of socio-economic rights will not be realised without a broader political vision of the developmental strategy required to realise these commitments. Second, a mechanism must be put in place to ensure that economic and budgetary policy and decisions are aligned to the purposes and values of socio-economic rights. This mechanism should ideally be created in the Constitution itself, failing which, in subsidiary legislation. The objectives of socio-economic constitutionalism will not be achieved if economic policy and budgetary decisions are insulated from accountability to the obligations imposed by socio-economic rights. Finally, careful attention must be paid to designing state institutions and governmental processes that are capable of implementing socio-economic rights effectively and consistently with human rights values.

The South African experience suggests that the project of socio-economic constitutionalism can benefit significantly from the recognition of justiciable socio-economic rights. However, the full potential of this model of socio-economic constitutionalism will remain unrealised in the absence of an overarching vision, a concrete strategy and concomitant state capacity for embedding the normative commitments of socio-economic rights in state social policies and practices. These are the challenges that must be confronted if the broader project of socio-economic constitutionalism is to make a meaningful contribution to redressing the social and economic disparities and insecurities at the heart of many contemporary crises.

Acknowledgments This work is based on the research supported in part by the National Research Foundation of South Africa (Grant Number 150027). My gratitude goes to helpful comments from two anonymous reviewers of this article, which helped improve the final project as well as several discussions on the themes of this article with Gideon Basson and other colleagues in the Department of Public Law, Stellenbosch University.

References

Albertyn C (2007) Substantive equality and transformation in South Africa. SA J Hum Rights 23: 253–276

[151] Langford et al. (2014); Wilson (2021).

Albertyn C, Goldblatt B (1998) Facing the challenge of transformation: difficulties in the development of an indigenous jurisprudence of equality. SA J Hum Rights 14:248–276

Basson G (2023) Poverty discrimination under the Promotion of Equality and Prevention of Unfair Discrimination Act: a transformative substantive equality approach. SA J Hum Rights 39:26–51

Bilchitz D (2007) Poverty and fundamental rights: the justification and enforcement of socio-economic rights. Oxford University Press

Boonstra WJ, Söderberg N (2024) Theorising resistance in times of fossil fuel: ecological grief, righteous anger and interaction rituals in Sweden's energy regime shift. Energy Res Soc Sci 116. https://doi.org/10.1016/j.erss.2024.103652

Botha H (2012) Representing the poor: law, poverty and democracy. In: Liebenberg S, Quinot G (eds) Law and poverty: perspectives from South Africa and beyond. Juta & Co, pp 79–99

Brand D (2004) In: Botha H, Van Der Walt A, Van Der Walt J (eds) The proceduralisation of South African socio-economic rights jurisprudence, or 'what are socio-economic rights for?'. SUN Press, Stellenbosch, pp 33–56

Coggin T (2021) There is no right to property: clarifying the purpose of the property clause. Const Court Rev 11:1–37

Culwick Fatti C, Khanyile S (2023) South Africa's power crisis: going off the grid words for the wealthy – but could deepen injustice for the poor. The Conversation, 22 February 2023 (available online: https://theconversation.com/south-africas-power-crisis-going-off-the-grid-works-for-the-wealthy-but-could-deepen-injustice-for-the-poor-200288)

Davis DM, Klare K (2010) Transformative constitutionalism and the common and customary law. SA J Hum Rights 26:403–509

De Vos P (2001) A bridge too far? History as context in the interpretation of the South African Constitution. SA J Hum Rights 17:1–33

De Vos P et al (eds) (2021) South African constitutional law in context, 2nd edn. Juta & Co

Dugard J (2014) Urban basic services: rights, reality and resistance. In: Langford M, Cousins B, Dugard J, Madlingozi T (eds) Socio-economic rights in South Africa: symbols or substance? Cambridge University Press, pp 275–309

Dugard J (2019) Unpacking section 25: what, if any, are the legal barriers to transformative land reform? Const Court Rev 9:135–160

Gabriel RD, Klein M, Pessoa AS (2022) The political costs of austerity. Available at SSRN: https://ssrn.com/abstract=4160971 or https://doi.org/10.2139/ssrn.4160971

Gargarella R (2006) Theories of democracy, the judiciary and social rights. In: Gargarella R, Domingo P, Roux T (eds) Courts and social transformation in new democracies: an institutional voice for the poor? Ashgate, pp 13–34

Gargarella R (2018) Latin America: constitutions in trouble. In: Graber MA, Levinson S, Tushnet M (eds) Constitutional democracy in crisis? Oxford University Press, pp 177–189

Goldblatt B, Rosa S (2014) Social security rights: campaigns and courts. In: Langford M, Cousins B, Dugard J, Madlingozi T (eds) Socio-economic rights in South Africa: symbols or substance? Cambridge University Press, pp 253–274

Graber MA, Levinson S, Tushnet M (eds) (2018) Constitutional democracy in crisis? Oxford University Press

Heywood M (2021) Economic policy and socio-economic rights in the South African Constitution, 1996 - 2021: why don't they talk to each other? Const Court Rev 11:341–377

International Covenant on Economic, Social and Cultural Rights (1966) 993 UNTS 3

Kaika M, Calvário R, Velegrakis G (2024) Austerity: an environmentally dangerous idea. J Polit Ecol 31:67–81

Klare K (1998) Legal culture and transformative constitutionalism. SA J Hum Rights 14:146–188

Klare K (2015) Self-realisation, human rights, and separation of powers: a democracy-seeking approach. Stellenbosch Law Rev 26:445–470

Landau D (2012) The reality of social rights enforcement. Harv Int Law J 53:190–247

Landau D, Dixon R (2019) Constitutional non-transformation? Socioeconomic rights beyond the poor. In: Young KG (ed) The future of economic and social rights. Cambridge University Press, pp 110–133

Langford M, Cousins B, Dugard J, Madlingozi T (eds) (2014) Socio-economic rights in South Africa: symbols or substance? Cambridge University Press

Ledger T (2021) Access to basic services: enabling progressive transformation or entrenching poverty and inequality. Public Affairs Institute Short Report. Available online at https://pari.org.za/short-report-access-to-basic-services/

Leijten I (2015) The German right to an *Existenzminimum*, human dignity, and the possibility of minimum core socioeconomic rights protection. German Law J 16:23–48

Liebenberg S (2010) Socio-economic rights: adjudication under a transformative constitution. Juta & Co

Liebenberg S (2019) The participatory democratic turn in South Africa's social rights jurisprudence. In: Young KG (ed) The future of economic and social rights. Cambridge University Press, pp 187–211

Liebenberg (2021) Austerity in the midst of a pandemic: pursuing accountability through the socio-economic rights doctrine of non-retrogression. SA J Hum Rights 37:181–204

Liebenberg S (2022) The art of the (im)possible? Justice Froneman's contribution to designing remedies for structural human rights violations. Const Court Rev 12:137–170

Liebenberg S (2023) Reasonableness review. In: Young KG, Langford M (eds) The Oxford handbook of economic and social rights. Oxford University Press. https://doi.org/10.1093/oxfordhb/9780197550021.013.48

Liebenberg S, Goldblatt B (2007) The interrelationship between equality and socio-economic rights under South Africa's transformative constitution. SA J Hum Rights 23:335–361

Liebenberg S, Kolabhai RL (2022) Private power, socio-economic transformation, and the Bill of Rights. In: Boggenpoel Z (ed) Law, justice and transformation. LexisNexis, pp 245–283

Lindsay MJ (2017) The presumptions of classic liberal constitutionalism. Iowa Law Rev 102:259–290

Lister M (2005) Marshall-ing social and political citizenship: towards a unified conception of citizenship. Gov Oppos 40:471–491

Marshall TH (1950) Citizenship and social class, and other essays. Cambridge University Press

Michelman FI (2015) Constitutionally binding social and economic rights as a compelling idea: reciprocating perturbations in liberal and democratic constitutional visions. In: García HA, Klare K, Williams LA (eds) Social and economic rights in theory and practice. Routledge, pp 277–293

Modiri J (2018) Conquest and constitutionalism: first thoughts on an alternative jurisprudence. SA J Hum Rights 34:300–325

Murcott M (2022) Transformative environmental constitutionalism. Brill/Nijhoff

National Development Plan: 2030, Our Future – Making it Work (2012), National Planning Commission, The Presidency

Ngcukaitobi (2018) The land is ours: South Africa's first black lawyers and the birth of constitutionalism. Penguin Books

Ngcukaitobi (2021) Land matters: South Africa's failed land reforms and the road ahead. Penguin Books

Patel L (2023) 47% of South Africans rely on social grants – study reveals how they use them to generate more income. The Conversation, 3 May 2023. Available online at: https://theconversation.com/47-of-south-africans-rely-on-social-grants-study-reveals-how-they-use-them-to-generate-more-income-203691

Pienaar JM (2014) Land reform. Juta & Co

Pieterse M (2004) Coming to terms with judicial enforcement of socio-economic rights. SA J Hum Rights 20:383–417

Pieterse M (2005) What do we mean when we talk about transformative constitutionalism? SA Publiekreg/Public Law 20:155–166

President Cyril Ramaphosa (2024) State of the Nation Address, 8 February 2024. Available online at: https://www.gov.za/news/speeches/president-cyril-ramaphosa-2024-state-nation-address-08-feb-2024

Rawls J (1993) Political liberalism. Columbia University Press

Ray B (2016) Engaging with social rights: procedure, participation and democracy in South Africa's Second Wave. Cambridge University Press

Reports of the Judicial Commission of Inquiry into Allegations of State Capture, Corruption and Fraud in the Public Sector Including Organs of State (2022). Available online at https://www.statecapture.org.za/site/information/reports

Rosa S (2012) Transformative constitutionalism in a democratic developmental state. In: Liebenberg S, Quinot G (eds) Law and poverty: perspectives from South Africa and beyond. Juta & Co, pp 100–123

Scott C, Macklem P (1992) Constitutional ropes of sand or justiciable guarantees? Social rights in a new South African Constitution. Univ Pa Law Rev 141:1–148

Seekings J, Nattrass N (2005) Class, race and inequality in South Africa. University of Kwa-Zulu-Natal Press

Sibanda S (2020) When do you call time on compromise? South Africa's discourse on transformation and the future of transformative constitutionalism. Law Democr Dev 24:384–412

Socio-Economic Rights Institute of South Africa (2013) Targeting the poor? An analysis of Free Basic Services (FBS) and municipal indigent policies in South Africa. Available online: https://www.seri-sa.org/images/Targeting_the_Poor_Nov13.pdf

South African Human Rights Commission Equality Report 2017/18 Achieving Substantive Economic Equality Through Rights-Based Radical Socio-Economic Transformation in South Africa (2018). https://www.sahrc.org.za/home/21/files/SAHRC%20Equality%20Report%202017_18.pdf

Stiglitz JE (2012) The price of inequality. Allen Lane

Taylor H (2019) Forcing the court's remedial hand: non-compliance as a catalyst for remedial innovation. Const Court Rev 9:247–281

Teitel R (2000) Transitional justice. Oxford University Press

Terreblanche S (2002) A history of inequality in South Africa: 1652 – 2002. University of Natal Press/ KMM Review Publishing

United Nations Committee on Economic, Social and Cultural Rights (1990) General Comment No. 3, The nature of States parties' obligations (art 2, para 1 of the Covenant), UN doc. E/1991/23

United Nations Committee on Economic, Social and Cultural Rights (2018) Concluding observations on the initial report of South Africa, UN doc. E/C.12/ZAF/CO/1

United Nations Committee on the Rights of the Child (2016) General Comment No. 19, Public budgeting for the realization of children's rights (art 4 of the Convention), UN doc. CRC/C/GC/19

Van der Walt A (2009) Property in the margins. Hart Publishing

Veriava F (2019) Realising the right to basic education: the role of the courts and civil society. Juta & Co

Warwick BTC (2019) Unwinding retrogression: examining the practice of the Committee on Economic, Social and Cultural Rights. Hum Rights Law Rev 19:467–490

Williams LA (2010) The role of courts in the quantitative-implementation of social and economic rights: a comparative study. Const Court Rev 3:141–199

Wilson S (2021) Human rights and the transformation of property. Juta & Co

Winkler T, Mahler C (2013) Interpreting the right to a dignified minimum existence: a new era in German socio-economic rights jurisprudence. Hum Rights Law Rev 13:388–401

World Bank (2020) Poverty & Equity Brief: South Africa, April 2020. Available online: https://databankfiles.worldbank.org/public/ddpext_download/poverty/33EF03BB-9722-4AE2-ABC7-AA2972D68AFE/Global_POVEQ_ZAF.pdf

The Welfare State and the Socio-Economic Constitution of Sweden

Olof Wilske

Contents

Abstract In this chapter, I wish to clarify the character of the Swedish socio-economic constitution as a matter of constitutional fact and as a consequence of EU law. Can the Swedish welfare state, due to its entrenched position across the political spectrum, be described as a socio-economic constitution of sorts, or does it owe its constitutionality to positive constitutional law at the EU and national levels?

In the twentieth century, the "welfare state" (the conceptualization of which may be discussed) may be regarded as the very *raison d'être* of Sweden as a nation-state. The term "folkhemmet" was coined in a social democratic context in 1928 and came to be the guiding principle for much of the activity across the political spectrum, despite being challenged from time to time. In contrast, constitutional rights have not until recently occupied a prominent position in the political or public conscience. The goals of the welfare state have been attained through regular statutes and legal precedent. The main constitutional document—the Instrument of Government—

O. Wilske (✉)
Uppsala University, Uppsala, Sweden
e-mail: olof.wilske@jur.uu.se

S. Hindelang et al. (eds.), *YSEC Yearbook of Socio-Economic Constitutions 2024,* YSEC Yearbook of Socio-Economic Constitutions (2025) 2024: 67–82, https://doi.org/10.1007/16495_2024_75, Published online: 28 January 2025

does however contain wordings which, if they are to be taken seriously, would define Sweden as a social welfare state in a constitutional sense.

In particular, the language of chapter 1, article 2 should be noted. But this article has rarely been invoked for the purpose of claiming social or welfare state rights. Instead, it has generally been regarded as an expression of guiding principles for the legislator or, at the most, guidelines for constitutional interpretation in certain cases as mentioned by the highest courts. Elsewhere, the protection of private property and the freedom of trade are constitutionally guaranteed. These have indeed been invoked and applied in some cases.

I would argue that social rights as a constitutional concept have become a reality only through the impact of European Union law and the European Convention of Human Rights. EU constitutional law is an integral part of Swedish constitutional law and therefore the socio-economic character of Swedish constitutional law is now a reality.

1 The Swedish Model

The "Swedish Model" as a system of socio-economic organization is, at least in Sweden, considered to be world-famous. It is probably fair to say that it is not completely unknown. For instance, French daily Le Monde quite recently declared that major reforms over the last 30 years had profoundly transformed the Nordic country known to be an egalitarian country with a strong welfare system.[1] It noted, in particular, that Sweden is one of the countries of Organization for Economic Cooperation and Development (OECD) where inequality has increased the most in recent decades, and that Sweden now has become "a paradise for the super-rich".[2] The seeds of this development were planted in the 1990s, when Sweden went through a serious financial and fiscal crisis and the public sector was opened up for reform and privatization—breaking, one could say, the patterns of the Swedish model as it had been known up until then.

The patterns of public-sector reform in Sweden are not unique in any way. Neither is, to be truthful, the "Swedish Model", which could in fact be said to be a Nordic model, at least in some aspects. But Sweden as a country and as a social model does seem to evoke certain interest from academics and politicians alike.[3]

As a concept, the "Swedish Model" is usually associated with such characteristics as political democracy, social welfare, and economic equality. It has a reputation already in the 1930s, when progressive intellectuals, especially in France and the

[1] Le Monde: *Suède: le lent déclin d'un "modèle" qui n'en finit pas de creuser les inégalités entre les riches et les pauvres.* 20th December 2022.

[2] Ibid.

[3] Esping-Andersen (1985, 1990).

United States, used the Swedish experience as a basis for arguments in their domestic debates.[4] One early classic is the book *Sweden: The Middle Way,* written by American journalist Marquis Childs in 1936, in which the author presents how Sweden attempts to tread a tricky path between communism and capitalism, which later became an integral part of Swedish self-image and of the construction of *folkhemmet* ("the people's home"), the name attached to the social democratic project of building the Swedish welfare state.[5] After the second world war, Sweden was in a particularly favoured position since neutrality had spared it from the devastation of war, and so was the position of Swedish social democracy. The labour movement could benefit from its own strength and from the perennial disunity among the non-socialist parties, managing to manufacture a national consensus around an economic and social model that was in essence social democratic. The industrial structure was dominated by large, heavily capitalized and concentrated firms, control of which were effectively concentrated in a few hands, and Swedish capitalists were rather easily persuaded to accept state participation in economic rationalization. There were also ample supplies of natural resources providing a cushion against the world economy. Most major labour conflicts had been resolved by the Saltsjöbaden agreement of 1938, whereby most of the labour law became a product of collective agreements rather than statutory law. These factors facilitated the realization of the social democratic postwar programme, which mostly ruled out nationalisation and instead emphasized aggressive wage-solidarity bargaining, active labour market policies and restrictive fiscal policies.[6] But for some parts of the labour movement, collective ownership of the means of production was the ultimate political goal. This is probably why concentration of ownership was seen as compatible with the long-term goals of the social democratic party. State ownership of corporations remained relatively limited, but in the late 1970s and early 1980s some legislative measures were taken, for example regarding union representation in corporate boards of directors and the Codetermination Act of 1976. The apex of this development was probably the introduction of "wage-earner funds" *(löntagarfonder)* in 1984 after an, by Swedish standards, epic political battle in which Swedish capital owners literally took to the streets.[7] In retrospect, it also seems like something of a turning point in the social democratic project.[8]

The welfare state project, in its various forms, was not a constitutional endeavour. And its opponents rarely used constitutional arguments. In fact, Swedish constitutionalism has some eccentric traits, one of them being its historically normative patchiness.[9] Especially during the formative decades of the Swedish model, the Swedish constitution of 1809 was indeed considered obsolete in some respects, and

[4]Lundberg and Tydén (2010).

[5]Childs (1936).

[6]Esping-Andersen (1985), pp. 227–236.

[7]Algotsson (2001).

[8]Henrekson and Jakobsson (2001); Vahlne-Westerhäll (2002); Blomqvist and Rothstein (2009).

[9]Zamboni (2022).

it did not play an important role in political debate or jurisprudence from 1920 until it was replaced in 1974. This period of time has been called the "constitution-less half-century" by a prominent Swedish constitutional scholar.[10] This, however, does not been that Sweden was not governed by law or constitutional principles. The principle of legality has very deep roots in Swedish legal and constitutional culture.[11] But "the Constitution" in a Swedish context has not fulfilled its role in an ideal-typical sense since the early twentieth century. When the current Instrument of Government (IG) was introduced in 1974, the main intention was to bring it up to date with the constitutional realities of the time, mainly parliamentarism and universal suffrage, which had been constitutional facts and practice since 1917 and 1920, respectively. The normative aspirations of this constitutional project were modest. In any case, since classic constitutionalism had come to be associated with the liberal and conservative movements, formal constitutional reform was not a part of the welfare state project.

In this context, it should also be noted that fundamental rights expressed as binding rules in a constitution with normative impact is something of a novelty in Swedish (and Nordic) constitutional culture, with the exception of the very detailed rules on freedom of the press and other media laid down in separate constitutional documents. There are numerous reasons for this, which will only be mentioned briefly here. One important factor is the persistent historical continuity of Swedish constitutionalism, where the principle of legality has been part of the normative deep structure since "forever".[12] Discursively formulated constitutional rules have not always been deemed necessary since they have been considered to be implicit in the legal order.[13] Another is that the constitutional documents traditionally have been concerned with the legitimacy and the functioning of the state, separation (or, in the case of the 1974 IG, non-separation) of powers, taxation et cetera. A third reason is the impact of Scandinavian legal realism in the twentieth century, which some have celebrated as the legal philosophy of the democratic and egalitarian Nordic welfare states and others scorn for having contributed to a state-apologetic and rights-sceptical Nordic political culture which has prioritised the "common good" over individual human rights.[14] A fourth explanation is that human rights did not play an important role as a mobilising concept during the formative years of the welfare state or even in the histories of democratisation of the Nordic region. Instead, narratives have focused on the historical egalitarianism of Nordic societies, the role of the Reformation in producing a strong state apparatus and trust in administration, or the homogeneity of Nordic populations.[15]

[10]Sterzel (2002).

[11]Debaenst (2024).

[12]The concept of "normative deep structure" is understood here as in Tuori (2002).

[13]Debaenst (2024).

[14]Strang (2018). The truth, as usual, is probably somewhere in between.

[15]Hagtvedt Vik et al. (2018).

It should also be noted that just because it is different, constitutionalism is not absent from Swedish and Nordic legal traditions. The stories of constitutionalism and of constitutional thought are usually told from Continental European or Anglo-Saxon viewpoints and presented matter-of-factly. The particularities of Nordic constitutionalism do not fit neatly into the standard narratives of constitutional theory and history. Furthermore, the weakness of constitutionalism in Sweden during the short twentieth century obfuscates an older constitutional heritage, which was very much a reality up until 1917 or so.[16] The reasons for the specific postwar development in Scandinavia are explored further below.[17] In a nutshell, Nordic constitutional law may be said to include a number of common "macro-elements", such as consensual democracy, cautious judicial review with an absence of separate constitutional courts, deference to the parliamentary legislator, a pragmatic and practical legal style, and constitutional flexibility.[18] The element of consensus is worth emphasizing in a Swedish context, because legislative work is traditionally built around legislative committees which often—perhaps naively—strive for a rationalistic "best solution" where policy issues are often transformed into technicalities. It is usually easier to reach agreements and make compromises on technicalities than on values, norms and ideals.[19]

1.1 What Is a Socio-Economic Constitution?

The term "socio-economics" seems to be understood in many different ways, but usually seems to put economics at the heart of social theory.[20] In a legal scholarship environment, especially in the US, it could also be understood as a recognition that other factors and disciplines than law must be taken into account in any endeavour to contemplate its meaning,[21] or as an ethical foundation for law-related economic analysis,[22] connected to the law and economics discourse. When used in constitutional context, the issue of socio-economic rights seems to be the most prevalent association.[23] But I do not believe any of these conceptions grasp the idea of socio-economic constitutions.

As I understand it, the socio-economic constitution of a country comprises the type of social model along the lines of which society functions in terms of economics and social interaction on a macro level. This may be both in a legal or constitutional

[16] Wilske (2024).

[17] Section 3 *infra.*

[18] Husa (2002).

[19] Bull (2014).

[20] Cf. Hellmich (2015).

[21] Ashford (1997).

[22] Ashford (2015).

[23] Cf. Taylor (2023).

sense, and in a wider social scientific meaning. Of course, the concept of a "constitution" is polychromatic and I adhere to the idea that constitutional norms need not be discursively formulated. According to my view, constitutional tradition and practice as well as the professional habits of lawyers can also be part of the constitution in a broader sense, though rarely explored in legal scholarship. One could speak of the constitution as a set of legal rules *and* a social contract concerning the moral fundamental structures of the political society that it regulates. The substance of the social contract thus determines how major social institutions should be designed and which kinds of political and economic action that can be regarded as consistent with the principles of justice in the social contract. In this way, the socio-economic constitution can be understood as the transformation of the social contract from moral and political philosophy (or grand political agreement) into the domain of law.[24]

Another distinction of interest is the one between normative and descriptive constitutionalism. In a strictly legal sense, constitutions are often understood as normative, or even that it is a necessary condition for a constitution to be normative. This is, however, not always the case. Constitutional texts can include any number of assertions, but the normative value often varies depending on the kind of provision. In Sweden, the 1974 Instrument of Government was at its creation even considered a codification of constitutional norms already in force. Sometimes, this distinction is characterized as one of 'legal' (normative) and 'political' (not-so normative) constitutionalism, where Sweden would be a case of the latter. When ascertaining where to insert socio-economic constitutions in these dichotomies, I will consider them to be mainly descriptive or political, although there may be some more legal or normative aspects to them as well.

In post-war Europe, constitution-makers were inspired by the success of American New Deal constitutionalism as well as elements of the (albeit failed) Weimar constitution. This entailed a mix of democratic reforms, civil and social rights, state interventionism and multilateralism which might qualify as a socio-economic constitutional model which also happened to become very successful, though with some significant shortcomings such as extensive bureaucratization.[25]

In the call for contributions to this volume of YSEC, the editors ask the question whether the conceptual pair of "socio-economic" and "constitutions" is at all associated with a constitutional concept or understanding in its own right, and if constitutional texts specifically address the balance between social concerns and the freedom to do business. As we shall see, the main constitutional document in Sweden, the Instrument of Government, does indeed concern itself somewhat with these issues, while the Swedish constitution in a broader sense to a significant extent is the product of what might be called old habits. Perhaps it can contribute to a broader understanding of the concept.

---

[24] Zetterquist (2007).

[25] Dani (2023).

1.2 What Is a Welfare State?

Like 'socio-economic constitutions', the concept of the welfare state is also subject to various definitions and understandings, and is perhaps even more prone to misunderstandings. In this chapter, it is understood as the comprehensive expansion of the duties and accomplishments of the state as a response to the complexity of living conditions in an industrial society. The welfare state-as-social state has taken on the task of providing social security for large parts of the population in the form of statutory health, unemployment, and retirement insurance, as well as standards regarding income, diet, health, housing and education. The welfare state has even assumed responsibility for economic growth and general prosperity, monetary stability, infrastructure for transport and communication, utilities and public service broadcasting, as well as cultural facilities such as theatres, museums and libraries.[26]

One, in legal scholarship sometimes overlooked, aspect of this development is the ever-increasing complexity of the state itself, such that the image of 'the state' as a single, superior, compact entity is not as accurate as in the classical liberal state. As Vesting puts it, "the previously vertical relationship between state and citizen, the original dependence of subjects on public authority, was transformed into a series of horizontal relationships of *communication* between a plurality of legal subjects, of whom the state was but one subject among many".[27]

The welfare state was the single most important societal and political endeavour of the Swedish twentieth century, and many aspects this project peaked some time in the 1970s. Interestingly, the central Swedish constitutional document, the Instrument of Government (IG), is from 1974. Apart from a few articles, however, the welfare state is largely absent from the IG, which is largely concerned with "classical" constitutional issues: civil rights, the organisation of the legislature, the administration, the judiciary and the executive, how laws and other legal rules are enacted, the state budget, constitutional control mechanisms, local and regional self-government and so forth. As stated above, the welfare state project was not constitutional in nature, at least not in the positive-discursive way. It was, however, *constitutive* for Sweden in the sense that it formulated the very identity of Sweden as a nation during the postwar years to a much greater extent than the actual constitution. The IG was the formal and legally binding constitution, to be sure. The elements of the Swedish welfare state were not constitutionally enacted; rather, they were implemented through a plethora of statutory laws. In this regard, social rights have been of utmost importance, but they have not been *constitutional* rights in the classical sense. Systematically, they belong to the domain of administrative or "social" law.

---

[26] Vesting (2023).

[27] Vesting (2023).

2 Socio-Economic Elements in the Instrument of Government

The Swedish constitution is a multi-textual one; that is, a constitution which is comprised of several separate documents. This may seem odd, but in fact it is far from unique in a global context.[28] There are four constitutional documents in Sweden: the Instrument of Government *(Regeringsformen)* of 1974, the Freedom of the Press Act *(Tryckfrihetsförordningen)* of 1949, the Fundamental Law on Freedom of Expression *(Yttrandefrihetsgrundlagen)* of 1991 and the Act of Succession *(Successionsordningen)* of 1810. The Instrument of Government (IG) is the most important one, since it includes the "constitutive" rules of the state, and the only one of interest in this context. Of course, the concept of "constitution" is contested and may include constitutional tradition and practice as well as other unwritten sources, and in the case of most European countries, ECHR and/or EU law also has constitutional implications. The European legal influence has been important in the case of the Swedish socio-economic constitution, a factor to which I will return later on. But first, I would like to present some of the socio-economic elements which have expressly been laid down in the IG. As mentioned in the previous section, the welfare state is largely absent in Swedish constitutional documents, but there are traces to be found, and during the past few decades civil rights have claimed an ever more important place in the IG.

2.1 Welfare as a Fundamental Aim of Public Activity

The first chapter of the IG is bears the title "Basic principles of the form of government" (in Swedish: "statsskickets grunder"). It contains the most fundamental elements of constitutional law, such that they may not be delegated to international organisations, for instance. The constitutional committee of the Swedish parliament has even made a "Solange" statement of its own, referring to the famous Solange judgment of the German constitutional court. Therefore, it is interesting to note that already in article 2, paragraph 2 of this chapter, the following is stated:

> The personal, economic and cultural welfare of the individual shall be fundamental aims of public activity. In particular, the public institutions shall secure the right to employment, housing and education, and shall promote social care and social security, as well as favourable conditions for good health.

This article was included at a very late stage of the constitutional reform work leading up to the IG of 1974. It was the result of a compromise: the nonsocialist parties had for some time been working towards a more explicit and detailed protection of fundamental rights in the constitution, whereas the social democratic

[28] Albert (2023).

position was that such protections were unnecessary because they could be an impediment to social welfare legislation and other important political reform work and because they believed that the most valuable protection for fundamental rights was the democratic system of government in itself. It is noteworthy that the social democratic party, which had been subscribing for government power for decades and still maintained it at the time, and also dominated the political agenda, did not favour binding rules on either political or social rights in the constitution.[29] It is plausible that the traditionally sceptical social democratic attitude towards *Rechtsstaat* and constitutionalism influenced this position.[30]

The committee preparing this specific article argued that a certain protection of social and economic rights would be necessary for the proper functioning of democracy. The article was also said to express fundamental values to which broad sectors of society agreed and that it could form a constitutional basis for the actual content of the legislative reform programme. However, the committee acknowledged that it would not be possible to guarantee the full accommodation of welfare to all citizens, and that the legislator would be bound to make trade-offs between competing interests and limited resources which could not be formulated in the constitutional text. However, the type of goal-oriented statements made in the article was thought to be in line with international conventions and the constitutions of other countries.[31]

Over the decades, the normative position of the provision in chapter 1, article 2 has shifted somewhat. It is still an expression of goals, but the Supreme Court *(Högsta domstolen)* has ruled that it can be used as an interpretive tool when applying statutory law and even constitutional provisions. It has been used in this manner to put Swedish law in line with requirements of international law.[32] Early attempts to invoke the article in court proceedings were usually dismissed on the grounds that it was directed to the legislator and subject only to political control. In this respect, the stipulations of the article have come to enjoy a higher constitutional status, despite the article itself being a product of a legal-political context very different to the one prevailing today.

2.2 Industrial Action

As mentioned in the introductory section, Swedish labour law is to a very large extent the result of collective bargaining and the jurisprudence of the Labour Court, which was created in 1929 and is the court of last instance in labour law matters . This is an integral part of the functioning of the Swedish labour market and may

[29]Lind p. 73.

[30]Neumann 1934 (1987).

[31]SOU 1975:75.

[32]For instance, NJA 2020 s. 3 (Swedish Supreme Court).

indeed be described as a constituent element of the Swedish socio-economic constitution, which from time to time has come into conflict with EU and continental perceptions of labour law. The special character of labour law is expressed in the provision in chapter 2, article 14 of the IG:

> A trade union or an employer or employers' association shall be entitled to take industrial action unless otherwise provided in an act of law or under an agreement.

Unlike other constitutional provisions in the IG concerning fundamental rights and freedoms, this one can be set aside not only statutory law, but by agreements. Moreover, it creates rights not only for individuals *vis-à-vis* the state, but also between individual legal subjects such as employers and employees. This was laid down in a decision by the Labour Court in 2003 and entails that industrial action may not be limited by a court without statutory or contractual authority.[33] Unfortunately, the *travaux préparatoires* which are usually so important in Swedish legal interpretation are mostly silent on this article of the IG. A conclusion might be that rights pertaining to industrial action are an integral part of the Swedish socio-economic constitution, but that its implications are so obvious that the constitutional protection is more or less symbolic.

2.3 Property Rights

Constitutional rights and liberties were a highly contested issue when the current IG was prepared. The issue of private property rights was right at the centre of this conflict. Socialists worried that property rights would stand in the way of social reform programmes, and non-socialists feared that the absence of constitutional guarantees for property would pave the way for socialism. The attempt to introduce

Be all that as it may, property has usually been considered to be a fundamental human right worthy of protection, not merely (or at all) as a protection of capitalist interests.

In the first case in which Sweden was found to be in breach of the European Convention of Human Rights (ECHR), property and expropriation were core issues, although the case actually concerned article 6 of the ECHR and the right to have expropriation cases tried by a court of law.[34] The IG did from the start contain a largely symbolic provision on property protection, but it was substantially reformed in 1993, and contains the following (chapter 2, article 15):

> The property of every citizen shall be so guaranteed that none may be compelled by expropriation or other such disposition to surrender property to the public institutions or to a private subject, or tolerate restriction by the public institutions of the use of land or buildings, other than where necessary to satisfy pressing public interests.

---

[33] AD 2003 nr 46 (Swedish Labour Court).

[34] Case of Sporrong and Lönnroth, 23 September 1982.

> A person who is compelled to surrender property by expropriation or other such disposition shall be guaranteed full compensation for his or her loss. Compensation shall also be guaranteed to a person whose use of land or buildings is restricted by the public institutions in such a manner that ongoing land use in the affected part of the property is substantially impaired, or injury results which is significant in relation to the value of that part of the property. Compensation shall be determined according to principles laid down in law.

The issue of wage-earner funds was mentioned in the introductory section. It was a matter of intense political debate during the 1980s, but only rarely were constitutional arguments invoked. Some opponents, however, claimed that the introduction of such funds entailed fundamental changes of the economic and political systems and that they therefore were "constitutionally unacceptable".[35] Protection of property seemed to be an integral part of the socio-economic constitution after all, notwithstanding the vague wording of the IG. In any case, the political process ended up in a stronger constitutional protection for property rights. The wage-earner funds were abolished by the non-socialist government of the early 1990's and successive social democratic governments have not attempted to reintroduce them.

2.4 *Copyright*

Copyright is a form of property right. Chapter 2, article 16 of the IG simply states that "Authors, artists and photographers shall own the rights to their works in accordance with rules laid down in law." The reason for copyright being protected separately is that it is considered important for the free formation of opinion.[36] Still, the constitutional protection of this right is comparatively feeble since it only states that the material content of copyright should be laid down in statutory law.

2.5 *Freedom of Trade*

Chapter 2, article 17 of the IG provides the following:

> Restrictions on the right to trade or practise a profession may be introduced only in order to protect pressing public interests and never solely in order to further the economic interests of a particular person or enterprise.

Freedom of trade is an integral part of any market economy and is usually considered one of the classic freedoms. The principles as such were introduced from the eighteenth century onwards in European countries. In Sweden, guilds lost their last privileges in 1864, but freedoms of trade and profession were not introduced in the constitutional text until 1994, 130 years later. This is another example of

[35] Algotsson (2001).

[36] Prop. 1975/76:209 p. 129.

an entrenched feature of Swedish society which has not been discursively formulated in constitutional documents until just recently.

Of course, limitations are possible through statutory law, and such regulations are ubiquitous in any modern society, not least for safety reasons. But the core of the freedom is to conduct business and to gain profit from it, and it would not be possible to limit businesses or trades as such.[37]

2.6 *Education and Research*

All children covered by compulsory schooling shall be entitled to a free basic education in the public education system, according to chapter 2, article 18 of the IG. Compulsory schooling has been a legal reality in Sweden since 1842, although basic education was provided well before that in many places. Education, of course, is a central feature of any modern society, and it is highly plausible that it would be a reality without formal constitutional protection. The latter was introduced in 1994. A provision on the freedom of research was added in 2010, motivated by the importance of free research in a democratic society.

2.7 *Conclusions*

The Swedish instrument of government contains a number of discursively formulated socio-economic elements. By no means do they present a comprehensive picture of a Swedish socio-economic constitution, nor does the IG normatively prescribe much at all with regard to socio-legal elements. It is, however, reasonable to conclude a few things by reading the IG.

First, there is no getting around the fact that Sweden is a welfare state (or a social state), considering chapter 1, article 2. The wording is surprisingly far-reaching; admittedly, none of the large political parties have seriously proposed dismantling the welfare state as such, but doing so would clearly imply constitutional reform. The Swedish labour model also seems rather constitutionally protected. Second, property and trade rights also seem entrenched to the point that a more radical socialist political program would require constitutional reform as well. To a certain extent, then, the socio-economic constitution is indeed protected by the IG, although the welfare state more has the character of grand political bargain.

In the next section, I will introduce some aspects of EU law impact on Sweden with regard to socio-economic aspects.

[37] Bexhed and Thorstensson (2018).

3 European Integration and Proxy Constitutionalism

The issue of European Community membership was first introduced in the early 1970s, but Swedish non-alignment policy was considered a major hurdle. After the fall of the Berlin Wall, the political context changed and Sweden applied for membership after a consultative referendum in 1994. Major reasons, apart from the new situation in Europe, were a domestic economic crisis in the early 1990s and the desire to be a part of European decision-making. At the time, there were questions regarding the constitutionality of Swedish EU membership and also how it would impact the sovereignty of the Swedish parliament *(Riksdagen).* As for the European Convention on Human Rights (ECHR), it was ratified by Sweden early on but failed to make much of a domestic impact until the early 1980s and under a fair amount of political and legal controversy.

In the Scandinavian countries, European integration has led to a constitutional transformation that to a large extent has brought them closer to the constitutional traditions of their continental neighbours, as Rehling Larsen has noted.[38] As in the UK, European integration has led to a kind of 'constitutionalism by proxy' in Scandinavia.[39] The idea of popular sovereignty as entrenched in the Swedish constitution has been challenged by the federal European constitutional development of union law and human rights law. Because of the success of social democracy in Scandinavia, which set it apart from the rest of continental Europe, the Nordic countries were tardy and reluctant participants in the project of European integration. Whereas the reconstitution of Europe after the second world war was shaped by the centre-right Christian democrats, Scandinavia remained mostly social democratic.[40] In the view of Christian democratic constitutionalists, democracy needed to be constrained in order to avoid a constitutional collapse such as the fall of the Weimar republic in Germany in 1933, and in other European countries for that matter. European integration was a constitutive part of this constitutional endeavour, which saw the constitution as an order of values and democracy was interpreted in substantive rather than procedural terms. But in Scandinavia, where democracy was first and foremost understood as majority rule, the protection of fundamental rights by counter-majoritarian institutions seemed very foreign. One reason for this was the social democratic view that the rise of fascism was a result of capitalist excess and economic inequality. Society would, in this view, be best protected by social and economic policies in order to limit the impact of cyclical economic crises. For this reason, constitutional reform was not high on the agenda of for Scandinavian social democrats.[41] Neither were constitutionally protected rights.

The ECHR became something of a battering ram for the protection of constitutional rights in Sweden. From the 1990s, the supreme courts in Sweden have less

[38] Rehling Larsen (2023).

[39] Rehling Larsen (2021).

[40] Rehling Larsen (2023).

[41] Rehling Larsen (2021).

disinclined to consider ECHR law than domestic constitutional law, partly because of constitutional limits to judicial review that were repealed in 2010. The current situation is that the stature of the IG has grown and Sweden is slowly becoming more of a constitutional democracy in the continental sense. But perhaps even more important than the ECHR is the massive impact of European Union law. This is partly due to the sheer volume of EU regulation, but also to the fact that the IG does not accurately portray how laws and other regulations are created. Instead of the archetypical national parliamentary sovereignty, plenty of regulation is now handed down from Brussels for national authorities to implement. In chapter 10 of the IG, which concerns international relations, the procedures for transfer of decision-making authority to the European Union are quite clear. But the actual normative influence of the EU does not appear in the IG or in any other discursive constitutional document. The European aspect of the Swedish constitution is therefore not very transparent.

More importantly in the context of this chapter is the introduction of a distinctly socio-economic element via the EU treaties into the Swedish constitution. As Lind observed already in 2009, the creation of the European Social Charter introduced an entirely new dimension of justiciability of rights in Sweden, thus judicializing the and moving it in a constitutional direction, away from the national political project it had been in the twentieth century.[42]

4 Conclusions

The "welfare state" is still an integral part of Swedish national identity and as such also of its socio-economic constitution. However, some of its distinctly national traits have had to give way to the insight that Sweden is not unique in its socio-economic enterprise, although it has probably been distinctly more political than legal (or constitutional) in Sweden (and the rest of Scandinavia) than in continental Europe. To a great extent, the judicialization and constitutionalisation of rights is an effect of ECHR and EU law, but not entirely. As shown above, welfare state elements were included early on in the IG when it was new in 1974 as a matter of political and constitutional aim. These aims are no longer a matter of national political or constitutional affairs, but rather a part of the greater European political and constitutional project.

References

Albert R (2023) Multi-textual constitutions. Va Law Rev 109:1629

[42] Lind (2009).

Algotsson K-G (2001) Äganderätt och demokrati. Svensk grundlagsdebatt under 1990-talet. SNS förlag, Stockholm
Ashford R (1997) Socio-economics: what is its place in law practice? Wis Law Rev 1997:611
Ashford R (2015) Introduction to socio-economics: an ethical foundation for law-related economic analysis. Akron Law Rev 49:287
Bexhed M, Thorstensson A (2018) Näringsfrihet och vinstbegränsning. Svensk juristtidning, p 128
Blomqvist P, Rothstein B (2009) Välfärdsstatens nya ansikte. Atlas, Stockholm
Bull T (2014) Constitutional identity – a view from Sweden. Retfaerd årgang 37 nr. 4/147
Childs M (1936) Sweden: the middle way. Yale University Press, New Haven
Dani M (2023) The Democratic and Social Constitutional State as the paradigm of the post-World War II European constitutional experience. In: Dani M et al (eds) The legitimacy of European constitutional orders. Edward Elgar Publishing, Cheltenham
Debaenst B (2024) Du gamla, du nya. 1974 års regeringsform ur ett rättshistoriskt perspektiv. In de Lege: Regeringsformen 50 år 1974-2024. Iustus, Uppsala
Esping-Andersen G (1985) Politics against markets. The social democratic road to power. Princeton University Press, Princeton
Esping-Andersen G (1990) The three worlds of welfare capitalism. Princeton University Press, Princeton
Hagtvedt Vik H, Jensen S, Lindkvist L, Strang J (2018) Histories of human rights in the Nordic countries. Nord J Hum Rights 36(3):189–201
Hellmich SN (2015) What is socioeconomics? An overview of theories, methods and themes in the field. Forum Soc Econ 46:1–23
Henrekson M, Jakobsson U (2001) Where Schumpeter was nearly right – the Swedish model and capitalism, socialism and democracy. J Evol Econ 11:331–358
Husa J (2002) Nordic reflections on constitutional law. A comparative Nordic perspective. Peter Lang Europäischer Verlag der Wissenschaften, Frankfurt am Main
Lind A-S (2009) Sociala rättigheter i förändring. En konstitutionellrättslig studie. (Social rights undergoing changes. A study in constitutional law). Doctoral dissertation, Uppsala University
Lundberg U, Tydén M (2010) In search of the Swedish model. Contested historiography. In: Matsson H, Wallenstein S-O (eds) Swedish modernism. Architecture, consumption, and the welfare state. Black Dog Publishing, London, pp 36–41
Neumann F (1987) Rechtsstaat, the division of powers and socialism. In: Tribe K (ed) Social democracy and the rule of law. Allen & Unwin, London. Reprinted by Routledge 2020. First published under the pseudonym Leopold Franz as 'Rechtsstaat, Gewaltenteilung und Sozialismus', Zeitschrift für Sozialismus Jg. 1, 1934, pp 254–261
Rehling Larsen S (2021) Varieties of constitutionalism in the European Union. Mod Law Rev 84: 477
Rehling Larsen S (2023) Constitutional pathways in Scandinavia. In: Dani M et al (eds) The legitimacy of European constitutional orders. Edward Elgar Publishing, Cheltenham
Sterzel F (2002) Ett kvartssekel efter "det författningslösa halvseklet": Har Sverige nu en författning? In: Grundlagens makt. Konstitutionen som politiskt redskap och som rättslig norm. SNS förlag, Stockholm, pp 77–98
Strang J (2018) Scandinavian legal realism and human rights: Axel Hägerström, Alf Ross and the persistent attack on natural law. Nord J Hum Rights 36(3):202–218
Taylor W (2023) The social constitution. Embedding social rights through legal mobilization. Cambridge University Press, Cambridge
Tuori K (2002) Critical legal positivism. Ashgate, Aldershot
Vahlne-Westerhäll L (2002) Den starka statens fall? En rättsvetenskaplig studie av svensk social trygghet 1950-2000. Norstedts juridik, Stockholm
Vesting T (2023) State theory and the law. Edward Elgar Publishing, Cheltenham
Wilske O (2024) Is there a Swedish constitutional exceptionalism? In: Scandinavian studies in law, vol 70. Stockholm Institute for Scandinavian Law, Stockholm

Zamboni M (2022) The role of constitution in Sweden: addressing its patchy legal legitimacy and its (half-way) transition from political to legal constitutionalism. Faculty of Law, Stockholm University Research paper

Zetterquist O (2007) A European social contract? In: Scandinavian studies in law, vol 52. Stockholm Institute for Scandinavian Law, Stockholm

The Constitutionalisation of the Economy in France, Germany and Belgium: Enshrining the Market Order, Rationalising the Social State

Guillaume Grégoire

Contents

Abstract In legal literature, a specific theory prevails on the issue of the economic order accepted or imposed by supreme norms: the economic neutrality of national constitutions. The constitutional orders of European states would be mostly open to various options of economic policy, be they more interventionist or more liberal, depending on the choices made by the elected lawmakers. This thesis of 'economic neutrality' is attractive: it is straightforward and consistent with the position of judicial self-restraint put forward by the constitutional courts themselves.

Nevertheless, it remains superficial—at least for the German, French and Belgian legal orders. Even leaving aside the (albeit decisive) influence of EU law, the interpretation given to both economic liberties and social rights most often reveals a neoliberal mindset. Enshrined by constitutional courts through classical economic liberties, the market order is used by these same supreme courts as a 'factual

G. Grégoire (✉)
University of Liège, Liège, Belgium
e-mail: Guillaume.gregoire@uliege.be

S. Hindelang et al. (eds.), *YSEC Yearbook of Socio-Economic Constitutions 2024*, YSEC Yearbook of Socio-Economic Constitutions (2025) 2024: 83–136,
https://doi.org/10.1007/16495_2024_72, Published online: 31 January 2025

constraint' that justifies the ongoing rationalisation of the social state.

1 Introduction—The 'Economic Neutrality' of National Constitutions: A Veil of *Judicial Self-Restraint*

While the 'economic constitution' has become a cardinal concept in EU law studies,[1] it is also increasingly used in analyses of national constitutional law.[2] However, since at least the seminal decision of the German Federal Constitutional Court (FCC) of 20 July 1954,[3] the generally accepted view has been that national constitutions are 'economically neutral'—at least in Western Europe. In other words, there is no 'economic constitution', since no explicit constitutional choice has been made about the economic system. As the German Constitutional Court stated in the above-mentioned judgment:

> The Basic Law neither guaranteed the "economic neutrality" (*wirtschaftspolitische Neutralität*) of government and legislative powers nor a "social market economy" that could only be managed with market-compliant means (*martktkonforme Mittel*). The "economic neutrality" of the Basic Law only consists in the fact that the constituent power has not expressly taken a decision for a particular economic system.[4]

This stance of economic neutrality of the Constitution (and of the Constitutional Court) was reiterated in the *Mitbestimmung* decision of 1 March 1979.[5] Consequently, the Constitutional Court is 'open' to the various economic orientations of the legislature, be they social(ist) or (neo)liberal. Most European constitutional courts have implicitly or explicitly followed this approach. The first decisions of the French Constitutional Council in economic matters are generally regarded to reflect such *judicial self-restraint*:[6] this court confirmed the constitutionality of the *Nationalisations* in 1981 (subject to an upward revaluation of the compensatory indemnities),[7] but also of the *Privatisations* in 1986.[8] Other constitutional courts, such as the Belgian Constitutional Court, regularly emphasise the wide 'margin of

[1] Streit and Mussler (1994); Joerges (2005); Hatje (2010); Kaupa (2016).

[2] Grégoire and Miny (2022).

[3] BVerfG, 20 July 1954, *Investitionshilfe*, 1 BvR 459, 484/52.

[4] *Ibid.*, §§37–38.

[5] BVerfG, *Mitbestimmung*, 1 March 1979, 1 BvR 532/77.

[6] Rabault (2000); Dussart (2015).

[7] Cons. const., 16 January 1982, *Nationalisations I*, No. 81-132 DC; 11 February 1982, *Nationalisations II*, No. 82-139.

[8] Cons. const., 25–26 June 1986, *Privatisations*, No. 86-207 DC.

appreciation' left to the legislature in economic and fiscal matters,[9] which may be seen as an implicit endorsement of the doctrine of 'economic neutrality'.

A minor caveat, which may seem self-evident, is nevertheless generally added by the constitutional courts, namely that the legislature is free... as long as it does not violate the Constitution. This is clearly expressed by the FCC in the 1954 decision: 'This enables the legislature to pursue the economic policy it deems appropriate, provided it observes the Basic Law' (*Grundgesetz*, hereafter GG)[10]—and 'in particular fundamental rights', as it added in the *Mitbestimmung* decision in 1979.[11] Since the fundamental rights cover both 'liberal' freedoms and 'social' rights, the literature argues that 'economic neutrality' is not absolute: total 'socialisation', as well as complete 'privatisation' and 'liberalisation' of the economy, would be ruled out. Between the two extremes, however, parliament is said to be free to act.

This thesis of 'economic neutrality' is attractive: it is straightforward and consistent with the position of judicial self-restraint put forward by the constitutional courts themselves. Nevertheless, it remains superficial. Even leaving aside the (albeit decisive) influence of EU law,[12] the interpretation given to both economic liberties and social rights most often reveals a specific 'economic referential',[13] i.e., a relatively homogeneous doctrinal model of how the economy would and should work. More precisely, a neoliberal economic referential emerges. Based on an analysis of the German, French and Belgian situations, this is what I would like to argue here.[14] These three States were chosen because their constitutional courts all subscribe, implicitly or explicitly, to the 'economic neutrality' thesis, while at the same time having specific features that can shed light on the issue under study. These dimensions of comparison are: the historical tradition regarding the balance of powers (legicentrism vs. constrained legislature); the structure of the State (centralism vs. federalism); the period of adoption of the constitution currently in force (nineteenth century vs. post World War II); the original function of the constitutional review (arbiter of the distribution of powers vs. guardian of fundamental rights); the composition of the constitutional court ('experts' vs. 'politicians'); etc. The underlying assumption is that if a convergent way of dealing with economic issues emerges from such different legal configurations, one may infer that the cause is not primarily (or exclusively) legal, but rather has to do with extra-legal factors, including a shared worldview—an 'economic referential'—that implicitly guides the interpretation and application of

[9]Cour const., 17 September 2009, No. 143/2009, B.5; 10 October 2012, No. 118/2012, B.6.2; 8 May 2014, No. 78/2014, B.5.

[10]BverfG, 20 July 1954, *Investitionshilfe*, *loc. cit.*, §38.

[11]BverfG, 1 March 1979, *Mitbestimmung*, *loc. cit.*, §141.

[12]See Grégoire (2025a).

[13]Muller (2010).

[14]For a more systematic analysis, see Grégoire (2025b).

constitutional law.[15] This is precisely what is argued in this paper. Enshrined by the three constitutional courts through classical economic liberties (Sect. 2), the market order is used by these very same supreme courts as a 'factual constraint' that justifies the ongoing rationalisation of the social state (Sect. 3).

2 The Extension of Economic Liberties or the Constitutionalisation of the Market

There are three classic economic liberties: freedom of contract, property rights and economic freedom *sensu stricto*. As subjective rights of the economic agent, they represent, from the physiocrats to Friedrich Hayek, the essential legal pillars of the market institution. In the three legal orders studied, these classic economic liberties have been increasingly enshrined and protected by the constitution in recent decades. Although freedom of contract is also relevant, it will be left aside here, due to the practical limits of this contribution. An analysis of the development of the right to property and economic freedom is sufficient to reveal the tendency of constitutional judges to legally enshrine the market. The right to property has been continuously (re)affirmed and gradually expanded by the respective constitutional courts of the states studied, to such an extent that it has even served as a bulwark against any extensive socialisation or nationalisation of the economy, even by the indirect means of redistributive taxation (Sect. 2.1). The freedom to pursue an economic activity was also enshrined by the supreme courts, which even drew from it the existence of a constitutional duty to protect the competition order, in a kind of implicit reception of EU law (Sect. 2.2). The result, at the constitutional level, is the advent of an 'objectivised' market order (Sect. 2.3).

[15] Other European States could have been included. Among them, two categories would have been of particular interest: the Eastern European states (of the former 'Soviet bloc'), on one hand; and the Southern European countries, on the other hand. Some of the former adopted new constitutions in the 1990s, which explicitly refer to the (social) market economy (e.g. in Hungary and Poland). Some of the latter were subjected to the 'conditionality' and 'structural reforms' imposed by the European stability mechanisms and the Memoranda of Understanding of the Troika (i.e. the International Monetary Fund, the European Central Bank and the Commission). For instance, apart from the paradigmatic case of Greece, Italy would also have been a very relevant case to study, given its rich history of economic constitutionalism, both in terms of positive law and academic literature.

2.1 *The Right to Private Property: An Instrument for Rationalising the Legislature's Economic Interventionism*

In the liberal tradition initiated by Locke, the right to property is the foundation of individual freedom. Sieyès, the founding father of modern constitutionalism, extended this idea by making private property the source of 'active' citizenship and the foundation of a new social organisation. This explains why most modern constitutions have explicitly endorsed the central place of the right to private property within their own legal systems, even if only in the form of limits on expropriation. But it is the constitutional courts that have drawn out all the legal and axiological implications. On one hand, the right to property has been developed and refined: various patrimonial rights have been subsumed under the guarantee of private property, while certain restrictions have been accepted on the basis of the 'socially bound' nature of property (Sect. 2.1.1). Despite these restrictions, the 'essence' of property rights was considerably strengthened and used to limit the legislature's economic interventionism (Sect. 2.1.2), be it to limit the possibility of large-scale nationalisation or to rationalise fiscal policies by prohibiting 'confiscatory' taxation.

2.1.1 Development and Constitutional Refinement of the Right to Private Property

Each of the three constitutional courts has confirmed the constitutional rank of the right to property. In France, it was affirmed in the decision *Nationalisations* (1981), through Articles 2 and 17 of the 1789 '*Déclaration des droits de l'Homme et du Citoyen*' (DDHC), which is included in the 'constitutional block' (*bloc de constitutionnalité*) built up since the 1970s.[16] In Belgium, the Constitutional Court used its 'combination method', which merges the fundamental rights protected by the Constitution and by international and EU law into an 'indissociable whole', to extend the guarantee against expropriation provided by Article 17 of the Constitution to the full protection of property offered by Article 1 of the First Additional Protocol to the European Convention on Human Rights (hereafter Art. 1P1).[17] For its part, the FCC clarified the reasoning by which the right to property becomes an 'elementary fundamental right' and an 'axiological decision of particular importance':[18] as an expression of human dignity (Art. 1 GG),[19] the right to property (Art. 14 GG)

[16]Cons. const., 16 July 1971, *Liberté d'association*, No. 71-44 DC; 27 December 1973, *Taxation d'office*, No. 73-51 DC.

[17]Rosoux (2015), pp. 53–57 and pp. 136–147.

[18]BverfG, 7 August 1962, *Feldmühle-Urteil*, 1 BvL 16/60, §53.

[19]BverfG, 23 April 1991, *Bodenreform I*, 1 BvR 1170/90, §131.

guarantees in the patrimonial sphere an area of individual freedom (Art. 2 GG) against possible encroachment by the community.[20] Moreover, in each of the three States, the protection of property is extended to other 'economic rights that function economically like property',[21] including rights of claim or intangible rights over intellectual creations (copyright, industrial and commercial property, etc.).

While extending the scope of the right, the three highest courts take into account new restrictions on private property, due to the evolution of the 'general interest', which must adapt to social changes. This was explicitly stated by the Constitutional Council in the landmark decision *Nationalisations*.[22] The Belgian Constitutional Court also refers to this idea when 'measuring' the 'fair balance', i.e., the proportionality, of the infringement of the right to property.[23] The German Constitutional Court agrees, but gives the reason for such limitations:[24] the 'socially bound' nature of property (*Sozialbindung des Eigentums*),[25] a legacy of Article 153 of the Weimar Constitution.[26]

Despite these proclaimed limits, constitutional judges are applying increasingly strict controls, even when it's not a case of 'expropriation' (which implies deprivation) but only of 'restriction', i.e., of regulation of the use of right to property. Under the dissolving effect of the principle of proportionality, the FCC is blurring this structuring distinction[27] that it had previously helped to forge.[28] The same is true in Belgium, where 'restrictions' may give rise to compensation.[29] In France, the strengthening of control was strikingly reflected in the decision to declare unconstitutional the so-called '*Loi Florange*', which provided for a system to prevent profit-based layoffs (*licenciements boursiers*).[30] The alleged disproportion was not only the obligation to sell (although only in cases where the business is completely shut down while still generating profits), but also, and more fundamentally, the fact that the law would substitute the judge for 'the business owner of a company, who is not

[20] BverfG, 18 December 1968, *Hamburgisches Deichordnungsgesetz*, 1 BvR 638/64, §94; 1 March 1979, *Mitbestimmung*, *loc. cit.*, §145.

[21] Badura (2011), p. 39. For France: Colly (2022), p. 596. For Belgium: Pâques and Vercheval (2011), p. 793.

[22] Cons. const., 16 January 1982, *Nationalisations I*, *loc. cit.*

[23] Cour const., 22 September 2011, No. 145/2011, *loc. cit.*, B.56.

[24] BVerfG, 1 March 1979, *Mitbestimmung*, *loc. cit.*, §§167 to 170.

[25] On this concept, see Leisner (1972).

[26] Kirchheimer (1930).

[27] Wilhelm (2000).

[28] BVerfG, 15 July 1981, *Nassauskiesung*, 1 BvL 77/78.

[29] Cour const., 1 October 2015, No. 132/2015, B.8.1. For a fuller presentation of the Constitutional Court's reasoning, see: Rosoux (2015), pp. 873–894.

[30] Cons. const., 27 March 2014, *Loi visant à reconquérir l'économie réelle*, No. 2014-692 DC. See also: Cons. const., 7 December 2000, *Loi relative à la solidarité et au renouvellement urbains*, No. 2000-436 DC.

in [financial] difficulty, for economic choices relating to the management and development of that business'.[31]

2.1.2 Protection of the 'Essence' of Property as an Instrument for Limiting the Economic Action of Legislative Power

The constitutions must guarantee the 'very core' of the right of property, its 'essence' (*Wesengehalt*), in the words of the German Basic Law (Art. 19, para. 2). Even if the use of the right can be regulated by the legislature, the owner must ultimately retain control over the (tangible or intangible) object to which the right is attached. The French constitutional judges are also familiar with this idea: the prohibition of the 'denaturation' of the right to property[32] appears to be the functional equivalent of the guarantee of the 'essence' in the German constitutional system. This threshold limit can also be found in Belgian constitutional case law,[33] through the interpretation given by the European Court of Human Rights (ECtHR) to Article 1P1.[34] From this so-called 'essence' of the right to property, the constitutional judges have derived certain significant limits on the legislature's power to organise the economy: they infer a maximum threshold for nationalisation of the economy (Sect. 2.1.2.1) or 'discover' tax rates above which taxation becomes 'confiscatory' and therefore unconstitutional (Sect. 2.1.2.2).

2.1.2.1 Property Rights as an Obstacle to Nationalisation and Socialisation

Today, the trend is mainly towards the privatisation and liberalisation of public services. But not so long ago, the path seemed inexorably to lead to ever wider collectivisation of national economies. Basically, such collectivisation can take two forms: either 'nationalisation', which involves the transfer of ownership and control of the company to the state; or 'socialisation', which involves the collective control of the workers over (certain) companies or branches of the economy. Each of these options of course entails a challenge to the rights of the 'owners' of the companies concerned, i.e., the shareholders.[35] Neither nationalisation nor socialisation has been addressed by the Belgian constitutional court, but the former is not unknown to the French constitutional order (Art. 9 of the 1946 Preamble) (Sect. 2.1.2.1.1). The latter

---

[31] Fabre (2014).

[32] Cons. const., 29 July 1998, *Loi d'orientation relative à la lutte contre les exclusions*, No. 98-403 DC, Rec. 7.

[33] E.g., Cour const., 24 March 2004, No. 54/2004, §B6.

[34] ECtHR, 23 September 1982, *Sporrong and Lönnroth v. Sweden*, No. 7151/75, §63; ECtHR, 19 June 2006, *Hutten-Czapska v. Poland*, Req. No. 35014/97.

[35] Strictly speaking, shareholders are not the owners of companies, but only of the shares constituting the entities that give legal form to these companies.

is present in the Basic Law (Art. 15 LF) but has so far never been implemented, except in the watered-down form of 'codetermination' (*Mitbestimmung*) (Sect. 2.1.2.1.2).

Property Rights as an Obstacle to Nationalisation in France

With regard to nationalisation in France, the law of 18 December 1981, adopted shortly after François Mitterrand's accession to the presidency, led the Constitutional Council to settle the issue of the relationship between the act of nationalisation (Art. 9 of the 1946 Preamble) and the right of private property. The *Conseil* concluded in two stages[36] that nationalisations were constitutional in principle, but that the amount of compensation had to be adjusted, which *de facto* hindered any future similar initiative, due to the excessively high cost that this would entail for public finances. To reach this conclusion, the judges neutralised the imperative nature of Article 9 of the Preamble,[37] but also implicitly established a maximum threshold for nationalisation of the economy,[38] although it gave no indication of the precise boundaries of the 'field of private property' that cannot be infringed. Stating the existence of such an absolute constitutional limit was the main objective set from the outset by the rapporteur of the decision, Georges Vedel.[39]

However, the judges' reasoning was not self-evident. On one hand, the position of property rights in the hierarchy of norms was hotly debated at the time.[40] On the other hand, the extension of the 'expropriation' rules of Article 17 of the French Constitution to nationalisation was not as inevitable as it might seem. Conceptually, these two measures do not necessarily overlap.[41] First, the assets transferred to the State are not *a priori* the same: traditional expropriation concerned immovable properties, whereas nationalisation concerns 'enterprises', i.e., means of production involving a collective of workers. Second, the notion of 'general interest' underlying the idea of nationalisation could be interpreted more broadly than in the case of expropriation, because paragraph 9 implies an anti-capitalist conception of the economy. Third, expropriation is generally an operation of the executive power via the administration and under the control of the courts, whereas nationalisation is an act of the legislature itself, which could justify setting aside or at least restraining judicial control. This would have opened the way for a different assessment of the

---

[36] Cons. const., 16 January 1982, *Nationalisations I, loc. cit.*; 11 February 1982, *Nationalisations II, loc. cit.*

[37] See also: Cons. const., 25–26 June 1986, *Privatisations*, No. 86-207 DC, Rec. 55–61; 9 April 1996, *Loi portant diverses dispositions d'ordre économique et financier*, No. 96-375 DC, Rec. 2–6; 16 May 2019, *Loi relative à la croissance et la transformation des entreprises*, No. 2019-781 DC, Rec. 43–47.

[38] Rivero (1982), p. 210; Luchaire (1982), pp. 71–72.

[39] Archives of the Cons. const. session of 12 December 1981 (Dec. No. 81-132 DC, *Nationalisations I*), pp. 4–5.

[40] Favoreu (1982), p. 43.

[41] Beaud (1994).

'adequacy' of the compensatory indemnity, potentially downwards rather than upwards. After all, there was a very significant historical precedent in favour of this interpretation: just two months after the adoption of the DDHC on 26 August 1789, the nationalisation of the Catholic Church properties was pronounced by the very same National Constituent Assembly (on 2 November 1789), with no compensation other than the transfer to the State of the costs of worship and upkeep of its ministers.[42] From a legal point of view, nationalisation and expropriation were therefore two distinct legal mechanisms according to the author of the DDHC itself. More recently, the distinction was also drawn by the ECtHR in the *Lithgow* case regarding the nationalisation of aeronautical and naval industries by the United Kingdom in 1977.[43] According to the Strasbourg Court, nationalisation implies a broad discretion for the State as to the opportunity of the operation, but also a wide discretion in laying down the terms and conditions of the transfer, including the amount of compensation—at least when nationalisation by the State concerns the assets of its own nationals.[44] The Constitutional Council had solid legal bases for developing such a solution. Besides Article 9 of the Preamble, Article 34 of the Constitution gives the legislature jurisdiction over 'nationalisation of companies and the transfer of ownership of companies from the public to the private sector', as well as over the 'system of ownership' itself. It could therefore be argued that the means of production may be subject to a system of 'private' as well as 'social' or 'state' ownership. Such an interpretation would certainly not have been more ideologically neutral. Conversely, the reasoning followed by the Constitutional Council is far from 'economic neutrality'. Rather, it is part of a liberal doctrine that seeks to protect the market economy against the possible collectivisation of the economy.

Property Rights as a Limit to Socialisation (and Co-determination) in Germany

Large-scale collectivisation of the economy had previously been advocated by certain German intellectuals, on the basis of constitutional arguments. In the early years of the Federal Republic, Wolfgang Abendroth defended the 'socialist

[42] Bodinier and Teyssier (2000). See Sueur (1991).

[43] Colly (1998), pp. 194–195.

[44] ECtHR, 8 July 1986, *Lithgow*, No. 9006/80, §§ 111–122. The issue is more controversial when nationalisation applies to non-nationals, who may invoke the protection of the 'general principles of international law', according to the wording of Article 1P1. But even in this case, and despite the clash between Western and developing countries on this issue, a distinction between nationalisation and expropriation seems possible, if not *in the general and abstract written rules* (UN General Assembly resolution 1803 (XVII) of 14 December 1962: 'Permanent sovereignty over natural resources'; UN General Assembly resolution 3281 (XXIX): 'Charter of Economic Rights and Duties of States'), at least *in the practice* of international relations and *in international arbitral awards* (LIAMCO v. Libya, International Law Reports, vol. 62, 1982, p. 140). The proliferation of bilateral investment treaties can be seen as a result of this distinction: it is precisely to prevent the circumvention of the rules on expropriation (including the amount of compensation) by acts of nationalisation that specific rules have been established by treaty. For an introduction to this complex issue, see Ruzza (2013).

potential' of the Basic Law,[45] based mainly on the constitutional provision devoted to 'socialisation'. Article 15 GG states that 'Land, natural resources and means of production may, for the purpose of nationalisation, be transferred to public ownership or other forms of public enterprise by a law that determines the nature and extent of compensation', provided that '[w]ith respect to such compensation the third and fourth sentences of paragraph (3) of Article 14 [dedicated to expropriation] shall apply, *mutatis mutandis*'. However, the *Bundestag* has so far never made use of this constitutional provision. Some authors suggest that Article 15 GG is no more than a 'constitutional fossil in the age of globalisation',[46] despite the fact that the housing crisis in Berlin has revived the issue.[47] Even a possible defensive effect was denied to Article 15 LF by the FCC,[48] paving the way for large-scale privatisation following the reunification[49] and the privatisation of public services decided at the European level.[50]

This does not mean, however, that no changes have occurred in the balance of powers within the private economic sector in Germany. In a way, the extension in 1976 of the system of 'co-determination' (*Mitbestimmung*) to all companies with more than two thousand employees represented a (much less ambitious) variation of the idea behind socialisation. Introduced in 1951 in the mining and steel industries, this system implies not giving all the power to the workers but, at the very least, to counterbalance the power of the employers by giving the employees greater influence over company decisions through their representatives on the supervisory boards.[51] In the famous decision of 1 March 1979,[52] the FCC had to decide whether such an arrangement was compatible with the Basic Law, and in particular with the right to property. The Court validated the Co-determination Act, but the reasoning followed nevertheless seriously undermines the assertion of economic neutrality.

On one hand, the Constitutional Court accepts that the 'social obligation' of property ownership justifies imposing significant limitations on it.[53] From this perspective, the system of co-determination remains within the admissible limits. On the other hand, however, co-determination passes the test of proportionality because of the twofold fact that it contributes to 'politically securing the market economy', and that, on the other hand, 'the decisive influence and the right of final decision remain with the shareholders'.[54] This gives us a glimpse of the threshold

---

[45] Abendroth (1954).

[46] Froese and Depenheuer (2018), §§4 et seq.

[47] Ipsen (2019); Röhner (2020).

[48] BVerfG, 7 May 1961, *Volkswagenprivatisierung*, 1 BvR 561, 579/60, 114/61, §40. See Leisner (1975).

[49] Böick (2018).

[50] Albach and Witte (2002).

[51] McGaughey (2016).

[52] BVerfG, 1 March 1979, *Mitbestimmung*, *loc. cit.*, §§140–141.

[53] *Ibid.*, §§152–156.

[54] *Ibid.*, §§167 to 170.

beyond which a more ambitious reform of the right of property of the means of production would risk constitutional censure.

2.1.2.2 The Prohibition of 'Confiscatory' Taxation: The 'Essence' of Property as an Instrument of Fiscal Rationalisation

Rather than depriving shareholders of power over the means of production, an *indirect* collectivisation of the economy may consist in redistributing the 'purchasing power' to citizens, through 'confiscatory' taxation. Here too, the constitutional courts have intervened to limit the action of the legislature, whether in Germany, France or Belgium—albeit in varying degrees.

The FCC as the Legislature's 'Authoritarian praeceptor*' in Tax Matters*

Traditionally, taxes were not considered to be an infringement of property rights,[55] as they represented abstract debts (not directly linked to concrete assets).[56] However, faced with the extension of the 'fiscal state' to cover the widespread interventions of the 'social state', certain scholars, including the future constitutional judge Paul Kirchhof (1987–1999), argued in favour of limiting taxation by means of the constitutional protection of property.[57] The FCC eventually endorsed this position.[58] In a groundbreaking decision of 22 June 1995,[59] drafted by Kirchhof as judge-rapporteur, the FCC relied on both the principle of equality before the law (Art. 3 FL) and the right to property (Art. 14 FL) to overturn a century-old tax: the net wealth tax, introduced in 1893 in Prussia and extended to the Reich in 1922.[60] Behind the developed arguments emerges a genuine general theory of (confiscatory) taxation in a capitalist market economy.

First, the Court decided to immunise taxpayers' existing assets: no taxation, even wealth tax, can ever be levied on acquired capital, but only on the income from that capital.[61] Moreover, it is not only the acquired capital that must be guaranteed, but also half of the taxpayers' income (from work *and* capital) must be immune from any levy. The legal basis for this decision lies in a highly controversial interpretation of the second sentence of Art. 14, para. 2 GG, according to which the property use

[55]BVerfG, 20 July 1954, *Investitionshilfe, loc. cit.*, §34; 29 July 1959, *(Großer) Erftverband*, 1 BvR 394/58, §90; 10 May 1960, *Familienlastenausgleich* I, 1 BvR 190/58, §63.

[56]It could even be argued that, conceptually, tax is prior to property. As a subjective right enforceable against others, property necessarily presupposes a collective institution (the state), which itself inevitably requires a minimum pooling of resources, i.e., a (tax) 'contribution' (Murphy and Nagel 2002).

[57]Kirchhof (1981).

[58]Kirchhof (2003).

[59]BVerfG, 22 July 1995, *Vermögensteuer*, 2 BvL 37/91.

[60]Vogel (1996); Flick and Schauhoff (1996).

[61]BVerfG, 22 July 1995, *Vermögensteuer, loc. cit.*, §§49–50.

'shall also (*zugleich*) serve the public good'. The Court gives the adverb '*zugleich*' (literally 'at the same time') a quantitative meaning, as if the words used had been '*zu gleichen Teilen*', i.e., 'in equal shares'.[62] The Court drew from this (meager) argument an ultimate constitutional limit to the 'insatiability of the Leviathan':[63] the 'fifty-percent rule' (*Halbteilungsgrundsatz*),[64] according to which the total tax burden on income must remain close to a fifty-fifty split between the private and public spheres.[65]

Justice Böckenförde strongly denounced the implications of such a decision. He offered a fierce critique of the Court's reasoning.[66] He condemns the imposition of framework criteria on the legislature, based moreover on a provision (section 14) that was not even raised by the applicants. Echoing Justice Holmes' resistance in the US Supreme Court's Lochner decision,[67] he criticised the lack of judicial self-restraint of the Court and accuses the latter of becoming an 'authoritarian *praeceptor*' for legislative power. Böckenförde then highlights the ideological nature of the reasoning followed. The specific protection of property over acquired capital would represent in this respect a 'privilege for the (very) wealthy'. The new tax dogma, which has no constitutional basis and even contradicts previous FCC case law, now leaves the State powerless 'against the inherent dynamics of accumulating capital', since the limits imposed were more or less equivalent to the existing tax rates. At the particularly critical time of German reunification, it was therefore the social state that would ultimately be jeopardised. The constitutional limitation of state (taxation) revenue implied that expenditure (including social benefits) had to be 'rationalised', i.e., curtailed.

On the very same day,[68] the FCC extended its general theory of (confiscatory) taxation to inheritance law.[69] It relied on the doctrinal authority of the conservative scholar of constitutional law (and future President of the FCC) Hans-Jürgen Papier[70] to establish the principle that 'the tax burden must not make the inheritance appear economically useless (*ökonomisch sinnlos*) from the point of view of an owner thinking in economic terms (*wirtschaftlich denkenden Eigentümers*)'.[71] The Court then drew the legal consequences of this economic criterion: '[t]he burden of inheritance tax must be calculated in such a way that the continuation of the business is not jeopardised for tax purposes'.[72] Although the Court does not specify the

[62] Grosclaude (2002), p. 53.

[63] Vogel (1996), p. 44.

[64] Seer (1999).

[65] BVerfG, 22 July 1995, *Vermögensteuer, loc. cit.*, §51.

[66] BVerfG, 22 July 1995, *Vermögensteuer*, dissenting opinion of Justice Böckenförde, §§83 et seq.

[67] US Supreme Court, 17 April 1905, *Lochner v. New York*, 198 U.S. 45 (1905).

[68] BVerfG, 22 June 1995, *Erbschaftsteuer*, 2 BvR 552/91.

[69] Vogel (1996).

[70] Papier (1994).

[71] BVerfG, 22 June 1995, *Erbschaftsteuer, loc. cit.*, §20.

[72] See also: BVerfG, 30 October 2010, 1 BvR 3196/09, §17; 7 April 2015, 1 BvR 1432/10, §§8–9.

threshold of 'economic uselessness', it is clear that private property over the means of production is the keystone of the functioning of the (market) economy in the FCC's economic referential. The close scrutiny (and subsequent invalidations) of later reforms to business inheritance tax confirm the importance of the constitutional guarantee of private property for the objective of preserving the 'competitiveness' of German (small and medium-sized) businesses in a competitive global market.[73]

The Constitutional Council's Capping of Tax Rates: A Work of 'Economic Rationality'

The question of the maximum tax threshold has also been submitted to the Constitutional Council on several occasions. In a decision of 24 July 1991, the Council laid down the principle that a tax measure shall not, 'by its effects on taxpayers' assets, infringe the right of property'.[74] However, a constitutionality review has generally been carried out on the basis of the principle of equality before public burdens, set out in Article 13 of the French Constitution.[75] But this principle is in fact permeated by the right to property.[76] According to the Constitutional Council, the protection afforded by Article 13 of the DDCH entails a prohibition of 'confiscatory taxation'.[77] Yet, the possible confiscatory effect of taxation presupposes the guarantee of the taxpayer's right of property over his taxed assets and income.

Until 2012, however, the Council did not use this prohibition on confiscatory taxation to invalidate a measure. It repeatedly stated that such a limit existed, while noting in the specific case that it had not been breached. The Council exercised its veto power and sketched out a constitutional framework for taxation that suggested the existence of a maximum tax threshold.[78] Famous mainly for having invalidated the 75% tax on very high incomes promised by François Hollande during his presidential campaign, the censure was in fact based on a technical reason. But in the same decision, other provisions were overturned on the grounds that they were excessive or confiscatory. The decisive change is now to reason on the basis of the aggregate marginal tax rate. Previously, each measure was assessed separately, on the basis of its individual marginal tax rate. Henceforth, the excessiveness of the tax measure is measured against the 'maximum marginal tax rate' obtained by

[73] BverfG, 7 November 2006, *Erbschaftsteuer*, 1 BvL 10/02; 17 December 2014, *Steuerprivilegien für Firmenerben*, 1 BvL 21/12. See Krumm (2015).

[74] Cons. const., 24 July 1991, *Loi portant diverses dispositions d'ordre économique et financier*, No. 91-298 DC, Rec. 25.

[75] Fouquet (2011).

[76] De Crouy-Chanel (2011).

[77] Cons. const., 29 December 1998, *Loi de finances pour 1999*, No. 98-405 DC; 19 December 2000, *Loi de financement de la sécurité sociale pour 2001*, No. 2000-437 DC; 28 December 2000, *Loi de finances rectificative pour 2000*, No. 2000-441 DC; 29 December 2005, *Loi de finances pour 2006*, No. 2005-530 DC; 16 August 2007, *Loi en faveur du travail, de l'emploi et du pouvoir d'achat*, No. 2007-555 DC.

[78] Collet (2014a).

aggregating the various taxes. In this case, the level obtained was close to 75% for the three invalidated measures. It is still difficult to determine the exact level of the confiscatory tax threshold used by the Constitutional Council, but the *Conseil d'État* has concluded that there is a 'risk of censure by the constitutional judge' when the aggregated marginal tax rate is 'higher than a ratio of two-thirds'.[79]

Should this be confirmed over the long term, the consequences of this decision cannot be overstated. In 1924, the marginal rate on the highest incomes in France was 90%, for budgetary reasons. This was also the case in the United States under the administration of Franklin D. Roosevelt and until the mid-1960s, for social justice reasons this time. More recently, the multiple presidential candidate Jean-Luc Mélenchon, who came close to the second round in 2022, also proposed imposing a marginal rate of 90% on the part of individual incomes over €400,000 a year. Yet, according to the guidelines laid down by the Council, such a rate would be unconstitutional.

But that's not all. There also seems to be an *absolute* limit to the taxation of assets: the acquired capital. Following the example of FCC's case law, the limit could be summarised as follows: income from capital is taxable, but the capital itself is sacred. The Constitutional Council does not express this so explicitly, but its decisions on 'wealth tax' do imply this tenet.[80] Tax measures that indirectly oblige taxpayers to sell part of their assets in order to pay the amount of tax due are considered confiscatory and contrary to the principle of equality before public burdens.[81] This rule is already implied in the decision of 9 August 2012.[82] Here, the Council 'surreptitiously'[83] constitutionalised the legal method consisting in capping wealth tax by adjusting it to the income actually available after income tax, in order to immunise the net acquired capital. What is remarkable is that the Council's reasoning includes the criterion used by the FCC. As it admits in its own commentary on the decision,[84] the 'economic rationality' of the taxpayer's behaviour guides the approach taken by the *Conseil*.[85]

---

[79] French C.E. fr, A.G. (Finance Section), Advisory Opinion No. 387402 of 21 March 2013, *Demande d'avis relative aux conditions de constitutionnalité d'une contribution sur les très hauts revenus*.

[80] Cons. const., 30 December 1981, *Loi de finances pour 1982*, No. 81-133 DC, Rec. 4–12; 29 December 1998, *Loi de finances pour 1999*, *loc. cit.*, Rec. 24–28.

[81] Grosclaude (2002); Wanda (2005).

[82] Cons. const., 9 August 2012, *Loi de finances rectificative pour 2012 (II)*, No. 2012-654 DC, Rec. 33.

[83] Collet (2014b).

[84] Official commentary on Decision No. 2012-654 DC of 9 August 2012, p. 21. See Collet (2014a), pp. 42–46.

[85] Collet (2014a), pp. 42–46; Martinez (2022), p. 398.

The (Timid) Recognition of a 'Confiscatory' Inheritance Tax by the Belgian Constitutional Court

It was also on the basis of the principle of 'equality of citizens before public burdens', as applied to taxation (Art. 172 of the Constitution), that the Belgian Constitutional Court (then 'Court of Arbitration') came to declare a tax unconstitutional. According to some scholars, this decision paved the way for 'the establishment of a system of judicial review of confiscatory taxation.[86] The overturned provision concerned inheritance tax and provided for a marginal rate of 90% on the part of the inheritance exceeding €175,000 when the legatee was not related to the deceased by blood or marriage.[87] However, unlike its German and French counterparts, the Belgian Constitutional Court does not reason at an aggregate level. Instead, it focused on the marginal tax rate of the contested measure alone. Insofar as this rate exceeds 80% and is motivated solely by budgetary reasons—and not by an objective of encouraging or deterring specific taxpayer behaviours—the provision is declared incompatible with the constitutional principle of equality before the law.[88] The question nevertheless arises as to which reason the Court would have accepted: would the fight against an excessive concentration of wealth through inheritance (for all or, as in this case, solely for extra-familial inheritance) be capable of justifying such rates?

However, it cannot be denied that the Belgian Constitutional Court is far less aggressive than the FCC and the Constitutional Council when it comes to 'confiscatory taxation'... for now. In the future, though, it may well follow suit, given its tendency to embrace the interpretations of the ECtHR, which has begun to enforce[89] the prohibition of 'disproportionate and excessive burdens'.[90] As one commentator has observed, the latter is now inclined to consider that 'an excessively high tax, which undermines the economic viability of the taxpayer, would be regarded as expropriation and not taxation'.[91]

If the Constitutional Court has made less use of the right of ownership and the principle of equality before public burdens to develop a strict control of taxation, it is perhaps also because it has developed other tools, especially the principle of 'economic and monetary union' between the different entities of the State (federal authority, regions and communities). Derived from a very thin legal basis, this principle helped the Court to declare unconstitutional a tax of the Walloon Region which officially pursued an ecological objective but dissimulated economic protectionism vis-à-vis the Flemish Region.[92] Rather than taking offence at this bold

[86] Bourgeois (2005).

[87] Cour const., 22 June 2005, No. 107/2005, B.15.7.

[88] Cour const., 22 June 2005, No. 107/2005, B.15.4.

[89] ECtHR, 14 May 2013, *NKM v. Hungary*, No. 66529/11.

[90] ECtHR, 14 December 1988, *Wasa Liv Ömsesidigt v. Sweden*, No. 13013/87.

[91] Baker (2013), p. 393.

[92] Cour const., 25 February 1988, No. 47/88, 6.B.4. and 6.B.5.

interpretation, the parliament strengthened its legal basis. It incorporated this new principle of 'economic and monetary union' in a quasi-constitutional norm that requires special majorities to be adopted and amended,[93] together with other 'liberal' tenets: the 'free movement of persons, goods, services and capital' and the 'freedom of trade and industry'. For some authors, the consequence of the Court's decision has therefore been to 'give concrete form to the coherence of the economic system, to establish it legally'[94]—and not just any economic system: the 'market economy'.[95] Indirectly, it also contributed to elevate the legal value of the freedom of trade and industry, i.e., the second classic economic freedom that the constitutional courts have used to constrain the legislature's decisions in economic matters.

2.2 From Economic Freedom to Free Competition: Institutional Protection of the Market

Since the French Revolution, 'economic freedom' has gradually conquered Europe, and far beyond, under various names: freedom of trade and industry (*liberté du commerce et de l'industrie*; *Handels-und Gewerbefreiheit*), freedom to choose an occupation (*liberté professionnelle*; *Berufsfreiheit*), entrepreneurial freedom (*liberté d'entreprendre*; *Unternehmensfreiheit*) or freedom of competition (*liberté de concurrence*; *Wettbewerbsfreiheit*). Beyond the semantic distinctions, what is more important conceptually is that economic freedom has a dual dimension: on one hand, the freedom to *access* the market, i.e., to set up a business and choose a profession; and on the other hand, the freedom to *operate on* the market, i.e., to be free from unfair restrictions imposed on the way we run our business or exercise our occupation.

Historically, classical liberals focused on the first dimension, assuming that free competition would follow. The various neoliberal currents then moved to the second dimension, to protect the competitive structure of the market not only against public intervention, but also against private monopolies and cartels. This shift is the result of the existential crisis of the liberal economic order in the first decades of the twentieth century, due to the democratisation of parliament and the rise of labour law, but also to the cartelisation of the economy—i.e. the abolition of the competition by endogenous market forces (capitalist firms). In response, liberal intellectuals undertook an *aggiornamento* of their doctrinal base. The key question they addressed was as follows: how could and should the mechanism of competition be

[93] Article 6, §1, VI, paragraph 3 of the Special Law on Institutional Reforms (LSRI) of 8 August 1980, amended by the Special Law on Institutional Reforms of 8 August 1988. The principle of 'economic and monetary union' is also enshrined in another fundamental Special Law, i.e., the Special Financing Law of 16 January 1989 (Piron 2022).

[94] Schoonbroodt (1990), p. 9.

[95] Yernault (2013), p. 932.

guaranteed institutionally and legally? The various currents that have come to be known as 'neoliberalism(s)' were born out of this very question.[96] Despite their many differences, their common answer was that the state should not refrain from intervening in the market, but that this public intervention should be conditional on the protection of competition—i.e., not against the market, but for the market. Put simply, what distinguishes liberalism from *neo*liberalism is the shift from the defence of individual freedom to the search for a structural guarantee of competition.

A similar shift can be seen in the constitutional jurisprudence of the three States studied: the subjective dimensions of economic freedom were first enshrined (Sect. 2.2.1), and then the constitutional courts gradually developed an institutional guarantee of competition in the market (Sect. 2.2.2).

2.2.1 Enshrinement and Development of 'Economic Freedom' by National Constitutional Courts

In France, the freedom of trade and industry, proclaimed by the *décret d'Allarde* of 2-17 March 1791, is even older than the establishment of the Republic. Since the beginning of the twentieth century, it has played a major role in the supervision of state interventionism by the *Conseil d'État*.[97] However, this administrative control did not apply to the legislature itself.[98] The situation changed radically with the decision *Nationalisations* of 16 January 1982. The Constitutional Council 'discovered' a constitutional basis for 'entrepreneurial freedom', even though it had not been invoked by the applicants. According to the Council, this basis is to be found in the general protection of freedom set out in Article 4 DDHC.[99] This new economic freedom is then linked to the right to property (Art. 2 and 17 of the DDHC) to together provide protection against the implicit 'collectivism threshold'[100] beyond which the State could not proceed to nationalisation.[101] To some extent, this provided the 'basis for capitalist activity'[102] and the foundation for the 'market economy'.[103] Since then, the *Conseil* has made it clear that entrepreneurial freedom protects both the freedom of access to the market and the free exploitation of activity on the market.[104] Moreover, constitutional control has been considerably strengthened over time. Initially confined to a loose control of 'denaturation' or 'manifest

[96] Audier (2012, 2022).

[97] French C.E., 29 March 1901, *Casanova*; 30 May 1930, *Chambre syndicale du commerce en détail de Nevers*; 22 June 1951, *Daudignac*; 28 October 1960, *Sieur de Laboulaye*.

[98] Savy (1977), p. 100.

[99] Cons. const., 16 January 1982, *Nationalisations I*, *loc. cit.*, 16.

[100] Vedel and Delvolvé (1992), p. 640.

[101] Cons. const., 16 January 1982, *Nationalisations I*, *loc. cit.*, Rec. 20.

[102] Jurion (2017), pp. 78–80.

[103] Savy (1983), p. 107.

[104] Cons. const., 30 November 2012, *Storms*, No. 2012-285 QPC, Rec. 7.

error',[105] it then gradually evolved into a full and complete control of proportionality,[106] which led to the invalidation of certain legislation.[107] In 2002, the Council struck down one of the key measures of the left-wing government in charge at the time: the tightening of the legal criteria for 'economic redundancies'.[108] The reasoning was based on a very explicit market logic:[109] the measure was hindering economic expectations and the room for manoeuvre of entrepreneurs in their efforts to make their businesses more attractive in a context of increased competition. As several authors have pointed out, this decision marks the beginning of a process of 'market objectivisation',[110] whereby the market is no longer seen as a socially and legally embedded institution, but as an external (or natural) fact that precedes the legal organisation of society. In this respect, the decision *Florange* of 27 March 2014 can be analysed as a direct extension of the 2002 decision. It represents a new stage in the process of 'fundamentalisation of liberal order':[111] the system to prevent profit-based layoffs is said to have a disproportionate impact on the ability of business owners 'to anticipate economic difficulties and to make economic trade-offs'.[112] The primacy of shareholders over other stakeholders is therefore constitutionally enshrined here.[113]

The same logic, but stated even more explicitly, emerges from the judgments of the FCC. Unlike France, Germany has a constitutional provision that is directly linked to the idea of free economic activity: the guarantee of 'freedom to choose an occupation' (*Berufsfreiheit*), laid down in Article 12 GG. It is not entirely clear whether *Berufsfreiheit* was originally conceived as a generic recognition of economic freedom or not.[114] But what is clear is that the FCC made it the 'principal fundamental right of free economic activity'[115] and the 'cornerstone of the constitutional order from the economic point of view'.[116] The seminal decision is the

[105] Cons. const., 4 July 1989, *Loi modifiant la loi n° 86-912 du 6 août 1986 relative aux modalités d'application des privatisations*, No. 89-254 DC, Rec. 5; 10 June 1998, *Loi d'orientation et d'incitation relative à la réduction du temps de travail*, No. 98-401 DC, Rec. 26–28; 13 January 2000, *Loi relative à la réduction négociée du temps de travail*, No. 99-423 DC, Rec. 24–34.

[106] Cons. const., 20 March 1997, *Loi créant les plans d'épargne retraite*, No. 97-388 DC, Rec. 51; 27 July 2000, *Loi modifiant la loi n° 86-1067 du 30 septembre 1986 relative à la liberté de communication*, No. 2000-433 DC, Rec. 40.

[107] Cons. const., 7 December 2000, *Loi relative à la solidarité et au renouvellement urbains*, *loc. cit.*, Rec. 20.

[108] Cons. const., 12 January 2002, *Loi de modernisation sociale*, No. 2001-455 DC, Rec. 47–50.

[109] Feldman (2002).

[110] Garnier (2004); Martinez (2022), pp. 374–379.

[111] Sachs and Vernac (2014).

[112] Cons. const., 27 March 2014, *Loi visant à reconquérir l'économie réelle*, *loc. cit.*, Rec. 19–21.

[113] Chazal (2014), pp. 1102–1103.

[114] Jungbluth (2018), pp. 217–218.

[115] Ossenbühl (1990), p. 5.

[116] Oppermann (1985), p. 83.

decision on pharmacies (*Apotheken-Urteil*) of 11 June 1958.[117] Most of the principles that have underpinned the abundant constitutional case law in economic matters can already be found here. It is even the founding decision of the 'principle of proportionality', which forms the cornerstone of the German approach to fundamental rights and, by extension, of the 'global constitutionalism' that spread around the world in the second half of the twentieth century.[118] After an in-depth presentation of legal history and social philosophy, the *Apotheken-Urteil* comes to the conclusion that *Beruf* ('occupation' or 'profession') is an act of individual self-determination in the economic sphere, which must therefore be particularly protected. As a result, *Berufsfreiheit* is generally considered as 'the most important right in economic life' and even an 'objective decision on constitutional values' (*objektiv-rechtliche Wertentscheidung*).[119] Moreover, the term *Beruf* is interpreted very broadly, to include any form of economic activity, whether self-employed or employed, and whether in the private sector or the public sector. Subsequently, the freedom to choose an occupation was further extended both in terms of activities covered (professional education[120]) and of right holders (all legal entities, including corporations[121]).

It was also in the decision on pharmacies that the FCC extended the freedom to choose an occupation to free exercise of the economic activity. It developed its constitutional review on the basis of a 'three-level theory' (*Drei-Stufentheorie*). Considerations of political expediency may intervene in the regulation of exercise (first stage), but the room for manoeuvre is restricted when it comes to limiting access to an occupation. Here, only *subjective* admission criteria (i.e., related to the educational background of candidates) are tolerated, provided they remain proportionate (second stage). By contrast, the objective criteria (over which the individual has no control, even if all the individual conditions set are met) are prohibited, unless it can be demonstrated that this 'crudest and most radical means' is the only one capable of preventing 'demonstrable or highly probable serious dangers to an overridingly important common good' (third stage). On the basis of a detailed economic analysis of the pharmacy market and of the 'rational' behaviour of pharmacists, the FCC concluded that the objective restrictions on the establishment of new pharmacies in Bavaria was disproportionate and therefore unconstitutional.

As in France, the extension of *Berufsfreiheit* is further consolidated by its link with the right to property (Art. 14, para. 1 GG), which provides a genuine guarantee of 'entrepreneurial freedom' (*Unternehmerfreiheit*).[122] Endorsing a distinction proposed in academic circles,[123] the FCC expresses the close functional association

[117] BVerfG, 11 June 1958, *Apotheken-Urteil*, 1 BvR 596/56. See Tettinger (1983).

[118] Stone Sweet and Mathews (2008).

[119] Scholz (2022), §4.

[120] BVerfG, 18 July 1972, *Numerus clausus I*, 1 BvL 32/70.

[121] BVerfG, 4 April 1967, *Arbeitsvermittlungsmonopol*, 1 BvR 84/65, §15.

[122] Meyer (2006), p. 222.

[123] Wittig (1967), p. 2188.

between the two 'liberal' provisions as follows: 'Art. 14 para. 1 GG protects what has been acquired, i.e., the result of the activity, while Art. 12 para. 1 GG protects the acquisition, i.e., the activity itself'.[124] Moreover, the combination of the two fundamental economic liberties give rise to new derivative freedoms: freedom of internal organisation of the business and labour management,[125] freedom of production,[126] freedom of advertising,[127] freedom of pricing[128] and freedom to contract.[129] This deep-rooted connection between *Berufsfreiheit* and the right to property would therefore have a 'systemic significance for the economic constitution'.[130]

Against this background, German *Dogmatik* deploys a colossal effort to maintain, as best it can, the theory of the 'economic neutrality' of the Basic Law. The result, however, looks more like an Orwellian exercise in 'doublethink'. It argues that the market order does not result from an objective structural choice set out in the constitution, but from a consistent application of subjective fundamental rights: the decentralised market system would be able to optimise these individual freedoms. But the schizophrenic nature of this stance is apparent even in the FCC's most important decisions. The decision *Mitbestimmung* once again provides a good illustration of the very relative economic neutrality of the Basic Law as interpreted by the Court of Karlsruhe. The constitutionality of the law depends both on the fact that the power of decision remains in the hands of the business owners and on the fact that the scope of the companies concerned is limited to large companies, where the personal aspect of self-determination is less significant for business owners than in small and medium-sized enterprises. Yet the Court might have just as well advanced another argument in support of its declaration of constitutionality: the fact that, according to its own jurisprudence, *Berufsfreiheit* is also recognised for workers, since that freedom has 'the same value and dignity for all'.[131] What is even more interesting is that the FCC mentions this, albeit very cursorily, when it states that 'the holders of the fundamental right can only exercise the guaranteed freedom with the help of others, the workers, who are also holders of the fundamental right under Art. 12 para. 1 GG'.[132] However, the reasoning is immediately interrupted, probably to avoid taking the point further than intended. For, once workers are vested with the same dignity and value in their occupation, it could be assumed that they (should) have a right to an equal share in the management and direction of the

---

[124] BVerfG, 16 March 1971, *Erdölbevorratung*, 1 BvR 52/66, §122. This dictum has been reiterated on several occasions: 24 April 1991, *Warteschleife*, 1 BvR 1341/90, §90; 10 March 1992, *Akademie-Auflösung*, 1 BvR 454/91, §73.

[125] BVerfG, 1 March 1979, *Mitbestimmung*, *loc. cit.*, §§166–169.

[126] BVerfG, 8 January 1959, *Strafbarkeit der Arzneiproduktion*, 1 BvR 425/52, §30.

[127] BVerfG, 7 November 1991, *Werbung für Lohnsteuerhilfevereine*, 1 BvR 1469/86, §25.

[128] BVerfG, 17 December 2002, *Arzneimittelfestbeträge*, 1 BvL 28, 29, 30/95, §111.

[129] BVerfG, 24 April 1991, *Warteschleife*, *loc. cit.*, §58.

[130] Scholz (2022), §86.

[131] BVerfG, 11 June 1958, *Apotheken-Urteil*, *loc. cit.*, §52.

[132] BVerfG, 1 March 1979, *Mitbestimmung*, *loc. cit.*, §198.

means of production to which they bring their workforce. The size of the company would moreover be irrelevant here. The solution adopted is quite different: *Berufsfreiheit* guarantees shareholders' ultimate power of decision over the means of production, despite the proclaimed economic neutrality.

The 'freedom to choose an occupation' is also mentioned in the Belgian Constitution since the adoption in 1993 of an Article 24*bis* (now Article 23) dedicated to 'economic, social and cultural rights'. Despite the plea of a few scholars to infer from this a guarantee of entrepreneurial freedom,[133] the Constitutional Court refused to use the provision.[134] It did so not because it refused to recognise the constitutional nature of this economic freedom, but because in the meantime it had favoured another legal basis.[135]

The 'combination method' of reasoning gave the Court the possibility to constitutionalise the legislative principle of 'entrepreneurial freedom' (Art. II.3 and II.4 of the Economic Law Code) by connecting it to the principle of equality and non-discrimination (Art. 10 and 11 of the Constitution) and to the quasi-constitutional norm already mentioned (Art. 6, para. 1, VI, 3° of the Special Law on Institutional Reforms of 8 August 1980)—to which it sometimes even adds the EU fundamental freedoms of movement.[136] As the current President of the Court observes, the Court played an active role in establishing entrepreneurial freedom 'as a normative and unifying paradigm of economic activity' in Belgium.[137]

Yet, while the Constitutional Court protects both the freedom to access the market and the freedom to operate on the market,[138] it has so far made only very moderate use of its power of censure. Sometimes, however, the Constitutional Court does carry out a 'concrete examination'[139] of the facts of the case. For example, regarding the prohibition on tobacco advertising, the Constitutional Court used the economic analysis produced by the legislature to conclude that the measure did not jeopardise the 'financial viability of the sector'.[140] Nevertheless, cases of unconstitutionality have so far been concentrated on those 'where the entrepreneurial freedom is not

133 Delpérée (1995), p. 290.

134 Cour const., 21 May 2015, No. 66/2015, B.11.2. On Article 23 of the Constitution, *see below*, 2.

135 Cour const., 30 April 2015, No. 50/2015, B.8. This basis has since been confirmed on several occasions: Cour const., 21 December 2017, No. 150/2017, B.11.2 to B.11.4; 5 July 2018, No. 90/2018, B.7.3; 21 January 2021, No. 10/2021, B.36.1 to B.36.4; 30 September 2021, No. 119/2021, B.11.2; 9 December 2021, No. 177/2021, B.42.4.

136 Cour const., 22 December 2010, No. 149/2010, B.11; 18 October 2012, No. 119/2012, B.5.2; 12 December 2021, No. 177/2021, B.42.6.

137 Nihoul (2022), p. 545.

138 For the freedom to access the market: Cour const., 14 December 2005, No. 188/2005; 9 December 2010, No. 135/2010; 23 January 2014, No. 6/2014; 28 April 2011, No. 56/2011. For the free exercise of economic activity on the market: Cour const., 18 October 2012, No. 119/2012, *loc. cit.*

139 Depré (2002), p. 372.

140 Cour const., 30 September 1999, No. 102/99, B.21.2.

simply limited, but actually suppressed or rendered practically impossible'.[141] The Belgian Constitutional Court thus left the legislature a relatively wide margin for manoeuvre concerning the regulation of entrepreneurial freedom, at least greater than that in the German and French cases.

2.2.2 From a Subjective Economic Freedom to the Institutional Guarantee of the Competitive Order

Protection against legislative interference is only one side of the coin, the other is protection against possible infringement by other individuals. There is thus a shift from the subjective economic freedom to a principle of equality in competition—and the shift affects all three legal orders studied (Sect. 2.2.2.1). And that's not all: for France and Germany at least, entrepreneurial freedom and *Berufsfreiheit* seem to be gradually superseded by an institutional guarantee of competition (Sect. 2.2.2.2).

2.2.2.1 Free and Fair Competition as an Economic Implication of the Principle of Equality

Still latent in the decision on pharmacies, the competitive dimension of the *Berufsfreiheit* was explicitly taken into account in the decision *Erdölbevorratung* (*oil stocks*) of 16 March 1971.[142] The case concerned the obligation imposed on the oil industry to build up stocks in order to guarantee sufficient energy supplies, as required by a European directive. A number of importing companies, which lacked the infrastructure (such as refineries) possessed by companies also involved in the production process, challenged this stock-holding obligation before the FCC, as it affected their competitiveness. The FCC ruled in their favour: since the business structure of a company is linked to the freedom of internal organisation of economic activity, and since the latter is one of the freedoms derived from *Berufsfreiheit*, imposing a burden on a company that would considerably impair its competitiveness due to its own internal structure would be contrary to Art. 12 GG, read in conjunction with the principle of equality (Art. 3, para. 1 GG). The general principle of equality thus permeates the economic freedom to create a kind of principle of free and fair competition.

In France, the linking of free competition with the principle of equality[143] began explicitly in a decision of the Constitutional Council on 28 December 1998.[144] The

---

[141] Vanderstraeten (2015), p. 25. See e.g.: Cour const., 28 April 2016, No. 56/2016, B.12.; 6 April 2000, No. 40/2000, B.43.

[142] BVerfG, 16 March 1971, *Erdölbevorratung*, *loc. cit.*

[143] Mongouachon (2017).

[144] Cons. const., 29 December 1998, *Loi de finances pour 1999*, *loc. cit.*, 36.

Council then confirmed, in two decisions in 2001,[145] that free competition is seen as 'an implication or corollary'[146] of the general principle of equality in the economic sphere. Without being explicitly mentioned, this 'competitive implication' of the principle of equality is also at work in the decision of 21 January 2011.[147] On that occasion, the Court used it to justify, on the basis of general interest, the restriction on entrepreneurial freedom caused by the authorisation given to the administrative authority to impose a weekly rest period on all establishments exercising the same profession in the same geographical area. A few months later, the same reasoning was applied to justify the restriction on entrepreneurial freedom resulting from the prohibition on Sunday working in Alsace-Moselle.[148] It expressly states there that 'the control of conditions of competition' is a reason of general interest. Although free and fair competition does not (yet) exist as an autonomous principle of constitutional value[149] that can be invoked directly by individuals before a court, it nonetheless permeates the constitutional case law of the Constitutional Council, leaving open the possibility of a future 'constitutionalisation' through the combination of the principle of equality and entrepreneurial freedom.

In Belgium, the principles of equality and non-discrimination (Art. 10 and 11 of the Constitution) constitute the cornerstone of the constitutional protection of fundamental rights, and freedom of enterprise is no exception. The state's intervention in the economy must therefore comply with these principles. The effect of this is 'to prevent the public authorities from taking charge of an economic activity by attaching to it means of action which are (...) likely to distort unduly or disproportionately the normal process of competition on the market'.[150] Of course, this does not mean that the legislature cannot depart from the principle of competition, either to replace it with public services or to temper its functioning or effects for reasons of general interest. But the connection of the principle of entrepreneurial freedom to those of equality and non-discrimination implicitly makes the competitive order the rule, exceptions to which must be duly justified and remain proportionate (to the scale of values established not by the legislature but by the Constitutional Court). Moreover, as I have already mentioned, free competition further strengthens its constitutional status through its combination with the quasi-constitutional principle

[145] Cons. const., 11 July 2001, *Loi portant diverses dispositions d'ordre social, éducatif et culturel*, No. 2001-450 DC, Rec. 10; 27 November 2001, *Loi portant amélioration de la couverture des non salariés agricoles contre les accidents du travail et les maladies professionnelles*, No. 2001-451 DC, Rec. 34.

[146] Jurion (2017), p. 104.

[147] Cons. const., 21 January 2011, *Société Chaud Colatine*, No. 2010-89 QPC, Rec. 4–5.

[148] Cons. const., 5 August 2011 *Société SOMODIA*, No. 2011-157 QPC, Rec. 7.

[149] Debré (2014), p. 9.

[150] Nihoul (2022), p. 556.

of 'economic and monetary union' (Art. 6, para. 1, VI, 3° LSRI)[151] and the EU's fundamental freedoms of movement.[152]

2.2.2.2 The Constitutional Principle of Competition, the Heart of Economic Public Policy

Less than a year after the *Erdölbevorratung* decision, the FCC reached a new milestone by proclaiming that 'the existing economic constitution (*sic*) contains the fundamentally free competition of entrepreneurs acting as suppliers and demanders on the market as one of its basic principles'.[153] Admittedly, the FCC concluded in this case that the prohibition on unfair competition in the headstone market remained within the bounds of the restrictions authorised by the regulation of the exercise of the economic activity. Yet the Court nonetheless affirmed in this decision the paramount importance of competition in the constitutional economic order. Abandoning the undoubtedly overly ideologically-charged expression 'economic constitution' (*Wirtschaftsverfassung*), the FCC repeated this idea five years later with the following formula: 'Within the existing *economic order* (*Wirtschaftsordnung*), the behaviour of entrepreneurs in competition is a constituent part of their professional activity'.[154] This does not prevent the State from intervening in the market, but such intervention must in principle be designed to improve competition, not to counter it. Hence the Court recognition of the essential role of the State in controlling and providing accurate information to consumers and economic operators, as a condition of free and fair competition.[155]

The advent of the principle of competition can also be observed in France. Here, the protection of the 'competitive functioning of the market',[156] as well as 'the need to maintain a balance in commercial relations',[157] is deduced from the broader constitutional objective (*objectif à valeur constitutionnel*) of preserving the 'economic public order'.[158] It was on this basis that provisions were validated that were particularly prejudicial to entrepreneurial freedom in the French territory of New Caledonia (obligation of prior authorisation for mergers, possible injunction to sell

[151] Cour const., 2 February 1995, No. 4/95, B.5.7. See also: Cour const., 10 November 2011, No. 166/2011, B.10; 28 April 2011, No. 56/2011, *loc. cit.*, B.8.2.

[152] Cour const., 25 April 1995, No. 37/95, B.7.3; 21 December 2000, No. 136/2000, B.49; 4 November, No. 2015/159, B.12.

[153] BVerfG, 8 February 1972, *Steinmetz*, 1 BvR 170/71, §19.

[154] BVerfG, 12 October 1977, *Direktruf*, 1 BvR 216/75, §45.

[155] BVerfG, 26 June 2002, *Glykol-Fall*, 1 BvR 558/91, §59.

[156] Cons. const., 12 October 2012, *Société Groupe Canal Plus et autre*, No. 2012-280 QPC, Rec. 11.

[157] Cons. const., 13 May 2011, *Société Système U Centrale Nationale et autre*, No. 2011-126 QPC, Rec. 5.

[158] Pez (2015); Laget-Annamayer (2018).

off assets, etc.).[159] A very high degree of economic 'concentration' and the formation of 'economic powers' led to 'insufficient competition in many markets', so that the State was deemed to be entitled to act to protect 'economic public order'. On the other hand, the Constitutional Council ruled that the legislative intervention to impose the 'competitive functioning of the market' may under no circumstances go so far as to oblige 'to modify, supplement or terminate agreements or acts, or to dispose of assets even though the dominant position of the company or group of companies may have been acquired *on its merits* and no abuse has been found'.[160] Otherwise, there would be a risk of 'manifestly disproportionate' interference in entrepreneurial freedom (and the right to property). The provision of the so-called 'Macron law' of 2015, which gave the regulatory authorities the power to tackle dominant positions in the retail sector, regardless of the existence of any abuse, was therefore declared unconstitutional. Yet, this defence of 'competition on the merits' is a far cry from the claimed 'economic neutrality'. Forged in Germany in the 1930s,[161] the concept of 'competition on the merits' (*Leistungswettbewerb*) refers to a set of discussions that drive theoretical controversies among neoliberals and that have permeated European competition law.[162]

Whether or not the members of the Constitutional Council are aware of the ideological underpinning of their reasoning, they are in any case gradually incorporating the principle of competition as the fundamental constitutional principle governing the economic order. Of course, constitutional objectives other than the preservation of the competitive functioning of the market may justify a restriction of entrepreneurial freedom—for example, the protection of employment,[163] health[164] or, more recently, the environment.[165] It is also true that the objective of preserving the competitive functioning of the market can only be used by the legislature to justify an infringement of entrepreneurial freedom, but it cannot be invoked directly by individuals to challenge the economic intervention of public authorities. However, the many recent decisions mentioned above suggest that competition may soon be formally recognised as an autonomous 'constitutional requirement' (*exigence*

---

[159] Cons. const., 1 October 2013, *Loi du pays relative à la concurrence en Nouvelle-Calédonie*, No. 2013-3 LP, Rec. 11–15. For other examples, see: Cons. const., 11 December 2015, *Syndicat réunionnais des exploitants de stations-service et autres,* No. 2015-507 QPC, Rec. 8; 7 November 2019, *Loi relative à l'énergie et au climat*, No. 2019-791 DC, Rec. 6–12.

[160] Cons. const., 5 August 2015, *Loi pour la croissance, l'activité et l'égalité des chances économiques*, No. 2015-715 DC, Rec. 32 (emphasis added).

[161] Nipperdey (1930); Böhm (1933).

[162] Mongouachon (2015).

[163] Cons. const., 10 June 1998, *Loi d'orientation et d'incitation relative à la réduction du temps de travail, loc. cit.*, cons 26–28.

[164] Cons. const., 4 August 2016, *Loi pour la reconquête de la biodiversité, de la nature et des paysages*, No. 2016-737 DC, Rec. 39.

[165] Cons. const., 31 January 2020, *Union des industries de la protection des plantes*, No. 2019-823 QPC, Rec. 4.

constitutionnelle),[166] thereby providing a genuine 'constitutional matrix' for 'competition law'.[167] A former member of the Constitutional Council, who was still in office at the time he spoke, even admitted that in the eyes of the Council members, their task is to 'set limits' and 'determine the conditions for the efficiency' of the legislature in its work to 'preserve the structures of the market and protect it against abusive or collusive behaviour'.[168] What is more, according to the same judge, this task of protecting competition, driven by EU law, would have an implicit major effect: it would overturn the 'economic neutrality' of the Constitution. This does not mean that free competition is now the only principle governing the economic constitutional order, but it does at least suggest a general trend towards the constitutional enshrinement of the competitive market economy.

By contrast, the Belgian constitutional court does not seem to have developed an explicit independent conception of the principle of competition. But it simply has little need to do so, given its much greater openness to European law,[169] which offers it, via the 'combination method', a tailor-made legal framework in this area. Its review has nonetheless a dissuasive and 'prudential' effect on legislative action.[170] By gradually 'constitutionalising' the different aspects of economic freedom, it has established the essential basis for controlling government action in economic matters.

2.3 *Intermediate Outcome: An 'Objectivised' Market Order*

At the present stage of our analysis, it appears that both of the classic economic liberties that underpin the market system have been endowed with well-established constitutional status. Far from being particularly 'open' or 'neutral' in economic matters, the case law of the three legal orders studied convey a neoliberal referential, albeit to varying degrees. Even if the constitutional judges are probably not consciously endeavouring to translate into legal terms a specific economic theory, they convey a certain economic *Weltanschauung* based on a competitive market order that must be organised and guaranteed by the public authorities. A maximum threshold for the collectivisation of the economy must be imposed. Income from economic activities must be protected from confiscatory taxes. Acquired capital must be immune from any levy. The rational expectations of business owners seeking to maximise their investments in a competitive environment must be preserved. The competitive structure of the market itself must be guaranteed, if necessary against private powers attempting to abuse their dominant positions.

[166] Martinez (2022), pp. 427–432.

[167] Martucci (2015).

[168] Canivet (2014), p. 158.

[169] Verdussen (2011).

[170] Vanderstraeten (2015).

The protection of economic liberties has therefore led to the advent, at constitutional level, of a competition paradigm, which has become the core of 'economic public order'. However, these classic economic liberties represent only one side of national economic constitutions. The economic and social rights constitute another, which must also be analysed if we hope to draw up an overall assessment of the way in which national constitutional judges interpret (and condition) the legal ordering of the economy.

3 The Limitation of Economic and Social Rights or the Rationalisation of the Social State

Social constitutional thought can take two main paths, potentially cumulative: on one hand, it can be derived from an objective principle identifying the state as 'social'; on the other hand, it can be expressed through subjective fundamental rights, via a catalogue of 'economic and social rights' (Sect. 3.1). However, beyond their gradual recognition, their scope is limited on both sides by the three constitutional courts. The justiciability of the social state principle or economic and social rights remains partial, notably due to a liberal reinterpretation of the idea of solidarity, which leads the constitutional courts to endorse the current rationalisation of the social state (Sect. 3.2).

3.1 Paths of the Social State: Objective Meta-Principle or Subjective Fundamental Rights

From Lorenz von Stein in the nineteenth century to Hermann Heller in the first decades of the twentieth century, the idea of 'social state' (*Sozialstaat*) was particularly conceptualised in Germany. It found its first concrete expression in the economic section of the Weimar Constitution, in which the fundamental principles of economic liberalism, though confirmed, were embedded and enclosed in objectives of (distributive) social justice.[171] After the Nazi tragedy, the 'social' nature of the new Federal Republic of Germany was reaffirmed by the Parliamentary Council responsible for drafting the new 'basic norm'. Introduced in Art. 20 para. 1 and Art. 28 para. 1 GG, the 'meta-principle' of the 'social state'[172] is binding on all public authorities, whether federal or federated (Art. 20, para. 3 GG). Besides, this 'social statehood' (*Sozialstaatlichkeit*) also extends to the constitutional legislator, since the principles set out in Articles 1 and 20 GG are rendered intangible by the 'eternity

[171] Grégoire (2022).

[172] Heuschling (2013).

clause' (Art. 79, para. 3 GG), as confirmed by the FCC.[173] But due to the almost unanimous reluctance of the Parliamentary Council to include a catalogue of social rights, the Basic Law contains very few provisions giving concrete form to the social state.[174] It therefore fell to the FCC to gradually define the constitutional implications of the social state. On one hand, 'liberty-rights' were recognised for workers: the freedom of coalition,[175] the (derived) freedom of collective bargaining (*Tarifautonomie*)[176] and the right to 'industrial dispute' (*Arbeitskampf*)[177] (Art. 9, para. 3 LF). On the other hand, the 'radiating effect' (*Ausstrahlungswirkung*) of the social state principle on traditional fundamental rights has specific legal implications, including the strengthening of existing guarantees[178] or even the recognition of genuine 'claim-rights' or 'rights to benefits'[179]—which must first have been implemented by the legislature.[180]

The 'social' character of the Republic is also proclaimed in the French Constitution of 1958, in the very first sentence of its first Article. However, this principle of the 'Social Republic' has been largely neglected, both by legal literature and by the Constitutional Council. The reason for this omission lies in the fact that, unlike Germany, a catalogue of economic and social rights exists in France, *via* the Preamble to the 1946 Constitution, which has been recognised by the Constitutional Council as part of the '*bloc de constitutionnalité*' since the seminal decision *Liberté d'association* in 1971.[181] Therefore, as Alain Supiot has observed, 'the Social Constitution of the Fifth Republic is to be found in the 1946 Preamble, which sheds light on the concept of the "Social Republic"',[182] thereby dispelling the

[173]BVerfG, 23 April 1991, *Bodenreform I, loc. cit.*, §131; 14 May 1996, *Sichere Drittstaaten*, 2 BvR 1938/93, §209; 30 June 2009, *Lissabon*, 2 BvE 2/08, §249.

[174]Niclauß (1974). See also Thurn (2013).

[175]BVerfG, 30 November 1965, *Dortmunder Hauptbahnhof*, 2 BvR 54/62, §20.

[176]BVerfG, 18 November 1954, *Hutfabrikant*, 1 BvR 629/52, §25; 30 November 1965, *Dortmunder Hauptbahnhof, loc. cit.*, §20; 1 March 1979, *Mitbestimmung, loc. cit.*, §205. See: Sodan (1998).

[177]BVerfG, 6 May 1964, *Hausgehilfinnenverband*, 1 BvR 79/62, §40; 26 June 1991, *Aussperrung*, 1 BvR 779/85, §35; 4 July 1995, *Kurzarbeitergeld*, 1 BvF 2/86, §§112–116.

[178]BVerfG, 18 July 1972, *Numerus clausus I, loc. cit.*, §67 (right of admission to university education); 28 February 1980, *Versorgungsausgleich I*, 1 BvL 17/77; 16 April 1985, *Krankenversicherung der Rentner*, 1 BvL 5/80, §124 (protection of specific social security benefits, including pensions, based on the right to property); 7 October 1980, *Präklusion I*, 1 BvL 50/79, §61 (equal distribution of social security benefits).

[179]BVerfG, 18 June 1975, *Waisenrente II*, 1 BvL 4/74, §44; 29 May 1990, *Steuerfreies Existenzminimum*,1 BvL 20/86, §104; BVerfG, 6 December 2005, *Gesetzliche Krankenversicherung*, 1 BvR 347/98; 9 February 2010, *Hartz IV*, 1 BvL 1/09; 18 July 2012, *Asylbewerberleistungsgesetz*, 1 BvL 10/10; 5 November 2019, *Sanktionen im Sozialrecht*, 1 BvL 7/16.

[180]BVerfG, 18 July 1967, *Jugendhilfe*, 2 BvF 3/62, 2 BvR 139/62, §87.

[181]Cons. const.,16 July 1971, *Liberté d'association, loc. cit.* Regarding the Preamble, see Rivero and Vedel (1947), Koubi (1996).

[182]Supiot (2021), pp. 144–145.

'obscure' and 'enigmatic' character of the latter.[183] Besides the duty of nationalisation set out in Article 9,[184] the Preamble of 1946 contains a list of several economic and social rights. These rights are of two kinds: first, the economic rights of workers,[185] which focus on individual 'liberty rights' but exercised collectively (collective bargaining,[186] right to strike[187] and trade-union freedom[188]); second, the social rights of citizens,[189] which take the form either of 'principles of social policy' (public health,[190] employment[191] and housing[192]) that may justify legislative interference with (liberal) fundamental rights, or of 'claim rights' that may be invoked by individuals to guarantee a minimum level of 'material benefits' attached to Articles 10 and 11 of the Preamble.[193]

In Belgium, the 'social' nature of the State has never been explicitly enshrined in the Constitution. For a long time, the 'economic and social rights' therefore remained outside the scope of this 'model constitutional state'[194] of nineteenth-century liberalism. It was not until 31 January 1994 that a specific constitutional clause was adopted: Article 23 (Art. 24bis at the time). This provision states that:

> Everyone has the right to lead a life in keeping with human dignity.

---

183 Rabault (2015).

184 See above, Sect. 2.1.2.1.1.

185 Ogier-Bernaud (2003); Gay (2014).

186 Cons. const., 5 July 1977, *Loi portant diverses dispositions en faveur de l'emploi des jeunes et complétant la loi n°75-574 du 4 juillet 1975 tendant à la généralisation de la sécurité sociale*, No. 77-79 DC.

187 Cons. const., 25 July 1979, *Loi modifiant les dispositions de la loi n°74-696 du 7 août 1974 relatives à la continuité du service public de la radio et de la télévision en cas de cessation concertée du travail*, No. 79-105 DC.

188 Cons. const., 20 January 1981, *Loi renforçant la sécurité et protégeant la liberté des personnes*, No. 80-127 DC.

189 Gay (2020).

190 Cons. const., 22 July 1980, *Loi sur la protection et le contrôle des matières nucléaires*, No. 80-117 DC, Rec. 4; 8 January 1991, *Loi relative à la lutte contre le tabagisme et l'alcoolisme*, No. 90-283 DC, Rec. 5–15.

191 Cons. const., 28 May 1983, *Loi portant diverses mesures relatives aux prestations de vieillesse*, No. 83-156 DC, Rec. 4; 16 January 1986, *Loi relative à la limitation des possibilités de cumul entre pensions de retraite et revenus d'activité*, No. 85-200 DC, Rec. 4.

192 Cons. const., 29 May 1990, *Loi visant à la mise en œuvre du droit au logement*, No. 90-274 DC, Rec. 13; 19 January 1995, *Loi relative à la diversité de l'habitat*, No. 94-359 DC, Rec. 5–7; 29 May 2015, *Société SAUR SAS*, No. 2015-470 QPC.

193 Cons. const., 18 December 1997, *Loi de financement de la sécurité sociale pour 1998*, No. 97-393 DC, Rec. 33 (family allowance); 23 July 1999, *Loi portant création d'une couverture maladie universelle*, *loc. cit.* (healthcare insurance); 14 August 2003, *Loi portant réforme des retraites*, No. 2003-483 DC (retirement pensions); 29 December 2009, *Loi de finances pour 2010*, No. 2009-599 DC, Rec. 101 (social assistance); 15 November 2018, *Loi portant évolution du logement, de l'aménagement et du numérique*, No. 2018-772 DC, Rec. 36 (disability allowance).

194 Marx and Engels (1948a, b).

> To this end, the [federal] laws [and] federate laws [...] guarantee economic, social and cultural rights, taking into account corresponding obligations, and determine the conditions for exercising them.
>
> These rights include among others:
>
> 1° the right to employment and to the free choice of an occupation within the context of a general employment policy, aimed among others at ensuring a level of employment that is as stable and high as possible, the right to fair terms of employment and to fair remuneration, as well as the right to information, consultation and collective negotiation;
>
> 2° the right to social security, to health care and to social, medical and legal aid;
>
> 3° the right to decent accommodation;
>
> 4° the right to the protection of a healthy environment;
>
> 5° the right to cultural and social fulfilment;
>
> 6° the right to family allowances.

Here again, the provision contains both certain 'liberty rights' for workers and social 'claim rights' for all citizens. Moreover, the wording 'among others' implies that the list is not exhaustive.

However, in each of the three legal orders, the issue is not only that of the recognition of such 'economic and social rights' by the constitutional courts (whether directly in a catalogue or indirectly through a meta-principle), but also that of their concrete effects, i.e., their justiciability.

3.2 *The Limited Justiciability of Economic and Social Rights*

A distinction is traditionally drawn between 'objective' and 'subjective' justiciability: The former concerns a dispute over the validity of a standard and leads to a judicial review of conformity with higher provisions and rules; the latter is used to guarantee individual exercise of a right (*via* financial or in-kind compensation).[195] Even if the question is highly controversial in legal literature, the courts and tribunals usually consider that constitutional social and economic rights only entail an 'objective' justiciability. Because of their 'programmatic' nature and their alleged lack of 'direct effect', they should be first implemented by the legislature to gain 'subjective' justiciability, at least when it concerns 'claim rights' providing material benefits to individuals. But there is more: even the precise contours of 'objective' justiciability are difficult to determine. Two main effects, which may be cumulative, can be expected: prohibiting (in principle) any regression in the protection of economic and social rights previously recognised by the legislature ('standstill effect'); accepting some regression but establishing a minimum threshold of protection that the legislature may under no circumstances cross ('essence' or 'hard core').

Only the Belgian Constitutional Court has followed the first path (Sect. 3.2.1), although in reality this does little to hinder the legislature in its efforts to 'rationalise' public social spending. As in France and Germany, a 'proviso of the possible' appears, which gives priority to budgetary considerations over the implementation

[195] De Schutter (2013).

and defence of economic and social rights (Sect. 3.2.2). The sole exception concerns the second effect mentioned, i.e., cases where the 'essence' or the 'hard core' of a right is affected, but this has so far only been put into practice in Germany—and albeit very tentatively (Sect. 3.2.3).

3.2.1 The *Standstill* Obligation, a Principle of (Relative) Non-regression: The Belgian Exception

The standstill effect is the main tool for 'the legal effectiveness of the enshrinement of economic, social and cultural rights'[196] in Belgium. Also known as the 'ratchet effect' (*effet-cliquet*), it involves an 'obligation not to reduce the level of protection already guaranteed by the laws',[197] i.e., a prohibition on 'the public authorities from legislating against the guaranteed rights, and thus reducing the level of protection acquired'.[198] The legislature may therefore amend the legislative framework implementing economic and social rights, but it must maintain a substantially comparable level of guarantees.[199] On the contrary, a reduction in the level of guaranteed rights means, in principle, that any person affected has the right to have the legal provision in question invalidated (or, at least, not applied in the case). The Constitutional Court has gradually deployed the standstill effect to all the rights covered by Article 23 of the Constitution: the right to social assistance,[200] to a healthy environment,[201] to decent accommodation,[202] to legal aid,[203] to work and to fair remuneration,[204] to social security and family allowances,[205] as well as, more recently, to the protection of collective negotiation[206] or to cultural and social fulfilment.[207] In addition, rights not explicitly mentioned in Article 23 of the Constitution could be given a standstill effect in the future, since the list is not exhaustive.

The principle of non-regression applies to both legislative and executive norms.[208] This is of prime importance in the field of social security, which is largely

---

[196] Fierens (2000).

[197] Vandeburie (2008), p. 40.

[198] Hachez (2000), p. 30.

[199] Maes (2006).

[200] Cour const., 27 November 2002, No. 169/2002, B.6.4.-B.6.6.

[201] Cour const., 28 September 2006, No. 145/2006, B.5.1.

[202] Cour const., 10 July 2008, No. 101/2008.

[203] Cour const., 14 February 2013, No. 7/2013, B.68.3.

[204] Cour const., 17 July 2014, No. 107/2014, B.22-B.23; 19 March 2015, No. 36/2015, B.15.1-B.15.3.

[205] Cour const., 13 October 2016, No. 130/2016, B.15.1; 13 October 2016, No. 129/2016, B.20.2.

[206] Cour const., 14 May 2020, No. 67/2020, B.33.

[207] Cour const., 30 September 2021, No. 117/2021, B.26.1 and B.27.1.

[208] Cour const., 17 March 2016, No. 42/2016, B.13.3.

shaped by royal or ministerial decrees. The problem, however, is to determine which norm should be weighed against the contested norm, in other words to define the 'point of reference' from which the ratchet effect operates. Should the comparison be made with the rules in force in 1994, when Article 23 of the Constitution was adopted ('fixed point' theory[209]), or with the rules in force as they existed immediately prior to the adoption of the new contested legislation ('mobile point' theory[210])? The Constitutional Court has vacillated between the two solutions: first it took the adoption of Article 23 as the point of reference,[211] then it finally adopted the 'mobile point' theory.[212] Each new piece of regulation in the field of economic and social rights should thus create an additional detent in the 'ratchet', a new 'non-return barrier' in the protection provided.[213]

However, the reasoning is not flawless, because irreversibility is relative in two respects. On one hand, only 'substantial' or 'significant' deteriorations of the protection are prohibited.[214] On the other hand, even these 'substantial' or 'significant' deteriorations may be validated if they are justified by reasons of general interest. It is thus up to the constitutional court to assess the proportionality of the measure. But this review appears to be anything but consistent: sometimes it checks only for the existence of a reason of general interest (and always endorses the one given by the legislature) before validating the deterioration,[215] sometimes it carries out the aptitude test but not those of necessity and proportionality in the narrow sense.[216] Against this background, the 'mobile point' theory may paradoxically lead to a lower level of protection than the 'fixed point theory', if several reforms are undertaken to (significantly) lower the overall level of protection of an economic and social right but in small successive (and individually non-significant) reductions. This situation is not merely hypothetical: it was the scenario in the case of the two-stage restriction on material aid to asylum seekers.[217] Hence the call from some scholars to use as the 'point of reference' the one that provided the highest level of

[209] Brems (1995); Van Drooghenbroeck (1997).

[210] De Feyter (1994); Hachez (2000).

[211] Cour const., 27 November 2002, No. 169/2002, B.6.5; 14 January 2004, No. 5/2004, B.14.6 and B.25.3.

[212] Cour const., 28 July 2006, No. 123/2006, B.14.3; 28 September 2006, No. 145/2006, B.5.1.

[213] Hachez (2008), pp. 360–362.

[214] Cour const., 14 September 2006, No. 137/2006, B.7.3 (healthy environment); 27 July 2011, No. 135/2011, B.4.-B10 (assistance to asylum seekers); 30 June 2014, No. 95/2014, B.5.-B.12 (assistance to asylum seekers); 1 October 2015, No. 133/2015, B.7.1 (assistance to foreigners legally residing in the territory); 18 May 2017, No. 61/2017, B.10.1 (assistance to foreigners legally residing in the territory); 23 January 2019, No. 6/2019, B.8. (assistance for seniors).

[215] Cour const., 19 March 2015, No. 36/2015, *loc. cit.*, B.15.3; 27 January 2016, No. 12/2016, B.5.3; 14 May 2020, No. 67/2020, *loc. cit.*, B.33; 30 September 2021, No. 117/2021, *loc. cit.*, B.27.3.

[216] Cour const., 30 June 2014, No. 95/2014, *loc. cit.*, B.5.-B.12.

[217] Cour const., 27 July 2011, No. 135/2011, *loc. cit.*, B.4.-B10; Cour const., 30 June 2014, No. 95/2014, *loc. cit.*, B.5.-B.12. See: Hachez and Vincent (2015).

protection (regardless of when it was adopted and whether or not it is still in force) and not the law in force before the adoption of the contested norm.[218] So far, however, the Constitutional Court has always refused to do so.

The question of the existence of a principle of non-regression also arose in the two other states under scrutiny, but it was answered negatively by both the Constitutional Council and the FCC. In France, the debate focused on the effects to be given to the prohibition of 'depriving constitutional requirements of legal guarantees', as stated by the Council when it reviews possible infringements of the rights to material benefits derived from Articles 10 and 11 of the Preamble (family allowances, health insurance, pensions, etc.).[219] In certain isolated decisions dating from the 1980s and 1990s,[220] the Council seemed to recognise a sort of 'ratchet effect' with regard to freedom of communication[221] and the right of asylum.[222] But then it backed down and abandoned this 'standstill obligation' in subsequent decisions.[223] Since then, the rejection of such a principle is clear and has been expressed many times: the legislature may lower the level of protection, provided however—and here lies the absolute limit—that it does not purely and simply deprive legal guarantees attached to a constitutional right or objective. The ultimate (and only true) guarantee attached to 'claim-rights' derived from economic and social rights is therefore solely the protection of a 'minimum content', i.e., of its 'essence' or intangible 'hard core'... yet to be defined, as we shall see below. But the recent example of pensions can give an indication of the (weak) scope of such protection: because of the lack of a 'standstill effect', the Council approved the gradual extension of the statutory retirement age from 60 to 64, despite the reduction in the social right to retirement that it implies;[224] by contrast, extending it to an age close to the average life expectancy or reducing the amounts allocated (after a full career) to a level well below the poverty line should probably be regarded as a 'deprivation of legal guarantees' of a constitutional requirement (national solidarity)—and therefore declared unconstitutional.

---

[218] Hachez (2008), pp. 361–362; Dumont (2017), p. 80.

[219] Boyer (2011).

[220] Cons. const., 11 October 1984, *Loi visant à limiter la concentration et à assurer la transparence financière et le pluralisme des entreprises de presse*, No. 84-181 DC, Rec. 37; 13 August 1993, *Loi relative à la maîtrise de l'immigration et aux conditions d'entrée, d'accueil et de séjour des étrangers en France*, No. 93-325 DC, Rec. 81.

[221] Cons. const., 11 October 1984, *Loi visant à limiter la concentration et à assurer la transparence financière et le pluralisme des entreprises de presse*, No. 84-181 DC, Rec. 37.

[222] Cons. const., 13 August 1993, *Loi relative à la maîtrise de l'immigration et aux conditions d'entrée, d'accueil et de séjour des étrangers en France*, No. 93-325 DC, Rec. 81.

[223] Cons. const., 29 July 1986, *Loi portant réforme du régime juridique de la presse*, No. 86-210 DC; 22 April 1997, *Loi portant diverses dispositions relatives à l'immigration*, No. 97-389 DC, P. 6271.

[224] Cons. const., 9 November 2010, *Loi portant réforme des retraites*, No. 2010-617 DC; 14 April 2023, *Loi de financement rectificative de la sécurité sociale pour 2023*, No. 2023-849 DC.

Just before the issue began to be discussed in France, the FCC had already settled the question by stating that, given the 'breadth and vagueness' of the social state principle, 'it is not possible to infer from it that social benefits must be granted to a certain extent', except when the 'minimum conditions for living in human dignity' are at stake.[225] It thus endorsed the view of the legal philosopher Robert Alexy who argued that, because of the need to 'balance' (*Abwägung*) conflicting principles, there could be no 'ratchet effect' (*Rückschrittsverbot* or *Verschlechterungsverbot*) in the German constitutional order that would prevent the legislature from rolling back social and economic rights, including existing 'rights to benefits'.[226]

3.2.2 The 'Proviso of the Possible' or the Primacy of Budgetary Constraints

The denial of any 'standstill obligation' in France and Germany is actually the consequence of a 'proviso of the possible', i.e., a kind of 'reality principle' conceded by the constitutional courts, whereby 'the state cannot be forced to comply with its obligations in the framework of social rights if it does not possess the economic means to do so'.[227] Such a 'proviso of the possible' (*Vorbehalt des Möglichen*) stems from the FCC's decision of 18 July 1972 concerning the *numerus clausus* for medical studies and was from the outset explicitly linked to the requirements of macroeconomic equilibrium set out in Art. 109, para. 2 LF.[228] The right to access university education, granted with one hand, has therefore been partially withdrawn with the other, as some scholars have sarcastically pointed out.[229] The FCC has then used this 'proviso of the possible' on several occasions,[230] including in cases on allowances for disabled children[231] and on tax exemption for minimum living incomes.[232] The state of public finances thus becomes a criterion of

[225] BVerfG, 29 May 1990, *Steuerfreies Existenzminimum, loc. cit.*, §§88 and 104.

[226] Alexy (1986), pp. 454–472.

[227] According to the formula used by the ECtHR (*Da Silva Carvalho Rico v. Portugal*, 1 September 2015, No. 13341/14, §44).

[228] BVerfG, 18 July 1972, *Numerus clausus I, loc. cit.*, §70. On this 'proviso of the possible' in German constitutional law, see: Munaretto (2022).

[229] Isensee (1980), p. 372.

[230] BVerfG, 7 July 1992, *Trümmerfrauen*, 1 BvL 51/86, §122; 10 March 1998, *Kindergartenbeiträge*,1 BvR 178/97, §58; 8 October 1997, *Integrative Beschulung*, 1 BvR 9/97, §§71–72; 3 April 2001, *Pflegeversicherung III*, 1 BvR 1629/94, §46; 9 November 2004, *Opferentschädigungsgesetz*, 1 BvR 684/98, §§51 and 61; 19 November 2021, *Bundesnotbremse II (Schulschließungen)*, §§53–56.

[231] BVerfG, 18 June 1975, *Waisenrente II, loc. cit.*, §44.

[232] BVerfG, 29 May 1990, *Steuerfreies Existenzminimum, loc. cit.*, §94. For other examples of the 'proviso of the possible', see also: 7 July 1992, *Trümmerfrauen*, 1 BvL 51/86, §122; 10 March 1998, *Kindergartenbeiträge*, 1 BvR 178/97, §58; 8 October 1997, *Integrative Beschulung*, 1 BvR 9/97, §§71–72; 3 April 2001, *Pflegeversicherung III*, 1 BvR 1629/94, §46; 9 November 2004,

constitutionality—and sound budgetary management a valid reason for reducing the guarantees of 'claim-rights'. The 'proviso of the possible' thus operates as a 'precept of judicial self-restraint'[233] with regard to policies of public expenditure rationalisation.

The French Constitutional Council also quickly acknowledged the necessity of curbing healthcare costs as a reason of general interest justifying restrictions on the rights enshrined in the 1946 Preamble.[234] It even endorsed 'the financial equilibrium of social security' as a constitutional requirement derived from Article 11 of the Preamble.[235] Various measures have suffered the consequences of this constitutional incorporation of financial equilibrium. Regarding successive increases in the retirement age, from 60 to 62 and then from 62 to 64, the Council considered that 'by adopting the law under review, the legislature wished to preserve the pay-as-you-go pension system, which is facing major funding difficulties', due in particular to the increase in life expectancy.[236] It was also on this basis that the successive reductions in the system of access to healthcare for illegal aliens (state medical aid) were also validated by the Constitutional Court.[237] The latter now recognises the 'constitutional objectives of proper use of public funds and fight against social protection fraud'.[238] Behind these various formulas lies the idea of 'proviso of the possible'.[239] Although implicit in the Council's decisions, this 'reality principle'[240] emerges expressly in the words of the former President of the Council, Pierre Mazeaud. At a meeting of the Venice Commission in 2005, he delivered a speech on 'the place of extra-legal considerations in the exercise of constitutionality review'.[241] On that occasion, he set out, in the clearest possible terms, the Council's reasoning on social rights:

> Several rights or principles expressly mentioned in the 1946 Preamble (or deduced from it) have been described as "constitutional objectives". [...] Conferring such a qualification on these rights has served to temper their effect, despite the affirmation of their constitutional

---

Opferentschädigungsgesetz, 1 BvR 684/98, §§51 and 61, 19 November 2021, *Bundesnotbremse II (Schulschließungen)*, §§53–56.

[233] Gaier (2013).

[234] Cons. Const., 16 January 1991, *Loi portant dispositions relatives à la santé publique et aux assurances sociales*, No. 90-287 DC.

[235] Cons. Const., 18 December 1997, *Loi de financement de la sécurité sociale pour 1998*, *loc. cit.*, Rec. 25; 12 August 2004, *Loi relative à l'assurance maladie*, No. 2004-504 DC, Rec. 5, 8 and 48.

[236] Cons. const., 9 November 2010, *Loi portant réforme des retraites*, No. 2010-617 DC, *loc. cit.*, Rec. 9 (see Bernaud 2011); 14 April 2023, *Loi de financement rectificative de la sécurité sociale pour 2023*, No. 2023-849 DC, Rec. 92.

[237] See: Cons. const., 29 December 2003, *Loi de finances rectificative pour 2003*, No. 2003-488 DC, Rec. 14–20; 28 December 2010, *Loi de finances pour 2011*, No. 2010-622 DC, Rec. 31–37.

[238] Cons. const., 27 December 2019, *Finance Act for 2020*, No. 2019-796 DC, Rec. 123–129, especially Rec. 126.

[239] Gay (2020), p. 422.

[240] Ribes (2008).

[241] Mazeaud (2005).

> status. They must be regarded as not being absolute in nature, as not being directly applicable and as being addressed not to individuals but to the legislature, for whom they constitute obligations of means and not of result. In particular, they are not subjective rights with direct justiciability. *Realism has obviously dictated this solution: as the level of benefits provided by the "welfare state" is conditioned by the economic situation*, it would be unreasonable to fix it rigidly at constitutional level.[242]

Regressions in social benefits (health, unemployment, pensions, etc.) are therefore justified by the legislature and endorsed by the Constitutional Council on the basis of an objectivised 'economic situation' characterised by the alleged need for austerity in times of 'permanent crisis'.[243]

Even in Belgium, the standstill obligation is of little use in the face of successive reforms designed to rationalise the cost of the social state,[244] particularly under the ongoing pressure of the European Semester.[245] As mentioned above, it covers neither non-significant reductions nor significant ones justified by reasons of general interest. Yet, the latter also include sound budgetary management and the desire to combat social fraud or abuse of social aid. Hence the approval of numerous reforms relating to assistance for immigrants[246] or minimum social assistance,[247] as well as the validation of the new sliding-scale allowance system for unemployment insurance[248] or the 'index jump' involving the temporary neutralisation of the automatic indexation of wages and social benefits to inflation.[249] The standstill principle serves above all as an 'instrument for rationalising the legislative process in social matters':[250] the less justified the reforms are, the stricter and more rigorous the review will be; the clearer they are motivated, the greater the judicial self-restraint of the constitutional court will be.[251] In other words, the effect of the Court's decisions would be to 'encourage a form of evidence-based lawmaking'[252] regarding the conversion of the so-called prodigal 'welfare state' into a financially sound 'social state'. However, the strict proportionality control attached to this kind of 'duty of

[242] Emphases added. Regarding the 'realism' of the Constitutional Council: Ribes (2007).

[243] Borgetto and Lafore (2019), pp. 294–312.

[244] Schoukens (2016).

[245] Detienne (2024).

[246] Cour const., 17 January 2002, No. 17/2002, B.4.3.-B.4.4; 30 June 2014, No. 95/2014, *loc. cit.*, B.5.-B.12. See: Hachez and Vincent (2015), pp. 77–80.

[247] Cour const., 14 January 2004, 4/2004; 28 July 2006, No. 123/2006, *loc. cit.*

[248] The legal framework for unemployment insurance is contained in a Royal Decree and implemented by a Ministerial Decree, so that the reforms were not referred to the Constitutional Court but to the Council of State. The latter dismissed the action for annulment on the basis of lack of legal interest of the applicants (Belgian C.E., 20 December 2012, *Vlaams netwerk van verenigingen waar armen het woord nemen t. Belgische Staat*, No. 221.853, unpublished), using an extremely formalistic argument (Dumont 2013).

[249] Cour const., 13 October 2016, No. 130/2016.

[250] Dumont (2019a, b).

[251] Cour const., 1 October 2015, No. 133/2015, *loc. cit.*; 18 May 2017, No. 61/2017, *loc. cit.*; 6 May 2021, No. 70/2021.

[252] Dumont (2019b), p. 627.

thoroughness' (*devoir de minutie*) in social reforms[253] is only applied to symbolic measures that have limited budgetary consequences. Once a more fundamental measure (potentially) restricting economic and social rights comes into consideration, the Court maintains a position of deference vis-à-vis the legislature, as in the 'index jump' case.[254] Here, the Court refused to verify the existence of a significant reduction in the protection of the right to fair remuneration and the right to social security. It only points to the fact that the reason of general interest invoked (improving the competitiveness of Belgian companies in a context of international competition) is legitimate and that it would not be for the Constitutional Court to supersede the legislature's assessment in economic matters.

The reason why the Belgian Constitutional Court grants parliaments so much room for manoeuvre in social matters lies in its very particular conception of solidarity. The decision of 28 April 2016 on the Treaty on Stability, Coordination and Governance (TSCG) in the Economic and Monetary Union[255] represents a prime example of the neoliberal interpretation given by the Court to this idea. A number of citizens and NGOs had brought an action against this treaty imposing the adoption of a national balanced budget rule coupled with an automatic correction mechanism. In their view, the strict budgetary objectives set out in the TSCG could result in the public authorities no longer being able to meet their constitutional obligations with regard to fundamental social rights. The Court dismissed the applicants' claims for lack of legal interest, but nevertheless endeavoured to develop several elements tending to justify the merits of the TSCG in the light of Belgian constitutional law. Besides the fact that 'the legislature has a broad discretionary power when determining its socio-economic policy, in particular as regards the budget and debt management', the Court mentioned a quite original argument: intergenerational solidarity.[256] Yet, while the concept is enshrined in a new Article 7*bis* of the Constitution adopted in 2007, this provision was not intended to protect fiscal discipline but to ensure 'sustainable development'. Even more surprising is the fact that the Court actually turned the applicants' argument against them, since they had invoked this Article to support the unconstitutionality of the measure, because of the limits on public investment that the new 'budgetary straitjacket' would inevitably impose.[257] In so doing, but without any supporting evidence from the preparatory work of the law of assent, the constitutional judges unexpectedly altered the ecological and social rationale underpinning Article 7*bis*. Instead, it explicitly endorses the neoliberal idea of 'budgetary' intergenerational solidarity,[258] according to which

[253]Remiche (2017), pp. 251–255 and 296–327.

[254]Cour const., 13 October 2016, No. 130/2016, *loc. cit.*, B.17.2.-B.17.4.

[255]Cour const., 28 April 2016, *TSCG*, No. 62/2016. See Gérard and Verrijdt (2017).

[256]Cour const., 28 April 2016, No. 62/2016, *loc. cit.*, B.8.4-B.8.6. See: Behrendt and Miny (2018), pp. 22–23.

[257]For the impact of these new rules on the investment strategies of public authorities, see: Piron (2024).

[258]El Berhoumi et al. (2017), pp. 573–575.

public debt must be seen as a burden imposed on future generations (and not, for example, as the counterpart of bequeathed infrastructures).[259] Hence the conclusion that strict budgetary discipline is not a threat to current economic and social rights, but the necessary condition for their preservation over time.

Even more striking, the judges also refer here to the 'economic context' as a factual constraint that requires the legislature to self-impose the 'golden rule of fiscal policy'. Any possibility of an alternative Keynesian policy is thereby eliminated. In support of its reasoning, the Court here adds a reference to the 'corresponding obligations' of economic and social rights, as provided for in Art. 23 para. 2 of the Constitution. It reiterated this argument in its decision on the law of 16 March 2021 approving the decision on the EU system of own resources.[260] From this point of view, the need to reduce the budget in order to achieve financial equilibrium would ultimately be the collective counterpart of the individual economic and social rights. The problem is that the Court ignores the two conditions it had previously laid down justifying the strengthening of these 'corresponding obligations', namely that they contribute to the general objective of human dignity (enshrined in Art. 23 para. 1 of the Constitution) and that they are proportionate to that objective.[261] While it is difficult to find a legal argument for this 'omission', it is easier to understand the practical reason behind it: the link between the austerity measures and the guarantee of human dignity is very thin, to say the least, so the easiest (or only) solution for the Court was simply to overlook these conditions.[262] As a result, 'corresponding obligations' are tending now to become the constitutional basis for the shift 'towards an active social state'.[263] This is further confirmed in the Court's recent decisions on 'structural pension reforms'.[264]The neoliberal reversal of the idea of 'solidarity' is thus matched by a growing emphasis on individual responsibility as a prerequisite for access to economic and social rights, at least when it concerns rights to benefits.

3.2.3 Guarantee of the Essence and Right to Minimum Benefits: A (Timid) Limit to the Rationalisation of the Social State?

Although it is used by contemporary German ordoliberals,[265] the 'intergenerational argument' has not (yet) entered the German constitutional order, despite several calls

[259] Buchanan (1958), pp. 31–47.

[260] Cour const., 30 September 2021, No. 127/2021.

[261] Cour const., 10 July 2008, No. 101/2008, *loc. cit.*, B.33.1. and B.33.2.

[262] Dermine (2016), pp. 471–472.

[263] Dumont (2008). See: Cour const., 27 July 2011, No. 135/2011, *loc. cit.*, B.8.3.3.; 30 June 2014, No. 95/2014, *loc. cit.*, B.7.

[264] Cour const., 28 September 2017, No. 104/2017, B.13.1; 6 May 2021, No. 70/2021, *loc. cit.*, B.6.; 29 September 2022, No. 117/2022, B.14.4.

[265] Vanberg (1994); Goldschmidt (2009).

for it to do so.[266] However, the FCC's enshrinement of 'intergenerational equity' regarding climate issues[267] may well pave the way for a revolution in fundamental rights dogma in many areas, including economic and social matters.[268] On the other hand, the Court very clearly endorsed the shift towards individual responsibility initiated by the legislature in the field of social assistance. Underway since the 1970s, the shift was accentuated in the early 2000s with the adoption of the Hartz reforms, which implemented a vast programme to make the labour market more flexible and to contain social spending.[269] Among various new regulations, the 'fourth Law for Modern Services on the Labour Market' (Hartz IV) was specifically aimed at simplifying the unemployment benefit system. This system was reduced to two pillars: on one hand, benefits financed by contributions in proportion to the unemployed person's previous salary, based on the 'social insurance' model (*Arbeitslosengeld I*, ALG I); on the other hand, benefits financed by taxation, provided once eligibility for ALG I has expired, based on the 'public assistance' model (*Arbeitslosengeld II*, ALG II).[270] ALG II was a flat-rate monthly allowance: €345 for the beneficiary, €311 for dependent adults and €207 for dependent children up to the age of 14. These amounts were in fact equal to social assistance (*Sozialhilfe*), provided for people who are totally unable to work and support themselves and their families.[271] The idea was therefore to provide temporary support for unemployed people, but at a much lower level than a (low) wage, in order to encourage them to return to work.[272] This retreat of the welfare state, justified on budgetary grounds, nevertheless raised serious constitutional objections. Although the FCC has never recognised any 'ratchet effect', it does seem to have established a 'floor effect', i.e., a threshold in the form of 'minimum conditions for living in human dignity' that must be maintained for every individual.[273] In a sense,

[266] Kahl (2014); Schlegel (2021).

[267] BVerfG, 24 March 2021, *Klimaschutz*, 1 BvR 2656/18, §148. See: Lenz (2022); Grosche (2022).

[268] Hailbronner (2022).

[269] Trube (2004).

[270] On the shift from the 'social insurance' model (*Versicherung*) to the 'public assistance' model (*Fürsorge*) brought about by the Hartz IV reform, see: Knuth (2006).

[271] In addition to the basic flat rate benefit, there may also be other allowances for housing, heating or more occasional assistance.

[272] It should be noted that at the time there was no uniform statutory minimum wage and the decision was left to collective bargaining in the various sectoral branches on the basis of Article 9 LF. However, a law of 11 August 2014, introduced as part of legislation to strengthen collective bargaining, changed the situation by enshrining a minimum wage. Starting at €8.5 gross/hour, it has since been raised several times by decree following agreements reached within the Minimum Wage Commission (on which both unions and employers are represented). Since October 2022, it has been set at €12 gross/hour, i.e., around 60% of the German median wage, through further intervention by the legislature, before the Commission again became responsible for subsequent determinations.

[273] BVerfG, 18 June 1975, *Waisenrente II*, *loc. cit.*, §§44–45; 29 May 1990, *Steuerfreies Existenzminimum*, *loc. cit.*, §104. See: Neumann (1995).

this represents the 'social' expression of the guarantee of the 'essence' (*Wesensgehaltsgarantie*) of fundamental rights (Art. 19, para. 2 LF).

After a first validation of the reform by the Federal Social Court (*Bundessozialgericht*),[274] the FCC had to review the constitutionality of Hartz IV. More specifically, it had to assess the method used to determine the amount of ALG II, as well as the adequacy of this amount to the vital needs of beneficiaries.[275] From the outset, the Constitutional Court confirmed the existence of a 'fundamental right to the guarantee of a subsistence minimum in line with human dignity' (*Grundrecht auf Gewährleistung eines menschenwürdigen Existenzminimums*).[276] Based on Article 1 GG, it gives rise to a genuine 'right to benefits' of two kinds: the 'minimum [physical] subsistence' *sensu stricto* (food, clothing, housing, heating, health, etc.); the 'socio-cultural subsistence' ensuring the 'possibility to maintain inter-human relationships and a minimum of participation in social, cultural and political life'. On the other hand, the Court takes great care to directly set out the limits of this right it has just created: the *Existenzminimum* 'only covers those means which are vital[277] to maintain an existence that is in line with human dignity'. It limits its scope even further by adding that, as this right is inevitably imprecise, it must necessarily be 'safeguarded by a statutory claim' (*gesetzlichen Anspruch*), thus determined 'by a parliamentary statute which contains a concrete benefit claim on the part of the citizen towards the competent benefit institution', in order to 'cover social reality in a manner that is appropriate to the present day and realistic'.[278]

As a result, the FCC confines itself to a limited review regarding the amount of benefits, but not regarding the calculation methods. They are subject to meticulous verification, since 'the assessment of the benefits must be clearly justifiable on the basis of reliable figures and plausible methods of calculation'[279]—which are themselves open to continuous reassessment according to the actual basic needs of individuals. As in Belgium, the legislature's obligation is therefore transformed into a constitutional requirement for extensive methodological justification.[280] Once these abstract principles had been applied to the concrete case, the FCC validated both the amounts of the ALG II and the method of calculation.[281] There were nevertheless two minor criticisms levelled by the Court against the reform: first, the legislature deviated from the chosen method on several occasions, without justification and without any solid substitutable criteria; second, only the usual vital needs were taken into account, whereas specific occasional needs may

[274]BSG, 23 November 2006, B 11b AS 1/06 R. See: Giesen and Ricken (2007).

[275]BVerfG, 9 February 2010, *Hartz IV*, *loc. cit.* See: Seiler (2010); Egidy (2011).

[276]*Ibid.*, §§133–135.

[277]In the German version, the words used are '*unbedingt erforderlich*', which literally means 'strictly necessary'.

[278]*Ibid.*, §136–138.

[279]*Ibid.*, §142.

[280]*Ibid.*, §§137 and 144.

[281]*Ibid.* at §§151–156 and §§159–169.

exist.[282] It is therefore the 'random estimates' that have been declared unconstitutional,[283] in particular the 40% haircut applied to children up to the age of 14, without any empirical basis, as if they were 'small adults', whereas they actually have specific needs, for instance in terms of schooling.[284]

Despite this methodological objection, the FCC refused to 'determine a specific amount of benefit on its own on the basis of its own assessments and evaluations'.[285] It gave the legislature until 31 December 2010 to adjust its methods of calculation, but stated it was not 'obliged under constitutional law to set higher benefits' as long as the procedure was well justified.[286] According to the FCC, the core of the Hartz IV reform is therefore constitutional, but the details can be improved. And, indeed, after the methodological corrections made by the legislature, it fully endorsed the ALG II regime.[287]

This raises the question of the true significance of the *Hartz IV* decision for the constitutional principle of social statehood. Some wonder whether the declaration of unconstitutionality does not ultimately represent a 'Pyrrhic victory'[288] for the *Existenzminimum*, since the FCC did approve the (very low) amounts of 'vital needs' estimated. Others draw the conclusion that the social state is 'reduced to its most basic form: people should not starve in Germany'.[289] Above all, at the methodological level, i.e., the only one where the Court really exercises its review, the statistical model used (and approved by the FCC) is a snake biting its own tail: the amount of the minimum subsistence level is deducted from the consumption expenditure of the poorest households (excluding those benefiting from social assistance). But there is no guarantee that they are not already living below the threshold of human dignity. In addition, before the introduction of a minimum wage,[290] this method gave rise to the risk of a 'race to the bottom'. The reduction in the amount of social benefits under ALG II was likely to lead to a decrease in the wages of the working poor, since even underpaid jobs (but exceeding ALG II) were made 'attractive' to the 'reserve army' of jobseekers. And this income decrease could then have a negative impact on the consumption expenditure of the working poor, and subsequently on the estimated level of the *Existenzminimum*, leading to a possible downward adjustment of wages on the unqualified labour market—and so on. Hence the self-congratulation of 'social-democrat' Chancellor Gerhard Schröder in 2005 at the World Economic Forum in Davos, where he boasted of having 'built

[282] *Ibid.*, §146.

[283] *Ibid.*, §§171–182, especially §171.

[284] *Ibid.*, §§190–198.

[285] *Ibid.*, §212.

[286] *Ibid.*, §211.

[287] BVerfG, 23 July 2014, *Sozialrechtliche Regelbedarfsleistungen*, 1 BvL 10/12; 27 July 2016, 1 BvR 371/11.

[288] Butterwegge (2011), p. 19.

[289] Rammer (2010).

[290] See above, footnote 272.

up one of the best low-wage sectors in Europe'.[291] In the end, the only category of vulnerable individuals to benefit indirectly from the Hartz IV decision was asylum seekers (and other foreigners with a temporary right of residence). The FCC obliged the legislature to increase their allowances, which were more than 35% lower than the minimum social assistance benefits for the explicit purpose of discouraging immigration.[292]

The tension between the protection of the *Existenzminimum* and the liberal shift of the welfare state towards individual responsibility reaches its climax when ALG II beneficiaries do not respect the obligation to cooperate. The sanction consisted of a temporary reduction (for three months) of 30% of the amount granted, then 60% for the second breach, before outright withdrawal in the event of a further breach. Here too, the FCC was attempting to strike a balance.[293] On one hand, the 30% haircut was approved, except insofar as it provided for a fixed period of three months, regardless of the subsequent cooperation of the sanctioned recipient. On the other hand, the harsher provisions were declared incompatible with the Basic Law, given the 'lack of compelling evidence regarding the suitability and necessity of a reduction in benefits on this scale', which 'extends far beyond the minimum subsistence guaranteed by fundamental rights'.[294] Two readings of the decision are possible. Some point to the fact that the judgment proves that the *Existenzminimum* is truly effective and binding on the legislature.[295] Others are quite surprised that the legislature is authorised to go beyond the limit of the *Existenzminimum*, yet supposed to express the essence not only of the principle of social state, but also of the (no more) intangible right to human dignity.[296] While acting as the guarantor of a minimum 'right to benefit', the FCC therefore endorses the idea that the protection of human dignity has to be earned—and thereby confirms the 'activating' inflection of the social state.

The reaction of the German public authorities to Covid-19 may give the impression of a 'solidarist' realignment of the social state, which has proved to be of 'systemic importance' in the face of the crisis. And it is true that the FCC systematically rejected actions against the many restrictions introduced by the German Protection Against Infection Act (*Infektionsschutzgesetz*—IfSG), including measures to close businesses,[297] schools and crèches,[298] or to impose social

[291] Schröder (2005).

[292] BverfG, 18 July 2012, *Asylbewerberleistungsgesetz*, *loc. cit.* See: Tiedemann (2012); Schreiber (2018).

[293] BverfG, 5 November 2019, *Sanktionen im Sozialrecht*, *loc. cit.* See: Nettesheim (2020).

[294] *Ibid.*, §§189–209, especially §190 and §200.

[295] Gantchev (2020).

[296] Schmidt (2020).

[297] BVerfG, 28 April 2020, 1 BvR 899/20.

[298] BVerfG, 9 June 2020, 1 BvR 1230/20.

distancing,[299] curfews[300] and compulsory vaccinations.[301] The Court then gave final approval to the measures taken, in particular regarding freedom of movement and children's right to education,[302] emphasising that they were also subject to the 'proviso of the possible'. Above all, the legislature has lifted the debt brake to be free to inject hundreds of billions into the economy to prevent a complete collapse.[303] However, the recent decision, on 15 November 2023, to invalidate the reallocation of 60 billion euros of unused funds for pandemic-era aid to the climate and transformation fund (*Klima- und Transformationsfonds*—KTF)[304] demonstrates the FCC's determination to restore—whatever it takes—economic orthodoxy.[305]

Despite all that, the fact remains that, through the *Existenzminimum*, the FCC has at least given concrete form, albeit modestly, to the guarantee of the 'essence' of economic and social rights. The French Constitutional Council has not gone so far. Of course, the French Parliament has never carried out such a far-reaching rationalisation of the social state as the *Bundestag* did with the Hartz reforms. The guarantee of the essence seems nevertheless to exist in the French constitutional order. The prohibition of 'depriving constitutional requirements of legal guarantees' set by the Constitutional Council regarding the rights to benefits derived from Articles 10 and 11 of the Preamble (family allowances, health insurance, pensions, etc.) correspond to a threshold below which the legislature is not allowed go. Nevertheless, this threshold currently remains purely theoretical. The Constitutional Court has invalidated certain legal provisions for breach of the equality principle in access to social benefits, but never for breach of the 'essence' of the right contained in paragraph 11 of the Preamble. In other words, the legislature is 'authorised to replace existing provisions with less protective ones, provided that they do not fall below a minimum threshold of protection... which has yet to be defined'.[306]

The situation is much the same in Belgium. Because of its double relativisation, we already know that the standstill obligation 'does not, strictly speaking, guarantee the preservation of the social acquis'.[307] But is there an absolute limit to the possible erosion of economic and social rights? Does Article 23 of the Constitution entail, alongside the 'ratchet effect', a 'floor effect', i.e., a protection of the 'essence' of economic and social rights? Some authors suggested this idea by claiming the existence of a right to irreducible minimum benefits, on the basis of the human

[299] BVerfG, 15 July 2020, 1 BvR 1630/20.

[300] BVerfG, 5 May 2021, 1 BvR 781/21.

[301] BVerfG, 10 February 2022, 1 BvR 2649/21.

[302] BVerfG, 19 November 2021, *Bundesnotbremse I (Ausgangs- und Kontaktbeschränkungen), loc. cit.*, p. 223; 19 November 2021, *Bundesnotbremse II (Schulschließungen), loc. cit.*

[303] Dorn et al. (2020).

[304] BVerfG, 15 November 2023, *KTF*, 2 BvF 1/22.

[305] Meickmann (2023).

[306] Bauduin (2020), p. 5.

[307] Hachez (2015), p. 313 and p. 322.

dignity protected by Art. 23, para. 1.[308] Other legal scholars have argued that each of the economic and social rights recognised in Article 23 contains a 'hard core' which cannot be affected, even when the standstill obligation failed to prevent the reduction of the rights.[309] Nevertheless, at the present time, the Constitutional Court has never referred to such an *Existenzminimum* or to the guarantee of the 'essence' of the economic and social rights as a possible limit to the rationalisation of social spending. Yet, the 'combination method' would provide a powerful argument for this guarantee: Article 4 of the United Nations International Covenant on Economic, Social and Cultural Rights,[310] as well as the European Committee of Social Rights,[311] include the protection of the 'hard core' of these rights.

4 Conclusion: The Economy as a 'Factual Constraint' Ordered by Constitutional Courts

Stone by stone, decision by decision, each of the three national constitutional courts has built up a body of case law outlining the contours of a social state based on economic and social rights, albeit using different reasoning and interpretative methods. However, rather than the advent of effective protection of economic and social rights, social constitutional jurisprudence tends mainly to accommodate and marginally adjust the rationalisation of welfare state costs. In each of the constitutional orders, a 'proviso of the possible' emerges, which surreptitiously reduces economic and social rights to their alleged programmatic status. Even the standstill obligation, recognised in Belgium, is of little use against 'budgetary imperatives'. The legislature is all the more justified in undertaking reforms on the grounds of the 'economic context' that the very idea of solidarity is shifting in favour of an intergenerational equity reduced to its financial expression, i.e., balanced budgets. To ensure its long-term sustainability, the social state should be reoriented towards 'activation' of aid recipients—something that constitutional judges accept without further difficulty through the 'corresponding obligations' of economic and social rights or via the principle of 'individual responsibility'.

It could be argued, though, that in so doing the constitutional courts are merely exercising judicial self-restraint, in accordance with the economic neutrality of national constitutions. This argument might be convincing if it did not obscure the practice of double standards vis-a-vis classic economic liberties. Apart from the requirement for 'methodological justification', the 'proviso of the possible' is used to validate all the social state reforms. In contrast, the 'economic context' is simply

[308] Jamoulle (2001); Fierens (2015).

[309] Vogel-Polsky (1995); Dumont (2017).

[310] Limburg Principles on the Implementation of the International Covenant on Economic, Social and Cultural Rights (UN Doc. E/C.12/2000/13, 2 October 2000), No. 56.

[311] ECSR, 23 May 2012, *GENOP-DEI and ADEDY v. Greece*, No. 65/2011; 23 May 2012, *GENOP-DEI and ADEDY v. Greece*, No. 66/2011. See: Hachez (2014).

ignored at the other end of the ideological spectrum of fundamental rights, that is, the right to private property and economic freedom. Yet these classic economic liberties too have a significant cost,[312] which is never mentioned and even less taken into account.

In France, nationalisations are reduced to simple expropriation without any explanation of the reasoning behind the decision, even though the nationalisation of the property of the clergy provided a historical precedent. The judge here substitutes his own assessment of the 'fair value' of the compensation without hesitation. Similarly, the Constitutional Council substitutes its assessment for that of the legislature as to whether the socio-economic context justifies a system to prevent profit-based layoffs. According to the Council, the judge cannot take the place of the business owners... but it can take the place of the legislature, apparently. Finally, the tax increase on the wealthiest, based on the principle of solidarity (which is supposed to be strengthened in times of economic crisis), was censured because of a new constitutional threshold for taxation. Here, the 'essence' of the fundamental right does not appear to be merely an abstract principle. The same phenomenon can be seen even more clearly in Germany, where the basic norm is interpreted in a very creative way, to say the least. The FCC has identified a fourfold prohibition: depriving shareholders of the ultimate power of decision within their companies; taxing net acquired capital; taxing income (from work and capital) at more than 50% (*Halbteilungsgrunsatz*); taxing inheritances or gifts in a way that 'appears economically useless from the point of view of an owner thinking in economic terms'. In the end, only the Belgian Constitutional Court seems (at first glance) to have maintained a certain consistency in its judicial self-restraint, even if it is not exempt from innovative interpretations in order to define the (broader) contours of a 'confiscatory tax' on inheritance or to pull out of its hat a constitutional principle of 'economic and monetary union' within the Belgian territory, in order to counter any protectionist impulses.

In any case, there is no trace of any 'proviso of the possible' in the protection of classic economic liberties. On the contrary, the interpretation given to the latter suggests that the market order is the only real horizon of possibility for the legislature. It appears as an extra-legal (natural) fact in the various national constitutional jurisprudences. Whatever denomination is chosen to describe this phenomenon ('objectivisation', 'factualisation' or 'naturalisation'), it operates at two levels. On one hand, normative consequences are deduced from these objectivised economic 'facts': net acquired capital, which is the core element of capitalist economy, should be immune from any form of taxation; a company's dominant position obtained 'on its merits' cannot be forced to sell its assets; the competitive context of the economy implies that the business owner should always be able to 'anticipate economic difficulties and make economic trade-offs', which means that it is constitutionally impossible for the legislature to impose a judicial assessment of the appropriateness of profit-based layoffs—or to prescribe a genuinely equal sharing of decision-

[312] Holmes and Sunstein (2000).

making power with the workers; etc. On the other hand, the 'economic impact' of legal norms is taken into account when assessing their constitutionality: the validation of nationalisations depends on the degree of collectivisation of the economy they induce; the 'continuation of economic activity' and the 'economic usefulness of the transfer' become a criterion for judging the appropriateness of the level of business inheritance taxation; etc. Moreover, it is not just any kind of market that is being objectivised: it is the *competitive* market order. Competition is considered now as 'one of the fundamental principles of the economic constitution' (Germany), or at least as the core of 'economic public order' (France).

Ultimate 'cunning of reason' in economic constitutionalism: narrowing the scope for legislative (fiscal) intervention in the economy contributes, indirectly but inevitably, to extending the budgetary limit of the 'proviso of the possible' imposed on the social state. The new constitutional dogma in fiscal matters inevitably affects the State's potential for social correction and wealth redistribution, as the German judge Böckenförde rightly pointed out. In a European context already marked by the framework for budgetary discipline within the Economic and Monetary Union, this constitutional 'proviso of the possible' is far from being economically neutral—as demonstrated by the Belgian constitutional court's decision on the TSCG.

One thing seems therefore to be clear: the economic neutrality of national constitutions is a *myth*. Albeit that it is true that national constitutional texts are open to a variety of interpretations and are, in this sense, relatively 'open', the 'authentic interpreters' have considerably curbed the room for manoeuvre of the legislature, revealing a specific economic 'referential'. The stance of judicial self-restraint adopted by the judges is easily explained, either by their concern to conceal their creative power in the absence of an explicit choice laid down by the *pouvoir constituant*, or by their genuine belief in the objectivity or naturalness of the economic world-view that they hold—for a choice is not supposed to be legally circumscribed if it is only factually constrained. However, such a stance does not stand up to analysis, provided that the various positions adopted by constitutional courts are linked and compared, depending on whether they apply to the guarantees of the market order or of the social state. In a nutshell, the founding norms of the market are granted normative primacy over social provisions at the constitutional level. The former are the principle, the latter the exception. Behind this statement, there is no denying the 'factual' constraint placed nowadays on society and the State by the market. But the decisive point is that such 'market constraints' ultimately stems from contingent legal frameworks. Yet, despite path-dependency, these frameworks are never immutable… not even if they are constitutional.

References

Abendroth W (1954) Zum Begriff des demokratischen und sozialen Rechtsstaates im Grundgesetz der Bundesrepublik Deutschland. In: Hermann A (ed) Aus Geschichte und Politik. Festschrift zum 70. Geburtstag von Ludwig Bergsträsser, Düsseldorf, pp 279–300

Albach H, Witte E (eds) (2002) Privatisierung von öffentlichen Unternehmen. Unternehmenstheorie und praktische Erfahrungen. Gabler Verlag, Wiesbaden
Alexy R (1986) Theorie der Grundrechte. Suhrkamp, Frankfurt am Main, pp 454–472
Audier S (2012) Néo-libéralisme(s): une archéologie intellectuelle. Grasset, Paris
Audier S (2022) L'invention du néolibéralisme: histoire, concepts, controverses, 2 vol. Le Bord de l'Eau, Lormont
Badura P (2011) Wirtschaftsverfassung und Wirtschaftsverwaltung. Mohr Siebeck, Tübingen
Baker P (2013) Some recent decisions of the European Court of Human Rights on tax matters. Eur Tax 52(6):393–395
Bauduin B (2020) Le droit de la protection sociale face à la QPC. La Semaine Juridique Social 3088(48)
Beaud O (1994) Nationalisation et souveraineté. La nationalisation comme acte de puissance publique. Les Petites Affiches 141:11–18
Behrendt C, Miny X (2018) La Cour constitutionnelle belge et face aux enjeux budgétaires. Revue de la Faculté de Droit de l'Université de Liège 1:17–30
Bernaud V (2011) Le Conseil constitutionnel et la réforme des retraites: une inertie discutable. Droit social 3:305–310
Bodinier B, Teyssier É (2000) L'événement le plus important de la Révolution. La vente des biens nationaux. Éditions du Comité des Travaux Historiques et Scientifiques, Paris
Böhm F (1933) Wettbewerb und Monopolkampf. Carl Heymanns Verlag, Berlin
Böick M (2018) Die Treuhand: Idee - Praxis - Erfahrung (1990-1994). Wallstein Verlag, Göttingen
Borgetto M, Lafore R (2019) Droit de la sécurité sociale, 19th edn. Dalloz, Paris
Bourgeois M (2005) De l'impôt confiscatoire selon la Cour d'arbitrage. Journal des Tribunaux 6205:797–803
Boyer C (2011) L'"effet cliquet" à l'épreuve de la question prioritaire de constitutionnalité. Actualité Juridique. Droit Administratif 30:1718–1725
Brems E (1995) De nieuwe grondrechten in de Belgische Grondwet en hun verhouding tot het Internationale, inzonderheid het Europese recht. Tijdschrift voor Bestuurswetenschappen en Publiekrecht:619–636
Buchanan JM (1958) Public principles of public debt. a defense and restatement. Richard D. Irwin, Homewood
Butterwegge C (2011) Ein noch rigideres Armutsregime? Deutschland im Übergang zu Hartz V. Gesundheits- und Sozialpolitik 65(2):9–20
Canivet G (2014) Prolégomènes à l'étude de la doctrine du Conseil constitutionnel en matière de concurrence. In: Behar-Touchais M, Charbit N, Amaro R (eds) À quoi sert la concurrence? Institut de droit de la concurrence, Paris, pp 153–159
Chazal J-P (2014) Propriété et entreprise: le Conseil constitutionnel, le droit et la démocratie. Recueil Dalloz 19:1101–1106
Collet M (2014a) L'impôt confisqué. Odile Jacob, Paris
Collet M (2014b) Le plafonnement de l'ISF ou la naissance clandestine d'un principe constitutionnel. Grief 1(1):146–153
Colly F (1998) Le Conseil constitutionnel et le droit de propriété. Revue de droit public:135–197
Colly F (2022) La Constitution économique de la France et la jurisprudence économique du Conseil constitutionnel. In: Grégoire G, Miny X (eds) The idea of economic constitution in Europe. Genealogy and overview. Brill/Nijhoff, Leiden/Boston, pp 567–616
De Crouy-Chanel E (2011) Le Conseil constitutionnel mobilise-t-il d'autres principes constitutionnels que l'égalité en matière fiscale? Les Nouveaux cahiers du Conseil Constitutionnel 33:15–26
De Feyter K (1994) De juridische gevolgen van de internationale en nationale erkenning van economische, sociale en culturele rechten. In: Mensenrechten. Maklu, Antwerpen/Apeldoorn, pp 161–178
De Schutter O (ed) (2013) Economic, social and cultural rights as human rights. Edward Elgar, Cheltenham/Northampton

Debré J-L (2014) Constitution, liberté d'entreprendre et concurrence. Concurrences 2:7–11
Delpérée F (1995) Les droits économiques, sociaux et culturels. In: Ergec R (ed) Les droits économiques, sociaux et culturels dans la Constitution. Bruylant, Brussels, pp 287–290
Depré S (2002) L'exercice d'une activité professionnelle au regard de la Convention européenne des droits de l'homme et de la liberté du commerce et de l'industrie. Revue Trimestrielle des Droits de l'Homme 50:369–383
Dermine P (2016) La discipline budgétaire européanisée à l'aune de la Constitution belge. Journal des Tribunaux:471–472
Detienne Q (2024) Next Generation EU ou le nouveau «pouvoir de la bourse» de la Commission en matière sociale. L'exemple des retraites en Belgique. In: Adalid S (ed) Relance et Transition(s): le nouvel âge de l'intégration. Bruylant, Paris, forthcoming
Dorn F, Fuest C, Neumeier F (2020) After the great economic collapse: Germany's stimulus package to recover the economy in times of Covid-19. CESifo Forum 21(2):38–46
Dumont D (2008) Vers un État social "actif"? Journal des tribunaux 6300:133–139
Dumont D (2013) Dégressivité accrue des allocations de chômage versus principe de standstill. Journal des tribunaux 39:769–776
Dumont D (2017) Le "droit à la sécurité sociale" consacré par l'article 23 de la Constitution: quelle signification et quelle justiciabilité? In: Dumont D (ed) Questions transversales en matière de sécurité sociale. Larcier, Brussels, pp 11–98
Dumont D (2019a) Le principe de *standstill* comme instrument de rationalisation du processus législatif en matière sociale: Un plaidoyer illustré (I.). Journal des Tribunaux 138(30):601–611
Dumont D (2019b) Le principe de *standstill* comme instrument de rationalisation du processus législatif en matière sociale: Un plaidoyer illustré (II.). Journal des Tribunaux 138(31):621–628
Dussart M-L (2015) Constitution et économie. Dalloz, Paris
Egidy S (2011) Casenote - the fundamental right to the guarantee of a subsistence minimum in the Hartz IV Decision of the German Federal Constitutional Court. German Law J 12(11): 1961–1982
El Berhoumi M et al (2017) La Cour constitutionnelle face au Pacte budgétaire européen: un arrêt sans intérêt? Journal des Tribunaux 6699:565–582
Fabre A (2014) La promesse présidentielle de "Florange" à l'épreuve du droit de propriété et de la liberté d'entreprendre. Constitutions. Revue de droit constitutionnel appliqué 2:204–210
Favoreu L (1982) Une grande décision. In: Favoreu L (ed) Nationalisations et Constitution. Economica, Paris, pp 19–55
Feldman J-P (2002) Le Conseil constitutionnel et la liberté d'entreprendre. Revue trimestrielle des droits de l'homme 52:1089–1090
Fierens J (2000) L'efficacité juridique de la consécration des droits économiques, sociaux et culturels. In: Scholsem J-C (ed) Le point sur les droits de l'homme. Commission Université-Palais, Liège, pp 167–213
Fierens J (2015) Existe-t-il un principe général du droit au respect de la dignité humaine?, note sous Cass., 18 novembre 2013. Revue Critique de Jurisprudence Belge 4:358–382
Flick H, Schauhoff S (1996) Einheitswert, Vermögen- und Erbschaftsteuer — Anforderungen an eine verfassungsgemäße Besteuerung. Zeitschrift für Rechtspolitik 29(3):101–106
Fouquet O (2011) Le Conseil constitutionnel et le principe d'égalité devant l'impôt. Les Nouveaux cahiers du Conseil Constitutionnel 33:7–14
Froese J, Depenheuer O (2018) Kommentierung von Art. 15 GG. In: von Mangoldt H, Klein F, Starck C (eds) Kommentar zum Grundgesetz, 7th edn. C.H. Beck, Munich, pp 1543–1559
Gaier R (2013) Der Vorbehalt des Möglichen als Gebot richterlicher Selbstbeschränkung. In: Bäuerle M, Dann P, Wallrabenstein A (eds) Demokratie-Perspektiven. Festschrift für Brun-Otto Bryde zum 70. Geburtstag. Mohr Siebeck, Tübingen, pp 367–379
Gantchev V (2020) Welfare sanctions and the right to a subsistence minimum: a troubled marriage. Eur J Soc Secur 22(3):257–272

Garnier R (2004) La pénétration des exigences économiques dans la jurisprudence du Conseil constitutionnel. Revue du droit public et de la science politique en France et à l'étranger 2:457–480
Gay L (2014) Droit de grève et liberté syndicale dans la jurisprudence constitutionnelle: des libertés "particulières"? Les Nouveaux cahiers du Conseil Constitutionnel 45:35–49
Gay L (2020) Des droits à part (entière)? La justiciabilité inaboutie des droits sociaux en droit constitutionnel français. Cahiers de Droit 61(2):397–425
Gérard P, Verrijdt W (2017) Belgian Constitutional Court adopts national identity discourse. Eur Const Law Rev 13:182–205
Giesen R, Ricken O (2007) Regelleistungen und Anrechnungsvorschriften nach SGB II verfassungsgemäß. Neue Zeitschrift für Arbeitsrecht 12:677–678
Goldschmidt N (ed) (2009) Generationengerechtigkeit. Ordnungsökonomische Konzepte. Mohr Siebeck, Tübingen
Grégoire G (2022) The Economic Constitution under Weimar: Doctrinal Controversies and Ideological Struggles. In: Grégoire G, Miny X (eds) The Idea of Economic Constitution in Europe. Genealogy and Overview. Brill/Nijhoff, Leiden/Boston, pp 53–93
Grégoire G (2025a) The EU's neoliberal constitutionalism(s). Eur Law Open, forthcoming
Grégoire G (2025b) La Constitution économique. Enquête sur les rapports entre économie, politique et droit, Bibliothèque de la pensée juridique. Classiques Garnier, Paris, forthcoming
Grégoire G, Miny X (eds) (2022) The idea of economic constitution in Europe: genealogy and overview. Brill/Nijhoff, Leiden/Boston. Available on https://brill.com/view/title/63005
Grosche N (2022) Recht und Intertemporale Gerechtigkeit: Berichte und Kritik. Der Staat 61(1): 113–128
Grosclaude J (2002) De l'inconstitutionnalité de l'imposition de la fortune en Allemagne et en France. In: Gouverner, administrer, juger, Liber Amicorum Jean Waline. Dalloz, Paris, pp 49–58
Hachez I (2000) L'effet de standstill: le pari des droits économiques, sociaux et culturels? Administration publique:30–57
Hachez I (2008) Le principe de standstill dans le droit des droits fondamentaux: une irréversibilité relative. Bruylant/Sakkoulas/Nomos, Brussels/Athens/Baden-Baden
Hachez I (2014) Le Comité européen des droits sociaux confronté à la crise financière grecque: des décisions osées mais inégalement motivées. Revue de droit social 3:249–279
Hachez I (2015) L'acquis social: quelle(s) protection(s) juridique(s)? In: Iliopoulos-Strangas J (ed) The future of the constitutional welfare state in Europe. Nomos, Baden-Baden, pp 307–336
Hachez I, Vincent S (2015) Principe de standstill et droit à l'accueil des demandeurs d'asile. De l'ABC d'une méthodologie à l'allégorie de la grenouille. Administration publique 1:72–81
Hailbronner K (2022) Gerichtlicher Rechtsschutz intertemporaler Freiheitssicherung künftiger Generationen durch Klimaschutz – die Aufgabe dogmatischer Grundlagen für die Rolle der Gerichte beim Grundrechtsschutz durch das BVerfG im Klimabeschluss. Zeitschrift für öffentliches Recht 77(3):607–611
Hatje A (2010) The economic constitution within the internal market. In: von Bogdandy A, Bast J (eds) Principles of European constitutional law. Hart Publishing/Verlag CHBeck, Oxford/München, pp 589–622
Heuschling L (2013) Le méta-principe de l'État social (*Sozialstaat*) dans la jurisprudence de la Cour constitutionnelle fédérale allemande. In: Burgorgue-Larsen L (ed) La justice sociale saisie par les juges en Europe. Pédone, Paris, pp 83–104
Holmes S, Sunstein CR (2000) The cost of rights: why liberty depends on taxes. W. W. Norton & Company, New York
Ipsen J (2019) Sozialisierung und Übermaßverbot. Neue Zeitschrift für Verwaltungsrecht 8:527–529
Isensee J (1980) Verfassung ohne Grundrechte: Ein Wesenszug des Grundgesetzes. Der Staat 19(3):367–384

Jamoulle M (2001) L'article 23 de la Constitution belge dans ses relations avec les droits sociaux fondamentaux, le droit du travail et la sécurité sociale. In: Van Limberghen G, Salomez K (eds) Liber Amicorum Maxime Stroobant. Gand, Mys & Breesch, pp 121–147
Joerges C (2005) What is left of the European economic constitution? A melancholic eulogy. Eur Law Rev 30:461–489
Jungbluth D (2018) Die Entwicklung des deutschen Wirtschaftsverfassungsrechts: Von Weimar bis zum Investitionshilfeurteil. Springer, Wiesbaden
Jurion R (2017) La jurisprudence économique du Conseil constitutionnel. Metz, Université de Lorraine, 20 September 2017
Kahl W (2014) "Soziale Gerechtigkeit" oder Generationengerechtigkeit? Zur Notwendigkeit der Wiederbelebung einer verfassungspolitischen Debatte aus aktuellem Anlass. Zeitschrift für Rechtspolitik 47(1):17–21
Kaupa C (2016) The pluralist character of the European economic constitution. Hart Publishing, Oxford
Kirchheimer O (1930) Die Grenzen der Enteignung: Ein Beitrag zur Entwicklungsgeschichte des Enteignungsinstituts und zur Auslegung des Art. 153 der Weimarer Verfassung. De Gruyter, Berlin
Kirchhof P (1981) Besteuerung und Eigentum. Veröffentlichungen der Vereinigung der Deutschen Staatsrechtslehrer 39:213–285
Kirchhof P (2003) Der Grundrechtsschutz des Steuerpflichtigen: Zur Rechtsprechung des Bundesverfassungsgerichts im vergangenen Jahrzehnt. Archiv des öffentlichen Rechts 128(1): 1–51
Knuth M (2006) "Hartz IV" – die unbegriffene Reform. Sozialer Fortschritt 55(7):160–116
Koubi G (ed) (1996) Le préambule de la Constitution de 1946: antinomies juridiques et contradictions politiques. PUF, Paris
Krumm M (2015) Bewertung und Verschonung von sog. großen (Familien-) Unternehmen nach der Entscheidung des BVerfG v. 17.12.2014 zur Erbschaftsteuer. FinanzRundschau 97(11): 481–496
Laget-Annamayer A (ed) (2018) L'ordre public économique. LGDJ, Issy-les-Moulineaux
Leisner W (1972) Sozialbindung des Eigentums. Duncker & Humblot, Berlin
Leisner W (1975) Der Sozialisierungsartikel als Eigentumsgarantie. JuristenZeitung 30(9):272–277
Lenz S (2022) Der Klimabeschluss des Bundesverfassungsgerichts Eine Dekonstruktion: Abhandlungen und Aufsatze. Der Staat 61(1):73–112
Luchaire F (1982) Doctrine, nécessité ou poésie. In: Favoreu L (ed) Nationalisations et Constitution. Economica, Paris, pp 65–85
Martinez J (2022) Conseil constitutionnel et économie. L'Harmattan, Paris
Martucci F (2015) Constitution économique et concurrence: En quête d'une matrice constitutionnelle du droit de la concurrence. Concurrences 1:13–25
Marx K, Engels F (1948a) Der 'Musterstaat' Belgien. Neue Rheinische Zeitung, No. 68, 7 August 1848
Marx K, Engels F (1948b) Der 'konstitutionelle Musterstaat'. Neue Rheinische Zeitung, No. 123, 22 October 1848
Maes G (2006) Het standstillbeginsel in verdragsbepalingen en in art. 23 G.W.: progressieve (sociale) grondrechtenbescherming. Rechtskundig Weekblad: 69(28):1081–1094
Mazeaud P (2005) La place des considérations extra-juridiques dans l'exercice du contrôle de constitutionnalité. Erevan. Available on https://www.conseil-constitutionnel.fr/sites/default/files/as/root/bank_mm/pdf/Conseil/20051001erevan.pdf
McGaughey E (2016) The codetermination bargains: the history of German corporate and labor law. Columbia J Eur Law 23:135–176
Meickmann TV (2023) Das Ende der Großzügigkeit. Verfassungsblog, 15 November 2023
Meyer HM (2006) Vorrang der privaten Wirtschafts- und Sozialgestaltung als Rechtsprinzip: Eine systematisch-axiologische Analyse der Wirtschaftsverfassung des Grundgesetzes. Duncker & Humblot, Berlin

Mongouachon C (2015) Ordolibéralisme versus néolibéralisme: antagonismes idéologiques et conséquences pratiques en droit européen de la concurrence. In: Dormont S, Perroud T (eds) Droit et Marché. LGDJ, Paris, pp 21–44
Mongouachon C (2017) Principe d'égalité et concurrence dans la jurisprudence du Conseil constitutionnel. La Revue des Droits de l'Homme:42–60
Muller P (2010) Référentiel. In: Boussaguet L, Jacquot S, Ravinet P (eds) Dictionnaire des politiques publiques, 3rd edn. Presses de Sciences Po, Paris, pp 555–556
Munaretto L (2022) Der Vorbehalt des Möglichen. Öffentliches Recht in begrenzten Möglichkeitsräumen. Mohr Siebeck, Tübingen
Murphy L, Nagel T (2002) The myth of ownership: taxes and justice. OUP, New York
Nettesheim M (2020) Anmerkung: BVerfG, Urteil v. 5.11.2019 - 1 BvL 7/16. JuristenZeitung 75(3):153–156
Neumann V (1995) Menschenwürde und Existenzminimum. Neue Zeitschrift für Verwaltungsrecht 5:426–432
Niclauß K (1974) Das parlamentarische Rat und das Sozialstaatspostulat. Politische Vierteljahresschrift 15:33–52
Nihoul P (2022) Constitution et économie en Belgique. In: Grégoire G, Miny X (eds) The idea of economic constitution in Europe. Genealogy and overview. Brill/Nijhoff, Leiden/Boston, pp 543–566
Nipperdey HC (1930) Wettbewerb und Existenzvernichtung. Kartell-Rundschau 28:127–152
Ogier-Bernaud V (2003) Les droits constitutionnels des travailleurs. Economica, Paris
Oppermann T (1985) Aussprache. Veröffentlichungen der Vereinigung der Deutschen Staatsrechtslehrer 43:82–84
Ossenbühl F (1990) Die Freiheiten des Unternehmers nach dem Grundgesetz. Archiv des öffentlichen Rechts 115(1):1–32
Papier H-J (1994) Art. 14 GG. Grundgesetz-Kommentar. Munich, C.H. Beck, § 297
Pâques M, Vercheval C (2011) Le droit de propriété. In: Les droits constitutionnels en Belgique - Les enseignements jurisprudentiels de la Cour constitutionnelle, du Conseil d'état et de la Cour de cassation. Larcier, Brussels, pp 789–818
Pez T (2015) L'ordre public économique. Les Nouveaux Cahiers du Conseil constitutionnel 49(4): 43–57
Piron D (2022) The Special Financing Law: tax competition and fiscal consolidation at the heart of Belgium's material economic constitution. In: Grégoire G, Miny X (eds) The idea of economic constitution in Europe. Genealogy and overview. Brill/Nijhoff, Leiden/Boston, pp 659–686
Piron D (2024) Governing public investment in Europe: the politics of off balance-sheet policymaking, the rise of Eurostat and contrasted regional policies in Belgium. Compet Change 28(3–4):494–514
Rabault H (2000) La constitution économique de la France. Revue française de droit constitutionnel 44:707–745
Rabault H (2015) Une "république sociale"? Le paradoxe des droits "économiques et sociaux". In: Gambino S (ed) Diritti sociali e crisi economica Problemi e prospettive. G. Giappichelli editore, Turin, pp 133–143
Rammer G (2010) Bloß nicht verhungern. Blätter für deutsche und internationale Politik 5:31–33
Remiche A (2017) La justiciabilité des droits économiques, sociaux et culturels en Belgique, thèse de doctorat en sciences juridiques, ULB
Ribes D (2007) Le réalisme du Conseil constitutionnel. Les Cahiers du Conseil Constitutionnel 22: 195–207
Ribes D (2008) L'incidence financière des décisions du juge constitutionnel. Les Cahiers du Conseil Constitutionnel 24:104–108
Rivero J (1982) Ni lu, ni compris? Actualité Juridique. Droit Administratif 4:209–214
Rivero J, Vedel G (1947) Les problèmes économiques et sociaux et la Constitution du 27 octobre 1946. Droit social:13–35

Röhner C (2020) Eigentum und Vergesellschaftung in der Wohnungskrise. Zur Aktualität von Art. 15 GG. Kritische Justiz 53(1):16–29

Rosoux G (2015) Vers une «dématérialisation» des droits fondamentaux? Bruylant, Brussels

Ruzza A (2013) Expropriation and Nationalization. In: Wolfrum R (ed) Max Planck encyclopedia of public international law, 9th edn. Oxford University Press, Oxford

Sachs T, Vernac S (2014) La fondamentalisation d'un ordre libéral. À propos de la décision du Conseil constitutionnel du 27 mars 2014, Loi sur la reconquête de l'économie réelle. Revue de droit du travail 9:528–536

Savy R (1977) Droit public économique. Dalloz, Paris

Savy R (1983) La Constitution des juges. Recueil Dalloz:105–110

Schlegel R (2021) Der Sozialstaat in und nach der Covid-19-Pandemie. Neue Juristische Wochenschrift 38:2782–2788

Schmidt L (2020) Verfassungsmäßige Sanktionen im Sozialrecht: Ein Dilemma der bundesverfassungsgerichtlichen Menschenwürdejudikatur. Göttinger Rechtszeitschrift 2:107–114

Scholz R (2022) GG Art. 12. Grundgesetz-Kommentar, 98e ed. C.H. Beck, Munich

Schoonbroodt E (1990) L'union économique et l'unité monétaire dans les lois de réformes institutionnelles. Courrier hebdomadaire du CRISP 34:1–30

Schoukens P (2016) The right to social security in the Belgian Constitution. In: Egorov A, Wujczyk M (eds) The right to social security in constitutions of the world: broadening the moral and legal space for social justice. International Labour Organization, Genève, pp 7–19

Schreiber F (2018) Die Reichweite der Gewährleistung des menschenwürdigen Existenzminimums aus Art. 1 Abs. 1 GG iVm. Art. 20 Abs. 1 GG als Menschenrecht. Soziales Recht 8(5):181–194

Schröder G (2005) Rede von Bundeskanzler Gerhard Schröder vor dem World Economic Forum am 28. Januar 2005 in Davos», Bulletin der Bundesregierung, No.08-2, 28 January 2005 (available on https://www.bundesregierung.de/breg-de/service/bulletin/rede-von-bundeskanzler-gerhard-schroeder-792094)

Seer R (1999) Der sog. Halbteilungsgrundsatz als verfassungsrechtliche Belastungsobergrenze der Besteuerung. FinanzRundschau 1999:1280–1291

Seiler C (2010) Das Grundrecht auf ein menschenwürdiges Existenzminimum: Zum Urteil des Bundesverfassungsgerichts vom 9. 2. 2010. JuristenZeitung 65(10):500–505

Sodan H (1998) Verfassungsrechtliche Grenzen der Tarifautonomie: Ein Beitrag zur Auslegung des Art. 9 Abs. 3 GG. JuristenZeitung 53(9):421–430

Stone Sweet A, Mathews J (2008) Proportionality balancing and global constitutionalism. Columbia J Transnatl Law 47:72–164

Streit ME, Mussler W (1994) The economic constitution of the European community: from Rome to Maastricht. Const Polit Econ 5(3):319–353

Sueur J-J (1991) Le Conseil constitutionnel français et le droit économique: essai d'interprétation. Revue Internationale de Droit Économique 3:271–311

Supiot A (2021) La "Constitution sociale" de la Ve République. Revue politique et parlementaire 1098:144–162

Tettinger PJ (1983) Das Grundrecht der Berufsfreiheit in der Rechtsprechung des Bundesverfassungsgerichts. Archiv des öffentlichen Rechts 108(1):92–133

Thurn JP (2013) Welcher Sozialstaat? Ideologie und Wissenschaftsverständnis in den Debatten der bundesdeutschen Staatsrechtslehre 1949–1990. Mohr Siebeck, Tübingen

Tiedemann P (2012) Verfassungswidrigkeit der Leistungssätze des Asylbewerberleistungsgesetzes. Neue Zeitschrift für Verwaltungsrecht:1024–1033

Trube A (2004) Die neue deutsche Arbeitsmarktpolitik und der Wandel des Sozialstaats. Sozialer Fortschritt 53(3):62–68

Van Drooghenbroeck S (1997) "Mendicité, ordre public et proportionnalité", obs. sous C.E., 8 octobre 1997, No. 68.735. Revue belge de droit constitutionnel 4:418–436

Vanberg VJ (1994) Rules and choice in economics: essays in constitutional political economy. Routledge, London; New York

Vandeburie A (2008) L'article 23 de la Constitution. Coquille vide ou boîte aux trésors? Lacharte, Brussels

Vanderstraeten M (2015) La liberté d'entreprendre dans la jurisprudence de la Cour constitutionnelle et du Conseil d'État. In: La liberté d'entreprendre ou le retour en force d'un fondamental du droit économique. Bruylant, Brussels, pp 7–41

Vedel G, Delvolvé P (1992) Droit administratif, tome 2. PUF, Paris

Verdussen M (2011) La Cour constitutionnelle, partenaire de la Cour de justice de l'Union européenne. Revue belge de droit constitutionnel:81–109

Vogel K (1996) BVerfG, 22. 6. 1995 — 2 BvL 37/91. Zur Bemessung der Vermögen- und Erbschaftsteuer auf Grundbesitz. JuristenZeitung 51(1):31–45

Vogel-Polsky É (1995) La reconnaissance en droit international des droits économiques, sociaux et culturels de la personne et son interrelation avec l'article 23 de la Constitution. In: Ergec R (ed) Les droits économiques, sociaux et culturels dans la Constitution. Bruylant, Brussels, pp 43–92

Wanda M (2005) L'impôt de solidarité sur la fortune à l'épreuve de la Constitution. Recueil Dalloz 19:1257–1260

Wilhelm J (2000) Zum Enteignungsbegriff des Bundesverfassungsgerichts. JuristenZeitung 55(19): 905–913

Wittig P (1967) Der Erwerb von Eigentum und das Grundgesetz. Neue Juristische Wochenschrift:2185–2188

Yernault D (2013) L'État et la propriété: le droit public économique par son histoire (1830-2012). Bruylant, Brussels

Balancing Act: Exploring Switzerland's Neutrality in the Context of Its Economic Constitution

Phil Baumann and Marc M. Winistörfer

Contents

Abstract As an open economy, Switzerland is dependent on foreign market access and open trade relations with other countries. This openness is underpinned by an economic constitution favoring a market economy and, fundamentally, being oriented toward competition. In the past, Switzerland's neutrality has not only

P. Baumann (✉)
Faculty of Law, University of Basel, Basel, Switzerland
e-mail: phil.baumann@unibas.ch

M. M. Winistörfer
Faculty of Law, University of Lucerne, Lucerne, Switzerland
e-mail: marc.winistoerfer@unilu.ch

S. Hindelang et al. (eds.), *YSEC Yearbook of Socio-Economic Constitutions 2024*, YSEC Yearbook of Socio-Economic Constitutions (2025) 2024: 137–170,
https://doi.org/10.1007/16495_2024_71, Published online: 26 February 2025

contributed to its security, but also to its economic success and stability. Switzerland's neutrality consists of the law of neutrality and neutrality policy. Whereas the former contains the main obligations and rights of a neutral country the later refers to measures serving the credibility of Switzerland's neutrality abroad. In implementing neutrality, Switzerland is regularly subject to pressure from abroad to restrict or authorise certain economic activities such as war material exports. Against this background, Switzerland has enacted several laws regarding critical transactions with certain countries. Although these regulations typically affect the fundamental rights of economic freedom and guarantee of ownership, they are not contrary to the guiding principle of economic freedom enshrined in Switzerland's economic constitution. Whereas Switzerland has thus legislation in place regarding export controls and sanctions, a comprehensive regulation of its significant commodities trading sector is still lacking. This poses the risk of future regulations based on emergency law that harm Switzerland's reputation as stable and predictable business location.

1 Introduction

Switzerland's economy is highly globalized and heavily involved in international trade.[1] Over two thirds of Switzerland's gross domestic product stem from exports. In 2022, Switzerland exported services in the amount of US$ 146 billion and goods worth US$ 402 billion.[2] In certain economic sectors or for specific products, such as watches, chocolate or pharmaceuticals, Swiss companies are among the global leaders. With CHF 2300 billion of foreign assets under management Switzerland is also the world's leading offshore wealth management centre.[3] In addition, Switzerland has become a key player in global commodities trading. Raw materials precious metals and gemstones now account for over 20% of exports and imports.[4] In this context, international investments play a pivotal role in Switzerland's economic growth and prosperity, with Swiss companies not only exporting goods and services but also capital, primarily through direct investments. Against this background, securing access to foreign markets is one of the most important Swiss foreign policy concerns.[5]

Switzerland is internationally known not just for its chocolate and watches, but also for its neutrality. Neutrality is a main tool for preserving Switzerland's territorial

[1] See Wegmüller and Schmidiger (2022).

[2] See WTO (2003), pp. 60 and 62; Bundesamt für Zoll und Grenzsicherheit (BAZG) (2023), p. 5.

[3] See BCG (2023), p. 4.

[4] Cf. https://www.eda.admin.ch/aboutswitzerland/de/home/wirtschaft/uebersicht/export.html.

[5] Lehne (2023), n. 39.

sovereignty, national cohesion and independence.[6] In the past, maintaining neutrality has also been instrumental for Switzerland's economic welfare and for becoming a major financial and commodity trading centre.[7] However, maintaining neutrality is not a simple endeavour for an open economy such as the Swiss one. Keeping economic relations with certain countries that are involved in conflicts can be seen as taking sides. Switzerland and its economy can also come under pressure if exports of certain goods to belligerent countries are restricted for reasons of neutrality. These challenges in dealing with neutrality became particularly apparent again in the course of Russia's military aggression against Ukraine. In particular, Switzerland has come under scrutiny for insufficiently regulating its commodity trading market. A lack of monitoring and transparency requirements are said to allow Russia to circumvent international sanctions and thereby finance its war against Ukraine. Furthermore, Switzerland's refusal to authorise the re-export of arms to Ukraine irritated key trading partners abroad.[8]

Measures to maintain neutrality can also be problematic in relation to the requirements of Switzerland's economic constitution that stipulates largely a market economy in which the state is not involved in business activities.[9] If for the sake of neutrality companies are restricted in their business activities, the question arises to what extent this is compatible with the requirements of the Swiss economic constitution.

Against this background, this chapter aims to analyse the relationship between Swiss neutrality and the Swiss economic constitution. For this purpose, it will discuss in a first part the pillars of the Swiss economic constitution. The next section provides an overview of Switzerland's neutrality and its components. Subsequently, certain neutrality-related regulations are briefly described and contextualised within the economic constitution. Building on the previous analyses, the following part addresses current challenges regarding Switzerland's neutrality. The chapter concludes with a synthesis of the analysis.

2 Pillars of the Swiss Economic Constitution

The following section aims to outline the cornerstones of the economic constitution. It is crucial to acknowledge that the economic constitution must not be considered in isolation but rather in dynamic interaction, occasionally even in conflict, with other

[6] See Villiger (2023), n. 325–332; Ziegler (2019), p. 579.

[7] Etzensperger and Maurer (2008), p. 26.

[8] See press release by the Federal Council, No approval for the transfer of Swiss war material to Ukraine, 3 November 2022. https://www.admin.ch/gov/en/start/documentation/media-releases.msg-id-91146.html.

[9] Baumann (2019), n. 24–32.

partial constitutions (such as the environmental or social constitution).[10] In cases where equally ranked constitutional norms collide, neither norm should supersede the other; instead, the provisions and principles should coexist in the spirit of practical concordance.[11]

2.1 *Key Aspects of the Economic Constitution*

Formally, the economic constitution is placed in Section 7 "Economy" (Articles 94–107 of the Federal Constitution of the Swiss Confederation (Const.) of April 18, 1999; Systematische Sammlung des Bundesrechts (SR) 101). Article 94 Const. sets out the principles of the economic system, which constitute the fundamental objectives of the economic constitution. In this regard, special attention is given to the principle of economic freedom as the guiding principle for economic policy in the Const.

The subsequent articles organize the constitutional federal competences in economic law according to policy areas. Commencing this is the competence to legislate on economic activities in the private sector (Article 95 para. 1 Const.). This grants the Confederation not only competence to legislate on the access to a profession and its pursuit but also the authority to financially support private economic activities.[12] Furthermore, Article 95 para. 2 Const. embodies the so-called "internal market function" of the economic constitution: The Confederation shall seek to create a unified Swiss economic area.[13]

The Federal government also holds legislative competences in the field of competition policy (Article 96 Const.), consumer protection (Article 97 Const.), financial market law, including banking, stock exchange, and private insurance law (Article 98 Const.), monetary policy (Article 99 Const.), economic policy to achieve a balanced economic development, and in particular to prevent and combat unemployment and inflation (Article 100 Const.), foreign economic policy (Article 101 Const.), national economic supply (Article 102 Const.), structural policy (Article 103 Const.), and agriculture (Articles 104 and 104a Const.). Additionally, federal responsibility extends to alcohol legislation (Article 105 Const.), gambling (Article 106 Const.), and legislation on weapons and war material (Article 107 Const.).

Outside the formal economic constitution, the Confederation possesses other relevant economic competences, for instance, to legislate on Swiss film production and cinema (Art. 71 Const.). Essential elements of the substantive economic constitution include economic-related fundamental rights, the guarantee of property

[10] See Rhinow et al. (2011), § 4 n. 28; Richli (2007), n. 55–57 and 65.

[11] See BGE 129 I 173 E. 5.1 = Decision of the Federal Supreme Court, Book 129, Volume I, Page 173, Consideration 5.1; BGE 126 III 129 E. 8a.

[12] See Bundi (2016), p. 124.

[13] See Winistörfer (2021), pp. 124–127; Häfelin et al. (2020), n. 622.

(Article 26 Const.), economic freedom (Article 27 Const.), and the above-mentioned principle of economic freedom (Article 94 Const.). Overall, the economic constitution is regarded as favoring a market economy and, fundamentally, being oriented toward competition.[14]

2.2 *Guarantee of Ownership*

Article 26 Const. protects private property from governmental encroachments. According to its para. 1, the right to own property is guaranteed. Protected by Article 26 para. 1 Const. is individual ownership against state interventions. The owner has the right to retain, utilize, and dispose of their specific property and assets. By means of Article 26 Const., the owner has a legal claim that government refrains from interfering with their property rights.[15] This fundamental right can be invoked by both individuals and legal entities alike.[16] Private property within the meaning of Article 26 Const. is broadly defined. It includes all proprietary rights in civil law, including real estate and contractual rights as well as intellectual property rights, the so-called duly acquired rights based on public law, and the actual conditions of property use against de facto restrictions.[17]

The guarantee of ownership specifically protects private property as an important legal institution established by the Swiss legal system. Furthermore, Article 26 para. 1 Const. safeguards property as a legal institution from erosion or de facto abolition, e.g., confiscatory taxation, i.e., taxes of such an elevated level that they effectively result in the appropriation of assets by government.[18] Article 26 para. 2 Const. contains a value guarantee. Hence, expropriations and any restriction on ownership equivalent to expropriation, e.g. when the restriction is particularly severe or imposes a special sacrifice, shall be compensated in full. For less severe restrictions, no compensation is required.[19]

Any restrictions on the guarantee of ownership must have a legal basis, be justified in the public interest or for the protection of the fundamental rights of others and be proportionate (Article 36 para. 1–3 Const.).[20] Severe restrictions must have their basis in a formal act, whereas, for less severe restrictions, an ordinance is sufficient. Any public interest may justify an interference with property, as long as the intended objective is not purely of fiscal nature or in violation of other

[14] See Rhinow et al. (2011), § 3 n. 94; Richli (2007), n. 52–54; Winistörfer (2021), pp. 304–306.
[15] Häfelin et al. (2020), n. 594.
[16] Rhinow et al. (2011), § 6 n. 9; Vallender et al. (2006), § 6 n. 5.
[17] See BGE 145 II 140 E. 4.2; Rhinow et al. (2011), § 6 n. 7f.; Häfelin et al. (2020), n. 597.
[18] BGE 143 V 254 E. 6.4.1; BGE 127 I 60 E. 3b; Vallender et al. (2006), § 6 n. 27f.
[19] See BGE 149 I 49 E. 6; BGE 145 II 140 E. 4.1; Häfelin et al. (2020), n. 606.
[20] See BGE 146 I 70 E. 6.1; BGE 145 II 70 E. 3.5; Rhinow et al. (2011), § 6 n. 11.

constitutional norms.[21] The institutional guarantee of ownership aligns with the core content of this fundamental right, which, in line with Article 36 para. 4 Const., is sacrosanct and cannot be limited under any circumstances.[22]

The guarantee of ownership is a decision in favor of private property and considered a fundamental prerequisite for the exercise of other fundamental rights, particularly economic freedom.[23] The legislator must protect private property as an institution within the legal framework, define its elements, and consider the function of private property as much as possible in the legislation.[24]

2.3 Fundamental Right of Economic Freedom

Article 27 para. 1 Const. guarantees economic freedom. This fundamental right includes the freedom to choose an occupation as well as the freedom to pursue a private economic activity (para. 2). The fundamental right of economic freedom protects privately conducted economic activities, whether primary, secondary, or occasional.[25] It protects Swiss individuals, foreign nationals permitted to work in Switzerland and legal entities against interference by government in their economic endeavors.[26] Whoever acts on behalf of government, particularly public authorities, as well as private entities entrusted with government tasks, is, in accordance with Article 35 para. 2 Const., bound by and under a duty to contribute to the implementation of the economic freedom.[27]

Components of the freedom to pursue a private economic activity include, among others, freedom of contract, free choice of resources and personnel, organizational freedom, freedom of competition, and freedom in foreign trade.[28] Another guarantee deriving from the economic freedom is the principle of equal treatment of competitors. This principle plays a crucial role, connecting the fundamental right to economic freedom and the legal requirement of competition neutrality by public authorities.[29] Both aim to ensure that the federal and cantonal governments treat

---

[21] See Rhinow et al. (2011), § 6 n. 16; Hangartner (1989), p. 715; Richli (2007), n. 114.

[22] Richli (2007), n. 109; different opinion cf. Rhinow et al. (2011), § 6 n. 17 and 26.

[23] Rhinow et al. (2011), § 6 n. 3; Richli (2007), n. 101; Hangartner (1989), p. 712.

[24] Hangartner (1989), p. 714; Vallender et al. (2006), § 6 n. 3.

[25] See Winistörfer (2021), pp. 127–141; Häfelin et al. (2020), n. 628f.; Richli (2007), n. 132; BGE 143 I 403 E. 5.6.1; BGE 142 I 99 E. 2.4.1.

[26] See Winistörfer (2021), pp. 179–191; Vallender et al. (2006), § 5 n. 11–21; BGE 142 I 162 E. 3.2.1.

[27] See Winistörfer (2021), pp. 191–196; Häfelin et al. (2020), n. 272–277.

[28] See Winistörfer (2021), pp. 141–159; Häfelin et al. (2020), n. 640–649; Vallender et al. (2006), § 5 n. 27–68.

[29] See BGE 143 II 425 E. 4.2; BGE 142 I 162 E. 3.2.1; BGE 138 I 378 E. 6.1.

direct competitors in a competition-neutral manner and do not interfere in ongoing economic competition.

The fundamental right of economic freedom can be restricted if the conditions of Article 36 para. 1–4 Const. are respected. Additionally, the principle of economic freedom and Article 94 para. 4 Const. must be considered.[30] Whether a restriction of Article 27 Const. is in accordance with the principle of economic freedom ultimately depends on the equal treatment of direct competitors. It is not without reason that the requirement for equal treatment among competitors is embodied in Article 94 para. 1 Const.[31]

2.4 Principle of Economic Freedom

Article 94 para. 1 Const. imposes an obligation on both the Confederation and Cantons to abide by the principle of economic freedom, forming the basic orientation of the economic constitution. Other than Article 27 Const., this provision does not confer any individual rights but establishes a binding economic policy directive for authorities at both federal and cantonal levels.[32] The principle of economic freedom extends guides state actions in broader economic contexts and legislative processes. Furthermore, it calls for the creation of an appropriate legal and institutional framework by the legislator.[33]

Constitutional jurisprudence has significantly contributed to defining and elaborating upon the principle of economic freedom, allowing for the identification of its various components. Essentially, Article 94 para. 1 Const. establishes the foundation for a market economy, emphasizing individual responsibility, market principles, and economic competition while rejecting central economic planning.[34] The coordination of the economy is carried out by the private sector and not by government. Distortions of competition are prohibited. Furthermore, Article 94 para. 1 Const. guarantees non-discriminatory market access. Moreover, this constitutional provision establishes the principles of state autonomy, competitive neutrality, and the cohesion of the Swiss economic landscape. It emphasizes the primary role of private entities in economic coordination, barring state interference that distorts competition. Additionally, it guarantees non-discriminatory market access. By enshrining the principle of economic freedom and highlighting its significance through Article

[30] See BGE 143 I 395 E. 4.1; BGE 142 I 162 E. 3.2.2; BGE 136 I 17 E. 3.3.

[31] Rhinow et al. (2011), § 5 n. 41; Reich (2011), n. 960–962; Vallender et al. (2006), § 5 n. 85.

[32] See BGE 143 I 388 E. 2.1; BGE 143 I 403 E. 5.1; BGE 138 I 378 E. 6.2.3; Reich (2011), n. 834; Winistörfer (2021), p. 235f.

[33] See Winistörfer (2021), pp. 270–273; Rhinow et al. (2011), § 4 n. 84f.; Richli (2007), n. 40f.

[34] Häfelin et al. (2020), n. 623; Winistörfer (2021), p. 259f. and 267–270; Vallender et al. (2006), § 4 n. 1; BGE 145 I 183 E. 4.1.1; BGE 138 I 378 E. 6.1.

94 para. 4 Const., the economic constitution endorsed a rule-based approach to economic policy.[35]

The principle of economic freedom cannot be restricted as such; non-compliance with this principle results in a so-called deviation. Examples are protectionist measures to deny market access, distortions of competition, the elimination of the market mechanism, and the control of market structure by government.[36] Article 94 para. 4 Const. determines under which conditions deviation from the principle of economic freedom is permissible. Accordingly, any deviation from the principle of economic freedom, and in particular measures designed to restrain competition, shall be permitted only if they are provided for in the Federal Constitution or justified by cantonal monopoly rights. The authorizations to deviate from the principle of economic freedom mentioned in Article 94 para. 4 Const. are found in various constitutional provisions, notably in the foreign economic policy competence of the Federal Constitution. Article 101 Const. empowers the Confederation to safeguard Swiss economic interests abroad (para. 1), allowing measures that deviate from economic freedom to safeguard the interests of the Swiss economy abroad (para. 2). The legislature is permitted to take any conceivable measure, namely import permits, quantity regulations, tariffs, import monopolies.[37] However, they are constrained by international obligations, including WTO commitments and agreements with the EU, limiting protectionist actions.[38]

3 Switzerland's Neutrality

The roots of Switzerland's neutrality date back to the sixteenth century.[39] In international law, Switzerland's neutrality was for the first time recognised in Article 3 of the Treaty of Paris of 20 November 1815.[40] Following Napoleon's abdication, the major European powers recognised Switzerland's permanent neutrality and declared that its neutrality and integrity, and its independence from any foreign influence are in the true interest of European policy as a whole.[41] Since then, Switzerland's permanent neutrality has been several times reaffirmed and enshrined in international law such as in the Treaty of Versailles of 28 June 1919 and shortly after in the London Declaration by the League of Nations of 13 February 1920.[42] As

[35] See Winistörfer (2022), pp. 29–38.

[36] See Winistörfer (2021), pp. 318–326; Reich (2011), n. 864–877; Richli (2007), n. 428–457.

[37] See Federal Council (1996) Message on the new Federal Constitution, p. 309.

[38] See Vallender et al. (2006), § 16 n. 4.

[39] See Schindler (1938), p. 413; Villiger (2023), n. 271–289.

[40] See further Ricklin (1991), pp. 3f., 13 and 15.

[41] Federal Council (2022) Report in response to Postulate 22.3385, p. 11; Villiger (2023), n. 298 and n. 324–340, see further Ziegler (2019), pp. 565–566; Ricklin (1991), pp. 30–58.

[42] Egli and Holzgang (2022), pp. 604f.; Petrig (2024), p. 421.

Switzerland is committed to the monistic system, binding international treaties do not need to be transformed into national law, but automatically become valid domestically.

The main characteristics of Switzerland's neutrality are that it is (i) of its own choosing, meaning that Switzerland could abandon its neutrality at any time; (ii) permanent, meaning that Switzerland remains neutral in any armed conflict between other states; and (iii) armed, as Switzerland has its own forces to defend its independence and territorial integrity.[43]

The Swiss neutrality consists of the law of neutrality and neutrality policy.[44] These two components must be distinguished to better understand Swiss neutrality.[45] Law of neutrality and neutrality policy are interrelated.[46] The legal obligations and rights of a neutral state are defined by the law of neutrality. However, these remain a dead letter if they are not backed up by a credible neutrality policy that convinces other countries that Switzerland will remain neutral in the event of war.[47]

3.1 Law of Neutrality

On the one hand, the law of neutrality, as enshrined in international agreements and customary international law, stipulates the rights and obligations of states with neutral status.[48] The law of neutrality is part of international law and is mainly based on the two Hague Conventions V and XIII of 1907.[49] The Hague Conventions of 1907, which were ratified by Switzerland in 1910, codified the customary international law of neutrality that had applied until then.[50] Since the ratification of the Hague Conventions the law of neutrality has further evolved under customary international law.[51]

---

[43] Federal Council (1993) White Paper on Neutrality, pp. 6–7; FDFA (2022), p. 6.

[44] Sassòli (2021), p. 525.

[45] FDFA (2022), p. 4; see also Federal Council (2007) Report on Neutrality, p. 5557.

[46] See Federal Council (2022) Report in response to Postulate 22.3385, p. 4, where the interrelationship is explained by referring to an atom. Accordingly, the law of neutrality is the nucleus of an the atom as its rights an obligations are like the protons and neutrons. Like an electron shell neutrality policy orbits flexibly around the law of neutrality.

[47] Federal Council (2022) Report in response to Postulate 22.3385, p. 7.

[48] Federal Council (2007) Report on Neutrality, p. 5558; see also Federal Council (2022) Report in response to Postulate 22.3385, p. 6f.

[49] Federal Council (2007) Report on Neutrality, p. 5557; Federal Council (2022) Report in response to Postulate 22.3385, p. 4.

[50] Egli and Holzgang (2022), p. 602.

[51] See for the importance of the customary international law that has developed since then as a source of law Egli and Holzgang (2022), p. 606; see also Sassòli (2021), p. 525.

Under international law neutrality is defined as the legal status of a state which is not participating in an armed conflict between other states.[52] This status comes with rights and obligations. Essentially, the neutral state has the right to remain unaffected by the conflict but at the same time is under the obligation to not participate and remain impartial.[53]

The law of neutrality only applies to international armed conflicts and not to internal conflicts such as civil wars between different ethnicities or religious groups.[54] Pursuant to the law of neutrality, a neutral state may not participate in international armed conflicts. In particular, it is prohibited from supporting belligerent states with military material or troops or from making its territory available to them.[55] The Hague Conventions only prohibit state supplies of military material but do not contain an obligation to restrict exports and transits of military material by private companies.[56] However, it is argued that pursuant to customary international law a neutral state is also obliged to prohibit private trade with military material with the belligerent states.[57] At least, a neutral state has an obligation of non-discrimination where restrictions apply to the private export of military goods. Restrictions have to apply without difference for both belligerent parties.[58] Furthermore, a neutral state must ensure the inviolability of its own territory, as far as such defence measures are feasible under the circumstances.[59] Finally, permanent neutral states must not do anything in peacetime that prevents them from complying with their obligations in the event of war, such as joining military alliances that involve mutual assistance obligations or require the deployment of armed forces.[60]

The law of neutrality also guarantees a neutral state's rights. The neutral state has the right to territorial integrity, meaning that belligerent parties are prohibited from transporting troops, ammunition or food convoys across the territory of a neutral state.[61] Further, the neutral state has the right to self-defence, including by military means and the right to trade freely, as long as these trading activities do not serve military purposes.[62]

---

[52] Federal Council (2022) Report in response to Postulate 22.3385, p. 2; Fleck (2021), p. 602.

[53] Fleck (2021), p. 602; see further Petrig (2024), p. 420.

[54] Federal Council (2022) Report in response to Postulate 22.3385, p. 4; Egli and Holzgang (2022), p. 606.

[55] Egli and Holzgang (2022), p. 607 et seq.

[56] See Art. 7 Hague Convention V.

[57] Egli and Holzgang (2022), p. 609; Egli (2005), p. 672f.; see further Fleck (2021), p. 615f.

[58] Federal Council (2007) Report on Neutrality, p. 5558; Federal Council (2022) Report in response to Postulate 22.3385, p. 5; Petrig (2024), p. 421f.

[59] Fleck (2021), p. 613.

[60] Federal Council (2022) Report in response to Postulate 22.3385, p. 5; Fleck (2021), p. 607f.

[61] Art. 1 and 2 Hague Convention V; Federal Council (2022) Report in response to Postulate 22.3385, p. 5.

[62] Federal Council (2022) Report in response to Postulate 22.3385, p. 5; see further Petrig (2024), p. 422.

However, the law of neutrality is by no means as clear as it seems in this brief overview. Rather, it leaves considerable scope for interpretation, in particular when applying the long-established rules to contemporary situations.[63] Generally, it is argued that the law of neutrality is outdated in many respects, as it dates back to a time when war was not yet prohibited as a means of international relations.[64]

3.2 *Neutrality Policy*

On the other hand, neutrality policy includes any measures taken by a state on its own initiative and irrespective of the obligations associated with the law of neutrality to ensure the predictability and credibility of its permanent neutrality.[65] A credible and coherent policy of neutrality serves above all to convince other states of the ability and willingness of the state concerned to remain neutral in the event of future armed conflicts.[66] In this regard a neutral state has to avoid creating interdependencies in peacetime that would make compliance with the law of neutrality at wartime more difficult.[67] In contrast to the law of neutrality, neutrality policy is not subject to legal obligations and therefore has more flexibility to adapt to current circumstances. Indeed, the Swiss neutrality policy has undergone significant changes during the last 30 years.[68]

Neutrality policy is of particular importance on matters on which the law of neutrality stays silent, but where policy actions have an indirect effect on neutrality.[69] Several areas in international relations that touch on neutrality are not governed by the law of neutrality.[70] These include internal armed conflicts with global implications such as the civil war in Syria or economic sanctions imposed on Russia in response of the Ukraine war.[71] In such cases other countries may expect a neutral state to take adequate measures such as expelling diplomats, imposing travel bans or freezing accounts.[72]

[63] Federal Council (2022) Report in response to Postulate 22.3385, p. 5.

[64] Sassòli (2021), p. 525; see also Egli and Holzgang (2022), p. 602; Fleck (2021), p. 605; see further Federal Council (1993) White Paper on Neutrality, p. 8f.

[65] Federal Council (2007) Report on Neutrality, p. 5558; see also Federal Council (2022) Report in response to Postulate 22.3385, p. 6f.

[66] Federal Council (2007) Report on Neutrality, p. 5558.

[67] Federal Council (2022) Report in response to Postulate 22.3385, p. 7.

[68] Sassòli (2021), p. 526.

[69] Federal Council (1993) White Paper on Neutrality, p. 8f.; Federal Council (2022) Report in response to Postulate 22.3385, p. 6.

[70] Federal Council (2022) Report in response to Postulate 22.3385, p. 7.

[71] See Petrig (2024), p. 423.

[72] Federal Council (2022) Report in response to Postulate 22.3385, p. 7.

3.3 The Role of Neutrality in Swiss Foreign Policy

Pursuant to Article 54 Const., foreign relations are the responsibility of the Confederation. Article 54 para. 2 Const. lists several objectives of the Swiss foreign policy. Explicitly, Switzerland's independence and welfare shall be safeguarded. Further, Swiss foreign policy shall contribute in the alleviation of need and poverty in the world and promote respect for human rights and democracy, the peaceful co-existence of peoples as well as the conservation of natural resources.

Given the high profile of Switzerland's neutrality, it may come as a surprise that neutrality is not mentioned as an objective. In fact, the Const. only refers to neutrality twice. Article 173 para. 1 lit. a Const. states that the Federal Assembly has the duty and power for taking measures to safeguard external security and the independence and neutrality of Switzerland. Similarly, Article 185 para. 1 Const. obliges the Federal Council to take measures to safeguard external security, independence and neutrality of Switzerland. Pursuant to the interpretation of the Const. by the legal doctrine neutrality does not constitute an objective of foreign policy in itself.[73] Rather, it serves and has always served as a means to overriding foreign policy objectives.[74] Accordingly, neutrality is one of several instruments for safeguarding Switzerland's external security interests, in particular to preserve the existence and independence of the Swiss state.[75] This instrumental character of Switzerland's neutrality is crucial. Against this background, the Federal Council has repeatedly spoken out against further defining neutrality in constitution or law, as this would limit Switzerland's room to manoeuvre in foreign policy.[76]

4 Neutrality-Related Regulations

4.1 Historical Background

The neutrality-related laws described in this section are relatively young. This could give the impression that the associated challenges are also new. In fact, Switzerland had to face difficulties early on, particularly regarding the adoption of economic sanctions and safeguarding the needs of its own economy. Two crucial events in the history of neutrality-related regulations were the return to integral neutrality in the

[73] See Ehrenzeller and Portmann (2023), n. 36.

[74] See Portmann and Frei (2023), n. 22; see Petrig (2024), p. 418f.; see Federal Council (1996) Message on the new Federal Constitution, p. 398; Federal Council (1993) White Paper on Neutrality, p. 6.

[75] Federal Council (2022) Report in response to Postulate 22.3385, p. 1; see further Saxer and Brunner (2023), n. 29.

[76] FDFA (2022), p. 6.

aftermath of the Second Italo-Abyssinian War and the Hotz-Linder Agreement during the Cold War.

4.1.1 Second Italo-Abyssinian War and the Return to Integral Neutrality

In 1920, Switzerland became a member of the League of Nations, an organization established after the atrocities of World War I with the objective of ensuring lasting peace through arbitration of international conflicts, international disarmament and arms control, and a system of collective security.[77] Prior to joining the League of Nations, the compatibility of Switzerland's membership with its neutrality was intensely and controversially discussed within government, armed forces, and parliament. In particular, the adaption of economic sanctions gave rise to discussion.

According to a secret dispatch, the Chief of Staff of the Swiss Army, Gen. Theophil Sprecher von Bernegg, disagreed with the Federal Council, cautioning that neutrality would also be affected by economic sanctions. He argued that Switzerland's membership to the League of Nations would be incompatible with neutrality.[78] In its report to the Federal Council, the National Defense Commission, by majority, expressed the view that while economic sanctions could lead to conflicts, the so-called economic neutrality could be approached with far more latitude than other purely military matters.[79] The Swiss government ultimately took the position that Switzerland's neutrality, in a modified sense, was compatible with its membership to the League of Nations.[80] After the Great Powers explicitly exempted Switzerland from participating in military sanctions and recognized its neutrality in the London Declaration of February 13, 1920, the Federal Assembly and subsequently the people approved Switzerland's membership to the League of Nations.[81] The result was the so-called "differentiated neutrality". Henceforth,

[77] See Federal Council (1919) Message on Switzerland joining the League of Nations, p. 549f.

[78] See Dispatch of the The Chief of the General Staff of the Swiss Army, Th. von Sprecher, to the Head of the Political Department, F. Calonder, April 23, 1919 = Le Chef d'Etat-major général de l'Armée suisse, Th. von Sprecher, au Chef du Département politique, F. Calonder, 23 avril 1919. In: Documents Diplomatiques Suisses 7a(348):690–692.

[79] The Head of the Military Department, C. Decoppet, to the Head of the Political Department, F. Calonder, July 28, 1919 = Le Chef du Département militaire, C. Decoppet, au Chef du Département politique, F. Calonder, 28 juillet 1919. In: Documents Diplomatiques Suisses 7b (24):58–60.

[80] Cf. Federal Council, Minutes of the Meeting on August 4, 1919 = Conseil Fédéral, Procès-verbal de la séance du 4 août 1919. In: Documents Diplomatiques Suisses 7b(33):108–110, 108f.; Federal Council (1920) Message on Switzerland joining the League of Nations, pp. 334–363.

[81] See Stenographisches Bulletin der Bundesversammlung, Nationalrat, 1920 pp. 231–319; Stenographisches Bulletin der Bundesversammlung, Ständerat, 1920 pp. 13–39, 46; Ricklin (1991), p. 4; with further indications Jorio (2023), p. 218f.

Switzerland was required to adapt economic sanctions imposed by the League of Nations.[82]

The Second Italo-Abyssinian War from 1935 to 1937 and the ensuing economic sanctions posed a major challenge to Switzerland's neutrality. In 1932, Emperor Haile Selassie had begun promoting coffee exports to Switzerland to finance the purchase of weapons and ammunition. However, following the outbreak of the Second Italo-Abyssinian War in October 1935, the Federal Council prohibited these exports in line with sanctions imposed by the League of Nations against both Italy, the aggressor, and Ethiopia, the attacked nation.[83] The legal basis was the Federal Council decision on the export, re-export, and transit of weapons, ammunition, and war material to Abyssinia and Italy, dated October 28, 1935.[84] In addition, the Swiss government imposed financial sanctions against Italy and export restrictions for certain goods and natural resources.[85] The conflict between Italy and the Ethiopian Empire spurred a debate in Switzerland about the limits of the country's contribution to collective security due to its differentiated neutrality. Swiss export-oriented businesses still struggling under the Great Depression and the appreciation of the Swiss currency aimed to minimize sanctions against Mussolini's fascist regime which was an important trading partner.[86] The economic sanctions and consequently the concept of differentiated neutrality came under increasing pressure domestically. The escalating political situation in Europe prompted the Federal Council to request recognition of Switzerland's traditional neutrality from the League of Nations Council in April 1938.[87] The League of Nations Council acknowledged Switzerland's return to "integral neutrality" in a resolution on May 14.[88]

4.1.2 Cold War: Hotz-Linder Agreement

In 1949, North American and European countries established the North Atlantic Treaty Organization (NATO) as a collective defense alliance to counter the Soviet Union's growing influence and military power in post-World War II. Europe. Previously, the USA and its allies had imposed trade restrictions to weaken the Eastern Bloc. Switzerland and other neutral countries (e.g. Sweden, Austria, Finland) were drawn into the smoldering conflict between East and West as the USA, Great Britain and France, starting in late 1948, pressured them to act in the interest of

[82] See Petrig (2024), p. 427f.

[83] See Jorio (2023), pp. 223 and 225f.

[84] Amtliche Sammlung des Bundesrechts (AS) Vol. 51 (1935) 693.

[85] AS Vol. 51 (1935) 717 and 720.

[86] See Federal Council (1935) Report on the Italo-Abyssinian War, pp. 921–972.

[87] Cf. Federal Council (1938) Report on Neutrality, pp. 840–852; see Schindler (1938), p. 440f.; Jorio (2023), p. 226f.

[88] See Schindler (1938), p. 443.

the Western powers and restrict the deliveries of goods and resources that would be essential to the Soviet Union in case of war.[89] The NATO countries feared that the embargo could be circumvented via Switzerland which ultimately had to give in to foreign pressure.

In July 1951, Switzerland signed the Hotz-Linder Agreement, an informal and undocumented arrangement named after its negotiators, Harold Linder (USA) and Jean Hotz (Switzerland). It aimed to restrict Swiss trade in strategically important goods during the Cold War era with the Eastern Bloc.[90] This agreement compelled Switzerland to partially comply with the Coordinating Committee on Multilateral Export Controls (CoCom) regulations governing dual-use goods across all NATO countries and report to CoCom quarterly, making Switzerland's de facto membership in the CoCom highly controversial in terms of neutrality policies.[91] Otherwise, Swiss businesses would have been excluded from US high technology markets.[92]

The CoCom drafted different lists for the internationally traded goods. Strict export controls restricted the trade with certain dual-use goods to normal trade levels of previous years (so-called "courant normal"), while strategically important items were either entirely withheld from the Eastern Bloc or heavily limited to the so-called "courant essentiel".[93] The legal foundations for the monitoring and restriction of the import, export, and transit of such goods were established by the Federal Resolution on economic measures towards foreign countries of September 28, 1956, and later the Federal Act on External Economic Measures of June 25, 1982, whose measures were not specifically directed against the Eastern Bloc but applied to the import, export, and transit of strategically important goods to all countries.[94] Any measures taken required the precondition that substantial Swiss economic interests would be adversely affected otherwise.

CoCom's impact persisted, experiencing adjustments in the late 1950s, followed by relaxed US measures in the late 1960s and early 1970s. However, CoCom tightened its grip again in the early 1980s due to political upheavals in Poland and Afghanistan.[95] CoCom stayed in force until its abolition on March 31, 1994, even though it had become obsolete regarding the Cold War with the fall of the Iron Curtain in 1989/90.[96] As armed conflicts remained a significant threat to peace and security after the end of the Cold War, the conviction prevailed both internationally

[89] Jorio (2023), p. 380; Ricklin (1991), pp. 25 and 45; for additional information, see Schaller (1987), pp. 18–21.

[90] See Wyss (2018), p. 196.

[91] See Schaller (1987), pp. 208–213, for a critical analysis.

[92] Jorio (2023), p. 381; Ricklin (1991), p. 24f.; for more details, see Schaller (1987), pp. 60–94.

[93] See Wyss (2018), p. 196; Schaller (1987), pp. 2 and 22f.

[94] AS 1956 1553; AS 1982 1923; see Wyss (2018), pp. 198–200.

[95] See Jorio (2023), pp. 381 and 408–412; Wyss (2018), p. 196f.; Federal Council (1995) Message on the GCA, p. 1315.

[96] See Wyss (2018), p. 201.

and in Switzerland that export controls for weapons, military goods, and dual-use goods needed to be maintained.[97]

4.2 War Material Act

The relationship between neutrality law and neutrality policy plays an important role in the export of war material.[98] Article 107 para. 2 Const. states that the Confederation shall legislate on the manufacture, procurement and sale as well as the import, export and transit of war material. Article 107 para. 2 serves foreign policy, security policy and neutrality policy interests, which also include the preservation of the domestic defense industry. As the latter is a structural policy interest, the Confederation can even deviate from the principle of economic freedom in this regard.[99]

Based on Article 107 para 2 Const. and on the before mentioned Article 54 para. 1 Const., the War Material Act (WMA, SR 514.51) was enacted on 13 December 1996. Pursuant to Article 1 WMA, the purpose of the WMA is to fulfill Switzerland's obligations and uphold its foreign policy principles by controlling war materials. At the same time, it aims to maintain an industrial capacity in Switzerland that is suited to the needs of its national defense. The WMA provides for a two-layered authorization system. First, a basic authorization is required for anyone who wants to manufacture war material in Switzerland or to trade in war material on his own account or on the account of a third party or who wants to broker war material to recipients abroad on a commercial basis. In addition to the basic authorization, an individual authorization must be obtained for specific activities. The WMA distinguishes between authorizations for import, export, trade, or brokerage as well as for the conclusion of contracts concerning the transfer of intellectual property.[100] Pursuant to Article 22 WMA the manufacture, brokerage, export and transit of war material for recipients abroad are authorized if this does not conflict with international law, international obligations and the principles of Swiss foreign policy. This general rule is materialized in Article 22a WMA which contains criteria that must be taken into account for foreign transactions (rejection criteria) or that lead to a mandatory refusal of authorization (exclusion criteria).[101] When deciding on an approval request particularly the following rejection criteria are to be considered: maintaining peace, international security and regional stability; the situation in the country of destination; and the behavior of the country of destination towards the international community, in particular regarding compliance with international law.

[97] See Federal Council (1990) Report on Security policy, p. 864f.; Federal Council (1993) White Paper on Neutrality, p. 21f.; Federal Council (1995) Message on the GCA, p. 1319.

[98] Federal Council (2007) Report on Neutrality, p. 5558.

[99] Mohler and Müller (2023), n. 20; Winistörfer (2021), p. 421.

[100] Art. 12 WMA.

[101] Federal Council (2021) Message on the WMA, p. 31.

Pursuant to the exclusion criteria, approval requests are not approved, if the country of destination is involved in an internal or international conflict or if it seriously and systematically violates human rights. The same applies if there is a high risk in the country of destination that war material is going to be used against the civilian population or passed on to an unwanted final recipient.

When assessing applications for authorizations for war material Switzerland's neutrality must always be considered.[102] Besides neutrality law, neutrality policy is also of considerable importance in this regard.[103] This is reflected in the exclusion criteria by the fact that also foreign transactions by private companies to countries being involved in internal or international conflicts cannot be approved. Thus, this exclusion criteria goes beyond the obligations of neutrality law, which—although legal views differ in this regard—does not prohibit the export of war material by private companies to parties to a conflict, unlike exports by government agencies, but merely subjects them to the principle of equal treatment.[104] Further, the exclusion criteria also apply to internal conflicts whereas the law of neutrality only applies to international ones. Even if the respective country is not involved in an international or internal conflict, neutrality policy considerations may still lead to a refusal of authorization in cases where war material exports are perceived by the international community as clearly favoring a party to the conflict.[105]

The authorization requirements of the WMA restrict the fundamental right of economic freedom of companies or individuals involved in war material related business activities.[106] Such entities cannot freely sell or distribute war material. As the authorization requirements aim at fulfilling foreign and security policy interests these restrictions are however in accordance with the principle of economic freedom. Further, as the WMA aims also at safeguarding Swiss defense industry capacities the economic interests of companies active in this field are at least indirectly considered in the authorization process. Therefore, the fact that a respective company is critical for the Swiss defense industry capacities and is dependent on war material exports can be weighted in when applying the rejection criteria. In contrast, general references to the interests of the Swiss economy as whole or to the welfare and economic security of the Swiss population would not be a sufficient legal argument for approving war material exports.[107]

In practice, the individual economic interests of companies of the defense industry appear to have been given greater weight in the past than foreign policy objectives.[108] In response to a public initiative the authorization criteria were subsequently tightened. Stricter application of the authorization requirements

[102] Federal Council (2021) Message on the WMA, p. 31.

[103] See Villiger (2023), n. 444.

[104] Federal Council (2021) Message on the WMA, p. 34.

[105] See Federal Council (2021) Message on the WMA, p. 31.

[106] See Lanz (2020), n. 191.

[107] See Lanz (2020), n. 176.

[108] See Mohler and Müller, n. 18.

worsens the economic conditions for the Swiss defense industry and puts it at a competitive disadvantage to competitors in the EU and elsewhere.[109] The overall consequences for Switzerland are nonetheless limited, since export of war material is below one percent of the total Swiss exports.[110] It can even be argued that an application of the authorization requirements in line with the constitutional foreign policy objectives may help to promote stable international investment conditions that are favorable for Switzerland's open economy as a whole.

4.3 Goods Control Act

In 1997, the Federal Act on the Control of Dual-Use Goods, Specific Military Goods and Strategic Goods (Goods Control Act, GCA; SR 946.202) was established as part of the reorientation of export controls.[111] It provides a legal framework for a vast range of trade restrictions.

The Goods Control Act is intended to allow for the control of dual-use goods, i.e. goods usable for civilian and military purposes, specific military goods, and strategic goods (Article 1). The Goods Control Act applies to dual-use goods and specific military goods covered by international agreements. The Federal Council determines which items falling under non-binding international control measures, as well as strategic goods outlined in international agreements, are subject to this act. The act applies insofar as the War Materiel Act or the Atomic Energy Act is not applicable (Article 2 para. 1–3bis GCA). By aligning the Goods Control Act with international agreements and non-binding international control measures, the legislator ensured that Switzerland, as a significant exporter of dual-use goods, does not adopt a more restrictive policy than its primary competitors to prevent Swiss companies from facing disadvantages in international competition.[112]

According to Article 4 letters a and b GCA, for the purpose of implementing international agreements, the Federal Council may introduce authorization and reporting requirements and order supervisory measures for the research, development, manufacture, storage, transfer and use of goods, and the import, export, transit, and brokerage of goods and issue ordinances on inspections. Furthermore, in support of international control measures that are not binding under international law, the Federal Council may introduce authorizations and reporting requirements, and order supervisory measures in respect of the import, export, transit, and brokerage of goods (Article 5 GCA), provided such measures are also supported by Switzerland's most important trading partners.

[109] See Federal Council (2021) Message on the WMA, p. 40.

[110] Federal Council (2021) Message on the WMA, p. 40.

[111] See Federal Council (1995) Message on the GCA, pp. 1304–1306; Wyss (2018), pp. 201–203.

[112] See Wyss (2018), p. 204.

Authorizations will be denied if international agreements or non-binding control measures supported by Switzerland are violated, or if corresponding enforcement measures in accordance with the Embargo Act have been taken (Article 6 para. 1 GCA). Additionally, authorizations shall be refused if there is reason to believe that the activity covered may benefit terrorist groups or organized crime or constitute a danger to international critical infrastructure in which Switzerland participates (Article 6 para. 1bis GCA). Authorizations for specific military goods shall also be refused if the United Nations or states that participate with Switzerland in international export control measures prohibit the export of such goods, and if Switzerland's most important trading partners adhere to these prohibitions (Article 6 para. 2 GCA). The Federal Council shall regulate the refusal of authorizations for the export or brokerage of dual-use goods that can be used for internet and mobile telecommunications surveillance (para. 3).

The Federal Council can restrict authorizations for specific destination countries to implement international agreements, while also allowing exemptions or relaxations for countries involved in international agreements or non-binding control measures supported by Switzerland (Article 8 para. 1 and 2 GCA).

Similar to the War Material Act, the authorization requirements under this law restrict the fundamental right of economic freedom for entities involved in activities related to dual-use goods, specific military goods, and strategic goods. The Federal Council has extensive regulatory powers. This delegation of competences to the Federal Council is understandable for practical reasons, but not unproblematic, as restrictions of this fundamental right can be significant and may have profound impact on competition. The measures provided for in the Goods Control Act are intended to safeguard the foreign and security policy interests of Switzerland.[113] Furthermore, by referring to restrictions by the most important trading partners, these measures also help to secure good economic relations with them. The measures of the Goods Control Act are generally compatible with principle of economic freedom. However, the compatibility of the measures with the principle of economic freedom depends mainly on their design and whether they distort competition among direct competitors. As long as direct competitors are treated equally, the goods control regime is compatible with Article 94 para. 1 Const.

4.4 *Embargo Act*

The Federal Counsel already stated in its 1993 White Paper on Neutrality that neutrality itself does not prevent the adoption of economic sanctions, even if passed outside the UN system.[114] Since 1 January 2003 the Embargo Act (EmbA; SR

[113] Federal Council (1995) Message on the GCA, p. 1350.

[114] Federal Council (1993) White Paper on Neutrality, p. 21f.

946.231) serves as legal basis for the implementation of international sanctions.[115] Pursuant to Article 1 para. 1 EmbA the Confederation may enact compulsory measures in order to implement sanctions that have been ordered by the United Nations Organisation, by the Organisation for Security and Cooperation in Europe or by Switzerland's most significant trading partners and which serve to secure compliance with international law, and in particular the respect of human rights. Such compulsory measures include in particular restrictions on transactions involving goods and services, on payments and capital transfers, on the movement of persons and on scientific, technological and cultural exchange as well as prohibitions, authorisation and notification requirements (Article 1 para. 3 EmbA).

In its message on the EmbA the Federal Council pointed out that the EmbA does neither contain neutrality law regulations nor neutrality policy provisions.[116] While this is technically true, the implementation of sanctions certainly touches on Switzerland's neutrality.[117] In principle, the law of neutrality does not prohibit the participation in economic sanctions.[118] A neutral state must treat belligerent states equally only regarding bans on goods which are by their nature intended exclusively or essentially for military purposes. For other goods, a neutral state is left free to restrict economic transactions.[119] It is important to note, that that sanctions adopted by the Security Council on the basis of Chapter VII of the Charter are legally binding on Switzerland as a UN member in application of Article 25 of the Charter.[120] According to legal doctrine and established practice the application of resolutions of the Security Council is compatible with the law of neutrality.[121]

The Federal Council stated in its White Paper on Neutrality that the "international community will not respect a state's neutrality if one of the features of that neutrality is to maintain economic relations with a state sanctioned for breaking international law".[122] Moreover, sanctions that are imposed against a state breaking peace or violating international law serve peace and are thus "in accordance with the spirit of neutrality".[123] When deciding whether to participate in such sanctions, the risk of Switzerland being used for transactions circumventing the sanctions must also be taken into account.[124] Enabling the circumvention of sanctions could be seen by the international community as taking sides in favor of the sanctioned state.

[115] See Petrig and Sinz (2024), p. 344f, in detail for the scope of the EmbA.

[116] Federal Council (2000) Message on the EmbA, p. 1434.

[117] See Petrig and Sinz (2024), p. 386.

[118] Federal Council (1993) White Paper on Neutrality, p. 21.

[119] Federal Council (1993) Report on Neutrality, p. 231f.

[120] Federal Council (2007) Report on Neutrality, p. 5561.

[121] Federal Council (2007) Report on Neutrality, p. 5561; see also Petrig and Sinz (2024), p. 356.

[122] Federal Council (1993) White Paper on Neutrality, p. 21.

[123] Federal Council (1993) White Paper on Neutrality, p. 21.

[124] Federal Council (2000) Message on the EmbA, p. 1456.

Implementing international sanctions can thus be necessary under neutrality policy considerations to secure the credibility of Switzerland's neutrality.[125]

The sanctions imposed under the EmbA typically restrict the economic freedom and may also affect the guarantee of ownership of the persons concerned.[126] Sanctions based on the EmbG are not monetary, trade or economic policy measures; they are foreign policy measures in terms of their objective.[127] Prima vista, the EmbA seems to subordinate Switzerland's (economic) welfare under the other foreign policy objectives such as the promotion of human rights and the peaceful coexistence of peoples.[128] In particular, the Federal Council can ban the export of goods even if they would be beneficial for the Swiss economy as a whole and would contribute to the welfare of the Swiss population. However, it would fall short to assume there is a general conflict between the constitutional foreign policy objectives and the economic interests of Switzerland. As the EU imposes sanctions in response to violations of international law the adoption of such sanctions by Switzerland helps to enforce the global order. A global order based on international law allows international investments to be made and trade to be conducted. As an open economy, Switzerland thus has a great interest in a stable international legal order that promotes legal certainty and trust required for economic activities.[129] Further, the non-adoption of sanctions that have been ordered by Switzerland's most significant trading partners such as the EU or the US could deteriorate economic relations with them and thus cause damage to the Swiss economy. Ultimately, the adoption of sanctions serves the Swiss economy as a whole by maintaining global sourcing and export opportunities.[130] However, it must be examined in each case whether the resulting restrictions on economic freedom and the guarantee of property are proportionate.

4.5 *Act on Private Security Services Abroad*

In recent years the importance of private services provided in the military and security sector increased significantly internationally. At the same time, security companies operating from Switzerland providing security services abroad became more and more an issue at the national level.[131] Against this background, Switzerland enacted the Act on Private Security Services provided Abroad (PSSA; SR 935.41) on 1 September 2015. The PSSA applies to persons and companies that

[125] Petrig (2024), p. 437.

[126] See already Schürmann (1994), p. 291.

[127] Federal Council (2000) Message on the EmbA, p. 1450.

[128] In this sense Lanz (2020), n. 174.

[129] See Kley and Portmann (2014), n. 39.

[130] Schürmann (1994), p. 291.

[131] Federal Council (2013) Message PSSA, p. 1746.

provide private security services abroad from Switzerland or that provide services in Switzerland in connection with private security services provided abroad. Pursuant to Article 4 PSSA private security services include for example operating and maintaining weapons systems or advising or training members of armed forces. The PSSA ex lege prohibits certain activities related to direct participation in hostilities or serious human rights violations.[132] Further, it provides for a system of prohibitions that the competent authority can impose in specific cases. In order to monitor the activities carried out abroad, companies are required to notify the competent authority.[133] Activities that contradict the objectives of the law will be prohibited by the authority.[134]

According to Article 1 PSSA, the aim of the PSSA is to contribute to safeguarding the internal and external security of Switzerland, realizing Switzerland's foreign policy objectives (as mentioned in Article 54 para 2 Const.), preserving Swiss neutrality, and guaranteeing compliance with international law and, in particular, of human rights and of international humanitarian law. It seems worth noting that the PSSA—in contrast to the WMA or the EmbA—explicitly lists preserving Swiss neutrality as one of its aims. In this context, reference is made both to neutrality law and neutrality policy. As a consequence, activities falling in scope of the PSSA are to be checked for their compatibility with Switzerland's legal obligations as a permanently neutral state and—from a neutrality policy standpoint—regarding their effect on the credibility and effectiveness of Switzerland's neutrality.[135]

The PSSA restricts the economic freedom of the companies and person it applies to. However, this restriction is based on public interests as laid out in Article 1 PSSA such as preserving Swiss neutrality or realizing the general foreign policy objectives.[136] When assessing whether an activity is contrary to the aims of the PSSA, the competent authority must consider all the different objectives mentioned or referred to in Article 1 PSSA. In particular, it has to take into account whether the company in question is relevant for the Swiss defense industry and weigh in any effects of a prohibition on Swiss welfare and Swiss independence. Such a comprehensive weighing up of the mutually interdependent and sometimes conflicting public interests is essential for assessing each individual case.[137] The PSSA does not only provide for a legal assessment but also a political one. Activities which should be prohibited by the competent authority may by way of exception be authorized by the Federal Council if national interests prevail.[138] In such cases private economic and political interests may be aligned, if the company in question, is—due to its

[132] See Art. 8 and 9 PSSA.

[133] Article 10 para. 1 PSSA.

[134] Article 14 para. 1 PSSA.

[135] Federal Council (2013) Message PSSA, p. 1782.

[136] Federal Council (2013) Message PSSA, p. 1824.

[137] Federal Administrative Court B-3427/2019 of 7 January 2021, consideration 6.1.6.

[138] Article 15 BPS.

competences and capabilities—part of Switzerland's security-relevant technology and industrial base.[139]

5 Challenges

5.1 Swiss Response to EU Sanctions Against Russia

On 23 and 25 February 2022, in response to Russia's war of aggression against Ukraine the EU agreed on wide ranging sanctions against Russia targeting among others the financial sector, the energy and transport sectors, dual-use goods and certain Russian individuals. The position of the Swiss Federal Council remained unclear for several days. Initially, the Federal Council limited itself to taking measures aimed at preventing circumvention via Swiss territory.[140] Under considerable pressure from its international partners, finally, the Federal Council decided on 28 February 2022 to adopt the first and second package of EU sanctions against Russia in its entirety and subsequently also adopted the following sanction packages.[141] This decision by the Federal Council marked a significant change of course in Switzerland's foreign policy.[142] Regarding Russia's Crimea annexation in 2014 the Federal Council had only adopted the EU sanctions that directly related to the annexation. However, it did not adopt the additional EU sanctions against Russia, as it wanted to be seen as credibly mediator between the belligerents. It merely implemented certain measures to prevent Switzerland from being used as place to circumvent EU sanctions.[143]

To comply with its right of neutrality obligations Switzerland also placed restrictions on certain exports of military goods to Ukraine.[144] Beyond this, the Federal Council considers participation in economic sanctions to be compatible with the law of neutrality. This is because the law of neutrality does not recognise an obligation of economic neutrality. Therefore, Switzerland may impose economic sanctions against only one party to a conflict.[145]

Based on the Embargo Act, the Federal Council issued the corresponding measures on the ordinance level. In particular, the applicable ordinance provides for the

[139] See Federal Administrative Court B-3427/2019 of 7 January 2021, consideration 7.5.5.

[140] See Burckhardt and Lumengo Paka (2022), p. 267.

[141] Federal Council (2022) Report in response to Postulate 22.3385, p. 19; see Petrig and Sinz (2024), p. 385.

[142] See with reference to the reaction of the Swiss press Fauconnet (2022), p. 3; see further Petrig (2024), p. 436.

[143] Federal Council (2022) Report in response to Postulate 22.3385, p. 17; see Petrig (2024), p. 436.

[144] Federal Council (2022) Report in response to Postulate 22.3385, p. 19; see for the implementation Burckhardt and Lumengo Paka (2022), p. 268f.

[145] Federal Council (1993) Report on Neutrality, p. 237; see also Fauconnet (2022), pp. 9–16.

freezing of funds and economic resources owned or controlled by listed persons, companies, and organisations. This is accompanied by a reporting obligation for persons and institutions that hold or manage funds or know of economic resources that are likely to fall under the asset freeze.[146] The regulation also banned various financial transactions with links to Russia.[147]

These measures obviously interfered with the guarantee of ownership and often also with the economic freedom of the individuals and companies concerned, as they can no longer dispose of their property without restriction and are restricted in their business activities. The situation is less clear regarding the principle of economic freedom. Embargo measures are not a deviation of the principle of economic freedom. The aim of the sanctions is not of a protectionist nature as the Swiss economy is to be shielded from foreign competition. Rather, the sanctions are intended to put pressure on Russia to stop its war against Ukraine, which violates international law. At first glance, such sanctions could be contrary to the interests of the Swiss economy. This is because numerous companies are domiciled in Switzerland and wealthy Russians clients have significant accounts with Swiss banks and wealth managers. However, as the Federal Council already noticed in 1993, due to its location and its trading relationships with the EU, Switzerland could hardly ignore sanctions imposed by the EU.[148] Further, Swiss financial institutions may be obliged to comply with foreign sanctions anyway due to Swiss supervisory law.[149] Against this background, the adoption of the EU sanctions may well be in the interest of the Swiss economy as a whole as well as aligned with its foreign policy objectives.

5.2 *War Material Transfers*

In the course of the Ukraine war, Germany and Denmark requested authorisation from Switzerland to transfer Swiss war material to Ukraine.[150] As required under the WMA, at the time of the procurement both countries had signed a non-re-export declaration.[151] Due to the law of neutrality and the applicable provisions of the WMA Switzerland denied the requests.[152] The Federal Council was also of the opinion that such a transfer would require an adjustment to Switzerland's neutrality policy. However, Switzerland confirmed that Germany could re-export Swiss

[146] See Articles 15 and 16 of the Ordinance on measures in connection with the Situation in Ukraine (SR 946.231.176.72).

[147] See Burckhardt and Lumengo Paka (2022), pp. 270–272.

[148] Federal Council (1993) White Paper on Neutrality, p. 25.

[149] See Federal Supreme Court decision 4A_659/2020 of 6 August 2021, consideration 3.2.1.

[150] Federal Council (2022) Report in response to Postulate 22.3385, p. 20.

[151] See Article 18 WMA.

[152] Federal Council (2022) Report in response to Postulate 22.3385, p. 20.

military equipment to European countries, enabling them to replenish their war material inventories. Based on these considerations, the Federal Council approved the export of 25 main battle tanks to Germany under the assurance that the tanks will remain either in Germany, with NATO or with its EU partners.[153]

The Federal Council's restraint in authorizing war material transfers has led to partial criticism from legal doctrine. It is argued that the prohibition to export war material to countries engaged in an international armed conflict cannot apply to a country that is defending itself against a war of aggression in violation of international law.[154] This discussion leads back to the question of whether the law of neutrality—as stipulated in the Hague Conventions—is still appropriate under current international law.[155]

Fears have been voiced in Switzerland that the restrictive stance on re-exports will threaten the local defence industry in its existence, as foreign countries are not willing anymore to sign non-re-export declarations and will therefore procure war material elsewhere.[156] A proposal was introduced in parliament to waive non-re-export declarations with regard to Ukraine, but it was ultimately rejected.[157] If the non-re-export declarations actually result in a significant drop in orders from Swiss defence companies, adhering to a rigid application of the law of neutrality could in the end jeopardise Switzerland's obligation and capacity of armed neutrality.[158]

5.3 Commodity Trading Regulation

Switzerland has long been a key player in commodity trading, leveraging its strategic location, well-established financial infrastructure, and expertise in the sector. Renowned for its stability and neutrality, Switzerland has become a global hub for commodity trading, particularly in sectors such as energy, agriculture, and metals. In particular, due to Switzerland's neutrality and non-membership in international

[153] Cf. "Federal Council approves export of 25 main battle tanks to Germany", press release of 22 November 2023, online available at https://www.admin.ch/gov/en/start/documentation/media-releases.msg-id-98821.html.

[154] Mohler and Müller (2023), n. 94.

[155] See Sect. 3.1.

[156] See Neue Zürcher Zeitung, Parteien suchen Ausweg aus Waffen-Dilemma – Ständeräte wollen Weitergabe von Kriegsmaterial erlauben, February 3, 2023. https://www.nzz.ch/schweiz/parteien-suchen-ausweg-aus-waffen-dilemma-staenderaete-wollen-weitergabe-von-kriegsmaterial-erlauben-ld.1724455.

[157] See Parlamentarische Initiative "Änderung des Kriegsmaterialgesetzes. Lex Ukraine" (23.401). https://www.parlament.ch/de/ratsbetrieb/suche-curia-vista/geschaeft?AffairId=20230401.

[158] In fact, Germany is considering to apply a "swiss free" approach regarding procurement of war material (see Neue Zürcher Zeitung, "Swiss free", sobald es um Kriegsmaterial geht – wie die Schweiz ihre Rüstungsindustrie verlieren könnte, September 10, 2024. https://www.nzz.ch/pro/krise-der-schweizer-ruestungsbranche-exportverbote-und-souveraenitaet-ld.1847526.

organizations after 1945, the country was not obliged to adhere to embargoes.[159] Annual Revenues rose from CHF 2 billion in 2002 to over CHF 80 billion in 2022, as there are now over 900 commodity trading companies in Switzerland, employing 10,000 people and mostly located in the regions of Geneva, Zug and Lugano.[160]

In the last decades, Switzerland has been criticized both domestically and internationally for its lack of regulation of commodity trading. In Swiss Parliament, this criticism has led to numerous parliamentary motions calling for measures against corruption and money laundering, more transparency, a better protection of the environment, and the disclosure of the provenance of the traded commodities.[161] The commodities trading regulation—or the lack of such a regulation—came under further public scrutiny following the Russian attack on Ukraine. According to the critics, the absence of comprehensive commodities trading oversight had enabled the Russian Federation to fund its war efforts in Ukraine. The US and EU have repeatedly uttered allegations that Switzerland had not done enough regarding commodity trade regulation to ensure that the sanctions against Russia were effectively enforced.[162]

[159] See Haller (2021).

[160] See https://www.eda.admin.ch/aboutswitzerland/de/home/wirtschaft/taetigkeitsgebiete/rohstoffhandel.html; for more details, see https://www.bfs.admin.ch/bfs/de/home/statistiken/industrie-dienstleistungen/sektorielle-portraits/rohstoffhaendler.html.

[161] See e.g. Motion "Transparenz der Zahlungsströme von Rohstoff-Unternehmen" (12.3773); Motion "Aktionsplan Transparenz im Rohstoffhandel" (13.3422); Motion "Unterstellung von Edelmetallen unter das Geldwäschereigesetz" (13.3513); Motion "Schweizer Goldbranche. Sorgfaltsprüfungspflicht zum Schutz von Mensch und Umwelt" (18.4357); Motion "Rohstoffhandel stärker in die Pflicht nehmen mit einer unabhängigen Rohstoffmarktaufsicht. Korruption und Geldwäscherei reduzieren" (22.3031); Motion "Volle Transparenz beim Rohstoffhandel. Die Fehler vermeiden, die uns im Bankensektor teuer zu stehen gekommen sind" (22.3133); Motion "Schaffung einer Taskforce für die Sperrung von russischen und belorussischen Oligarchengeldern" (22.3236); see further FDFA (2013) Report on Commodities, pp. 16–22.

[162] See Berner Zeitung, Aus Anlass des Ukraine-Kriegs: Schweiz soll verschwiegenem Rohstoffhandel auf die Finger schauen, March 3, 2022. https://www.bernerzeitung.ch/die-gruenen-fordern-eine-starke-aufsicht-ueber-die-rohstoffhaendler-330823628932; Neue Zürcher Zeitung, Klumpenrisiko Rohstoffhändler? Die Schweizer Politik verschläft das nächste grosse Thema, May 10, 2023. https://www.nzz.ch/meinung/der-rohstoffhandelsplatz-ist-ein-juwel-und-ein-risiko-die-schweiz-sollte-mehr-wie-wayne-gretzky-sein-und-weniger-in-den-fussspuren-von-marc-rich-wandeln-ld.1736651; Tagesanzeiger, Riesige Gewinne: Kaum Zahlen zur Rohstoffbranche in der Schweiz – was steckt dahinter?, May 18, 2023. https://www.tagesanzeiger.ch/kaum-zahlen-zur-rohstoffbranche-in-der-schweiz-was-steckt-dahinter-231771138318; Neue Zürcher Zeitung, Nach den Banken geraten nun auch Schweizer Rohstoffhändler ins Visier der US-Regierung, July 19, 2023. https://www.nzz.ch/wirtschaft/us-delegation-nimmt-die-schweizer-rohstoffhaendler-unter-die-lupe-ld.1747620?reduced=true; Frankfurter Allgemeine Zeitung, Hilft die Schweiz Russland beim Umgehen von Sanktionen?, July 24, 2023. https://www.faz.net/aktuell/wirtschaft/vorwuerfe-von-us-beamten-hilft-die-schweiz-russland-beim-umgehen-von-sanktionen-19055487.html; Frankfurter Allgemeine Zeitung, Das heikle Geschäft der Schweiz mit Rohstoffen, November 8, 2023. https://www.faz.net/aktuell/wirtschaft/mehr-wirtschaft/rohstoffe-aus-russland-schweizer-handel-seit-ukraine-krieg-in-der-kritik-19297163.html#:~:text=Das%20heikle%20Geschäft%20der%20Schweiz%20mit%20Rohstoffen&text=Das

Several sanctions implemented by the Federal Council in its Ordinance on Measures in Connection with the Situation in Ukraine after the outbreak of the Russian attack on Ukraine have direct or indirect implications for commodity trading.[163] Since 29 June 2022, the purchase (when Switzerland is the destination) as well as the import, transit, and transportation into and through Switzerland of crude oil and petroleum products originating from the Russian Federation are prohibited (Article 12a para. 1).[164] Also prohibited is the provision of services of any kind, including financial services and brokerage, as well as the provision of funds in connection with these prohibited activities (para. 2). Exceptions to the prohibition apply, notably, for crude oil and petroleum products whose purchase price does not exceed the price cap of US$ 60 per barrel (para. 4 letter b). Further exceptions may be granted by SECO, especially if such activities are necessary to secure the energy supply of Switzerland or an European Economic Area (EEA) member state.

Similar restrictions for commodity trading apply to the trade in iron and steel products (art. 14a) and gold and gold products (art. 14d) from the Russian Federation or originating in the Russian Federation. Furthermore, Article 28b prohibits certain activities related to companies in the energy and mining sectors of the Russian Federation, including acquiring ownership interests, financing, establishing joint ventures, and securities services.

Despite these sanctions effecting commodities trading, Switzerland still lacks a comprehensive regulation of its commodities market. Both Article 95 and Article 101 Const. could serve as constitutional basis to regulate commodity trading. Article 95 para. 1 Const pursues predominantly so-called "police interests", specifically the protection of public safety, peace, order, health, and good faith in business dealings.[165] Regulatory measures based on this article should strictly adhere to the principle of economic freedom which limits the scope and type of the commodity trading regulation.[166] In contrast, Article 101 para. 2 Const. explicitly allows to deviate from the principle of the economic freedom under certain conditions. Measures based on this provision must serve the protection of the Swiss economy, e.g. when foreign economic sanctions against Swiss companies, protective tariffs on goods from Switzerland, or other market access barriers are imminent.[167] Therefore, commodity trading regulation, when implemented as a defensive measure to

%20birgt%20Risiken%20–%20die%20Regierung%20sollte%20genauer%20hinschauen.&text=Die%20Schweiz%20ist%20ein%20beliebter,die%20Ukraine%20richtig%20ins%20Bewusstsein.

[163] The commodities sector has also been subject to sanctions in the past (see FDFA (2013), Report on commodities, pp. 27–29.

[164] AS 2022 381.

[165] Biaggini (2017), Art. 95 n. 5; Vallender et al. (2006), § 17 n. 9; with further information on "police interests", see Rhinow et al. (2011), § 1 n. 20.

[166] Federal Council (1996) Message on the new Federal Constitution, p. 298; see Biaggini (2017), Art. 95 n. 5; Vallender et al. (2006), § 17 n. 9.

[167] Winistörfer (2021), p. 387f.; Rhinow et al. (2011), § 32 n. 24.

safeguard Swiss economic interests abroad, would not deviate from the principle of economic freedom.[168]

In case of urgency and when safeguarding the foreign policy interests of the country so requires, the Federal Council may issue ordinances and rulings with limited duration in direct application of Article 184 para. 3 Const. Furthermore, the Federal Council might take measures to safeguard external security, independence, and neutrality of Switzerland (Article 185 para. 1 Const.). It may in direct application of Article 185 Const. issue ordinances and rulings with limited duration in order to counter existing or imminent threats of serious disruption to public order or internal or external security. In the past, the Federal Council used these powers in different situations, probably most prominently during the Global Financial Crisis 2007/08 to bail out the UBS bank and in 2009 to authorize the Swiss Financial Market Supervisory Authority FINMA to disclose bank customer data to the US authorities.[169] Article 184 para. 3 and Article 185 para. 3 Const. constitute sufficient legal bases for the restriction of fundamental rights, provided that these restrictions are otherwise justified by a public interest and proportionate to the intended purpose.[170]

If foreign pressure on Switzerland to regulate commodity trading suddenly becomes too great and threatening to the Swiss economy, the Federal Council may feel inclined to pass emergency ordinances based on the competences in Articles 184 and 185 Const. However, such measures would be problematic with regard to the rule of law and would tarnish Switzerland's reputation as stable and predictable business location.

6 Conclusion

As a small country with an open economy Switzerland depends highly on global trade and on functioning cross-border supply chains as well as reliable relations with its trading partners. In fact, foreign market access is recognized as one of the key objectives of foreign economic policy, as addressed by Article 101 Const. In this context, maintaining neutrality seems to have proven to be useful for Swiss security and economic interests. Switzerland's commitment to neutrality is an important instrument for achieving foreign policy objectives. The use of this instrument,

[168] See Winistörfer (2021), p. 639; Richli (2007), n. 832; Vallender et al. (2006), § 16 n. 4.

[169] See Federal Council (2008) Message on Financial stability, pp. 8966–8969; Verordnung über die Rekapitalisierung der UBS AG vom 15. Oktober 2008 (AS 2008 4741); for further information, cf. Kley (2011), pp. 123–138; Federal Administrative Court B-1092/2009 of 5 January 2010 and Federal Supreme Court 2C_127/2010 of 15 July 2011; Müller and Jenni (2010), p. 104f.; Verordnung über die Wahrung der Vermögenswerte der Republik Zaire in der Schweiz vom 17. Mai 1997 (AS 1997 1149); Federal Supreme Court 1C_374/2009 of 12 January 2010.

[170] BGE 132 I 229 E. 10.1; see further BGE 137 II 431 E. 3; BGE 129 II 193 E. 5.3.3; BGE 141 I 20 E. 4; Lienhard and Zielniewicz (2012), pp. 111–142.

however, requires delicate balancing with the goals and principles of the Swiss economic constitution.[171]

For the understanding of the application of Switzerland's neutrality it is crucial to distinguish between the law of neutrality and the neutrality policy. The requirements of the law of neutrality and their implementation in statutory law are relatively clear, even if there are justified doubts as to whether the law of neutrality is still appropriate in its original understanding against the background of developments in international law. Neutrality policy, on the other hand, is much more difficult to grasp. Its application depends on the respective foreign policy environment and therefore requires correspondingly greater legal leeway.

The Swiss economic constitution allows for measures to comply with the law of neutrality and to pursue the policy of neutrality. It acknowledges that, under certain circumstances, restricting economic freedom or deviating from the principle of economic freedom may be necessary for the sake of reaching foreign policy goals and applying the instrument of neutrality for this purpose. However, neutrality-related measures are often in tension with the central tenets of the economic constitution as they restrict the fundamental rights of economic freedom and the guarantee of ownership. This is particularly evident in the case of sanctions. Switzerland is repeatedly under economic and political pressure to adopt the sanctions of its most important trading partners, in particular sanctions imposed by the EU. These sanctions restrict the fundamental rights of economic freedom and guarantee of ownership of individuals and legal entities. At the same time, they may well be appropriate or even necessary to strengthen the systemic content of the economic constitution, as they help to maintain good trade relations and thus add to the welfare and competitiveness of the Swiss economy as a whole. In addition, Switzerland, being an open economy, has a vital interest in a stable international legal framework that ensures security, peace, and mutual trust. Accordingly, it actively advocates for international rule of law, which is a fundamental prerequisite for effectively pursuing its foreign policy objectives.[172] Against this backdrop, the adoption of sanctions may also be necessary to prevent blatant violations of international law, such as those committed by Russia in its war against Ukraine. The Federal Council acknowledges this dilemma between neutrality, economic freedom, and foreign policy objectives faced by Switzerland with regard to sanctions—the risk of foreign sanctions and measures negatively impacting Swiss welfare versus the internal freedom and economic liberties retained.[173]

Many challenges with regard to Switzerland' neutrality are not of legal but predominantly of political nature. In other words, they are issues of neutrality policy and not the law of neutrality. Whether sanctions should be adopted is not a question that can be answered by applying the requirements of neutrality law. However, these political decisions affect the credibility of Swiss neutrality and thus ultimately also

---

[171] See Schaller (1987), pp. 200–206.

[172] Kley and Portmann (2014), n. 39.

[173] Cf. Federal Council (2000) Message on the EmbA, p. 1448f.

the extent to which the law of neutrality is upheld. In this regard it is important, that the legislator defines an overall framework legislation addressing aims, competences, procedural rules while leaving enough flexibility for the required balancing of interests by the competent authorities.

On the one hand, Switzerland has implemented such legislation in relation to war material, dual-use goods and security services. These legislations take into account Switzerland's dependence on its major trading partners and allow the Federal Council a wide margin of discretion in applying the restrictions. As these measures typically restrict economic freedom and the guarantee of property, they must be proportionate. On the other hand, there are no further regulations for commodity trading. This harbors the risk that if foreign pressure becomes too great, regulations will have to be issued based on emergency powers, as has already happened in the past. Recourse to emergency law would tarnish the rule of law and damage Switzerland's reputation as a stable and predictable business location. It is therefore advisable for Switzerland to take a proactive approach to the regulation of commodities trading.

Maintaining its neutrality while being an open, internationally connected economy is an exceptionally challenging task for Switzerland and its institutions. The interconnectedness of global economies and geopolitical realities underscore the difficulty of navigating this intricate terrain. The relationship between Switzerland's neutrality and its economic constitution remains complex and ambivalent. As Switzerland continues to be an active participant in globalized economy, it will also be facing challenges regarding its neutrality in the future. From a legal perspective, it is important to provide the necessary instruments and regulations in order to navigate through these challenges in a manner that is as credible and respectful of fundamental rights as possible and in line with foreign policy objectives and economic constitutional principles. Ultimately, the justification of Switzerland's neutrality also depends on the extent to which this will succeed.

References

Literature

Baumann P (2019) Wettbewerbsverzerrungen durch privatwirtschaftliche Staatstätigkeit. Schulthess, Zurich/Basel/Geneva

Biaggini G (2017) BV Kommentar: Bundesverfassung der Schweizerischen Eidgenossenschaft, 2nd edn. Orell Füssli, Zurich

Boston Consulting Group (BCG) (2023) Global Wealth Report 2023. https://web-assets.bcg.com/fb/64/e10897864913a480415d0e1fe3c6/bcg-global-wealth-report-2023-june-2023.pdf

Bundesamt für Zoll und Grenzsicherheit (BAZG) (2023) Jahresbericht Schweizer Aussenhandel 2022. BAZG, Bern

Bundi L (2016) System und wirtschaftsverfassungsrechtliche Zulässigkeit von Subventionen in der Schweiz und von Beihilfen in der EU. Schulthess, Zurich

Burckhardt P, Lumengo Paka N (2022) Schweizer Sanktionsrecht: Ein Überblick über die Massnahmen der Schweiz im Zusammenhang mit der Situation in der Ukraine. UKuR 1(17): 614–617
Egli P (2005) Rechtliche Schranken des Handels mit Kriefsmaterial. SZIER 2005:665–683
Egli P, Holzgang M (2022) Neutralitätsrecht und Neutralitätspolitik: Ein Überblick. AJP 2022:600–611
Ehrenzeller B, Portmann R (2023) Art. 54. In: Ehrenzeller B et al (eds) Die schweizerische Bundesverfassung, St. Galler Kommentar, 4th edn. Dike Zurich, St. Gallen, pp 1826–1847
Etzensperger C, Maurer C (2008) Die Schweiz als Drehscheibe des Rohstoffhandels. Die Volkswirtschaft 2008(9):25–27
Fauconnet Y (2022) Neutralitätsrechtliche Einordnung der schweizerischen Sanktionen gegen Russland im Ukraine-Krieg. Ex/Ante 2022(2):3–17
Federal Department of Foreign Affairs (FDFA) (2022) Swiss neutrality. FDFA, Bern
Fleck D (2021) The law of neutrality. In: Fleck D (ed) The handbook of international humanitarian law, 4th edn. Oxford University Press, Oxford
Häfelin U et al (2020) Schweizerisches Bundesstaatsrecht, 10th edn. Schulthess, Zurich/Basel/Geneva
Haller L (2021) Rohstoffhandel: Wie die Schweiz zur Drehscheibe wurde. Die Volkswirtschaft, Mai 28
Hangartner Y (1989) Besonderheiten der Eigentumsgarantie. In: Haller W et al (eds) Im Dienst an der Gemeinschaft. Helbing & Lichtenhahn, Basel/Frankfurt am Main
Jorio M (2023) Die Schweiz und ihre Neutralität: Eine 400-jährige Geschichte. Hier und Jetzt, Zurich
Kley A (2011) Die UBS-Rettung im historischen Kontext des Notrechts. ZSR 130(I):123–138
Kley R, Portmann R (2014) Vorbemerkungen zur Aussenverfassung. In: Ehrenzeller B et al (eds) Die schweizerische Bundesverfassung, St. Galler Kommentar, 3rd edn. Dike Zurich, St. Gallen, pp 1096–1113
Lanz M (2020) Bundesversammlung und Aussenpolitik, Möglichkeiten und Grenzen der parlamentarischen Mitwirkung. Dike, Zurich, St. Gallen
Lehne J (2023) Art. 101. In: Ehrenzeller B et al (eds) Die schweizerische Bundesverfassung, St. Galler Kommentar, 4th edn. Dike Zurich, St. Gallen, pp 2816–2838
Lienhard A, Zielniewicz A (2012) Zum Anwendungsbereich des bundesrätlichen Notrechts. ZBl 113:111–142
Mohler M, Müller RP (2023) Art. 107. In: Ehrenzeller B et al (eds) Die schweizerische Bundesverfassung, St. Galler Kommentar, 4th edn. Dike Zurich, St. Gallen, pp 2906–2933
Müller M, Jenni C (2010) Notrecht - ... abermals zur polizeilichen Generalklausel. Sicherheit & Recht 2010(2):101–109
Petrig A (2024) Die Vereinbarkeit von Sanktionen mit der Schweizer Neutralität. ZSR 143 (I):413–440
Petrig A, Sinz M (2024) Der Anwendungsbereich des Bundesgesetzes über die Durchsetzung von internationalen Sanktionen. SRIEL 2024(3):341–386
Portmann R, Frei C (2023) Vorbemerkungen zur Aussenverfassung. In: Ehrenzeller B et al (eds) Die schweizerische Bundesverfassung, St. Galler Kommentar, 4th edn. Dike Zurich, St. Gallen, pp 1807–1825
Reich J (2011) Grundsatz der Wirtschaftsfreiheit: Evolution und Dogmatik von Art. 94 Abs. 1 und 4 der Bundesverfassung der Schweizerischen Eidgenossenschaft vom 18. April 1999. Dike, Zurich, St. Gallen
Rhinow R et al (2011) Öffentliches Wirtschaftsrecht, 2nd edn. Helbing Lichtenhahn, Basel
Richli P (2007) Grundriss des schweizerischen Wirtschaftsverfassungsrechts. Stämpfli, Bern
Ricklin A (1991) Die dauernde Neutralität der Schweiz. Institut für Politikwissenschaft der Hochschule St. Gallen, St. Gallen
Sassòli M (2021) Die schweizerische Neutralität und der Fall Crypto AG. SRIEL 2021(4):523–540

Saxer U, Brunner F (2023) Art. 185. In: Ehrenzeller B et al (eds) Die schweizerische Bundesverfassung, St. Galler Kommentar, 4th edn. Dike Zurich, St. Gallen, pp 4323–4381
Schaller A (1987) Schweizer Neutralität im West-Ost-Handel: Das Hotz-Linder-Agreement vom 23. Juli 1951, Haupt, Bern/Stuttgart
Schindler D (1938) Die schweizerische Neutralität 1920–1938. ZaöRV 8:413–444
Schürmann L (1994) Wirtschaftsverwaltungsrecht, 3rd edn. Stämpfli, Bern
Vallender K et al (2006) Wirtschaftsfreiheit und begrenzte Staatsverantwortung, 4th edn. Stämpfli, Bern
Villiger ME (2023) Handbuch der schweizerischen Neutralität. Schulthess, Zurich
Wegmüller C, Schmidiger T (2022) Vielfältige Handelspartner für die Schweiz. Die Volkswirtschaft, November 23
Winistörfer MM (2021) Die Wirtschaftsfreiheit als Grundlage der Wirtschaftsverfassung: Grundrecht und Grundsatz im Lichte der Verfassungsdogmatik und der ökonomischen Theorie. Schulthess, Zurich
Winistörfer MM (2022) Der Grundsatz der Wirtschaftsfreiheit als Postulat für eine regelgebundene Wirtschaftspolitik. Ex/Ante 2022(1):29–38
World Trade Organization (WTO) (2003) World Trade Statistical Review 2023. WTO, Geneva
Wyss O (2018) Exportkontrollen strategischer Güter. Sicherheit & Recht 2018(3):195–207
Ziegler AR (2019) Der völkerrechtliche Status der Schweiz: Verträge, Schiedssprüche, Urteile und Erklärungen zur Sicherung der (territorialen) Souveränität (und der Neutralität) der Schweizerischen Eidgenossenschaft. SRIEL 2019(4):549–579

Federal Council Documents

FDFA (2013) Report on Commodities = Grundlagenbericht Rohstoffe, Bericht der interdepartementalen Plattform an den Bundesrat vom 27. März 2013
Federal Council (1919) Message on Switzerland joining the League of Nations = Botschaft des Bundesrates an die Bundesversammlung betreffend die Frage des Beitrittes der Schweiz zum Völkerbund vom 4. August 1919, BBl 1919 IV 541–680
Federal Council (1920) Message on Switzerland joining the League of Nations = Zusatzbotschaft des Bundesrates au die Bundesversammlung betreffend die Frage des Beitritts der Schweiz zum Völkerbund vom 17. Februar 1920, Bundesblatt 1920 I 334–363
Federal Council (1935) Report on the Italo-Abyssinian War = Bericht des Bundesrates an die Bundesversammlung betreffend die Anwendung des Artikels 16 des Völkerbundspaktes auf den italienisch-abessinischen Konflikt vom 2. Dezember 1935, BBl 1935 II 921–972
Federal Council (1938) Report on Neutrality = Bericht des Bundesrates an die Bundesversammlung über die Neutralität der Schweiz im Völkerbund vom 3. Juni 1938, BBl 1938 I 840–852
Federal Council (1990) Report on Security policy = Schweizerische Sicherheitspolitik im Wandel, Bericht 90 über die Sicherheitspolitik der Schweiz vom 1. Oktober 1990, BBI 1990 III 847–904
Federal Council (1993) White Paper on Neutrality = White Paper on Neutrality, Annex tot he Report on Swiss Foreign Policy for the Nineties of 29 November 1993 (Bericht über die Aussenpolitik der Schweiz in den 90er Jahren, Anhang: Bericht zur Neutralität vom 29. November 1993, BBl 1994 I 153–242). https://www.eda.admin.ch/content/dam/eda/en/documents/aussenpolitik/voelkerrecht/bericht-neutralitaet-1993_EN.pdf
Federal Council (1995) Message on the GCA = Botschaft betreffend das Bundesgesetz über die Kontrolle zivil und militärisch verwendbarer Güter (Güterkontrollgesetz, GKG) vom 22. Februar 1995, BBl 1995 II 1301–1357
Federal Council (1996) Message on the new Federal Constitution = Botschaft über eine neue Bundesverfassung vom 20. November 1996, BBl 1997 I 1–642

Federal Council (2000) Message on the EmbA = Botschaft zum Bundesgesetz über die Durchsetzung von internationalen Sanktionen (Embargogesetz, EmbG) vom 20. Dezember 2000, BBl 2001 1433–1465

Federal Council (2007) Report on Neutrality = Aussenpolitischer Bericht, Juni 2007, Anhang I: Neutralität vom 15. Juni 2007, BBl 2007 5557–5564

Federal Council (2008) Message on Financial stability = Botschaft zu einem Massnahmenpaket zur Stärkung des schweizerischen Finanzsystems vom 5. November 2008, BBl 2008 8943–9002

Federal Council (2013) Message PSSA = Botschaft zum Bundesgesetz über die im Ausland erbrachten privaten Sicherheitsdienstleistungen vom 23. Januar 2013, BBl 2013 1745–1826

Federal Council (2021) Message on the WMA = Botschaft zur Volksinitiative "Gegen Waffenexporte in Bürgerkriegsländer (Korrektur-Initiative)" und zum indirekten Gegenvorschlag (Änderung des Kriegsmaterialgesetzes) vom 5. März 2021, BBl 2021 623

Federal Council (2022) Report in response to Postulate 22.3385 = Klarheit und Orientierung in der Neutralitätspolitik. Bericht des Bundesrates in Erfüllung des Postulates 22.3385, Aussenpolitische Kommission SR, 11.04.2022

Economic Administrative Law and Socio-Economic Constitution in the Era of Globalization: Focusing on Korean Case

Kyung-Won Chang

Contents

Abstract In this chapter, the main content is to examine the specific meaning of Article 6 Paragraph 1 of the Constitution of Republic of Korea through the case of Korea concerning Economic Administrative Law and Socio-Economic Constitution in the Era of Globalization. The ruling covered in this chapter is the first case in which the Korean Supreme Court invalidated a domestic law based on a treaty and is a progressive ruling that is unprecedented in Korea. Even though Article 107 Paragraph 2 of the Korean Constitution provides for specific norm control, this case is a lawsuit confirming the invalidity of an ordinance under Article 107 Paragraph 3 of the Local Autonomy Act, which has the nature of abstract norm control, and is a matter of the relationship between domestic law and international law, especially the WTO Agreement. It raises important issues not only in academia but also in the judiciary regarding the issue of self-execution or direct applicability. In particular,

K.-W. Chang (✉)
University of Seoul Law School, Seoul, South Korea
e-mail: jang0503@uos.ac.kr

S. Hindelang et al. (eds.), *YSEC Yearbook of Socio-Economic Constitutions 2024,* YSEC Yearbook of Socio-Economic Constitutions (2025) 2024: 171–200, https://doi.org/10.1007/16495_2024_76, Published online: 23 January 2025

the judgment on the self-execution or direct applicability of Article 3 of GATT on the principle of national treatment, one of the most important provisions of the WTO Agreement, was made for the first time in this case. The legal principles presented in this case can be used not only in agreements between countries or in international treaties, but also in the discourse on economic integration around the world that will be discussed in the future. At this stage, it is difficult to talk about complete globalization of economic administrative law. However, international joint efforts to realize the rule of law in each country will become the cornerstone of the future globalization of economic activities and economic administrative law.

1 Introduction

Today, the term Glocalization (Globalization + Localization) is frequently used. In other words, we live in a rapidly changing environment where globalization is promoted on the one hand and localization is accelerated on the other. The world can now be said to be a global village, and international human and material exchanges are becoming very active.

In this situation, countries around the world are faced with a situation where they cannot rely solely on their own laws to regulate domestic economic activities. Norms created for exchange or cooperation between countries or activities at the level of international organizations require each country to comply with them. Currently, the rapidly progressing FTA negotiations between countries and the economic community agreements resulting from economic blocs not only have international legal effect between countries, but also require the citizens of each country to comply with them. For example, the WTO system, which was promoted at a global level in the past, can be said to be a multilaterally agreed upon international order that goes beyond national legal orders. In addition, in the case of FTA, as a bilaterally agreed upon inter-state order, it is a very important issue how to establish a relationship with each country's own national legal order.

According to the Korean Constitution, generally approved international laws and treaties have the same effect as Korean law.[1] International treaties sometimes contain restrictions on the fundamental rights of Korean citizens. Additionally, Article 60 Paragraph 1 of the Korean Constitution sets out the types of treaties that require the consent of the National Assembly.[2] In the case of these treaties, if the consent of

[1]Constitution of The Republic Of Korea (CROK) Article 6 (1) Treaties duly concluded and promulgated under the Constitution and the generally recognized rules of international law shall have the same effect as the domestic laws of the Republic of Korea.

[2]CROK Article 60 (1) The National Assembly shall have the right to consent to the conclusion and ratification of treaties pertaining to mutual assistance or mutual security; treaties concerning important international organizations; treaties of friendship, trade and navigation; treaties pertaining

the National Assembly is obtained, they are deemed to have equal effect as Korean law.

Today, international treaties are increasingly correlated with individual economic activities. Accordingly, the method of regulation under economic administrative law is changing in Korea, and the possibility that international treaties will become the subject of adjudication in constitutional trials or serve as trial norms in domestic trials is increasing.

In this regard, first, the status of international treaties in the domestic law system is an issue. If an international treaty has legal effect, it can only be the subject of unconstitutionality adjudication, but it is unlikely to become the standard for unconstitutionality adjudication. However, if an international treaty or inter-state agreement has a higher effect than the domestic constitution, it will act as a judicial norm in constitutional trials. And if an international treaty or inter-state agreement has the same effect as a law, a conflict may arise between the international treaty or inter-state agreement and domestic law. In the case of Korea, from the perspective of the Constitution, it is necessary to determine what domestic legal effect international treaties or inter-state agreements have, what their relationship is with the Constitution, and in what cases they can be directly applied by Korean courts.

In this chapter, the main content is to review the legislative precedents and interpretation theories of other countries regarding the specific meaning of Article 6 Paragraph 1 of the Korean Constitution through the case of Korea. When examining the specific meaning of Article 6 of the Korean Constitution, an approach from a comparative law perspective appears to be useful. To this end, this chapter deals with the meaning of legal integration through the example of European integration resulting from globalization and economic blocs. In addition, theories on the relationship between international law and domestic law and domestic enforcement of international legal norms are examined through examples from countries around the world. Furthermore, specifically focusing on the case of Korea, economic and administrative legal responses regarding how to establish the relationship between the legal order between countries and the legal order of their own country in the era of globalization will be examined. It also deals with how to interpret the meaning of the Korean Socio-Economic Constitution, which is the foundation of economic administrative law.

2 Economic Integration and Integration of Law

As the world's economy becomes a bloc through globalization and informatization, each country around the world is adapting its economic and administrative law regulations to suit this trend. A simple way to do this is to form blocs and establish

to any restriction in sovereignty; peace treaties; treaties which will burden the State or people with an important financial obligation; or treaties related to legislative matters.

a common legal system. Such an attempt was first made in Europe and continues to this day. There have been attempts to achieve economic integration in many continents, including East Asia.[3] However, these attempts were limited to forming an economic bloc and did not lead to integration at the legal level. It is almost impossible for East Asia or other continents to follow the same path of integration as the European Union, which was able to realize the integration experience after a long period of 70 years. European integration was achieved by breaking down the obsession of modern states and their borders.[4] On the other hand, countries on other continents are further solidifying their democracy and rule of law. The issue of integration must be resolved within each country's circumstances. A characteristic of European economic integration is the integration of the legal framework. These propositions are fundamental considerations along with discussions of community formation on other continents. Although the European Union initially began as an economic community, it would not have developed into the form of integration that continues and stably expands today, if the legal order for it had not been supported at the same time.[5] In this sense, the European Community is a legal community,[6] In this context, the EU legal order is a new autonomous legal order that applies before the laws of member states in conflict situations.[7]

This can be a good example for countries on other continents. This is because in the era of globalization, countries that advocate the rule of law today have similar legal systems. For countries that have not achieved legal integration like Europe, international agreements for international trade can become important legal resources in economic administrative law in each country. International agreements concluded by countries today often deal directly with issues related to individual rights and obligations. This is because the interests of countries often govern individual economic activities rather than ceremonial and political issues between countries as in the past. And when international agreements of this nature are concluded, domestic courts are inevitably faced with the question of whether to give direct effect to the provisions of such international agreements and whether to use such international agreements as a higher standard for judicial review of domestic law.

2.1 The Principle of "Direct Effect" in EU Law

The EU legal order was established through the preliminary ruling of Article 234 of the EC Treaty. The EU legal order refers to the supranational legal order formed

[3] Chang (2009), p. 306.

[4] Wieacker (1996), pp. 48–50; Chloros (1978), p. 11.

[5] Chang (2005), p. 172 f.

[6] Hallstein (1979), p. 341; Grunwald (1996), p. 43.

[7] EuGH, Rs. 6/64, Slg. 1964, 1251.

through the direct effect and supremacy of EU law in the relationship between EC law and the domestic laws of the Member States. The EU Treaties, including the three founding treaties of the EC, are more than just international treaties that set out the mutual obligations of the member states. The EU founding treaties set out the basic principles either in their own right or through legislative acts of the EU institutions. The EU has a set of rules that directly grant rights and impose obligations on the Member States and their natural and legal persons. The principles embodied in the Treaties establishing the EU have been continuously supplemented by new rules and implemented by various legislative acts of the EU institutions. And these contents were recognized by the EU courts through the ECJ ruling. The principle of direct effect is distinguished from direct applicability. Direct applicability means that EU law forms part of the domestic legal order of a member state without the domestic legislative procedures of the member state in implementing EU law. The direct effect of EU law means that individuals can directly file a suit in the domestic courts of a member state based on the provisions of the rights and obligations granted to them under EU law. While the direct application of EU law does not require additional legislative measures by the domestic institutions of the member states, the direct effect of EU law means that EU law has direct effect on individuals. In the Van Gend en Loos case, the ECJ held that a regulation must be clear and precise, leave no discretion to the authorities of the Member State, be unconditional, and require no further implementation by either the Community or the Member State to have direct effect.[8] This means that EU citizens can sue in domestic courts based on EU law. Through this, the EU protects the rights of EU citizens.

WTO law does not oblige EU member states to give direct effect to their domestic laws. It is up to the domestic courts to establish the specific relationship between WTO law and domestic law.[9] Since 1974, the ECJ has established that international treaties concluded by the Council under Article 218 of the Treaty on the Functioning of the European Union (TFEU) are an "integral part of the Community legal system".[10] Article 216, paragraph 2 of the Treaty on the Functioning of the European Union, which stipulates the principle of pacta sunt servanda, grants international treaties a higher status than secondary law. This applies to both GATT (1947) and WTO law.[11] However, the ECJ denies in principle the direct effect of GATT and WTO law within the EU legal order.[12]

[8]Case 26/62 NV Algemene Transport- en Expeditie Onderneming van Gend & Loos v Netherlands Inland Revenue Administration [1963) ECR 1; Case 104/81 Hauptzollamt Mainz v C.A. Kupferberg & Cie KG a.A.. [1982) BCR 3641, para. 23; Craig and de Búrca (2008), pp. 268, 273; Kuijper and Bronckers (2005), p. 1318.

[9]Cottier (2002), p. 103.

[10]Case 181/73 R. & V. Haegeman v Belgian State [1974] ECR 449, para. 5.

[11]Case C-61/94 Commission v Germany [1996) ECR 1-3989, para. 52; Tietje (2008), p. 58.

[12]Di Gianni and Antonini (2006), p. 777.

2.2 The "Direct Effect" of the WTO Agreement in Korea

According to Article 6, Paragraph 1 of the Constitution of Korea, treaties concluded and promulgated under the Constitution of Korea have the same effect as domestic law. Based on this, academic theories and case law recognize that Korea adopts a monistic stance in principle in the domestic application of international treaties. However, the Constitution is not included in "domestic law" here.[13] Therefore, the treaty is accepted as having legal effect.[14] In addition, when a treaty conflicts with a law of equal effect, general principles of legal interpretation, such as the principle of priority over new law or the principle of priority over special law, are applied.[15] Meanwhile, the Constitutional Court and the Supreme Court of Korea have recognized in principle that a treaty concluded and promulgated under the Constitution has domestic legal effect as a treaty itself, even in the absence of separate implementing legislation.[16] However, it seems that whether a treaty can be directly applied in domestic courts and whether a treaty can be directly invoked by individuals in domestic courts are treated as separate issues.[17]

Accordingly, the precedent handed down in 2005 by a Korean court led to new issues regarding the domestic legal effect of international law.[18] The ruling made by Korea's Supreme Court was about the direction in which each country's economic administrative law should move in the era of globalization. Korea's Supreme Court ruled that the 1994 General Agreement on Tariffs and Trade constituted part of WTO norms when local governments' school lunch ordinances mandating the use of Korean agricultural products in elementary and middle-high school lunches constituted part of WTO norms. 1994) was declared invalid on the grounds that it violated. This gave rise to controversy regarding the direct domestic effect of WTO law. The Korean Supreme Court judged that the relevant local government's ordinance violated WTO norms based on Article 6 Paragraph 1 of the Korean Constitution and invalidated its effect. This gave rise to much controversy regarding the domestic effect of international trade norms.

This ruling has a very important meaning as to whether it will be possible for individuals to file lawsuits in the future on the grounds that domestic law violates the WTO Agreement.

Below, with awareness of this problem, we examine the direct effect of WTO norms, focusing on the case of Korea. We also examine foreign practices related to

[13] As can be seen from the provision granting the same effect as domestic law only to "treaties concluded and promulgated under the Constitution of the Republic of Korea," the basis for the effect of a treaty is derived from the Constitution of the Republic of Korea.

[14] Constitutional Court of Korea 2001. 9. 27. 2000HunBa20.

[15] Sentenced on July 27, 2006 by the Seoul High Court of Korea, 2006-1.

[16] Constitutional Court of Korea, November 26, 1998, 97 Heon-Ba 65; 2000Heon-Ba20; Supreme Court of Korea, September 9, 2005, 2004Chu10.

[17] Supreme Court of Korea, March 26, 1999, Decision 96da55877.

[18] Supreme Court of Korea, September 9, 2005, Decision 2004Chu10.

the domestic effect of WTO norms. Through this, we identify the response patterns of economic administrative law in the era of globalization. Lastly, through the case of Korea, we examine the direction in which economic administrative law should move from the perspective of the socio-economic constitution.

3 Response of Economic Administrative Law to the Era of Globalization

3.1 Korean Local Government's Meal Ordinance Case

3.1.1 Details of the Case

Jeollabuk-do, a local government in Korea, enacted the 'Jeollabuk-do School Lunch Ordinance' for the purposes of improving students' health, understanding of traditional food culture, promoting consumption of Jeollabuk-do region agricultural products, and controlling supply and demand. According to this ordinance, excellent agricultural and livestock products produced in Jeollabuk-do, Korea and processed foods using them as ingredients are defined as 'excellent agricultural products', and excellent agricultural products produced in Jeollabuk-do are to be used preferentially for school meals. The Jeollabuk-do Superintendent of Education argued that this ordinance was invalid because it violated the national treatment principle of Article 3 of the '1994 General Agreement on Tariffs and Trade'.

In response, the Korean Supreme Court ruled that the General Agreement on Tariffs and Trade 1994 (GATT) and the Agreement on Government Procurement (AGP) are governed by Article 6 Paragraph 1 of the Korean Constitution. Since it has the same effect as domestic law, it was declared that ordinances enacted by local governments have no effect if they violate them. In other words, this ordinance, which contains provisions to prioritize the use of excellent agricultural products produced by local governments and processed foods using them as ingredients for school meals in elementary and middle-high schools in Korean local governments, stipulates the principle of national treatment. It is said to be ineffective because it violates GATT.

3.1.2 Issue of the Case

According to Article 117 Paragraph 1 of the Korean Constitution and Article 15 of the Korean Local Autonomy Act, ordinances of Korean local governments must be enacted within the scope of Korean law. If a local government's ordinance violates a higher law, it is illegal and invalid. In this case, the question was whether the WTO Agreement (GATT) became a superior law to the Ordinance. In other words, if the WTO Agreement is a treaty stipulated in Article 6 Paragraph 1 of the Korean

Constitution, the question arises as to whether the Korean courts must follow the WTO Agreement as a judicial norm according to this provision.

3.1.3 Possibility of Direct Application of the WTO Agreement to Judicial Norms in Korea

3.1.3.1 Issues of Direct Applicability and Direct Effect of Treaty and Article 6 Paragraph 1 of the Korean Constitution

Interpretation of Article 6 Paragraph 1 of the Korean Constitution

Article 6 Paragraph 1 of the Korean Constitution stipulates that "treaties concluded and promulgated under the Constitution and generally recognized international laws have the same effect as domestic law." Regarding the relationship between international law and domestic law, there is a conflict between dualism, which sees the two as belonging to separate legal systems, and monism, which sees them as belonging to the same legal system.[19] The majority view evaluates that Article 6 Paragraph 1 of the Korean Constitution is based on monism.[20] Korea's Supreme Court and Constitutional Court also take the same position.[21]

Theories

If we consider that Article 6 Paragraph 1 of the Korean Constitution adopts the monism that treaties that have been legally concluded and promulgated become domestic law without special modification procedures, the question arises as to whether direct applicability and direct effect should necessarily be recognized for such treaties. If monism and dualism are seen as criteria for determining direct applicability, international norms can be accepted as being directly applied without implementing laws.[22] In relation to this, Article 6 Paragraph 1 of the Korean Constitution adopts a monistic position regarding the domestic effect of treaties, and by this provision the treaty has been incorporated into domestic law, and furthermore, by viewing the treaty as having the same status as law, the direct effect. It is a view that acknowledges direct applicability.[23] On the contrary, there are conflicting views that this constitutional provision only acknowledges that it has been incorporated into Korean law through the conclusion and promulgation of a

[19] Noh (2022), p. 65.

[20] Kwon (2004), p. 174.

[21] Korea Supreme Court Decision 2002Da32523 Decided October 22, 2002; Korea Constitutional Court decision 97HunBa22, Decided July 6, 1998.

[22] Kim (2005b), p. 316.

[23] Kwon (2004), p. 178.

treaty, and whether it recognizes its direct effect or direct applicability in Korea is a separate issue.[24]

Under what conditions can a treaty concluded through due process be directly applied by the domestic law enforcement agencies, the executive and the judiciary? When an international treaty is concluded and promulgated, it has the same effect as domestic law without the need for any special legislative measures under domestic law. You can first think about whether it will work or not. Under the monistic legal system, which understands the relationship between international law and domestic law within a unified legal order, treaties are accepted under domestic law without requiring a conversion law into domestic law, while dualism starts from the premise of recognizing the autonomy of international law and domestic law respectively. This is because, under the (Dualism) legal system, it is accepted in the domestic legal order only after the conclusion of a treaty and the consent law, that is, the conversion of the treaty.

However, this conflict between monism and dualism has now been relativized, and not only is there no country where it is applied in its original form, but it is generally believed that its direct application must be judged through separate standards. In other words, the issue of whether a treaty is directly applied by domestic law enforcement agencies, that is, whether it has self-executing effects, cannot be distinguished based on monistic and dualistic systems and must be judged differently depending on the specific contents of the treaty. In other words, the intention of the contracting state regarding whether direct application is intended is the most important, and whether the treaty has an executive nature must be comprehensively judged on the nature of the treaty, the degree of specificity, and whether legal reservations by the state are specified. And as a result, a treaty that does not have self-enforcement power binds the relationship between states cannot be used as a judicial norm to force the execution of the executive branch within the domestic legal system.[25]

The Stance of Precedents of Korea

The Korean Supreme Court's position is that the treaty was incorporated into Korean law in accordance with the provisions of Article 6 Paragraph 1 of the Korean Constitution regarding the domestic effect of the treaty and interprets the treaty as having the same status as Korean law. As such, the general view is that the position of Korean courts regarding the interpretation of Article 6 Paragraph 1 of the Constitution is that treaties concluded and promulgated under the Constitution are consistently viewed as having the same effect under Korean law, and direct applicability are recognized.[26]

---

[24] Huh (2001), p. 171.

[25] Kim (2005b), p. 317.

[26] Constitutional Court of Korea, September 27, 2001, decision 2000HunBa20; Supreme Court of Korea, July 22, 2004, 2001Da58269.

Comparative Review

WTO members, including Korea, must ensure that their laws, regulations, and administrative procedures are consistent with the agreements annexed to the WTO Establishment Agreement. Therefore, in principle, domestic laws and regulations related to WTO norms of WTO member countries should be harmonized with the relevant WTO norms. However, in the process of implementing the WTO Agreement within member countries, there may be cases where certain domestic laws and regulations do not conform to relevant WTO norms. WTO member countries may adopt laws that are inconsistent with WTO norms or apply their own laws in a manner that is inconsistent with WTO norms for the purpose of protecting specific domestic industries exposed to competition. Alternatively, the domestic courts of member countries may make various interpretations in the interpretation of domestic laws related to WTO norms. Countries around the world appear to be taking the following stance on this:

United States: Denial of Self-Execution of WTO Agreement

Article VI, Section 2 of the United States Constitution states, "This Constitution, or any law of the United States made in pursuance of this Constitution, or any treaty made or hereafter concluded under the authority of the United States shall be the supreme law of the land." It stipulates that "the judges of each state are bound by the laws of that state, even if there are provisions to the contrary in the constitution or laws of that state."[27] Although this provision appears to adopt a monistic view of treaties, courts in the United States divide treaty provisions into self-executing treaty provisions and non-self-executing treaty provisions. It is divided into the doctrine of incorporation or adoption is applied to the former, and the theory of transformation is applied to the latter.[28] As a result, a 'treaty provision', if it is self-enforcing, can become one of the highest laws of the United States without the aid of implementing legislation. On the other hand, in the case of non-self-enforcing treaty provisions, they must undergo legislative transformation to become U.S. law, and until then, they are not considered legal binding on U.S. citizens or U.S. courts.

In particular, the United States treated the WTO agreement as an executive agreement rather than a treaty and enacted the Uruguay Round Agreement Act as a legislative measure to implement this agreement in domestic law. This law declared that any WTO agreement that conflicted with U.S. domestic law had no effect. It also stipulates that no one other than the U.S. central government may claim the WTO Agreement as a claim or use it as a defence in a lawsuit, and that the validity of the actions or omissions of the government and government agencies may

[27] Paust (1988), pp. 760–763.

[28] Ibid., pp. 765–770.

not be contested on the grounds that they violate the WTO Agreement.[29] In other words, the possibility of individuals directly invoking it through domestic legal procedures was explicitly excluded.

EU: Denial of Direct Effect of WTO Agreement

In the case of the European Communities ("EC"), on December 22, 1994, the EC Council denied the direct effect of the WTO Agreement, stating that the WTO Agreement cannot be directly invoked in the courts of the EC and member countries due to its nature.[30] This decision of the EC Council can be said to be a reciprocal response to the United States' denial of self-execution of the WTO Agreement and individual's right to action.

Following the decisions of the EC Council, the European Court of Justice ("ECJ") consistently denied the direct effect of not only the WTO Agreement but also the rulings of the WTO Dispute Settlement Body in the following three cases. First, in 1999, Portuguese Republic v. the Council case, the issue of direct applicability of the WTO Agreement was addressed. The issue in this case was whether an EC member state (Portugal) could invoke the WTO Agreement at the ECJ when contesting the legality of the EC Council's decision. In this case, it was decided that the WTO Agreement could not be invoked in determining the legality of the EC Board's actions.[31]

Next, in the Biret case in 2003 and the van Parys case in 2005, when an individual of a member country suffered financial damage due to a member country's failure to implement the decision of the WTO Dispute Settlement Body, the individual concerned claimed damages by invoking the decision of the WTO Dispute Settlement Body.[32] Whether a lawsuit can be brought to a member state's court was dealt with as a preliminary ruling. In both cases, the ECJ ruled that individuals cannot file lawsuits in the domestic courts of member states by invoking not only the WTO Agreement but also the rulings of the WTO Dispute Settlement Body.[33]

As above, the ECJ has consistently denied the direct applicability and direct effect of not only the WTO Agreement but also the final ruling of the WTO Dispute Settlement Organization in a series of cases. As mentioned above, the ECJ's negative attitude toward the direct applicability and direct effect of the WTO Agreement in general litigation cases clearly shows that the ECJ itself does not want to weaken the EC's negotiating power in international trade issues.

---

[29] Urguay Round Agreement (1994), Act 19 USC, s 3512 (b((2)(A).

[30] Council Decision 94/800/EC of 22 December 1994.

[31] Case C-149/96 Portugal vs. Council [1999] ECR I-8395, paras. 44–45; Case T-174/00 Biret International SA vs. Council of the European Union [2002] ECR ii-17, para. 23.

[32] Case C-377/02 *Van Parys v Belgische Interventie- en Restitutiebureau*, Judgment of 1 March 2005, para. 54.

[33] Chung (2006), p. 137.

Japan: Denial of the Direct Effect of GATT 1947

Article 98 Paragraph 2 of the Japanese Constitution stipulates that "Treaties concluded by Japan and established international laws must be faithfully observed." This provision appears to adopt monism in the relationship between treaties and domestic law.

In the 1984 Kyoto Necktie Case, the issue of the direct effect of the 1947 GATT was addressed. In this case, the Kyoto District Court, the court of first instance, decided that despite Article 98 Paragraph 2 of the Japanese Constitution, the 1947 GATT had no direct effect in Japanese domestic law.[34] The plaintiff who lost in this case appealed to the Osaka High Court and the Supreme Court against the original trial decision, but the plaintiff's appeal was dismissed. This attitude of the Japanese judiciary appears to be the same as that of the United States and the EC regarding the self-execution or direct effect of GATT.[35]

China: Denial of Direct Applicability of WTO Agreement

China became the 143rd member of the WTO on December 11, 2001. There are no provisions in the Chinese Constitution regarding the domestic effect of the WTO Treaty. Therefore, whether the direct applicability or direct effect of this treaty is recognized does not constitute a constitutional issue in China. However, in practice, the direct applicability of this treaty is denied in principle. Meanwhile, Article 142 of the 1986 Chinese Civil Law General Rules and Article 189 of the Chinese Civil Procedure Law stipulate that civil affairs treaties concluded by China have priority over domestic laws that conflict with it.[36] However, it is difficult to view the WTO agreement as a civil affairs treaty.

Due to these circumstances, in China, there is a conflict between the theory that the direct applicability of the WTO agreement is recognized and the theory that it is not recognized. However, when China joined the WTO in 2001, the Chinese government pledged to comply with the WTO agreement through 'revision of the country's current laws and new legislation.' And in the same year, Xiaoyang, President and Chief Justice of the Supreme People's Court of China, emphasized China's sovereignty and the dignity of domestic law in the relationship between the WTO Agreement and Chinese domestic law, and called for the 'transformation' of the treaty into domestic law. It was explicitly mentioned. It appears that the Chinese judiciary is, in principle, denying the self-execution or direct effect of the WTO agreement. Moreover, in 2002, Zhao Jianming, Vice President of the Supreme People's Court of China, said that the WTO Agreement stipulates the rights and obligations of member countries, not individuals. Considering these circumstances

[34] Mitsuo et al. (2003), p. 108.

[35] Iwasawa (1997), pp. 156–157.

[36] Lim and Chunn (2020), pp. 10–11.

comprehensively, China appears to deny the direct applicability and direct effect of the WTO Agreement in general litigation cases.[37]

Conclusion

Looking at the practices of countries around the world as above, even if a country adopts monism in the relationship between international law and domestic law, it does not necessarily recognize direct applicability and direct effect. On the contrary, just because a country adopts dualism does not mean that it completely denies it.[38] For example, Article 6 Paragraph 2 of the U.S. Constitution adopts monism like the Korean Constitution, but actual practice is divided into self-executing treaties and non-self-executing treaties. Article 98 Paragraph 2 of the Japanese Constitution, which is evaluated as adopting the principle of incorporation, also has the problem of distinguishing between self-executing treaties and non-self-executing treaties. Even in Britain, which adopts a strict dualism, treaties on the conduct of war or territorial cession, for example, are self-enforceable even without implementing legislation.[39] Considering these national practices, it is believed that theoretical discussions regarding monism or dualism in the relationship between international law and domestic law do not actually have a decisive influence on determining the domestic effect of international treaties.

3.1.3.2 Whether or Not the WTO Agreement Is Directly Applicable in This Case

The Stance of Precedent of Korea

According to Korean law, the GATT and WTO Agreements are treaties concluded under Article 6, Paragraph 1 of the Constitution, and therefore have the same status as domestic law without any special implementation legislation in accordance with the provisions of the Constitution. Korean courts recognize that treaties concluded with the consent of the National Assembly are directly applicable,[40] and therefore, GATT and WTO Agreements also have the same effect as domestic law. Korea enacted the 'Special Act on the Implementation of the World Trade Organization Agreement' as a law on the implementation of the WTO Agreement.[41] However, it does clarify the government's authority to enforce the agreement or provide for countermeasures against unexpected damage arising from the performance of the

[37] Ju (2005), pp. 37–38.

[38] Kim (2015), pp. 12–16.

[39] Ju (2005), p. 31.

[40] Seoul High Court of Korea, July 27, 2006, 2006To1; Constitutional Court of Korea, November 26, 1998, 97Hunba 65; 2000Hunba20.

[41] Korea Special Act on the Implementation of the World Trade Organization Agreement, Act No. 8681, December 14, 2007.

agreement's obligations.[42] In other words, this law only plays a limited role in supporting and assisting the implementation of the WTO agreement.

Meanwhile, in the case of 'Confirmation of the Invalidity of the Re-Decision on the Jeollabuk-do School Lunch Ordinance' regarding the domestic application of the WTO agreement in Korea, the Supreme Court of Korea ruled that the WTO agreement and its subsidiary agreements are treaties concluded under Article 6, Paragraph 1 of the Constitution and have the same effect as domestic laws.[43] Accordingly, GATT provisions are directly applied domestically. This ordinance is a subordinate law of GATT with the same effect as domestic law, and is in violation of the principle of national treatment stipulated in Article III:1 of GATT, so it is ruled out.[44] However, in a ruling on a case challenging the cancellation of the Korean government's anti-dumping duty imposition, the Korean Supreme Court did not recognize the direct effect of the WTO agreement.[45]

The contents of the ruling handed down by the Supreme Court of Korea [Confirmation of Invalidity of the Re-deliberation of the Jeollabuk-do School Lunch Ordinance] are as follows:

> [1]. The General Agreement on Tariffs and Trade 1994 (GATT) is a subsidiary agreement (multilateral trade agreement) of the Marrakesh Agreement Establishing the World Trade Organization (WTO) (Treaty No. 1265), which was approved by the National Assembly of Korea on December 16, 1994, ratified by the President on the 23rd of the same month, promulgated on the 30th of the same month, and entered into force on January 1, 1995. 'The Agreement on Government Procurement (AGP) is a treaty (Treaty No. 1363, Plurilateral Trade Agreement) that was promulgated and implemented on January 3, 1997 after obtaining the consent of the National Assembly on December 16, 1994. It has the same effect as domestic laws of Korea according to Article 6, Paragraph 1 of the Constitution. Therefore, if an ordinance enacted by a local government in Korea violates GATT or AGP, it is invalid.
>
> [2]. The ordinance of a local government in Korea that provides for the preferential use of excellent agricultural, livestock, and livestock products and processed foods (excellent agricultural products) produced by the local government for school meals provided at elementary, middle, and high schools in the local government and for selecting those who use such excellent agricultural products and supporting a portion of the food ingredients or food ingredient purchase costs is invalid because it violates the 'General Agreement on Tariffs and Trade 1994' that stipulates the principle of national treatment.

Since this ruling recognized the direct applicability and direct effect of the WTO Agreement, there is a view that private parties or foreign companies can claim violations of WTO norms. On the other hand, since this case was not filed by an

---

[42] Articles 3, 7, 8, 9, 11 and 12 of the Special Act on the Implementation of the World Trade Organization Agreement of Korea.

[43] Supreme Court of Korea, September 9, 2005, Decision 2004Chu10.

[44] The Supreme Court of Korea ruled that the content of the ordinance stipulating support for excellent agricultural products in Jeollabuk-do violated the principle of national treatment because it treated imported products unfavorably in order to protect similar domestic products under domestic laws, regulations, and requirements.

[45] Supreme Court of Korea, January 30, 2009, Decision 2008du17936.

individual, there is a different view that it cannot be seen as a recognition of direct effect, but only a recognition of direct applicability. Anyway, there is a consensus in Korea in that this precedent recognizes the direct applicability of the WTO Agreement.

Theories

In particular, regarding the 'scope' of direct application, there is a view that, respecting the purpose of the ruling, the WTO Agreement can be applied directly as an exception as an obligation to comply with the WTO Agreement borne by the state when it is an abstract normative control.[46] On the other hand, the recognition of the possibility of direct application does not depend on the relationship between upper-level and lower-level legislation, and the view that advocates direct application is for the guarantee of individual economic rights. In that view, abstract normative control is not related to concrete normative control. There is a view that the direct applicability of the WTO Agreement should be denied even in abstract normative control, in that there is less possibility to admit direct applicability.[47]

Even before this ruling was made, there was a view that it was desirable to deny direct applicability and direct effect to the WTO agreement.[48] And in this case of Korea, there is a view that direct applicability of the WTO agreement is possible in principle.[49] In addition, there are also other views that the court should decide on the direct applicability of the treaty by considering the purpose, content, and form of the treaty.[50]

Review

In fact, the WTO Special Implementation Act makes no mention of direct applicability or direct effect. In addition, considering the nature, purpose, and purpose of the WTO Agreement, it is difficult to find legal grounds that the direct applicability and direct effect of the WTO Agreement should be recognized.

Considering from a formal logical level, Article 6 Paragraph 1 of the Korean Constitution adopts monism, and the direct applicability and recognition of direct effect of a treaty ultimately depend on the judgment of the judiciary, so the Supreme Court not only controls abstract norms but also handles general litigation cases. Recognizing the direct applicability and direct effect of the WTO Agreement does not cause any constitutional problems. When it comes to the principle of reciprocity, which is one of the basic principles in international trade, Korea's major trading partners such as the United States, Europe, Japan, and China deny the direct

[46] Ibid., p. 31.

[47] Kim (2005b), p. 322.

[48] Kim (2005a), p. 188.

[49] Ju (2005), p. 41.

[50] Sung (1996), p. 19.

applicability and direct effect of the WTO Agreement in general litigation cases. Here exists a dilemma in Korea. But this case of Korea shows that, unlike other countries in the globalization trend, Korean courts are taking the lead in respecting agreements between countries.

3.2 Response of Economic Administrative Law to Globalization

Economic administrative law includes the laws and principles by which the government or administrative agencies regulate the economic activities of citizens. The purpose is to coordinate the relationship between national administration and people's economic activities and to lead to efficient and fair regulatory administration. The Economic Administrative law regulates the way administrative agencies exercise their authority, regulatory procedures, prevention of abuse of authority, and the rights and obligations of citizens, thereby playing an important role in maintaining social fairness and the rule of law.

Globalization has created an environment in which the legal systems of various countries can interact and conflict. It is important to harmonize international and national regulations. Through this, international treaties or international agreements must be harmonized with the legal order of member countries. Globalization requires transparency and accountability in national administration. It is necessary for the decision-making process of national and international organizations to be transparent and to actively provide information to citizens and stakeholders. This can secure public trust and further strengthen the rule of law. Advances in technology and digitalization have brought innovation to national administration. However, problems such as personal information protection and cyber security have also increased. These problems must be resolved through international standards and regulations, and technological advancements must be used to improve administrative efficiency. Cooperation between countries is essential here. To respond to international problems, cooperation between countries must be strengthened, and economic and administrative regulations and cooperation must be strengthened through international treaties and agreements. Globalization requires a mindset that respects and embraces diversity. We should create economic, administrative policies and laws that consider diverse cultures, languages, beliefs, etc., through which we will be able to maintain social stability and administrative efficiency at the same time. As for the direction of this change, it is important that economic administrative law and the rule of law respond to new environments and demands in a globalized world, while guaranteeing fundamental economic rights to citizens and achieving harmony between countries and international organizations.

In the globalized era, not only national legal systems but also the legal systems of international organizations have become important. The economic administrative laws of each country require regulation and cooperation at the international level as well. Therefore, we need to strengthen interaction with international organizations and find ways to harmonize legal systems at various levels. Economic administrative law must maintain a balance between efficiency and the rule of law. Globalization requires faster and more flexible responses, but this must not be done at the expense of the rule of law. In the flow of economic integration and globalization, the role of economic administrative law has become important in matters of conflict with domestic law due to the increase in cooperation between countries and international treaties. To respond to international conflicting problems, it is necessary to promote cooperation between countries and establish a legal basis for this. There may be instances where domestic trade policies conflict with international trade agreements. This may result in disputes with international trade organizations or other countries. If domestic administrative systems or laws are deemed to be contrary to democratic principles or the rule of law, they may be criticized internationally. The case of Korea discussed above shows that the domestic economic administrative legal issues are related and interact with the international community in a globalized world. In this situation, it is important to achieve harmony and balance between domestic economic administrative law and international law. Through this, international regulations and the country's internal circumstances will be harmonized, and national administration will be able to be trusted even in a globalized world.

However, in the face of globalization, Korean courts have other precedents regarding the GATT agreement in addition to the local government ordinance cases mentioned above.[51] The background of this incident is as follows. The Korean government imposed an anti-dumping tariff on a Korean importer, a tariff aimed at protecting the domestic industry. The company filed a lawsuit claiming that the imposition of anti-dumping duties violated the GATT agreement. In response, the Korean Supreme Court stated that the above agreement is an international agreement that establishes the relationship of rights and obligations between states, and in light of its contents and nature, the principle is that legal disputes related thereto shall be resolved by the WTO Dispute Settlement Body. It declared that the above agreement had no direct effect. In other words, it was decided that an individual cannot directly file a lawsuit in a domestic court seeking cancellation of a member government's anti-dumping imposition in a domestic court simply because the member government's anti-dumping imposition pursuant to the above agreement violates the WTO agreement.[52]

In other words, compared to previous precedents, the Supreme Court's position is that although the GATT Agreement has a certain effect domestically, it takes the form of an international agreement, and therefore individuals cannot make any claims to the country based on this. The imposition of tariffs to protect domestic products can be said to be part of a positive effort to secure the characteristics of member countries and national interests amid globalization, but in previous cases, the GATT agreement has the same effect as domestic law. It seems like a

[51] Supreme Court of Korea, January 30, 2009, Decision 2008Du17936.

[52] Ibid.

contradictory situation to rule that the ordinance is invalid and yet at the same time prevent the public from contesting the agreement domestically. Adopting a plan to protect its citizens while rejecting another plan that can protect its citizens in the form of a dispute is contradictory.

In the current situation, Korea is riding the trend of globalization, accepting global values as a member of the world, and accepting various exchanges and trade agreements. However, in practice, it cannot be said that international norms have been smoothly established without conflict with the existing Korean legal system. Therefore, Korea's economic administrative law and existing legal system must establish and harmonize a consistent stance on how to respond to globalization in the future. However, globalization is an atypical concept that is still in progress, and globalization and exchange with the international community are important to us. Therefore, although Korea's economic administrative law's response to globalization is still minimal, it will play a leading role in the world, if it develops and harmonizes the legal principles of the precedents mentioned above.

3.3 Conclusion

This ruling was the first case in which the Korean Supreme Court invalidated a domestic law because of a treaty. And it was a progressive ruling that is unprecedented in Korea. In the future, foreign companies will be able to implement lower-level laws and regulations, including presidential decrees, that are considered problematic from the perspective of the WTO Agreement. It was pointed out that there is a possibility of actively using Korean courts to invalidate government measures.

Even though Article 107 Paragraph 2 of the Korean Constitution provides for specific norm control, this case is a lawsuit confirming the invalidity of an ordinance under Article 107 Paragraph 3 of the Local Autonomy Act, which has the nature of abstract norm control, and is a matter of the relationship between domestic law and international law, especially the WTO Agreement. In relation to the issue of self-execution or direct applicability, important issues are being raised not only in academia but also in the judiciary. Even before the target ruling, the Supreme Court had made judgments on the self-enforcement or direct applicability of the treaty in several cases, especially self-execution of GATT Article 3 on the national treatment principle, one of the most important provisions in the WTO Agreement. The judgment on direct applicability was made for the first time in this case. In this respect, this ruling can be said to be a pioneering ruling regarding future domestic enforcement of the WTO Agreement by the Korean judiciary. Therefore, its importance and ripple effect are very large.[53]

Pursuant to Article 6 Paragraph 1 of the Korean Constitution, the Korean administration has the obligation to domestically implement the WTO Agreement.

[53] Ju (2005), pp. 22–23.

To faithfully comply with the WTO Agreement, the Korean government may file a lawsuit with the Supreme Court, if it determines that a local government's ordinance violates the WTO Agreement. In this case, the Korean Supreme Court should be seen as recognizing the self-execution of GATT Article 3 as an exception only in litigation to confirm the invalidity of ordinances with the nature of 'abstract norm control'. However, if the self-execution or direct effect of the WTO Agreement is an issue in general litigation cases in the future, it would be desirable to consider the principle of reciprocity in international commerce.

Today, as globalization progresses, there are cases where the actions of the executive branch are not bound only by the laws of Congress. There is a phenomenon in which specific standards for administrative legislation are delegated to international treaties and international cooperations or are further subject to the regulations of private international organizations. This phenomenon can be acknowledged from the perspective of the necessity of international cooperation and the efficiency of function performance. However, even here the values of rule of law and democracy cannot be abandoned. Unless international standards are established in the form of a treaty, there must be a basis for recognizing democratic legitimacy. In addition, the transparency of the standard establishment must be guaranteed, and it must be enacted in a way that does not completely exclude domestic administrative procedures.

The application of WTO norms in the unprecedented Korean Supreme Court ruling mentioned above shows the possibility that the function of the state as a political community will be formed biased in the process of globalization. However, globalization in the true sense is valuable only when it is realized not only with the globalization of economic administration, but also with the globalization of human rights, globalization of environmental protection, globalization that improves the quality of life, and globalization that respects cultural values and recognizes diversity. Until globalization in that sense is realized, the nation-state and its administration remain meaningful as a foundation for maintaining the balance of values. However, this emphasis on the nation-state does not mean excluding international cooperation externally and minimizing local autonomy internally. Nation-states must continue international cooperation under global governance based on legitimacy, and domestic local autonomy can control the tendency toward national uniformity by being recognized for its autonomy. This is because today we cannot live without acknowledging the multi-layered structure of human values, such as human rights, economic abundance, and the environment.

4 The Meaning of Socio-Economic Constitution in the Era of Globalization

The response of economic administrative law to the era of globalization is closely related to the economic constitution. This is because the constitution of a country is the highest level of law and serves to set the general direction and limits of economic administrative law. In this respect, clarifying the meaning of the economic order under the Korean Constitution is meaningful in suggesting the direction in which the Economic Administrative Law will move forward.

4.1 Korea's Socio-(Market)-Economic Constitutional Order

The economic order under the Korean Constitution basically guarantees the private property system (Article 23 of the Korean Constitution), freedom of choice of occupation (Article 15 of the Korean Constitution), and freedom of business activity in the area of economic life.[54] And it is based on the principle of private autonomy regarding economic activities.[55] It is also based on a free market economic order that respects free and fair competition.[56] In particular, the Korean Constitution stipulates the economy and economic order in Chapter 9, Articles 119 and below.

Article 119 Paragraph 1 of the Korean Constitution stipulates 'respect for the economic freedom and creativity of individuals and companies' as economic entities as the basic principle of the Korean economic order. And in Paragraph 2, the state is required to 'grow and stabilize the balanced national economy', 'maintain appropriate distribution of income', 'prevent market domination and abuse of economic power', and 'democratize the economy through harmony among economic entities'. It is defined for the purpose.[57] In order to achieve this

[54]The Korean Constitutional Court explained the freedom of business activities included in 'occupational freedom' in relation to Article 119 of the Korean Constitution. In other words, "Freedom of business activity is included in occupational freedom and means the freedom of the subject of occupational freedom to conduct business activities without interference or interference from the state in competition with other companies. This is in line with the purpose of Article 119 Paragraph 1 of the Constitution, which states that "the economic order of the Republic of Korea is based on respect for the economic freedom and creativity of individuals and companies."; Korea Constitutional Court decision 2002HunBa11, Decided September 29, 2005.

[55]Korea Constitutional Court decision 88HunGa13, Decided December 22, 1989; Korea Constitutional Court decision 2005HunBa96, Decided October 25, 2007; Korea Constitutional Court decision 2007HunBa39, Decided June 25, 2009; Korea Constitutional Court decision 2007HunBa135, Decided October 29, 2009. The Korean Constitutional Court explains the principle of private autonomy. In other words, the 'principle of private autonomy' is a basic principle derived from the principles of human self-determination and self-responsibility, and the formation of legal relationships is achieved through the will or actions of legal persons themselves, not through authority orders.: Korea Constitutional Court decision 2008HunBa87, Decided February 24, 2011.

[56]Kim (2001), p. 103; Korea Constitutional Court decision 88HunGa13, Decided December 22, 1989; Korea Constitutional Court decision 2008HunBa87, Decided February 24, 2011.

[57]The Korean Constitutional Court explains the meaning of 'democratization of the economy' as follows. The ideology of 'economic democratization through harmony among economic entities' stipulated in Article 119 Paragraph 2 of the Constitution is a national goal that can be pursued to form a just social order in the economic sphere and is a national goal that restricts the fundamental rights of individuals. It is a constitutional norm that justifies national actions.: Korea Constitutional Court decision 2001HunBa35, Decided November 27, 2003.

goal,[58] the government is actively granting the government a wide range of powers to regulate and adjust the economy.[59]

Although the Korean Constitution respects and guarantees the economic freedom and creativity of individuals and companies, the basic principle of economic order under the Constitution does not mean the pursuit of the so-called 'laissez-faire market economic order'.[60] In other words, the so-called 'laissez-faire market', which absolutely excludes all state intervention in the entire process of guaranteeing economic freedom protected by the Korean Constitution or forming and maintaining a free and fair economic order under the Constitution and is not restricted under any circumstances. It does not mean the pursuit of a 'completely autonomous competitive market economic order' between individual private economic entities either.[61] The Korean Constitutional Court also clearly states that various unintended economic contradictions and risks accompanying the free market economic order must be eliminated and improved. In other words, the Korean Constitutional Court emphasizes that human dignity and value must be guaranteed by overcoming the problems of capitalist society caused by absolute individualism and liberalism in the past and securing practical freedom and fairness.[62]

The current Korean Constitution clearly recognizes that the biggest economic risk and contradiction inherent in the market economic order is the emergence of market domination and monopoly through abuse of economic power. In particular, the market's ability to self-regulate against economic risks and contradictions is limited, and market freedom is limited due to the concentration of economic power and market dominance inherent in economic freedom.[63] Therefore, the formation and maintenance of a free and fair competitive order cannot be created by nature, so the

[58] Korea Constitutional Court decision 2001HunGa25, Decided July 24, 2003; Korea Constitutional Court decision 2002HunBa42, Decided July 15, 2004; Korea Constitutional Court decision 2003HunBa88, Decided December 22, 2005; Korea Constitutional Court decision 2007HunBa108, Decided September 24, 2009.

[59] Kim (2012), pp. 65–67: In particular, the Korean Constitutional Court explains the legislator's economic policy choices and policy judgments as follows: The legislator must take into account all circumstances, including the history of economic reality and prospects for the future, the economic and social costs required to achieve the goal, and the perception of the public or stakeholders regarding the economic problem in question, and make various measures as possible to ensure monopoly regulation and fair trade. Among the policies, you can choose the economic policy that you deem necessary. Such policy judgments and choices of legislators must be respected as an exercise of national regulatory authority regarding the economy, unless they can be seen as significantly lacking in rationality: Korea Constitutional Court decision 2001HunGa25, Decided July 24, 2003.

[60] Chong (2013), p. 227.

[61] Huh (2013), p. 168; Korea Constitutional Court decision 94HunMa113, Decided August 29, 1996.

[62] Constitutional Court of Korea, April 25, 1996, decision 92HunBa47.

[63] Constitutional Court of Korea, December 26, 1996, decision 96HunGa18.

formation and maintenance of a free and fair competitive order through the national legal order is continuously required.[64]

Article 119 of the Korean Constitution declares the guarantee of economic freedom for each individual economic entity as a basic principle, but also explicitly stipulates the basic national goals in the economic field that the state seeks to achieve through various economic policies and the constitutional tasks for this purpose.[65] This stipulates the constitutional basic principles regarding Korea's economic order,[66] the constitutional basis and purpose of state intervention to form and guarantee a free and fair economic order, and the state's responsibilities and tasks for the economy.[67]

First, the state guarantees the autonomous participation of economic entities in forming the economic order. Second, the state has an obligation to respect and guarantee individual economic freedom and fundamental economic rights, which set the limits of state action. Third, it defines the state's duties, responsibilities, and constitutional tasks for the overall development process of the national economy.[68] Subsequently, individual provisions (Articles 120 to 127) under Article 119 of the Korean Constitution present the basic direction and various specific tasks for state activities in the economic field. It grants the state the authority to actively realize this and pursue economic policies to ensure the smooth functioning of the constitutional economic order,[69] and its limits are also explicitly defined.[70]

4.2 The Socio-Economic Constitution as the Legal Basis for Economic Administrative Law

The Constitutional Court of Korea said, "The provisions of the Constitution on economic order help the 'fundamental economic rights' to guarantee the autonomous participation of individuals and society in the formation of the economic order

[64] Constitutional Court of Korea, December 26, 1996, decision 96HunGa18.

[65] Constitutional Court of Korea, July 24, 2004, decision 2001HunGa25.

[66] Constitutional Court of Korea, November 26, 2009, decision 2008HunMa711.

[67] Huh (2013), p. 168.

[68] Constitutional Court of Korea, November 27, 2003, decision 2001HunBa35; Constitutional Court of Korea, November 30, 2006, decision 2006HunMa489.

[69] For example, the Korean Constitutional Court explains the constitutional basis for national regulation and coordination regarding 'environment and economy' as follows: CROK Article 35 Paragraph 1 of the Korean Constitution…, Also, Article 119 Paragraph 2 of the Constitution…, Article 120 Paragraph 2 of the Constitution… It is stipulated that These provisions serve as a constitutional basis for national regulation and coordination of the environment and economy.: Constitutional Court of Korea, October 28, 2004, decision 99HunBa91; Constitutional Court of Korea, July 15, 2004, decision 2002HunBa42.

[70] Huh (2013), p. 169: Fundamental economic rights cannot be derived directly from the provisions of the 'Economy' chapter of the Constitution.

by setting limits on state actions, and state activities in the economic sphere. It consists of 'regulations on intervention and adjustment in the economy' (Article 119 et seq. of the Constitution) that presents basic directions and tasks and grants the state the authority to pursue active economic policies."[71] Therefore, the economic constitution not only guarantees the fundamental economic rights of individual economic entities based on the basic principles of the constitution, but also addresses the economic community tasks of promoting economic stability and development of the community as a whole and realizing economic justice, as well as the national tasks necessary to realize them. It can be understood as regulating roles, methods and even limits.

To guarantee fundamental economic rights, there is no choice but to limit the fundamental economic rights themselves. In light of the social relevance of the economy, especially the possibility of sharp conflict between economic interests and the need for harmony, and the request to realize economic community tasks, the possibility of broader restrictions on fundamental economic rights is recognized.[72] If the basic nature of the economic order under the Korean Constitution is seen as a socio market economic order, it is not simply that economic autonomy is guaranteed indefinitely and the state intervenes only in exceptional cases. Economic autonomy and state intervention are in a relationship in which they constrain and require each other at the same time.[73]

This socio market economic order is not an economic system according to some economic theory, a social phenomenon outside the norms, or a simple characterization of our economic constitution.[74] The socio-economic constitution can be said to be a norm that all members of the state and community must adhere to.[75] Therefore, state intervention that infringes on economic autonomy, and conversely, emphasis on economic autonomy (economic indulgence) that denies or neutralizes state intervention, can all be said to violate the socio market economic order.

Meanwhile, the Korean Constitutional Court rules as follows: The Korean Constitution provides for balanced growth and stability of the national economy, appropriate distribution of income, prevention of market domination and abuse of economic power, democratization of the economy through harmony among economic entities, and balanced regional economy in the chapter on the economy under Article 119 of the Constitution. By explicitly mentioning the national goals in the economic field, such as fostering the economy, protecting, and fostering small and medium-sized enterprises, and protecting consumers, the public interest that the state should achieve through economic policies is specified, and at the same time, the

[71] Constitutional Court of Korea, October 28, 2004, decision 99HunBa91.

[72] For more information on the discretion of economic legislation, its grounds and limitations, see below.

[73] In this respect, it is not appropriate to understand the relationship between Article 119 Paragraphs 1 and 2 of the Korean Constitution according to the 'principle-exception' theory.

[74] Han (2012), pp. 364–365.

[75] Choi (1998), p. 749.

restrictions on fundamental rights under Article 37 Paragraph 2 of the Constitution are specified. It embodies 'public welfare' in legal reservations for the benefit of the public.[76] Therefore, the ideology of 'economic democratization through harmony among economic entities' stipulated in Article 119 Paragraph 2 of the Korean Constitution is also a national goal that can be pursued to form a just social order in the economic sphere. It is a constitutional norm that justifies actions.[77]

Article 119 Paragraph 1 of the Korean Constitution ("The economic order of the Republic of Korea is based on respect for the economic freedom and creativity of individuals and companies") is the basic national goal in realizing the economic constitution and all state functions. Therefore, it is understood that Korea's economic order is specified in accordance with the constitutional standards or guidelines of Article 119 Paragraph 1. Conversely, violating economic freedom and creativity directly violates Article 119 Paragraph 1 of the Korean Constitution.[78] And in specifying Article 119 Paragraph 1, denying, or abandoning the goal under Paragraph 2 constitutes a violation of Paragraph 2. In other words, clause 2 can be a limitation of clause 1.

The state intervenes in the economy in accordance with the economic constitution, which is the highest legal order regarding the economy, and through this, has the obligation to realize the tasks set forth in the economic constitution. Therefore, the economic constitution provides the constitutional basis for economic administrative law. This economic constitution has as its supreme ideology the guarantee of economic life values, such as economic freedom and equality, as fundamental rights, and realizes this in accordance with the basic principles of the constitution, such as democracy, rule of law, and social state principles. And the various economic regulations in Chapter 9 of the Constitution are understood as the 'explicit economic constitution.'

The economic constitution may appear somewhat differently depending on the country's ideological foundation and economic reality, but it generally takes the form of a mixed economy. This is an economic constitutional requirement for a flexible response to economic reality. The Korean Constitution also shows the appearance of a mixed economy, and the nature of the Korean Economic Constitution is especially understood as a 'socio market economic order'. The socio market economic order can be said to be an economic order that is based on the guarantee of free economic activities, but at the same time, the understanding of the market economy changes depending on the social and national characteristics, and therefore requires a wide range of roles for the state.

Various economic regulations in Chapter 9, including Article 119 of the Korean Constitution, are constitutional goals regarding the national economy and have the character of national goal regulations or 'principles.' In other words, it is interpreted as having legal binding force on all state operations. Therefore, in principle,

[76] Constitutional Court of Korea, December 26, 1996, decision 96HunGa18.

[77] Constitutional Court of Korea, October 28, 2004, decision 99HunBa91.

[78] Constitutional Court of Korea, July 29, 1993, decision 89HunMa31.

constitutional economic regulations can become control norms, but the density of control can be relaxed depending on the limits of the separation of powers.

Guaranteeing the fundamental rights of economic freedom and equality is both the starting point and the limit of intervention under economic administrative law. Therefore, the state must ensure that individual economic entities can autonomously form their own economic lives and must not infringe on or take the lead in this. State economic intervention should in principle be supplementary. However, for the stability and soundness of the overall economy, exceptions to subsidiarity need to be recognized. The principle of subsidiarity also provides important constitutional limits to socio-state economic intervention.

According to the Korean Economic Constitution, the standards, guidelines, and directions for the formation of legal order regarding the economy include maintenance of the economic community, balanced growth and stability of the national economy, appropriate distribution of income, prevention of market domination and abuse of economic power, and democratization of the economy. It is a constitutional norm that presents. Therefore, it provides a constitutional basis for economic intervention, but at the same time, it also provides constitutional limits in a passive relationship that prohibits state action that violates or runs counter to this.

Broad discretion is granted to the state's intervention in the Economic Administrative law to carry out economic constitutional goals and tasks. Accordingly, the legislator of the Economic Administrative law has wide legislative discretion, and as a result, fundamental economic rights are likely to be broadly restricted. However, it can only be justified if it is consistent with the principle of proportionality under Article 37 Paragraph 2 of the Korean Constitution regarding restrictions on fundamental rights.

4.3 *Regulations and Fundamental Economic Rights Under the Economic Administrative Law*

An example of economic regulatory administration is the regulation of business activities by large retailers in Korea (hypermarket regulation). Korea's 'Distribution Industry Development Act' was revised in January 2012 and January 2013 to restrict business hours for large distribution companies, designate mandatory non-working days, and expand its scope. In other words, the goals sought to be achieved through the Distribution Industry Development Act are the establishment of a sound distribution order, the coexistence of large-scale distribution companies and small and medium-sized distribution companies, the revitalization of local commercial districts, and the protection of the health rights of workers in large-scale distribution companies. The contents of the regulations to realize this purpose are restrictions on business hours and designation of mandatory non-working days for large-scale and semi-large stores, which can be considered large-scale distribution companies.

Looking at the main contents of this law, in order to "establish a sound distribution order, workers' health rights, and the win-win development of large-scale stores, etc. and small and medium-sized distribution businesses, etc.," as stipulated by the relevant local government ordinance, the business hours of large distribution companies are changed to 0:00 a.m. Restrictions on business hours can be ordered from 1 to 8 a.m., and mandatory closure of business can be ordered from 1 to 2 days per month.[79]

The contents and meaning of this revision of the Distribution Industry Development Act are the contents of Article 119 Paragraph 2 of the Korean Constitution and the economic-related provisions thereunder, including preventing market domination and abuse of economic power, protecting, and fostering small and medium-sized businesses, fostering the local economy, and creating a balanced citizenry. It can be said to be the realization of economic growth and stability.

The Korean Distribution Industry Development Act attempted to realize these goals through support for the distribution industry and deregulation in the early stages of its enactment for the development of the distribution industry, establishment of a fair distribution order, and win-win development of large distribution companies and small and medium-sized distribution companies. However, currently, the abuse of economic power is intensifying as large distribution companies dominate the distribution market due to their strong economic power, distribution power, and capital power. This soon leads to the emergence of a monopoly by large distribution companies and a threat to the economic survival of small and medium-sized distribution companies. It has been done like that. In the end, a phenomenon that ran counter to the basic principles of economic order under the Korean Constitution occurred, and the amendment was made to strengthen regulations rather than deregulate the distribution industry.[80]

Economic activities that run counter to the free and fair economic order can be subject to constitutional restrictions. To regulate the abuse of market power and economic power that appears through the economic activities of large corporations, national regulation and coordination aimed at forming and maintaining a free and fair economic order is necessary. Relatively broad restrictions are possible on economic activities related to economically important public interests in relation to the economic activities of large corporations.

5 Conclusion

Korea has achieved rapid economic growth so far. However, behind this compressed growth, various problems in industrial society are being revealed. These problems are expressed today in the role of the state for economic democratization. Early constitutional states tried to overcome the feudal system and secure the prerequisites

[79] Reasons for revision of the Korea Distribution Industry Development Act.

[80] Constitutional Court of Korea, October 29, 1998, decision 97HunBa345; Constitutional Court of Korea, October 28, 2004, decision 99HunBa91.

to guarantee individual economic freedom and creativity. Representative examples included reorganization of the legal system, expansion of the education system to secure human resources, and securing physical infrastructure such as transportation, communication, and finance. In the twentieth century, the Constitution actively responded to the social and economic problems that emerged in industrial society.

Since 1948, the Korean Constitution has also recognized the importance of not only political democracy but also social and economic democracy and has prepared various constitutional provisions. On the other hand, the country worked hard to build human and material infrastructure for free economic activities, such as education and transportation, even in very poor circumstances. This became the basis for economic growth and political democratization.

At a time when concerns are growing about the polarization and entrenchment of socioeconomic structures, maintaining, and strengthening the public nature of social infrastructure such as education, housing, and mobility is the most basic task of the state. In constitutional discussions on economic order, an open and pragmatic approach is desirable, commensurate with the nature of the subject of discipline. Economic administrative law in the era of globalization also needs this open and practical approach.

As the world economy became a bloc through globalization and informatization, discussions on this issue in East Asia began officially in the late 2000s at the 'ASEAN plus Three'.[81] When discussing the integration issue of East Asia, East Asia has been called variously as East Asia, Northeast Asia, and Asia-Pacific. However, it was a discussion on the East Asian region focused on Korea, China, and Japan aside ASEAN. Academic efforts to group East Asia as a single unit of analysis have continued. However, it is almost impossible for East Asia to follow the same path as Europe, which achieved integration after a long period of 70 years. The integration issue of East Asia does not mean returning to the original European state like Europe. East Asian countries are in a situation where they are further strengthening their own democracy and rule of law. In this situation, this chapter intends to stimulate discussions on the legal system aspect as a basis for new integration

[81] The ASEAN+3 (APT) cooperation process began with an informal summit among the leaders of ASEAN, the Republic of Korea (ROK), China, and Japan as part of the Second ASEAN Informal Summit held in Malaysia in December 1997. The APT Summit was followed by the Joint Statement on East Asian Cooperation issued by the leaders at the Third APT Summit held in Manila, the Philippines in 1999. In this Joint Statement, the APT leaders resolved to strengthen and deepen East Asian cooperation, particularly at various levels and in various fields, including economic, social, political, and other areas. The Second Joint Statement on East Asian Cooperation, entitled "Building the Foundation for ASEAN+3 Cooperation," was adopted at the 11th APT Summit held in Singapore in 2007. This statement reaffirmed that the ASEAN+3 process would remain a key means for achieving the long-term goal of building an East Asian community with ASEAN as the driving force. At the 20th APT Commemorative Summit held in Manila, Philippines in November 2017, leaders adopted the Manila Declaration, pushing forward the implementation of the ASEAN Community Vision 2025 to lay the foundation for deeper regional integration in East Asia (https://aseanplusthree.asean.org/about-apt/history).

attempts in the era of globalization at the current stage, moving away from the political and economic aspects discussed so far.

From the perspective of economic administrative law, European integration has significant implications for us. A characteristic of European economic integration is the integration of the legal framework. This proposition is a basic consideration in economic cooperation between countries even in situations where it is not an economic community. If the effectiveness of agreements between countries cannot be maintained normatively, it is difficult for a country's economic activities to develop continuously in the era of globalization. In this sense, I believe that the Korean local government meal ordinance case presented in this chapter has international significance. Although it is the first ruling made in Korea, it can be said to be a progressive case that brings us one step closer to the era of globalization. The legal principles presented in this case can be used not only in agreements between countries or in international treaties, but also in the discourse on economic integration around the world that will be discussed in the future. This is because in the era of globalization, countries that advocate the rule of law today have similar legal systems. At this stage, it is difficult to talk about complete globalization of economic administrative law. However, our international joint efforts to realize the rule of law in each country will become the cornerstone of the future globalization of economic activities and economic administrative law.

References

Chang K-W (2005) Die Vergemeinschaftung des deutschen Wirtschaftsverwaltungsrecht. Köln/Berlin/München, S 172

Chang K-W (2009) Economic integration and integration of law. Adm Law J 24:306

Chloros (1978) Common law, civil law and socialist law: three leading systems of the world, three kinds of legal thought. Cambr Law Rev:11

Choi G-S (1998) Consideration on economic-related constitutional provisions. Const Rev 9:749

Chong J-S (2013) Constitutional law theory, p 227

Chung K (2006) Effect of local council ordinances in violation of the WTO Agreement. Gho Hwang Non-Jib 38:137

Cottier T (2002) A theory of direct effect in global law. In: von Bogdandy A, Mavroidis PC, Mény Y (eds) European integration and international co-ordination: studies in transnational economic law in honour of Claus-Dieter Ehlermann. Kluwer Law International, The Hague, p 103

Craig P, de Búrca G (2008) EU law: text, cases, and materials, 4th edn. Oxford University Press, Oxford, pp 268, 273

Di Gianni F, Antonini R (2006) DSB decision and direct effect of WTO law: should the EC courts be more flexible when the flexibility of the WTO system has come to an end? J World Trade 40(4):777

Grunwald (1996) Die EG als Rechtsgemeinschaft. In: Moritz Röttinger (Hg.) Handbuch der Europäischen Integration - Strategie, Struktur, Politik der Europäischen Union. Wien/Manz u.a. 1996, S 43

Hallstein (1979) Die EWG – eine Rechtsgemeinschaft, Ehrenpromotion, Universität Padua am 12. März 1962. In: ders. (Hg.) Europäische Reden. Stuttgart 1979, S 341

Han S-W (2012) Constitutional economic order. Study on major precedents in constitutional trials 2, pp 364–365

Huh Y (2001) Constitutional academy theory, p 171
Huh Y (2013) Korean constitution theory, pp 168, 169
Iwasawa Y (1997) Constitutional problems involved in implementing the Uruguay Round in Japan. In: Jackson JH, Sykes A (eds) Implementing the Uruguay Round. Oxford University Press, New York, pp 156–157
Ju J-Y (2005) A critical review of the domestic effect of the WTO Agreement in Korea. Seoul Int Law Rev 12(1):22–23, 37–38, 41
Kim M (2001) Socioeconomic order and property rights. Bupwonsa, p 103
Kim D-S (2005a) International law theory, pp 188, 254
Kim T-H (2005b) Globalization of national economic regulation. Seoul Law J 46(4):316
Kim M (2012) State and market under the Korean constitution. Korean Public Law Rev 41(1): 65–67
Kim D (2015) The relationship between international law and domestic law: theory and practice. Policy Res Ser 21:12–16
Kuijper PJ, Bronckers M (2005) WTO law in the European Court of Justice. Common Mark Law Rev 42(5):1318
Kwon Y (2004) Constitutional academy theory, p 174
Lim J.B./Chunn E.W. (2020) An analysis of China's WTO SPS disputes and policy implications, Trade Law J 149, 10-11
Mitsuo M et al (2003) The World Trade Organization-law, practice, and policy. New York: Oxford University Press, p 108
Noh K (2022) The legal effect of treaties and generally accepted international laws – focus on interpretation by the Constitutional Court and the Supreme Court. Law Policy Rev 22(4):65
Paust J (1988) Self-executing treaties. AJIL 82:760–763
Sung J-H (1996) Self-enforcement of treaties. Korea Int Law Rev 7:19
Tietje C (2008) The status of international law in the European legal order: the case of international treaties and non-binding international instruments. In: Wouters J, Nollkaemper A, de Wet E (eds) The Europeanisation of international law: the status of international law in the EU and its Member States. T.M.C Asser Press, The Hague, p 58
Wieacker (1996) Foundations of European legal culture. In: Gessner V, Hoeland A, Varga C (Hg.) European legal cultures. Dartmauth, pp 48–50

Towards a Common Constitutional Frame for Non-economic Values in Trade and Investment Agreements: Socio-Economic Constitutionalism in the Making

Wolfgang Weiß and Cornelia Furculita

Contents

Abstract Bringing trade and investment rules into conformity with the pursuit of often superior public policies is subject to intense debates in international economic law. While this topic has various facets and can be addressed from different angles, the present analysis demonstrates that specific tools to effectuate a better balance between trade and investment interests and non-economic policies have proliferated in trade and investment agreements that also give testimony of a considerable degree of convergence in the legal tools and their use. It could be shown that even though this on-going development is not straightforward but suffers from inconsistencies

---

W. Weiß (✉) and C. Furculita
University of Speyer, Speyer, Germany
e-mail: weiss@uni-speyer.de

S. Hindelang et al. (eds.), *YSEC Yearbook of Socio-Economic Constitutions 2024,* YSEC Yearbook of Socio-Economic Constitutions (2025) 2024: 201–246, https://doi.org/10.1007/16495_2024_77, Published online: 28 January 2025

and contradictory movements, one can observe considerable parallel and far-spread, even globally simultaneous developments. They concern both the textual means used in international agreements such as general exceptions, policy-specific chapters or confessions to regulatory autonomy of the states, and the jurisprudential interpretive approaches and control standards, even though in particular in investment treaty arbitration, practice develops very slowly. One can assess this as a muster of progressing and progressive constitutionalism in trade and investment policy in view of other public policies.

1 Introduction

The compatibility of states' trade interests with non-economic policy goals has long been a topic of discussion in international economic policy and world trade law. This topic has various facets and scholars have addressed it from different angles: Besides issue-specific research, pivotally on the interference between human rights, democracy and trade or environment policy and trade, some have engaged in analyzing the domestic or instrumental conditions for successful issue-interlinkage, whereas others researched into the positive effects of soft mechanisms or specific rules in international agreements.[1] In contrast to these approaches, the present contribution addresses the issue as to whether the relevant international hard law rules on making policy space available for non-economic policy issues in trade and investment policy testify a convergence in their formulation and application and hence allow for the establishment of a common legal framework for making way for non-economic issues in trade and investment policy across the globe. This issue has also been subject of legal research which demonstrated the convergence in rebalancing trade/investment interests with other public policies.[2] This chapter will look at the instruments used for this convergence and explore the latter's substantive and institutional dimension in greater detail. Thus, the present contribution adopts a rather constitutional perspective on the convergence issue which addresses the aspect of distributing regulatory authority among trading nations. For, researching the means that allow to consider non-economic issues in trade and investment policy relates to the question of how states shape their external economic relations in a way that is compatible with their own domestic non-economic policy objectives. If goods, services and their production processes at home have to meet certain requirements, for example in terms of quality, product safety or sustainability, then it is consistent with national policy to expect products and services from abroad to meet these requirements as well and to agree on corresponding clauses in their trade

[1]For a brief overview over the state of these research approaches with further references see Manchin et al. (2024), pp. 1 and 2–4; Ferrari et al. (2024), pp. 180 and 182–184.

[2]E.g. Cho and Kurtz (2018), pp. 179 ff and 197 f; Kurtz (2016); Newcombe (2011), pp. 355–365.

agreements. This problem becomes particularly relevant when international trade grows also qualitatively because states pursue progressive liberalisation and market opening. The ensuing nationally diverging requirements for products and production methods then come into view, and trade regulation faces the resulting trade barriers of the behind-the-border issues of national regulation.[3] Since the 1980s, the resulting non-tariff barriers to international trade have become core concerns for trade policy as tariffs had already been largely dismantled. The focus of trade policy globally has been shifting to the reduction of regulatory barriers, with the consequence that WTO rules and bilateral trade agreements contain an increasing number of provisions addressing domestic regulatory policies which is reflected in an ever broader issue coverage of trade agreements. This expansion of trade policy issues leads to an interaction between trade policy and other policy objectives and is reflected in an ever increasing level of non-trade issue coverage e.g. by social rights and environment commitments.[4] Furthermore, the characteristics of most global problems require the cooperation of states to solve them. Purely national attempts at solutions are usually not sufficient due to limited jurisdiction and transnational properties. The policy requirements implied in solutions may also have an impact on trade policy, for example when favouring trade in sustainable products. While in some areas it is national non-economic policy decisions that affect trade policy, in others it is global objectives that influence trade policy. In both cases, it is a matter of supplementing the economic success factors, conditions and requirements for trade between nations with paying attention to non-economic policies and bringing both into harmony. Free trade in the sense of a policy-free space that is guided only by economic objectives has probably never existed. In any case, under today's conditions of an interconnected world, trade relations are also the subject of undoubtedly legitimate non-trade objectives and policies. The same applies to investment relations in which the pertinent rules also have to factor in non-economic policies giving expression to the states' legitimate demand for regulatory leeway. The challenge that arises here—especially in the current state of international law, which works through the regulatory necessities in a silo-like manner in codifications and treaties specific to each policy field or issue, and thus in a rather fragmented manner (which is admittedly due to the complexities of international treaties being agreed between states)—is the question of the emergence of a basic legal framework or at least an approach that makes it possible to include respect for legitimate political objectives in the shaping of trade and investment relations.

In world trade law, this discussion has long been conducted under the heading of "trade and …". It is about a placement of non-economic goals in world trade law in the sense of a subject matter incorporation of these concerns,[5] and about a reinterpretation of the WTO rules aiming at overcoming the associated problems and a

---

[3]For the increasing relevance of these issues in international trade see Hoekman (2018), pp. 243–273.

[4]For their expansion in EU FTAs see Ferrari et al. (2024), pp. 180 and 188 f.

[5]See Cass (2005), p. 198.

corresponding reconceptualisation of the world trade order and its tasks, structures and processes. These discussions were closely linked to considerations of viewing WTO law as the global basis for regulating international economic relations and thus as a worldwide basic consensus. This triggered considerations and proposals for a constitutionalisation of the WTO, i.e. an understanding of the WTO and its basic principles as a kind of constitutional order of foreign trade. This interpretation perceives the WTO as a place for balancing and reconciling conflicting political goals and values, which in part has functions comparable to a national constitutional order. These ideas were primarily based on the rule-based functioning of the WTO and the success of its dispute settlement system, which was seen as a central building block of the WTO's rule-making and balancing function.[6] However, this is precisely where the current difficulties of the WTO become apparent: the rule-making function is only fulfilled to a limited extent, and dispute settlement has been paralysed at the Appellate Body level for several years now.

Nevertheless, the challenge of reconciling trade with other political objectives remains. The above-mentioned national and international dynamics to reconcile non-trade objectives with the basic rules of international trade have increased in recent decades due to the progress of trade liberalization, technical developments (reflected in the servitisation/servicification of trade[7]) and the deterioration of environmental and climate problems. This is reflected in the increase in bilateral attempts to find solutions to the "trade and …" problems in free trade agreements and thus outside the WTO. Beyond trade, investment protection standards in recent years became contested due to their alleged negative effects on domestic legislation in areas such as climate change, environment pollution and sustainability. The fear of the so-called "chilling effect" of international investment agreements restraining regulatory leeway and thus narrowing the necessary policy space[8] induced demands for more consistency of investment protection policies with other policies, and hence for amending investment rules to that effect. As will be discussed in more detail in this contribution, the EU also plays a significant role in this context with the trade and investment agreements it has concluded.

It is precisely in and through the EU that the discussion on the inclusion of non-economic policy objectives in trade and investment policy received new impetus. Already on the basis of primary law, trade and investment policy was recontextualised in the Treaty of Lisbon. But the issue of non-economic objectives

[6] Cass (2005), pp. 178 ff; Jackson (2006), pp. 144, 146, 208, and 224 ff; Shell (1995), pp. 833 f; Trachtman (2009), pp. 206 and 217. On the emergent development and transformation of the rule of law in GATT and WTO practice see Marceau (2015). For a critique see Howse and Nicolaidis (2001), pp. 227–252; Weiß (2020), pp. 85 ff.

[7] Low (2013), p. 63; Vandermerwe and Rada (1988), pp. 315 ff; Lanz R, Maurer A (2015) Services and global value chains: Some evidence on servicification of manufacturing and services network. WTO Staff Working Paper, No. ERSD-2015-03, pp. 2 ff; World Trade Organization (2019), World Trade Report 2019: The Future of Services Trade. http://www.wto.org/english/res_e/booksp_e/00_wtr19_e.pdf, pp. 67 f.

[8] Côté (2018), pp. 51–61; Tienhaara (2018), pp. 229–250.

also played an increasingly important role in the practical political orientation of EU external economic policy by the European Commission. This has been evident for some time in the so-called conditionality of the EU's trade benefits with regard to its market opening for third countries.

The developments on the inclusion of non-economic objectives in international economic law, and in bilateral trade and investment policy will be analysed in this chapter with a view to their convergence. The proposition of this chapter is that—based on the proliferating enshrinement of non-economic objectives in the pertinent provisions and agreements—the mechanisms by which external economic policy and non-economic objectives are brought into balance have converged. One of the pivotal mechanisms used to this end are exception clauses, which aim at balancing non-economic policy objectives with trade/investment interests in market opening and equal treatment. Beyond the converging development of the diverse rules merely on a textual level, the conceptualizations emerging from the practical application and interpretation of the rules in dispute settlement must be explored. According to the present contribution, a certain convergence can be observed, which thus provides the basis for identifying common mechanisms on the reconciliation of non-economic goals with trade and investment interests.

This chapter will trace the proliferation and significance of non-economic policy objectives in EU trade and investment policy and analyse the mechanisms used to ensure coherence between trade, investment and non-economic policies (see below Sect. 3), but before doing so, there is need to undertake this for the WTO texts as the international trade framework at first, identify the relevant rules in this respect and examine also their application by the WTO judiciary (see below Sect. 2). Finally, proliferation and significance of non-economic policies will be scrutinized with a view to bilateral and regional trade and investment agreements generally (see below Sect. 4), not only of the EU, in order to evaluate their substantive convergence. As part of these analyses, also the practical application and conceptualization of the convergence mechanisms in dispute settlement practice has to be elaborated in more detail, as the institutional dimension of balancing economic with non-economic policies has to be considered being an important factor of convergence.

2 WTO Law and Non-economic Policies

2.1 WTO Core Principles and Non-economic Policies

WTO law representing the almost globally accepted agreements on cross-border trade relations determines the frame for domestic trade policies of its members. In this capacity, the WTO rules do not only effectuate trade liberalization, in particular non-discriminatory market access and behind-the-border treatment, but also make space for the consideration of other, non-trade policy objectives. For, the WTO is not a mere trade agreement. The WTO rules are not merely dealing with trade issues as mere economic issues, but make room for considering their interference with public policy objectives that pursue non-commercial goals, too. WTO law is not limited to trade issues, nor is trade the "supreme common value that all WTO members must observe at any cost."[9] In contrast, WTO law is well aware of other objectives which may conflict with trade interests: In contrast to the time of GATT 1947, reference to non-trade concerns has increased tremendously after the Uruguay Round. The GATT 1947, in its preamble, merely referred to trade and economic issues such as full employment, real income and expanding production, which is understandable, given the devastation of the economic and living conditions in many parts of the world after World War II. Furthermore, some non-trade concerns (social progress and fair labour standards) have been dealt with in the Havana Charter on the International Trade Organization (see its Articles 1 and 7) so that their additional mention in GATT 1947 appeared to be unnecessary (as the GATT 1947 was supposed to enter into force together with the Havana Charter, see Article XXIX GATT). With the advent of the Marrakesh Agreement, this has considerably changed: The preamble to the WTO agreement though inspired by the GATT 1947 preamble, introduced a remarkable reference to other public policy aims (such as sustainable development and environment protection), and the negotiating history proves that this was done intentionally because the formulations of the preamble of the GATT 1947 were no longer seen as appropriate to the world trading system of the 1990s:[10] Thus, the WTO agreement recognizes the significance of other (non-economic) policy goals for trade issues and implies the awareness of inherent conflicts between e.g. trade and environment. The third recital of the WTO agreement preamble further states that the WTO agreements were entered into out of the desire of "contributing to these objectives", i.e. the policy aims listed in the first two recitals. Furthermore, the new, post-GATT 1947 agreements like the TBT and the SPS agreements reaffirm the right of WTO members to protect human, animal or plant life or health (see first recital of SPS preamble,[11] sixth recital of TBT preamble), the quality of its exports, the environment, the prevention of deceptive practices, or essential security interest (sixth and seventh recital to the TBT preamble). In the words of the Appellate Body, the SPS agreement is a "delicate and carefully negotiated balance … between the shared, but sometimes competing, interests of promoting international trade and of protecting the life and health of human beings."[12] GATS as well respects (recital 4 of the preamble) the right of WTO members to "meet national policy objectives" in a broadly conceived way as it contains no further qualifiers or limitations to the exercise of their regulatory autonomy. These statements establish that the WTO was not conceived to be an

[9] Grossmann G M, Horn H, Mavroidis P C (2012) Legal and Economic Principles of World Trade Law: National treatment. Research Institute of Industrial Economics IFN Working Paper No 917, p. 106; Mavroidis (2012), p. 326.

[10] Appellate Body, WT/DS58/AB/R, para 152—*US—Shrimp*. Cf. also Beise (2001), pp. 96 f.

[11] See Appellate Body, WT/DS321/AB/R, para 522—*Canada—Continued Suspension of Obligations in the EC—Hormones dispute*.

[12] Appellate Body, WT/DS26, 48/AB/R para 177—*EC—Hormones*.

international trade regulation that was blind of other legitimate public policy objectives.[13] Even though these statements are merely contained in preambles, the preambles add "colour, texture and shading"[14] to the interpretation of the individual provisions[15] as they identify the intentions of the negotiators and form part of the context (see Article 31 (2) VCLT). The preambles to the WTO agreement, the GATT 1994 and the TBT agreement reflect the object and purpose of these instruments[16] (in accordance with general international law rules of treaty interpretation[17]), and thus of the WTO in general.[18] Even more, the WTO objectives indicated in the preamble are incorporated into the text by the general reference in Article III:1 WTO Agreement to the objectives.

These recognized policy objectives are reflected also in the hard rules of WTO law. The protection of animal, plant and human life and health, for example, is recognized as a justification for trade restrictive measures in Article XX GATT, as is environmental protection (though not explicitly mentioned, but the grounds listed in Article XX b) and g) GATT contain the relevant goals for environmental protection and sustainable development). Consequently, the Appellate Body held that the important objective of environmental conservation and sustainable development (identified in the preamble) was reflected in Article XX g) GATT 1994[19] and concluded that the preamble showed that the signatories of the WTO agreement were fully aware of the importance and legitimacy of environmental protection as a goal of both national and international policy.[20] Hence, the right of WTO members

---

[13] See also van den Bossche and Zdouc (2022), pp. 93 f.

[14] Appellate Body, WT/DS58/AB/R, para 153—*US—Shrimp*.

[15] The Appellate Body used the preambles of WTO agreements for interpretive purposes. One example is the interpretation of Article 2.1 TBT Agreement. The Appellate Body referred to the sixth recital and opined that "[a]lthough the sixth recital does not explicitly set out a substantive obligation, we consider it nonetheless sheds light on the meaning and ambit of the "treatment no less favourable" requirement in Article 2.1, by making clear, in particular, that technical regulations may pursue legitimate objectives but must not be applied in a manner that would constitute a means of arbitrary or unjustifiable discrimination", Appellate Body, WT/DS381/AB/R para 213—*Measures Concerning the Importation, Marketing and Sale of Tuna and Tuna Products*; with regard to Article 2.2 TBT Agreement see ibid. para 316.

[16] See Appellate Body, WT/DS27/AB/ERW2/ECU, WT/DS27/AB/RW/USA, para 432—*EC-Regime for the Importation, Sale and Distribution of Bananas*—Second Recourse to Article 21.5 DSU; WT/DS269, 286/AB/R, para 241—*EC—Customs Classification of Frozen Boneless Chicken Cuts*; Panel, WT/DS58/RW, para 5.54—*US- Import Prohibition of Certain Shrimp and Shrimp Products*—Recourse to Article 21.5; WT/DS192/R, para 7.71, fn 257—*US—Transitional Safeguard Measure on Combed Cotton Yarn from Pakistan*.

[17] Panel, WT/DS135/R, para 8.47 and fn. 35—*EC—Measures Affecting Asbestos and Asbestos Containing Products*.

[18] Panel, WT/DS269/R, para 7.318—*EC—Customs Classification of Frozen Boneless Chicken Cuts*; Appellate Body, WT/DS246/AB/R, para 161, 168—*EC—Conditions for the Granting of Tariff Preferences to Developing Countries* (EC—GSP).

[19] Appellate Body, WT/DS246/AB/R, para 94 et seq—*EC—Conditions for the Granting of Tariff Preferences to Developing Countries* (EC—GSP).

[20] Appellate Body, WT/DS58/AB/R, para 129—*US—Shrimp*.

to take measures under Article XX GATT is reaffirmed and reinforced by the preamble to the WTO agreement.[21] The same holds true for Article XIV GATS and for Article 2.2 TBT Agreement. Article 2.2 TBT Agreement lists as "legitimate objectives" exactly the same as those mentioned in its preamble[22] which again repeats some of the wording of Article XX GATT,[23] and goes even beyond Article XX GATT as it is not exhaustive.[24] Thus, already the wording of WTO law is not blind for policy issues beyond mere trade, of which several are repeatedly mentioned in WTO law, and at least one of which (environmental conservation) has been denoted by the Appellate Body as "important objective".[25] Hence, in the Appellate Body's view, sustainable development and protection of the environment are among the objectives to be legitimately pursued in the international regulation of trade in the WTO, but also in domestic measures of WTO members under the exception clauses in which a WTO "Member's right to regulate is accommodated".[26]

That these objectives are reflected in exception clauses does neither mitigate their importance[27] nor legal effect, nor does it mean that in balancing trade against other concerns, trade has to prevail. For, the Appellate Body, but also panels, held that "WTO objectives" (sic!) "may well be pursued through measures taken under provisions characterized as exceptions",[28] without making any indication as to their alleged secondary rank or limited role which would contradict the significance of WTO members' regulatory autonomy in these policy areas. Instead, the Appellate Body held that the subparagraphs of Article XX GATT "comprise measures that are recognized as exceptions ... because the domestic policies embodied in such measures have been recognized as important and legitimate in character".[29] The Appellate Body judges both WTO obligations like non-discrimination and the recourse to exception provisions like Article XX GATT to be "rights" of WTO members; in this context the Appellate Body stresses the need to strike a right balance "between the *right* of a Member to invoke an exception under Article XX and the *duty* of that same

[21] See Panel, WT/DS58/R, para 7.52—*US—Shrimp*.

[22] Thus, Article 2.2 TBT agreement and recital four of its preamble are taken together in order to reason the regulatory autonomy of the WTO members insofar, Panel, WT/DS231/R, para 7.118–7.120—*EC—Trade Description of Sardines*.

[23] Panel, WT/DS135/R, para 8.55—*EC—Asbestos*.

[24] Cf. Appellate Body, WT/DS231/AB/R, para 286—*EC—Trade Description of Sardines*.

[25] Appellate Body, WT/DS246/AB/R, para 95—*EC—Conditions for the Granting of Tariff Preferences to Developing Countries* (EC—GSP).

[26] Appellate Body, WT/DS401/AB/R, para. 5.125—EC—Seal Products.

[27] Contra: Tietje and Lang (2021), p. 272.

[28] Appellate Body, WT/DS246/AB/R, para 94—*EC—Conditions for the Granting of Tariff Preferences to Developing Countries* (EC—GSP). See also panel, WT/DS431,432,433/R, para 7.114—*China—Measures related to the Export of Rare Earths*: WTO law must not "result in sovereign States being legally prevented from taking measures that are necessary to protect the environment or human, animal or plant life or health [as this] would likely be inconsistent with the object and purpose of the WTO Agreement".

[29] WT/DS58/AB/R, para 121—*US—Import Prohibition of Certain Shrimp and Shrimp Products*.

Member to respect the treaty rights of the other Members".[30] Thus, policy objectives stated in exceptions are not of lower rank and significance but do as well represent WTO objectives. Characterizing certain provisions as exceptions does not undermine these provisions' importance within the overall framework of the WTO.[31] Also the very existence of the SPS Agreement, establishing a clearer exemplification of a particular GATT "exception" for a specific category of technical barriers to trade, shows that Article XX b) GATT is not just an exception to an alleged core WTO principle of free trade. Otherwise, one would attribute the whole SPS agreement the value of an exception. In contrast, the SPS disciplines are not an exception but place additional, demanding obligations on WTO members with regard to particular health measures (in particular the requirement of a scientific risk assessment). The SPS agreement enshrines a careful way of balancing conflicting interests of health protection and of liberalised trade in the specific area of food and feed, and of dealing with the WTO members' overarching concern for human health, which require more elaborated and sophisticated rules than mere non-discrimination to counteract unnecessary trade restrictions. A simplistic rule exception dichotomy is not present there, and would not do justice to the complexities of reconciling trade interests and health concerns. Thus, the SPS agreement is a specific trade regime which provides for particular obligations additional to those of GATT 1994, and which prevail (Article 2.4 SPS).

Beyond exception clauses, the non-economic policies recognized in the preamble texts mentioned above also impact the interpretation of other WTO provisions, in particular the non-discrimination obligations.[32] Attempts to consider regulatory aims and intentions of domestic legislators and to open up regulatory space for them when adopting trade-impeding measures had for the first time been undertaken by the "aims and effects" test,[33] which, however, has been refuted under GATT 1994 by panels and the Appellate Body.[34] Subsequently, regulatory intention played a role in

---

[30] See Appellate Body, WT/DS58/AB/R, para 156—*US—Import Prohibition of Certain Shrimp and Shrimp Products* (emphasis in the original).

[31] Appellate Body, loc. cit. para 95. See also Appellate Body, WT/DS26/AB/R, WT/DS48/AB/R, para 104—*EC—Measures Concerning Meat and Meat Products* (EC—Hormones).

[32] For other examples of implicit recognition of a WTO Member's right to regulate in WTO case law see Mitchell (2023), pp. 465 ff. He ibid. 480 points out that besides exception clauses, a recognition of regulatory autonomy is also enshrined in rules whose "normative framework presupposes strong notions of regulatory purpose" or where the language "directly imports some degree of additional policy space", e.g. Art. 20 TRIPS.

[33] GATT panel, BISD 34S/83, para. 5.9 c)—Japan—Customs Duties, Taxes and Labelling Practices on Imported Wines and Alcoholic Beverages. Admittedly, the aims and effects test had not been considered with a view to the GATT preamble but with a view to employ Article III:1 GATT's anti-protectionism telos when interpreting the remainder of Article III GATT. But, and this is decisive in the present context, it was a first attempt to create greater room for domestic regulatory autonomy to balance trade and non-trade interests.

[34] After the Appellate Body (AB) had appeared to make room for WTO Member's regulatory autonomy to draw distinctions between otherwise like goods without granting less favourable treatment, see AB, WT/DS135/AB/R, para. 100—EC—Asbestos, it finally explicitly rejected the

interpreting the no less favourable treatment requirement in GATT and in the TBT non-discrimination obligations with a view to regulatory distinctions made by domestic legislators. After some Appellate Body reports gave the impression that the issue of regulatory intentions could be relevant in interpreting the no less favourable treatment requirement, the AB finally denied this for GATT Article III,[35] but confirmed the WTO Member's regulatory autonomy's significance for interpreting the non-discrimination clause of Article 2.1 TBT Agreement. With regard to Article 2.1 TBT Agreement, it was in particular the comparison to Article 2.2 TBT Agreement and the recognition of the WTO members' right to regulate in the TBT preamble which made the AB to conclude that Article 2.2 TBT does not operate as a prohibition of any obstacle to trade, but that the object and purpose of the TBT expressed in its recitals "explicit recognition of Members' right to regulate" requires the judiciary to strike a balance between trade liberalisation and the policies pursued by Members, with the effect that the interpretation of Article 2.1 TBT has to make way for legitimate regulatory distinctions.[36] The difference of the AB's approach to interpreting the non-discrimination obligations in the TBT as compared to GATT is reasoned by the AB with reference to the availability of a general exception clause under GATT and its lack for Article 2.1 TBT Agreement.[37] But still, the AB confirmed that the due balance between trade liberalisation and the WTO Members' regulatory autonomy under TBT is not different from GATT, where the non-discrimination obligation is qualified by the general exception provision of Article XX GATT.[38]

That the WTO is not solely about trade is confirmed by subsequent developments (contributing to the interpretation of international agreements, see Article 31 (3) VCLT), in particular the cooperation between the WTO and intergovernmental environmental organisations and the Ministerial Declarations of the WTO members.[39] In the Doha Ministerial, the WTO members expressed their conviction "that the aims of upholding and safeguarding an open and

---

aims and effects test, see AB, WT/DS27/AB/R, para. 241—EC—Bananas (with regard to Article XVII GATS), AB, WT/DS401/AB/R, paras. 5.117 ff EC—Seal Products (with regard to Article III:4 GATT); with regard to Article III:2 GATT see panel, WT/DS8/10/11/R, para. 6.16—Japan—Taxes on Alcoholic Beverages, impliedly confirmed by the AB, van den Bossche and Zdouc (2022), p. 399. For a closer analysis of the AB's turn in interpreting Article III:4 in relation to Article XX GATT between EC-Asbestos and EC- Seal Products see Weiß (2020), pp. 158 ff.

[35] See AB, WT/DS/400/R, para. 5.125—EC—Seal Products. For a detailed analysis of the turns in the interpretive approaches of the AB with regard to making way for regulatory autonomy in the no less favourable treatment standard, see Weiß (2020), pp. 160 ff.

[36] AB, WT/DS406/AB/R, para. 174—US—Clove Cigarettes; see also AB, WT/DS384, 386/AB/R, para 271—US—COOL.

[37] AB, WT/DS400, 401/AB/R, paras. 5.124 ff—EC—Seal Products. Ming Du (2016), p. 148.

[38] AB, WT/DS400, 401/AB/R, para. 5.122—EC—Seal Products.

[39] See e.g. with regard to environmental protection the 1994 Ministerial Decision at Marrakesh to establish a permanent Committee on Trade and Environment which took note of the Rio Declaration on Environment and Development and Agenda 21, as did the panel, WT/DS332/R, para 7.112,

non-discriminatory multilateral trading system, and acting for the protection of the environment and the promotion of sustainable development, can and must be mutually supportive".[40] Hence, sustainability and environment protection are considered as objectives of the WTO law; climate change has been an issue for the TRIPS Council since 2013. As regards labour rights, the Singapore Ministerial Declaration[41] provides some—very limited—guidance. The most decisive questions remained open, for example whether compliance with labour rights agreements entered into under the ILO may serve as an additional exception to WTO law allowing for a deviation from WTO trade obligations.

In conclusion, free trade is not the overarching WTO objective which would put competing policy objectives in second line. WTO law has a more holistic view and its founders were aware of the several drawbacks trade has on other not less legitimate public policy objectives.[42] The grounds itemized in the exception provisions are of high enough priority to supersede trade interests.[43] The objectives listed in exceptions such as Article XX GATT contribute to the overall picture of what the WTO is like. They codify objectives conflicting with trade interests and indicate the need for a balanced approach to trade liberalization.[44] Thus, the WTO's overall purpose neither is free trade nor deregulation, but trade liberalisation according to defined disciplines that include balancing conflicting interests.[45] Hence, the WTO's core disciplines of market access and non-discrimination[46] are complemented by provisions that require the balancing of trade interests with other policy objectives, enshrined in particular in the exception provisions, which themselves have meanwhile become basic rules of WTO law.[47] This understanding is confirmed by the interpretational approach regarding exceptions: The Appellate Body refuted the idea of a strict or narrow interpretation of exceptions (present in pre-WTO times) due to the significance and importance of the objectives enshrined therein.[48] Thus, exceptions function as a vehicle to equally foster both trade and

fn. 1193—*Brazil—Measures Affecting Imports of Retreated Tyres* and the Appellate Body, WT/DS58/AB/R, para 154—*US—Shrimp*.

[40] Para 6 of the Doha Ministerial Declaration, WT/MIN(01)/DEC/1.

[41] WT/MIN(96)/DEC, para 4, reaffirmed in para 8 of the Doha Ministerial Declaration. For the climate change discussions in the TRIPS Council meetings see https://www.wto.org/english/tratop_e/trips_e/cchange_e.htm.

[42] See again panel, WT/DS58/R, para 6.7—*US—Shrimp*.

[43] Farber and Hudec (1994), p. 1421.

[44] Qureshi (2015), p. 154.

[45] See Weiß (2020), pp. 98 ff. That the WTO is not about deregulation is also confirmed by an analysis of the consequences of some WTO disputes that induce WTO members to amend their regulations in an even more restrictive manner, see Lydgate (2017), pp. 562 f.

[46] These are the cornerstones of WTO substantive trade liberalisation, besides rules on unfair trade, see van den Bossche and Zdouc (2022), pp. 40 ff.

[47] See van den Bossche and Zdouc (2022), pp. 44 f.

[48] See Appellate Body, WT/DS26/AB/R, WT/DS48/AB/R, para 104—*EC—Hormones*; WT/DS246/AB/R, para 98—EC—GSP. See also Hilf (2001), p. 128 who rightly differentiates

non-trade objectives established in the WTO.[49] Admittedly, interpreting exceptions like Article XX GATT as objectives of the WTO is a novel reconstruction of the original reading of these GATT 1947 rules and their traditional conceptualisations (like rule-exception dichotomy, narrow interpretation of Article XX GATT[50] and the ensuing pro-trade bias[51]). But the contemporary interpretation and evolutionary conceptualisation of WTO provisions is legitimate and even necessary in face of current perceptions of the role of domestic regulation of WTO members. Furthermore, the old GATT 1947 rules have been placed in a completely new context, as GATT 1994 is legally distinct from GATT 1947 and as its rules became an Annex to the WTO agreement with its new objectives. Adapting the interpretation of formally unaltered legal provisions to current concerns and ideas, and reconsidering them in a changed societal and global context are conceptual approaches that can also be observed in the interpretation of core concepts of GATT/WTO law like non-discrimination, as already alluded to above.[52]

2.2 *Instruments for Effectuating the Consideration of Non-economic Policies*

The above explorations on the role of non-economic policy objectives in WTO law have already highlighted the mechanisms in place in WTO law to effectuate a balancing of trade interests with WTO Members' non-trade policies. WTO agreements on several occasions confirm the WTO Members' regulatory autonomy and their related right to regulate, both in explicit terms in their preambles, as well as, more or less impliedly, in their hard legal provisions. Regarding the latter, the itemized exceptions in the exception clauses such as Article XX GATT, Article XIV GATS are implicit references to a WTO Member's right to regulate in the named policy domains. The exception clauses provide for policy-based exceptions,[53] as they allow WTO Members to "condition … access to a Member's domestic market on whether exporting Members comply with, or adopt, a policy or policies unilaterally prescribed by the importing Member",[54] and thus effectuate the simultaneity of considering and balancing of trade and other interests. On an even more explicit account, Article 2.2 TBT Agreement refers to the fulfilment of

between economic and non-economic concerns; regarding the latter there is no convincing reason for a narrow interpretation.

[49] Qureshi (2015), p. 175.

[50] See GATT panel, DS 29/R (unadopted), para 5.38—*US—Import Restrictions on Tuna* (EEC).

[51] See Ming Du (2011), pp. 664–665 with further references.

[52] For different interpretive approaches insofar, see Weiß (2020), pp. 123 ff with regard to MFN; 143 ff, 155 ff with regard to NT.

[53] Mitchell (2023), p. 463.

[54] Appellate Body, WT/DS58/AB/R, para. 121—US—Shrimp.

"legitimate objectives" and indicates several of them which recognizes the legitimate right of WTO Members to regulate in these policy areas as long as the domestic legislation does not place unnecessary trade barriers. Article 2.2 TBT Agreement confirms the WTO Members' right to prepare, adopt or apply technical regulations. In the same way as the rights to market access and non-discrimination under WTO law only exist insofar as the WTO rules provide for them, likewise the right to regulate is recognized by the WTO judiciary only insofar as enshrined into the WTO Agreements. There is no general inherent right to regulate that could function as an overarching exception to any kind of WTO commitment, but the right to regulate of WTO Members does exist within WTO law only insofar as is explicitly or implicitly enshrined in WTO rules. As there are no market access or equal treatment rights outside WTO Agreements to be considered in WTO disputes, neither are there WTO Members' rights to regulate justifying departure from them outside those in WTO Agreements. Nevertheless, even though there is no overarching right to regulate principle which could work as a stand-alone justification in WTO law,[55] concerns over WTO members' regulatory autonomy have occasionally impacted the conceptualisation of WTO non-discrimination standards by the WTO judiciary.[56]

Thus, it is primarily through the exception clauses that WTO law provides for a way of balancing trade interests (i.e. market access and non-discrimination provisions) against other policy objectives. In this way, WTO law takes care that domestic policy measures are respected even though they may impede cross-border trade, as long as they themselves respect trade interests by not resulting in unnecessary trade impediments, while the trading rights of those WTO Members interested in market access must give way to those legitimate policy interests enshrined in exception clauses or other WTO provisions and not pursued in an excessive way. From the mutual consideration of these interests results the fundamental balance of trade and non-trade interests effectuated in WTO law. The exception clauses implement this balancing by, first, providing for more or less specifically itemized justification grounds, and sometimes, as in case of Article XX lit d) GATT ("including") or Article 2.2 TBT Agreement ("inter alia"), this list is not exclusive. Second, there is an additional qualifying condition which determines the specific relation between the itemized justifying policy ground and the domestic measure under scrutiny, e.g. a necessity requirement as in Article XX a) b) d) GATT, Article XIV a) b) c) GATS and Article 2.2 TBT, or a less demanding "relating to" requirement as in Article XX c), g) GATT. Thirdly, the introductory clause, i.e. chapeau of the exception clauses contain another layer of requirements: According to Article XX GATT, Article XIV GATS, the measures to be justified must not be "applied in a manner which would constitute a means of arbitrary or unjustifiable discrimination between countries where the same conditions prevail, or a disguised restriction on

[55] Appellate Body, WT/DS394, 395, 398/AB/R, paras. 303 ff—China—Measures Related to the Exportation of Various Raw Materials (China—Raw Materials). See also Mitchell (2023), pp. 478 f.

[56] See already above fn. 34; for the cases see Weiß (2020), pp. 155 ff.

trade". Recital 6 of the TBT agreement verbatim repeats this clause, which led the Appellate Body to infer that a legitimate regulatory distinction under Article 2.1 TBT Agreement must be designed and applied in an even-handed manner, i.e. not arbitrary or unjustifiable.[57] These requirements place a demand for good faith use of exceptions which has to be reflected in the consistency of the policies and their non-discriminatory practical application.

Consequently, these additional requirements clarify that the mere fact that a domestic measure giving rise to a trade impediment is rooted in or stems from a certain legitimate policy area is not sufficient for allowing a due balance between trade and non-trade interests. The regulatory autonomy to adopt measures in pursuance of the objectives is subject to further conditions. These policies must be designed and implemented in a consistent way and not create unnecessary impediments to trade. It is the WTO judiciary's approaches in conceiving the policy grounds in the exception clauses and the additional above-mentioned layers of qualifiers that must be met in order to pave the way for non-economic policies being capable of outweighing trade interests which decide about the regulatory leeway effectively available to states and hence about the sound balance between trade and non-trade interests. Therefore, the basic orientation and development of the WTO judiciary's case law with regard to their application of exception clauses will briefly be outlined now.

2.3 *Non-economic Policies in WTO Jurisprudence*

An analysis of the WTO judiciary's basic conceptualisation of the exception clauses shows, first, as already mentioned, that in contrast to pre-WTO times the itemized policy grounds are not conceived narrowly, but rather broadly, which enlarges the policy space of WTO Members. Even the allegedly closed list of enumerations in Article XX GATT/Article XIV GATS proves to be accessible to an expansive reading due to the broad terminology used. The most prominent examples are the contemporary and evolutionary, contextual interpretation of the term "exhaustible natural resources" in Article XX g) GATT[58] and the likewise broad conceptualization of the notion of protecting public morals or maintaining public order, as provided in Article XX a) GATT, XIV a) GATS which were interpreted to grant a particularly great leeway to WTO Members to define their domestic policies on what the public order requires. It can even include such diverse issues as respect of fundamental rights, censorship or protection against money laundering. Second, there are inherently open justifications as e.g. in Article XX d) GATT.[59] All of

[57] Appellate Body, WT/DS384/AB/R, para. 271—US—COOL. The same applies to the SPS Agreement, Weiß (2020), pp. 272 f.

[58] See e.g. Appellate Body, WT/DS58/AB/R, paras. 127 ff, 130—US—Shrimp.

[59] For a more detailed analysis see Weiß (2020), pp. 239 ff.

this allowed the WTO judiciary to develop the grounds for exception in the direction of greater regulatory autonomy for WTO members and broader policy space to pursue other policies than trade policy, and which have to be considered in attaining a balance between trade and other interests and values. The WTO judiciary also stressed that exception clauses lay down the unilateral right and prerogative for WTO Members to determine their legitimate policies and to define their level of protection to which WTO judiciary must defer in assessing the exception clauses' exigencies.[60]

Second, the necessity test as required in several of the itemized grounds in Article XX GATT, Article XIV GATS, but also in Article 2.2 TBT Agreement, has been developed into quite high a barrier for domestic policies to work as justification for trade impediments. For, the necessity test currently is conceived, after an initial understanding that a regulating WTO Member must choose appropriately available, least-trade restrictive policy means to attain its objectives, as a complex weighing and balancing exercise whose assessment depends on the importance of policy objectives pursued, the level of protection aimed at, and the measure's contribution to it and its impact on trade, implying diverse standards of weighing the objectives against its trade restrictive effects. The more important an objective or value is, the greater is the acceptable trade restrictiveness a measure may imply.[61] This interpretative development no longer accepts a rather simple necessity test in the form of the search for the reasonably available least trade-restrictive means to implement a certain level of protection, but stipulates a more burdensome test of the domestic measure which is more or less a search for the right balance between means and ends of a domestic policy coming close to a cost-benefit analysis or a proportionality test *strictu sensu*.[62] Irrespective of these developments, the case law of the WTO judiciary effectuates that non-economic policies are taken serious and that the previous blame under GATT 1947 that panels favour trade interests can no longer be upheld.[63]

Finally, the domestic policies must meet the exigencies of the exception clauses' chapeau (and of functionally comparable stipulations as with regard to Article 2.1 TBT Agreement). The dispute settlement practice of the WTO judiciary confirms that their stipulations are decisive as there have been several cases in which domestic policy measures that were necessary to attain legitimate policy objectives have finally failed because of arbitrary discrimination due to unreasonable carve-outs from the policy pursued.[64] The (new) role of the chapeaux as the final watershed for distinguishing WTO-compliant domestic measures from non-compliant ones has

---

[60] Appellate Body, WT/DS58/AB/R, para. 168—EC—Asbestos; WT/DS332/AB/R, para. 210—Brazil—Tyres.

[61] Cf. Appellate Body, WT/DS161, 169/AB/R, para. 162—Korea—Beef. For more on this development in WTO jurisprudence, see Weiß (2020), pp. 250 ff.

[62] Rigod (2015), pp. 139 f.

[63] Rigod (2015), p. 141. *Contra* Tietje and Lang (2021), p. 272.

[64] See Bartels (2015), p. 96.

surfaced as a consequence of the broad interpretation of the itemized justification grounds since the advent of the WTO.[65] Despite the different qualifiers used in the exception grounds to determine the required relationship between legitimate public policies pursued and the measure adopted (necessity versus less demanding "relating to" standards in Article XX GATT, whereas later agreements such as TBT and GATS use a uniform necessity approach), the rather identical requirements of the exception clauses' chapeaux appear to have streamlined, to a considerable extent, the exigencies that the pursuance of non-economic policies by WTO Members has to meet in order to finally justify trade-impeding policy measures under the requirements of the exception clauses. Even though the approach of the WTO judiciary in the review of the chapeaux' requirements sometimes is rather inhomogeneous, even incongruent, observers assess the pertinent WTO jurisprudence as turning the chapeaux into a "unifying force" for all the exceptions,[66] and this is indeed so as the chapeaux effectively demand consistency in the application of the domestic policies which may be hard to meet in case of unsuitable means or means that have disparate trade effects on different trading partners where the same conditions prevail.

Thus, exception clauses, confessions to regulatory autonomy of states and their consideration in the interpretation of WTO disciplines are the pivotal ways of bringing non-trade policy objectives into trade agreements, on a par level. The enshrined necessity test and the further consistency requirements for the domestic policies' implementation serve to rationalize the due balancing between trade interests in market access and non-discriminatory treatment of foreign products, on one hand, and the exercise of a state's regulatory autonomy, on the other, by making available criteria for a rational step-by step examination of the regulatory autonomy's interference with trade.[67]

From a global law perspective, the necessity test is a form of a proportionality analysis which gives Courts a decisive role in controlling domestic legislation or regulation[68] with regard to implementing the requirements of public policies against conflicting values such as human rights, or in the realm of WTO law, economic interests in open markets and non-discriminatory trade. Proportionality balancing then can become the master tool of governance,[69] and its intrusiveness in the legislative pursuit of public policy and thus a state's regulatory sovereignty by way of judicial control depends on the required steps of an arbiter's proportionality assessment, the density of their standard of review and thus the extent of deference to

---

[65] Weiß (2020), p. 278.

[66] Bhala (2005), para. 19-004. For the closeness of the chapeaus' requirements to a necessity test see also Rigod (2015), p. 147.

[67] Establishing consistency of a policy significantly adds to its meaningfulness and legitimacy, see van Engen et al. (2019), pp. 97–115. Thus, it is fundamental to its positive assessment by the judiciary.

[68] Von Bogdandy and Venzke (2013), pp. 49–72 = ACIL Research Paper 2012–10, pp. 10 ff.

[69] See Stone Sweet and Matthews (2019), pp. 2 and 4.

a regulatory state's assessments of what a given level of protection demands in terms of instruments for its attainment. Loose control standards regarding domestic factual assessments going hand in hand with a highly deferential attitude considerably mitigate the political powers an arbiter has over domestic regulatory choices and its intrusion into the balancing of conflicting policy objectives.[70] The standard of review and the related issue of how much deference to domestic assessments of law and fact will be granted by the WTO judiciary again is not subject of a conclusive approach. Rather, the applicable standard of review depends on whether mere factual assessments or issues of legal interpretation are at stake.[71]

3 EU CCP and Non-economic Policies

3.1 Coherence Between Trade and Non-economic Policies in the EU: From Political Practice to Constitutional Obligation

The incorporation of non-economic policies into trade policy started as early as in the 1990s with human rights clauses in the EU's trade and association agreements. On the level of its constitutional law, it was only with the advent of the Treaty of Lisbon in 2009 that trade policy not only became an explicit part of the EU's general external policy and the general objectives of EU foreign policy applied to EU trade policy (see Article 207 (1) TFEU according to which trade policy shall be conducted "within the framework of the principles and objectives of the Union's external action", in accordance with Articles 205 TFEU and 21 (3) TEU), but even more that, under Article 207(3) TFEU, trade policy must be compatible with EU internal policies and rules. Thus, trade policy has to be conducted in the context of the EU general external policy principles and objectives (indicated in Article 21 (1), (3) TEU) and the EU's values (Articles 3 (5), 21 (2) TEU)[72] and became subject to multiple policy coherence requirements. This re-contextualization of trade policy subsequently was implicitly emphasized by the European Commission in its 2015 Communication "Trade for All", where the Commission confirmed that trade policy should dovetail with the EU's sustainable development and foreign policies and the

[70]For proportionality control as an exercise of political power see Stone Sweet and Matthews (2019), ibid. Whether there can be a uniform control standard implying the always identical level of deference is highly doubtful, as proportionality tests are situated in different contexts, e.g. as regards multitude of treaty objectives and level of regulatory integration sought for by an international instrument.

[71]Lanovoy (2022), pp. 49 ff.

[72]Dimopoulos (2010), pp. 153–170; Cremona (2017), pp. 15 f.

external objectives of internal policies.[73] This re-orientation was sharpened recently by the Trade Policy Review of 2021 that implements the Green Deal into trade policy and brought about a determined shift towards a more robust trade policy formulation, oriented toward the assertive representation not only of the EU's economic, but also non-economic (regarding sustainability and labour rights) interests.[74] The objectives of trade policy thus go beyond the merely commercial policy objectives set out in Article 206 TFEU and comprise founding principles such as respect for democracy and human rights, and fundamental policy objectives such as sustainable development, respect for international law, and a cooperative and just world order (see Article 21(1) and (2) TEU). As the EU's Common Commercial Policy (CCP) is a continuation of the internal market concept, also from this perspective it must not contradict internal policy objectives.

This re-contextualization of trade policy in the Lisbon Treaty confirms the pre-Lisbon practice under which trade policy was not limited to trade issues[75] and continues with this traditional approach, giving a definite legal basis to the broad politicization of trade policy and its conditionality.[76] Contrary to the comprehensive policy objective orientation of trade treaty policy, the determination of significant distortions, injury margin and Union interest in the EU's autonomous trade policy until recently have been based on purely commercial interests. After some signs of a cautious change in the decision-making practice of the Commission in antidumping with regard to determining Union interest, the trade defence modernisation package of 2017/2018[77] finally enabled the incorporation of labour rights and environmental standards considerations in antidumping and antisubsidy decision-making when assessing distortions and calculating the injury margin.[78]

The commitment of the EU to determine and implement its trade policy in accordance with other non-economic policies and EU values is a constitutional obligation as these objectives are neither purely political assertions or agendas[79] nor mere declarations of intent.[80] Wording and context of Articles 3 (5) and 21 (3) TEU clearly speak in favour of granting them the same legal relevance, in particular binding force as other EU primary law provisions. Additionally, Article 21 (3) TEU explicitly provides that the EU has to 'respect the principles and pursue the objectives set out in paragraphs 1 and 2 in the development and implementation'

[73] European Commission (2015) Trade for All: Towards a More Responsible Trade and Investment Policy, COM(2015) 497 final, 3.

[74] European Commission (2021) Trade Policy Review: An Open, Sustainable and Assertive Trade Policy (Trade Policy Review), COM(2021) 66 final, 18 February 2021.

[75] See Opinion of Advocate General Wahl in Opinion 3/15, ECLI:EU:C:2016:657, para. 69. ff.

[76] Asteriti (2017), p. 124.

[77] See Trapp (2022).

[78] The new practice is mainly based on recital 4 of Regulation 2017/2321, Article 7 (d) BADR and Article 12 (1a) BASR. See Van Vaerenbergh (2022), pp. 846 ff.

[79] Krajewski (2012), p. 295; Müller-Ibold (2019), p. 150.

[80] Such was the Commission's position in CJEU, Opinion 1/78, International Agreement on Natural Rubber [1979] ECR 2871, 2884.

of its external policies and explicitly includes Part Five of the TFEU, which comprises trade policy.[81] The Court derived from Article 207 (1) sentence 2 TFEU the duty 'to integrate those objectives and principles into the conduct of its common commercial policy'.[82] Thus, Articles 3 (5) and 21 TEU provide for trade policy direction and orientation in conformity with other non-economic policy objectives, and they do so as legally binding obligations for the EU institutions.[83] Even long time before the Lisbon Treaty, the Court had opined that EU Treaty objectives are implemented through the policies and actions of the EU.[84] Articles 3 (5) and 21 TEU lay down constitutional obligations to respect these objectives, and not mere policy choices.[85] Accordingly, the CJEU clearly held that compliance of the EU with the objectives set out in Article 21 TEU is required of all actions of the EU.[86]

3.2 Considerable Leeway in Implementation

Confirming the EU objectives' binding force and legal obligation, however, does not conclusively clarify the resulting normative effect flowing from this obligation.[87] For, observing a legal stipulation can mean slightly different things: The normativity of a provision may require full compliance with it, but can also mean an obligation of mere consideration of it as an objective, which has to be pursued in the determination of a policy that has to serve also other interests. The precise normative content differs according to the wording used, the vagueness of the terminology employed, and again also depending on the context. Regarding the wording, the objectives do not provide for means and ways how they should be implemented. Insofar, the EU institutions have 'wide powers of assessment' in determining policies and their instruments, all the more as the formulations used in describing the objectives and principles of the EU grant leeway by using quite vague terms with considerable openness.[88] Consequently, trade policy has to consider a wide range of interests that

[81] The terminological shift from 'values' to 'principles' is without relevance insofar, see Cremona (2011), pp. 280 f.

[82] CJEU, Opinion 2/15, ECLI:EU:C:2017:376, para. 143.

[83] See also Kassoti and Wessel (2023), pp. 19–46; Larik (2016), pp. 64 ff, 154 ff; Sommermann (2013), paras. 3–6.

[84] CJEU, Case C-149/96, *Portugal v Council* [1999] ECR I-08395, EU:C:1999:574, para. 86. Admittedly, the focus of said statement may rather be the political discretion of the EU institutions in implementing the objectives, as will be addressed instantly.

[85] See Van Elsuwege (2021), p. 417; Kassoti and Wessel (2021), p. 244.

[86] CJEU, C-263/14, *EU Tanzania Agreement on Transfer of Pirates* ECLI:EU:C:2016:435, para. 47.

[87] Cannizarro (2021), p. 4; Kassoti and Wessel (2023), pp. 19–46, sub. III.

[88] See CJEU, Case C 5/73, *Balkan-Import-Export GmbH* [1973] ECR 01091, EU:C:1973:109, para. 27; Asteriti (2017), p. 130.

have to be balanced against each other, which imparts rather wide a discretion to the responsible institutions. The concrete formulation of the EU's trade policy strategy must therefore weigh up the various objectives according to current problems and needs (cf. the mandate to the European Council in Article 22 TEU and to the Council and the Commission in Article 207 (3) TFEU). None of the objectives set out in Articles 206 TFEU and Articles 3 (5), 21 TEU has any legal priority.

Despite this leeway for the EU, in particular for the Commission, to decide about ways and means of bringing trade policy in conformity with other policies and EU values, the constitutional obligation influences the interpretation of the EU's trade policy competence.[89] Hence, EU general objectives reflect in the substance of EU trade agreements, with the result that the EU's trade policy increasingly became linked to the pursuit of non-economic policy objectives.[90] As a most recent step, chapters on trade and sustainable development became part of the EU's trade treaties since the trade agreement with South Korea.[91] The classic example for non-economic policies reflected in trade agreements is the EU human rights conditionality. Following the introduction of this objective in the Maastricht Treaty, the EU relatively consistently began to include value clauses in agreements from 1992 onwards, in the form of commitments to democratic principles and human rights as the basis and condition ("essential elements") for cooperation and the respective agreement,[92] and these clauses are regularly accompanied by provisions laying down the consequences of serious non-implementation.[93] The EU UK Trade and Cooperation Agreement (TCA) contains a comparatively broad essential elements clause, under which not only rule of law, democracy and human rights, but also the fight against climate change (Article 764 TCA) and proliferation of weapons of mass destruction (Article 765 TCA) is part of the essential elements which in case of serious and substantial failure of fulfilment allow any Party to terminate or suspend the agreement (Article 772 TCA). Some agreements, however, are limited to mere preambular confessions to human rights, such as the recent free trade agreement with Singapore whose human rights conditionality only arises through its Article 16.18 in conjunction with the accompanying Partnership and Cooperation Agreement, Article 44 of which permits suspension in case of non-compliance.[94] Human rights conditionality also plays a role in autonomous trade policy allowing for unilateral measures such as granting tariff preferences in the GSP+ system in exchange for

[89] CJEU, Opinion 2/15, ECLI:EU:C:2017:376 paras. 142 ff, 239 ff.

[90] Bilal and Hoekman (2019), pp. 9 f.; Borchert I, Conconi P, Di Ubaldo M et al. (2020) The Pursuit of Non-Trade Policy Objectives in EU Trade Policy. EUI Working Papers, RSCAS 2020/26.

[91] Cremona (2018), pp. 242 f. See also Opinion procedure 1/17, Opinion of Advocate General Bot delivered on 29 January 2019, ECLI:EU:C:2019:72, paras. 177 f and 195; Case C-244/17, European Commission v. Council of the European Union, Opinion of Advocate General Kokott delivered on 31 May 2018, ECLI:EU:C:2018:364 para. 78.

[92] Bartels (2014), pp. 7 ff; Hoffmeister (1998).

[93] For more detail and a critical discussion see Beke et al. (2014), pp. 59 ff.

[94] For a critical analysis see Meissner and McKenzie (2017), pp. 832–849.

implementing certain ILO conventions and sustainable development commitments[95] or trade sanctions as a consequence of serious and systematic human rights violations.[96]

3.3 Instruments for Effectuating Coherence

The EU employs several instruments in order to implement a reconciliation between trade and non-trade policies. As mentioned, the conditionality requirements of trade policy with regard to human rights and sustainability commitments are implemented by pertinent clauses in autonomous instruments and the agreements (be it trade, cooperation or association agreements) that oblige EU trade partners to ratify and implement certain ILO conventions, international human rights agreements and instruments or conventions on climate and environmental standards, failure of which allows, by and large, for suspension, or termination of trade relations, or for the withdrawal of preferences granted. The specific TSD chapters in the more recent EU trade agreements,[97] however, do not provide for a suspension or termination of trade relations or other sanctions as a response to their non-compliance, in contrast to those of the US or Canada[98] (see *infra*), but are soft mechanisms mainly to foster cooperation and dialogue. The specific dispute settlement rules in these EU agreements do not provide for enforcement means such as remedies,[99] which stirred the EU reform process on EU TSD chapters.[100] As the suspension, termination or withdrawal options are rather rude "all or nothing" tools of merely sanctioning or counteracting severe non-performance of the respective obligations by the trade partner, they in practice are not very often used and actually do not allow for producing coherence between trade interests and other policy objectives. The clauses can be used to generally enforce predefined human rights, labor rights or environmental standards on the other party and usually are not implemented in a product-specific way. While they positively provide for common standards that the parties agree to apply in their domestic space, they do not allow the EU to restrain trade relations specifically in order to enforce certain goods or services of the other party

[95] Regulation (EU) No. 978/2012 of the European Parliament and of the Council of 25 October 2012 applying a scheme of generalised tariff preferences.

[96] Such sanctions can be based on different instruments and have the form of withdrawing GSP+ benefits, enacting issue-specific trade bans such as against trade in goods for torture, or adopting restrictive measures under Article 215 TFEU (actually outside trade policy). For more detail on these see Beke et al. (2014), pp. 30 ff.

[97] For an overview over their slightly different commitments see Beke et al. (2014), pp. 74 f.

[98] Claussen (2020), p. 33.

[99] Whether TSD chapters in EU FTAs can be enforced by recourse to general rules on countermeasures is heavily debated. In favour Bronckers and Gruni (2021), pp. 25–51; contra Weiß and Furculita (2020), pp. 881–882; Marín Durán (2020), p. 1047.

[100] Harrison et al. (2019), pp. 635–657.

being brought into conformity with the EU's policy choices by prescribing product or production requirements.

For the latter purpose, there are other instruments that the EU employs. Market opening and non-discrimination obligations in EU trade and/or investment agreements are subject to general exception clauses that verbatim imitate or explicitly refer to pertinent GATT/WTO exceptions such as Article XX GATT, Article XIV GATS which list unilateral measures that can be adopted and enforced without breaching the agreements. These general or sometimes issue-specific exception clauses allow a treaty party to depart from their market access and non-discrimination commitments in trade agreements and to raise barriers to trade which are necessary or at least related to a non-economic policy objective listed in the exception clause. The resulting trade barrier can be justified by the legitimate objective. In practice this means that the EU can lawfully block the import of foreign goods not in conformity with relevant domestic requirements flowing from the application of legitimate legislation. The same idea stands behind such provisions in investment agreements; they take care that market access and protection obligations for foreign investments do not counteract likewise legitimate domestic policies. In this way, policy space is created, as e.g. investment protection standards are not violated if a trade partner decides to adopt climate change or sustainability legislation, even though its consequences negatively interfere with the economic value of a protected investment.

Another tool used for the same purpose is the confirmation of each party's right to regulate in order to make space for the trade partners to implement domestic policies on subjects such as climate change, environment protection, or sustainability. While such rules in themselves may not have a specific legal consequence,[101] the due respect for the right to regulate impacts the way other provisions like market access, protection standards or an exception clause are to be interpreted and applied.[102] Interpreting an exception clause in view of respect for domestic regulatory autonomy might, for example, lower the requirements for a necessity test. Both of the above tools, general exception clauses as well as confirmation of each party's right to regulate do not provide for common standards, in contrast to the conditionality clauses mentioned above. Whereas conditionality clauses can be seen as instruments of positive integration, as treaty parties agree on common standards to be implemented or at least to engage in dialogue insofar, the other tools enable domestic legislative space which has to be respected by the other party even despite trade liberalization, so that one party can still unilaterally define its policies freely in the policy areas covered by exceptions and adopt the necessary unilateral measures. Hence, they are a tool of negative integration granting persisting regulatory freedom

[101] But see Art. 8.9 (2) CETA which provides that a Party's regulation that negatively affects an investment does not amount to a breach of investment protection standards; hence, it may operate comparable to an exception clause.

[102] Titi (2014), pp. 115 ff.

within the frame of basically non-discriminatory trade relations by securing deference to domestic legislation of the party adopting legitimate measures.[103]

With regard to investment agreements, a mechanism to ensure compliance of investment treaty obligations with regulatory policies, and thus preservation of public interests, is the conceptualization of the investment protection standards in international investment agreements in a manner that allows for domestic policy space and blocks an expansive interpretation of investor protection standards in a way that neglects legitimate regulatory interests. This means that the text of the substantive investment protection standards such as the protection against indirect expropriation or unfair treatment are defined more precisely in reflection of legitimate policy measures by the host state. The most-progressed EU example insofar is the CETA that in its Article 8.12 read in conjunction with its Annex 8-A defines indirect expropriation not to include "non-discriminatory measures of a Party that are designed and applied to protect legitimate public welfare objectives, such as health, safety and the environment", but with the qualifier that this applies "except in the rare circumstance when the impact of a measure or series of measures is so severe in light of its purpose that it appears manifestly excessive".[104] In most recent EU agreements, investment disciplines contain specific language and positive commitments such as regulatory cooperation or exchange of best practices in order to protect in particular climate change measures.[105]

Besides these main mechanisms for securing conformity of trade and investment relations with non-economic policies, there are other, softer instruments that contribute to a reconciliation of trade relations with other policies. These are positive commitments such as regulatory cooperation provisions as in CETA, or technical assistance rules.

---

[103]This categorization as instruments of negative integration does not apply to general exception provisions for trade barriers *within* customs unions or free trade areas that form integration communities, such as the EU or Mercosur (which are beyond the scope of this chapter). For, a liberalization reading of trade commitments attributing them a comprehensively deregulatory effect has an impact on how to conceive exception provisions as they play a different role in apportioning regulatory competences between the preferential area and its members compared to traditional FTAs with no or only a very limited liberalization agenda. For a comparison of EU to WTO jurisprudential developments insofar see Weiß (2020), pp. 53 ff.; for the positive integrationist function of the CJEU jurisprudence see Stone Sweet (2004), pp. 238 f. Nevertheless, convergences in applying general exception provisions, the underlying doctrines and thus in enabling regulatory autonomy can also be observed in the judicial conceptualisations by their adjudicatory institutions. See Wasilczyk (2023), pp. 149 f., 188 ff.

[104]This more or less verbatim reflects the definition in Annex B 13 (1) of the Canadian Model BIT 2004 or in Annex B of the US Model BIT 2012. Also the FET standard in Article 8.10 CETA, by and large, conforms to the one in US and Canadian BITs, see Dumberry (2022), paras. 4–8.

[105]Gehring and Tokas (2022), p. 811.

3.4 *Institutional Dimension of Effectuating Coherence*

Bringing trade and investment policy and other, non-economic policies into mutual conformity has also an institutional dimension that must be taken into account in the pursuit of coherence. This section will, admittedly briefly, reflect on the pertinent institutional actors.

3.4.1 The Role of Parliaments

A trade policy that addresses behind-the-border legislation interferes with the domain of domestic policy actors, in particular the legislative. Conversely, a domestic legislator that has also a decisive role in trade policy will use its powers in trade policy to strive for coherence with other domestic policies. Hence, both the institutional dimension of politics and the increasing interdependence of trade and domestic policies by trade policies addressing behind-the-border issues lead to trade policies becoming more intertwined with domestic policies. Consequently, the actors primarily responsible for national legislation, i.e. parliaments, advocate for their extended participation in determining trade policy, and rightly so for reasons of transparency, legitimacy and political inclusiveness. The interference of trade instruments with traditionally domestic policies increase the need for democratic legitimization of trade policies. Hence, for democratic legitimacy reasons, parliaments must be given greater leeway to participate in determining trade policy,[106] which again will increase transparency and information to the general public. Parliaments thus turn into actors of increasing coherence and positive consideration of non-economic policy objectives in trade policy, both on the level of the MS States and on the level of the EU, i.e. the European Parliament (EP).[107]

3.4.2 The Role of Dispute Settlement and Courts

As already mentioned in Sect. 3.1, despite the broad leeway for Council and Commission in implementing the constitutional obligation to bring trade policy into coherence with other policies, the CJEU as well plays a role in enforcing it. The Court determines the legal consequences of this constitutional obligation in defining the EU's trade policy in particular with a view to concrete legal acts enacting or implementing this policy that are challenged before it. Besides, the Court can be asked to issue binding opinions on the compliance of international

[106] Petersmann (2017), pp. 44 ff.; Young and Peterson (2006), pp. 795 and 797.

[107] Jančić (2017), pp. 204 ff; Weiß (2023), pp. 239 ff.

treaties with EU primary law including EU provisions enshrining values and objectives.[108]

A second layer of judicial control (or type of) flows from dispute settlement mechanisms provided for in international treaties. The EU and its treaty partners in (almost all[109] of) their trade and investment agreements agree on dispute settlement mechanisms (DSM),[110] usually in reflection of the well-known dispute settlement in the WTO. Investment treaties not only provide for state-to state DSM, but usually contain investor-state DSM (so-called ISDS).[111] All of these institutions decide in a usually binding way for the parties in case a dispute is brought before them in which the parties argue about the legality under the relevant international rules of measures taken by one party. This may in particular relate to measures a party adopted in order to bring its trade and investment relations into conformity with the requirements of other (mainly domestic) policies such as human rights or sustainability. Thus, it is the DS institutions' responsibility to act as a kind of final arbiter between the parties in determining which type of measures a party may adopt in compliance with the relevant international rules that are supposed to provide for coherence between trade, investment and other policies. Whereas the WTO DSM is enforceable, this is not necessarily the case with regard to FTA and investment treaty DSM, in particular as regards TSD chapters, as already mentioned.

The DS institutions therefore decide in a more or less final manner also about the interpretation of the instruments put in place for coherence between trade or investment liberalization and the requirements of other policy objectives set out above. Their jurisprudential application will be further explored in Sect. 4 where the pertinent disciplines in FTAs will be analysed in more detail. Concerns about a biased approach have been far-spread in particular in the area of ISDS in investment treaties. Safeguards for an unbiased balancing of investment and public interests therefore pertain to the broad legal qualification and expertise of the arbiters, and their independence and impartiality. Additionally, transparent procedures, the availability of appeals and the replacement of arbitration by public court-like investment dispute institutions will strengthen the quality of decisions and contribute to the due perception of public interests. These represent the institutional requirements necessary for a sound balance between investment and non-economic policies, and have been adopted by the parties in CETA's investment chapter by providing for a bilateral Investment Court system, and may become proliferated not least by the EU proposal for a permanent investment court.

---

[108] See e.g. for a control of an EU international treaty for its human rights compliance CJEU, Opinion 1/15, ECLI:EU:C:2017:592, para. 70—EU—Canada PNR Agreement.

[109] For the increasing proliferation of some type of DSM in FTAs globally see Furculiță (2021), pp. 15 f.

[110] For an overview over most recent EU FTA's dispute settlement mechanisms see Furculiță (2021), pp. 20 f, 31f, and 61 ff.

[111] Schill (2019), p. 113.

4 Bilateral and Regional Agreements and Non-economic Values

4.1 Non-economic Provisions in Free Trade Agreements

Not least with the shortfall of the WTO rule-making function and especially after the failure of the Doha Round, states began to actively pursue expanding the scope of trade policy with the help of bilateral and regional agreements. Thus, a myriad of free trade agreements (FTAs) proliferated in the last decade, with the EU and the US seemingly leading this movement.[112] Thus, the incorporation in FTAs of non-economic provisions, such as for example that of labour rights, environmental protection, human rights, democracy, transparency, and anti-corruption has been in a continuous ascent around the globe.[113] This trend has been especially prominent in the conclusion of recent mega-regional agreements,[114] such as that of the Comprehensive and Progressive Agreement for Trans-Pacific Partnership (CPTPP), which besides a chapter on exceptions contains dedicated chapters to labour, environment, development, transparency and anti-corruption.[115] Moreover, the range of specific non-trade issues has also greatly expanded over time. For example, more recent FTAs also address issues such as genetic resources, biodiversity, gender, indigenous rights.[116]

While the EU and the US approaches seem to converge with respect to actively including specific chapters on non-economic objectives in their FTAs, their exact content and legal value of doing so have been different.[117] Ever since the conclusion of the North American Free Trade Agreement (NAFTA), the US has included labour provisions in most of its FTAs and all of the FTAs concluded thereafter contain environmental provisions.[118] Nevertheless, unlike the EU, which adapts its norms to the specific context of each partner, the US has been imposing its approach on its trading partners, thereby ensuring a level playing field to its domestic producers.[119] Similar to the EU, the US has also been using conditionality, but with a focus on pre-ratification requirements,[120] thereby making certain domestic changes in the partner's policies a condition for FTA ratification. Another essential difference between US and EU approaches (at least until recently; the EU is changing its approach) has been with respect to the enforcement of these commitments, with

[112] Lee et al. (2021), p. 3.

[113] Milewicz et al. (2018), pp. 743 and 751; Claussen (2020), p. 29.

[114] Milewicz et al. (2018), pp. 743–744.

[115] Trans-Pacific Partnership Agreement (TPP) incorporated by the CPTPP, Art. 1.

[116] Velut et al. (2022), pp. 16 f.

[117] Horn et al. (2010), pp. 1565–1588; Postnikov (2019), pp. 181–183.

[118] Lee et al. (2021), pp. 2 f.

[119] Morin and Rochette (2017), pp. 624 and 632; Velut et al. (2022), p. 28.

[120] Moore and Scherrer (2017).

the US including strong enforcement mechanisms in its FTAs, allowing the imposition of sanctions. A telling example has also been the NAFTA's and, subsequently, the US-Mexico-Canada Agreement's (USMCA) approach with respect to the enforcement of labour provisions. NAFTA contained a special dedicated enforcement mechanism in a side agreement, the North American Agreement on Labor Cooperation (NAALC), which allowed for the imposition of sanctions in limited instances, and under which several investigations and consultations occurred but none of them reached the point of panel establishment.[121] As the instrument had been criticized for its ineffectiveness,[122] the USMCA introduced a new mechanism between the US and Mexico called the Rapid Response Labor Mechanism (RRM),[123] which is a facility-specific mechanism, containing expedited review with clear time frames allowing to speedily address violations of the freedom of association and collective bargaining rights.[124] Despite the clear disparities between the EU and American approaches, they are not contradictory and could reinforce each other, especially since they share certain commonalities, such as the exceptions for the conservation of natural resources, the promotion of domestic environmental norms, forest governance, biological diversity, or capacity building.[125]

While the trend set by the EU and the US to include provisions on non-economic objectives has been followed by many others, they did not do so to the same degree. Canada, New Zealand, and Switzerland, for example, have all committed to include specific provisions on sustainable development in all their FTAs concluded in the last decade.[126] On the other hand, big economies such as China, Japan, or Australia do not regularly link sustainable development with their trade agreements.[127] For example, the Japan–Australia Economic Partnership Agreement and Australia–Indonesia Comprehensive Economic Partnership Agreement do not contain labour and environment dedicated chapters. Chinese FTAs occasionally include environmental provisions and mostly neglect labour standards, and when they do address these non-economic issues, they do not do so in an ambitious manner.[128] Thus, the Regional Comprehensive Economic Partnership's (RCEP) does not include provisions on sustainability, except in the preamble.[129] Furthermore, the degree of enforceability of these non-economic provisions also greatly varies, as not all

[121]De La Cruz J (2022) Consequences of Non-compliance with USMCA Labor Provisions: Potential Effects on Exporting Firms. US International Trade Commission, Economics Working Paper Series Working Paper 2022-05-B, May 2022, p. 6.

[122]Ibid, 4.

[123]USMCA, Chapter 31, Annex A.

[124]Bonne (2022), p. 205; Bown C P, Claussen K (2023) The Rapid Response Labor Mechanism of the US-Mexico- Canada Agreement. Peterson Institute for International Economics 23-9 Working Paper, p. 14.

[125]Morin and Rochette (2017), pp. 623, 641, and 644; Leal-Arcas et al. (2020), p. 19.

[126]Velut et al. (2022), pp. 15–16.

[127]Ibid, p. 14.

[128]For more, see Wei and Rafael (2023), pp. 367–384.

[129]For more, see Duval and Natnicha (2023); Kettunen (2023), pp. 672–682.

agreements allow recourse to arbitration,[130] while those that do allow such recourse contain no or different remedies.[131] Accordingly, while there is a clear convergence when it comes to the increase of linkages between trade and non-economic issues, as well as that of the range of issues covered, not all countries engage in this conduct with the same zeal, nor in the same manner. The substance of the obligations regarding non-economic objectives and their enforceability are different.

Those FTAs that address non-economic policies usually incorporate one or more provisions of the types just mentioned. For example, about 97% of the WTO-notified Regional Trade Agreements include at least one environmental provision.[132] The majority of these, including older ones[133] but also some more recent, refer to sustainable development goals in their preambles, general objectives, and incorporate general GATT and GATS-type exceptions.[134] Thus, similar to EU FTAs, agreements such as Canada–Korea FTA, CPTPP, or USMCA expressly incorporate Article XX GATT and Article XIV GATS and their interpretative notes *mutatis mutandis* to limit the effect of market access and non-discrimination obligations.[135] Furthermore, seemingly emphasizing the particular importance of Article XX b) and g) GATT and avoiding any ambiguity in this respect, the agreements add that parties understand that 'environmental measures necessary to protect human, animal or plant life or health' and 'measures relating to the conservation of living and non-living exhaustible natural resources' fall under them, reflecting the interpretive approaches of WTO jurisprudence.[136] Similar to the EU, it is also common practice of states with ambitious FTAs having dedicated provisions to non-economic issues, such as the US, Canada, or Switzerland, to use provisions on the right to regulate.[137]

[130] Peru—Australia FTA, for example, contains only provisions on cooperation and consultations with respect to labour and environmental commitments. See Arts. 18.17, 19.5.

[131] For instance, EFTA model TSD chapter provides for panel review, but no remedies (https://www.seco.admin.ch/seco/en/home/Aussenwirtschaftspolitik_Wirtschaftliche_Zusammenarbeit/Wirtschaftsbeziehungen/Freihandelsabkommen/nachhaltigkeit/modellkapitelueberhandelundnachhaltigeentwicklung.html). Similarly does the UK—Japan Agreement for a Comprehensive Economic Partnership (Art. 16.18 (6)). Canada—Korea FTA, Art. 18.18 (4) provides for monetary assessment. CPTPP allows the imposition of the same trade remedies as in case of traditional trade disputes (TPP, Arts. 19.15 (12), 20.23).

[132] WTO, 'Trade and Climate Change', Information Brief No. 2, 2022, https://www.wto.org/english/news_e/news21_e/clim_03nov21-2_e.pdf, p. 4.

[133] Velut et al. (2022), p. 76.

[134] The Agreement Establishing the African Continental Free Trade Area (AfCFTA), for example, mentions the right to regulate in its preamble (recital 8), sustainable development is enshrined in the preamble to the Protocol on Trade in Services (recital 5) and the general objectives (Art. 3 (e); Protocol on Trade in Services, Art. 3 (2)(b)), and provides Art. XX GATT-like general exceptions (Article 26; Protocol on Trade in Services, Art. 15).

[135] Canada—Korea FTA, Art. 22.1(1); TPP, as incorporated by the CPTPP, Art. 29.1 (1); USMCA, Art. 32.1(1).

[136] Canada—Korea FTA, Art. 22.1(1); TPP, as incorporated by the CPTPP, Art. 29.1(2); USMCA, Art. 32.1(2).

[137] Velut et al. (2022), p. 18.

For example, the USMCA in its preamble recognizes the parties' 'inherent right to regulate', explicitly establishing that it should be exercised 'in accordance with the rights and obligations provided in this Agreement'. Accordingly, it makes clear that, as mentioned in Sects. 2.2 and 3.3, the right to regulate is not in itself enforceable, but might be useful as context for other disciplines, such as market access or exception clauses. In a manner evoking EU's instruments, FTAs across the globe also include 'non-derogation' clauses. Thus, FTAs regularly address the issue of using more relaxed non-economic policies to influence the level playing field by recognising the inappropriateness of encouraging trade by weakening or reducing the environment protections afforded by parties' domestic laws.[138] FTAs also enshrine parties' right to establish their own level of protection.[139] Newer FTAs go beyond mere preambular language and general exceptions and regularly make reference to multilateral environment agreements,[140] as well as to International Labor Organization (ILO) Declarations and Conventions,[141] encouraging their ratification or implementation.[142] Finally, trade agreements contain other non-economic rules such as those related to the public/civil society participation, cooperation, or implementation and dispute settlement.[143]

4.2 Non-economic Policies in Free Trade Agreements Jurisprudence

Dispute settlement mechanisms in FTAs, in general, have rarely been used until recently when the practice of the states suddenly has changed and several FTA disputes were initiated, especially by the EU and the US. This surge in FTA disputes could be due to the paralysis of the WTO Appellate Body since December 2019 or to the extensive FTA substantive coverage over non-WTO issues, especially non-trade policies, as most of the recent FTA disputes concern sustainable development commitments.[144]

The first ever sustainable development dispute resulting in a final panel report in 2017 was *US—Guatemala* labor dispute under the Dominican Republic-Central

[138] See, USMCA, Arts. 23.4, 24.4(3); TPP, Arts. 19.4, 20.3(6); UK—Australia FTA, Arts. 21.5, 22.3(6), 25.1(3).

[139] See, TPP, Art. 20.3(2); USMCA, Arts. 24.2(2), 24.3(1), Canada-Honduras Free Trade Agreement, Art. 18.1(1).

[140] For instance, US—Peru FTA, Art. 18.2; UK—Australia FTA, Art. 22.5.

[141] For example, Canada—Panama FTA, Art. 18.1; US—Panama Trade Promotion Agreement, Art. 16.6 (1).

[142] Velut et al. (2022), p. 79.

[143] WTO, 'Trade and Climate Change', Information Brief No. 2, 2022, https://www.wto.org/english/news_e/news21_e/clim_03nov21-2_e.pdf, pp. 5 and 9.

[144] Vidigal (2022), p. 569. Considering the growing number of disputes initiated under the USMCA's RRM, now most of the disputes are labour-related.

America-US Free Trade Agreement (CAFTA—DR).[145] The US initiated a myriad of labour disputes under the USMCA's RRM,[146] environmental consultations under the US—Peru Trade Promotion Agreement (TPA),[147] US—Korea FTA (KORUS),[148] and USMCA.[149] Neither of these disputes, however, has finalized with a panel report. In 2018, the EU initiated a dispute against Korea under EU—Korea FTA, which resulted in a panel report in early 2021.[150] In addition, the EU instituted a trade dispute against Ukraine related to its wood export ban which also resulted in a panel report,[151] where the panel considered the link between the FTA's TSD chapter and general trade exceptions. In what follows, we will consider the three panel reports with a focus on how trade and non-trade policies were reconciled.

In US—Guatemala labour dispute the panel found that at several worksites Guatemala failed to comply with its obligations with respect to the effective enforcement of its labor laws related to the right of association, the right to organize and bargain collectively, and acceptable conditions of work. Nevertheless, it held that these instances did not constitute a 'sustained or recurring course of action or inaction'[152] that was in a 'manner affecting trade',[153] a condition established by CAFTA-DR. Thus, the panel had to deal with the sensitive question with respect to the link necessary between trade and non-trade policies. It interpreted the latter phrase in a rather restrictive manner, referring to acts that confer 'some competitive advantage on an employer or employers engaged in trade between the Parties', this

---

[145] Guatemala—Issues Relating to the Obligations Under Article 16.2.1(a) of the CAFTA-DR (*US—Guatemala*), Final Report of the Panel, June 14, 2017.

[146] For a full list of cases brought under this mechanism see https://ustr.gov/issue-areas/enforcement/dispute-settlement-proceedings/fta-dispute-settlement/usmca/chapter-31-annex-facility-specific-rapid-response-labor-mechanism.

[147] USTR Requests First-Ever Environment Consultations Under the U.S.-Peru Trade Promotion Agreement (PTPA), 4 January 2019, https://ustr.gov/about-us/policy-offices/press-office/press-releases/2019/january/ustr-requests-first-ever#:~:text=Through%20these%20environment%20consultations%2C%20the,to%20a%20subordinate%20position%20within. The consultations resulted in an agreement reached between the parties. For more on the dispute see Pacheco Restrepo (2019), pp. 247–262.

[148] USTR to Request First-Ever Environment Consultations Under the U.S.-Korea Free Trade Agreement (KORUS) in Effort to Combat Illegal Fishing, 19 September 2019, https://ustr.gov/about-us/policy-offices/press-office/press-releases/2019/september/ustr-request-first-ever, following which Korea introduced several legislative amendments.

[149] 'USTR Announces USMCA Environment Consultations with Mexico', 10 February 2022, https://ustr.gov/about-us/policy-offices/press-office/press-releases/2022/february/ustr-announces-usmca-environment-consultations-mexico.

[150] Panel of Experts Proceeding Constituted under Article 13.15 of the EU-Korea FTA (*EU—Korea Labour*), 20 January 2021.

[151] Final Report of the Arbitration Panel, Restrictions applied by Ukraine on exports of certain wood products to the European Union (*EU—Ukraine Wood Export Bans*), 11 December 2020.

[152] *US—Guatemala* panel report (fn 145), paras. 590, 591.

[153] Ibid, para. 594.

being a question of fact and actual effects.[154] Since many other FTAs, including EU FTAs, contain similar language, the interpretation offered by the panel in this dispute questions the place of labour commitments within trade agreements.[155] The case at hand was received with criticism,[156] and used as an argument that using panels composed of trade experts is not the appropriate adjudication route for 'trade and…' disputes.[157] Moreover, it appears to set back the advancement of non-trade policy goals within FTAs witnessed in the last decades. The report was followed by the US addressing the interpretation of said phrase within the USMCA under negotiations at that time. Therefore, the USMCA defines the meaning of 'affecting trade' more broadly, seemingly referring to conduct simply related to trade, without the need to show actual effects on competition.[158] Furthermore, USMCA introduces a presumption that a failure is in a manner affecting trade, unless rebutted.[159] The application of this approach remains to be tested in practice.

The EU—Korea Labour dispute marked the first EU initiated dispute settlement procedure under its FTAs, being also the first to test its cooperative approach towards TSD chapters. The EU made two sets of claims: one concerning the consistency of Korea's measures with the FTA commitment to respect, promote, and realise, in parties' laws and practices, the principles concerning fundamental rights, and second concerning Korea's insufficient efforts towards the ratification of the core ILO Conventions.[160] In an attempt to achieve a result similar to that from US—Guatemala labour dispute, Korea raised a jurisdictional objection arguing that the TSD chapter's scope was limited by the FTA article defining it only to 'trade-related aspects of labour'.[161] By analysing the ordinary meaning of the terms of the article used as a ground for EU's claims read in their context and in light of the object and purpose of the TSD chapter, noting the explicit references to the ILO Constitution and the ILO Declaration with universal scope, and refuting the pertinence of US—Guatemala report to the case, the panel established that the article represented an exception to the more limited TSD chapter's scope, albeit without concluding that the matter at issue had no connection to trade.[162] Furthermore, seemingly supporting EU's ambitious pursuit of non-trade policies through FTAs,[163] the panel established

---

[154] Ibid, paras. 190, 192, 196.

[155] Claussen (2020), p. 33.

[156] See, for example, Ortino F (2021) Trade and labour linkages and the US—Guatemala panel report: Critical assessment and future impact. European Trade Union Institute (ETUI) Working Paper 2021.11, https://www.etui.org/publications/trade-and-labour-linkages-and-us-guatemala-panel-report.

[157] Claussen (2020), p. 36.

[158] See USMCA, fn. 4 to Art. 23.3(1), fn. 8 and 9 to Art. 23.4, fn. 11, 12 to Art. 23.5(1), and fn. 13, 14 to Art. 23.7.

[159] USMCA, fn. 5 to Art. 23.3(1).

[160] *EU—Korea Labour* panel report, para. 55.

[161] Ibid, para. 56.

[162] Ibid, paras. 63–68, 90–94.

[163] Novitz (2021), p. 4.

that in EU—Korea FTA measures implementing fundamental labour rights are 'inherently related to trade'.[164] This interpretation could be even said to change the object and purpose of the entire FTA, by putting TSD and trade commitments on equal footing.[165] Thus, despite some criticism with respect to panel's broad interpretation,[166] the panel converged with EU's approach and for the first time offered an opportunity for labour issues enshrined in FTAs to be treated separately from trade-related aspects.[167] Moreover, even without ratifying certain ILO Conventions, the panel held that Korea committed to ILO constitutional principles enshrined in the FTA, such as the freedom of association,[168] thereby making FTAs a potential means to enforce ILO Conventions to a certain degree, even when they have not been ratified. Still, with respect to EU's second set of claims, the panel established that Korea's efforts satisfied the exigencies of the provision, despite being 'less than optimal',[169] potentially incentivising other EU FTA partners to delay the ratification of ILO Conventions[170] and leading to calls for more stringent language to be used in TSD chapters.[171]

In EU—Ukraine Wood Export Bans dispute, the EU challenged Ukraine's wood export bans under the FTA provision prohibiting quantitative restrictions, in response to which Ukraine invoked the TSD chapter as a substantive justification.[172] Despite Ukraine's objection to jurisdiction arguing that the special TSD mechanism should have been used, the panel examined the dispute under the FTA's general dispute settlement mechanism, due to how the matter was identified by the EU and the untimely objection to that identification by the respondent.[173] This interpretation could be used to argue that in FTAs with different enforcement mechanisms for trade and non-trade issues the last could remain un-used if the complainant invokes the first, and the case is likely to make defendants raise timely objections. With respect to the invocation of the TSD chapter as a substantive justification, the panel concluded that TSD provisions 'are not in and of themselves self-standing or unqualified exceptions to justify measures that are in breach of other provisions', such as the prohibition on quantitative restrictions.[174] Rather, the panel established that the TSD chapter 'complements' the provisions of the Trade and Trade-related

---

[164] *EU—Korea Labour* panel report, para. 95.

[165] Vidigal (2022), p. 574.

[166] Ibid; Zhao (2022), pp. 950 ff.

[167] Boisson de Chazournes and Lee (2022), p. 345.

[168] *EU—Korea Labour* panel report, paras. 112 ff.

[169] Ibid, paras. 288, 291, 292.

[170] Han (2021), p. 543.

[171] For example, see Position Paper of the Green MEPs of the International Trade Committee on the Review of the 15-Point Action Plan, www.greens-efa.eu/files/assets/docs/20220428_inta_green_position_paper_on_tsd_def.pdf, p. 8.

[172] *EU—Ukraine Wood Export Bans* panel report, paras. 1, 137, 226.

[173] Ibid, paras. 25, 117–125, 132–138. For criticism see Kübek (2022), p. 285.

[174] *EU—Ukraine Wood Export Bans* panel report, paras. 244, 249, 251.

matters chapter; it used the first only as relevant context for the interpretation of the FTA general exception provision incorporating Article XX GATT.[175] Were the measure challenged under a TSD provision, the measure could have been considered under it, but since it was found to violate on its face a provision from the chapter dedicated to trade matters, the special provisions from that chapter interpreted in light of TSD commitments were used as potential justifications.[176]

Albeit in completely different circumstances, the approaches taken by the panels towards the status of non-trade policies within EU FTAs taken in EU—Korea Labour and EU—Ukraine Wood Export Bans could be perceived as contradictory, since the first seems to recognize the importance of TSD obligations, even without being trade related, while the last abnegates their self-standing importance.[177] Furthermore, EU—Ukraine Wood Export Bans was brought as an argument in favour of panelists with specific expertise to consider TSD commitments.[178] This dispute raised the question of the relationship between traditional general exceptions and specific chapters or rules dedicated to certain non-economic policy areas, answering it in favour of general exceptions being used as justifications for violations of chapters dedicated to trade. The panel did, however, give due consideration to the TSD chapter during the interpretation of Article XX GATT incorporated in the FTA, especially that of the necessity test, which within the WTO, as stated in Sect. 2.3, sets a considerable threshold for domestic policies. In light of the Ukraine's right to regulate its own level of environmental protection enshrined in the TSD chapter, the panel interpreted the weighing and balancing exercise with more flexibility by stating that the 'high trade restrictive effect inherent to an export ban cannot be considered to automatically outweigh the other elements', which led to a positive finding in favour of a provisional justification under paragraph (b) of Article XX GATT (which however finally failed due to lack of meeting the requirements of the chapeau).[179] Consequently, despite discrepancies in the two cases related to EU FTAs with respect to the status of TSD commitments within the agreements, both cases illustrate certain convergence when it comes to giving due consideration to non-economic policies enshrined in trade agreements, although to different degrees. Still, judging based on the three disputes, a clear trend in disputes related to 'trade and…' issues has not yet solidified, and it remains to see how things will evolve as more disputes will be solved. And in the same way as under WTO law, the chapeau of the exception clause is an important part in assessing whether the legitimate policy objectives enshrined in the exception clause can outweigh trade interests, with the panel following the WTO judiciary's approach.

---

[175] Ibid, para. 245.

[176] Ibid, paras. 245–249.

[177] Kübek (2022), p. 568.

[178] Vidigal (2022), p. 578.

[179] *EU—Ukraine Wood Export Bans* panel report, paras. 330–333, 344, 345 ff. Vidigal, nevertheless, argues that the declared flexibility had limited impact on the final result, Vidigal (2022), p. 577.

4.3 Non-economic Provisions in Investment Agreements

Over the last two decades the international investment regime was repeatedly criticized for not giving weight to non-investment concerns. Thus, the regime has been undergoing a legitimacy crisis underpinned by arguments that the system is inherently built in favor of investors, while states' public interests together with corresponding investors' obligations are given too little consideration within the agreements.[180] This asymmetry seems to even have led certain countries, such as South Africa, India, or Ecuador, to terminate especially older Bilateral Investment treaties (BITs).[181] However, in the last decade, states mostly revisited their approach to BITs design by including ever more special provisions promoting non-investment policy objectives, giving preference to more precise language, and ensuring states' regulatory space.[182] Thus, states are increasingly including provisions in their BITs to address such concerns as human and labour rights, environment protection, or public health.[183] Many innovations are clearly directed towards correcting, rejecting, and avoiding past controversial arbitral interpretations,[184] which led influential actors like the US and Canada to revise their BITs to give greater weight to host country interests.[185]

Non-investment policy concerns usually find their way in newer investment agreements through one of the means that have already been identified above Sect. 3.3. Thus, many agreements acknowledge the importance of non-investment concerns and include the right to regulate and non-relaxation commitments in their preambles,[186] or in specific treaty provisions.[187] The value of preambles or specific clauses, however, as argued in Sects. 2.2 and 3.3 with regard to WTO and EU agreements, is only to provide contextual language for the interpretation of other

[180] Giest (2017), p. 331; Marisi (2020), p. 284; Arcuri and Violi (2021), p. 2186.

[181] Giest (2017), p. 330; Marisi (2020), p. 285.

[182] UNCTAD World Investment Report 2020, Chapter III, https://unctad.org/system/files/official-document/WIR2020_CH3.pdf, p. 112; UNCTAD World Investment Report 2023, Chapter II, https://unctad.org/system/files/official-document/wir2023_ch02_en.pdf, p. 90.

[183] Acconci (2018), p. 315. For an analysis of the reason for the traditional omission of social values in BITs and their early change, see Kurtz (2016), pp. 171 f.

[184] Alschner (2022), p. 183. The COVID-19 pandemic has especially highlighted the need to regulate the relationship between public health and investment, see Duggal et al. (2021), pp. 133–146. Obviously, there have been other attempts of making available flexibility by reading NT obligations to cover non-economic concerns, but incompletely so, see Kurtz (2016), pp. 178 ff.

[185] Alvarez (2010), pp. 144 f.; Vandevelde (2009), p. 283.

[186] For example, Australia—Uruguay BIT, Preamble, recital 5; CPTPP, Preamble, recital 6, TPP, recitals 1, 9, 10, 12–14, 16; 2012 US Model BIT, preamble, recitals 5; 2019 Netherlands Model BIT, preamble, recitals 1, 3, 4, 5.

[187] For example, EFTA—Bosnia and Herzegovina FTA, 24 June 2013, Art. 1 (2) (e) on treaty objectives; Canada—Colombia FTA, Art. 815 on non-relaxation commitments; 2021 Canada Model BIT, Art. 3 on parties' right to regulate; 2019 Belgium-Luxemburg Model BIT, Arts. 1.2, 3.3, 14, 15 on levels of protection, right to regulate, treaty objective.

treaty norms without creating separate enforceable rights, leaving to the discretion of the arbitrators how to take them into account.[188] Only some agreements expressly clarify the legal effects of such provisions.[189] Many BITs contain general and security exceptions (the last usually akin to Article XXI GATT)[190] or specific clarifications, such as the exclusion of non-discriminatory measures designed and applied to protect legitimate policy objectives from the definition of expropriation[191] (as used within the definitions of indirect expropriation also in EU investment treaties, as shown above Sect. 3.3) or that of tobacco control measures.[192] The insertion of general exceptions in investment agreements is a growing practice which emerged only recently, in contrast to the international trade law context where it long became common practice. Unlike FTAs that generally follow the model of Article XX GATT, general exception clauses in BITs are less uniform. Some agreements contain exceptions inspired by Article XX GATT, containing a chapeau and an exhaustive list of legitimate policy objectives, with some paragraphs containing the necessity or 'relate to' tests.[193] Still, even Article XX GATT-like provisions contain different lists of objectives. For example, Japan's BITs do not except measures related to the conservation of exhaustible natural resources similar to Article XX g) GATT.[194] Other agreements also provide exceptions for health and environmental measures, but contain a very lenient language without replicating the chapeau or necessity test.[195] Interestingly, some BITs establish a rather genuine kind of a broad exception clause according to which 'nothing in this Chapter shall be construed to prevent a Party from adopting, maintaining or enforcing any measure *otherwise consistent* with this Chapter that it considers appropriate to ensure that investment activity in its territory is undertaken in a manner sensitive to environmental, health or other regulatory objectives' (emphasis added).[196] Strikingly, while the introductory language is construed as an exception to the entire investment chapter, such measures still have to be consistent with it. One has to wait and see

[188] Alschner W, Hui K (2018) Missing in Action: General Public Policy Exceptions in Investment Treaties. Ottawa Faculty of Law Working Paper No. 2018-22, p. 4; Choudhury (2020), p. 44; Zagel (2021), p. 16.

[189] Duggal et al. (2021), p. 142. For example, see the 2019 Netherlands Model BIT, Art. 2.2.

[190] For instance, 2021 Canada Model BIT, Art. 22; Australia—Hong Kong BIT (2019), Art. 19. For more on security exceptions in BITs and investment arbitration see Ranjan (2021), pp. 579–601. For early and diverse BIT practice in includeing general GATT-like exceptions, sometimes subject to slight changes, see Kurtz (2016), pp. 194 ff.

[191] For example, Benin-Canada BIT, Annex I, (c).

[192] TPP, as incorporated by CPTPP, Art. 29.5. For more see Sheargold and Mitchell (2021), p. 1854.

[193] See, for example, Australia—Hong Kong BIT, Art. 18; Israel—United Arab Emirates BIT (2020), Art. 15(1); Japan—Bahrain BIT (2022), Art. 18(1).

[194] Japan—Morocco BIT (2020), Art. 21(1); Japan—Georgia BIT (2021), Art. 15(1); Japan—Bahrain BIT, Art. 18(1).

[195] See, for example, Kenya—Mauritius BIT, Art. 12(1); Turkey—Zambia BIT, Art. 6(1).

[196] TPP, as incorporated by CPTPP, Art. 9.16; USMCA, Art. 14.16; UK—Australia FTA, Art. 13.7.

how such terminology might be interpreted with a view to its capacity for providing effective regulatory autonomy to the host state.

The inclusion of GATT-like general exceptions in BITs was claimed to not necessarily lead to the result desired by the states.[197] Investment arbitrators have previously conflated general exceptions with customary law by precluding the application of the police powers doctrine in the context of indirect expropriation when there was a general exception,[198] or by erroneously interpreting general exceptions restrictively by citing jurisprudence on customary law[199] (see below Sect. 4.4). It was also argued that customary law or reading traditional investment standards such as National Treatment or Fair and Equitable Treatment (FET) as accommodating regulatory objectives[200] might provide more flexibility to states, given the absence of a finite set of objectives or of a demanding 'necessity' test or chapeau similar to that under WTO general exceptions (see Sects. 2.2 and 2.3).[201] Nevertheless, the jurisprudence on the police powers doctrine or on reading standards flexibly is not uniform but filled with a high degree of uncertainty.[202] Furthermore, such flexibility pertains only to certain standards, not entire investment chapters. Accordingly, providing for general exception provisions, using more lenient language and clarifying the relationship with customary law could be the best route for attaining a better balance between investment and non-investment policies, as one can learn from the intricacies the WTO exceptions place in the interpretational approaches by the WTO judiciary with regard to the necessity test and the chapeau (see Sect. 2.3).

States also integrate non-economic issues in BITs through specific provisions, such as specifying the role of investment for the promotion of sustainable development, investor obligations, or corporate social responsibility,[203] which, nevertheless,

[197] For more see Alschner W, Hui K (2018) Missing in Action: General Public Policy Exceptions in Investment Treaties. Ottawa Faculty of Law Working Paper No. 2018-22.

[198] Alschner (2022), pp. 159–166. See *Bear Creek v. Peru*, ICSID Case No ARB/14/21, Award, 30 November 2017.

[199] For instance, in *Eco Oro v. Colombia*, ICSID Case No. ARB/16/41, Decision on Jurisdiction, Liability and Directions on Quantum, 9 September 2021, para. 83, supporting its interpretation by making reference to ILC Draft Articles on State Responsibility.

[200] For instance, *Pope & Talbot Inc.*, UNCITRAL, Award on the Merits of Phase 2, 10 April 2001, paras. 78, 81 interpreted the National Treatment standard as allowing differences in treatment that have 'reasonable nexus to rational government policies'. *Saluka Investments BV (The Netherlands) v Czech Republic*, Partial Award, UNCITRAL, 17 March 2006, para. 306 interpreted FETas 'weighing of the Claimant's legitimate and reasonable expectations on the one hand and the Respondent's legitimate regulatory interests on the other'.

[201] Lévesque (2013), pp. 363–370; Choudhury (2020), pp. 49–51. For more pros and cons of general exceptions see Marisi (2020), pp. 119–120.

[202] Alschner W, Hui K (2018) Missing in Action: General Public Policy Exceptions in Investment Treaties. Ottawa Faculty of Law Working Paper No. 2018-22, p. 14.

[203] See, for example, Morocco-Nigeria Reciprocal Investment Promotion and Protection Agreement, Art. 24; 2015 India Model BIT, Arts. 11, 12; Indonesia—Australia CEPA, Art. 14.17.

usually have a rather soft language.[204] Some agreements include contribution to non-investment policy objectives in the definition of investment, other types of investment falling outside the scope of the agreement.[205] Since most of the claims related to non-investment policies were based on the FET and indirect expropriation standards, many states, in following US and EU trends (see Sect. 3.3), refine BIT language to clarify that regulatory actions taken to protect legitimate policy objectives should not constitute violations of these standards.[206] Furthermore, they add more explicit language to provide what the grounds for a violation of these standards are,[207] or even exclude the FET standard altogether from the treaty.[208] Another recent trend in BIT drafting is to expressly allow counterclaims.[209] Finally, certain procedural reforms under consideration,[210] such as the EU-backed proposal to establish a permanent investment court with appeal mechanism could also help with balancing different interests more soundly.

Although treaty drafting cannot resolve the conflict between different policies alone, the states' approach in newer BITs clearly indicates upon a convergence with the inclusion of non-economic objectives in EU CCP and in the WTO and FTAs contexts with regard to the mechanisms used to effectuate a sound balance between trade/investment interests and non-economic policies and their objectives, i.e. by enshrining the respect for regulatory autonomy or right to regulate (in the investment context sometimes termed policy power doctrine) into the treaty text, objectives or preambles, by introducing general or specific exception clauses or policy specific chapters (with sometimes more lenient language favouring domestic policy decisions), and by employing stricter language with regard to traditionally rather generally drafted, more or less undefined investment protection standards (FET, indirect expropriation) in order to avoid too broad a leeway for arbitrators. The inclusion of the state's right to regulate in newer BITs serves different legal functions, i.e. as a treaty objective in the preamble, as a limitation of the scope of application, as a more or less explicit exception to investor protection standards or as their interpretive context.

[204] Duggal et al. (2021), p. 142.

[205] Morocco—Nigeria BIT, Art. 1(1).

[206] 2012 US Model BIT, Annex B, para. 4 (b); 2019 Netherlands Model BIT, Art. 12 (8).

[207] 2012 US Model BIT, Art. 5 (2); TPP as incorporated in CPTPP, Art. 9.6(2).

[208] 2015 India Model BIT, Art. 3 on treatment of investors instead of FET.

[209] TPP, as incorporated by CPTPP, Art. 9.19(2). For an analysis see Abel (2022).

[210] See the United Nations Commission on International Trade Law (UNCITRAL)'s Working Group III.

4.4 Non-economic Policies in Investment Arbitration Jurisprudence

As already alluded to, the legitimacy crisis of the international investment agreements is also related to the allegations that not only their text, but also the arbitrators in investor-state dispute settlement favour investors' rights over the states' right to regulate in the public interest.[211] International investment arbitrators dealt with numerous disputes that concerned also non-economic issues, such as human rights,[212] environment protection,[213] cultural sites,[214] or energy.[215] Due to the abundance of investment arbitral awards, being based on diverse BITs, and the absence of a permanent tribunal or a court of appeal which allows for harmonizing interpretive approaches, there is little consistency across arbitral awards dealing with non-investment issues. There are well-known cases, especially earlier ones, in which legitimate policy objectives raised by states as justifications failed and investors won the claims. For instance, in *Metalclad* the tribunal considered that the environmental motivation behind the state's measure was irrelevant for its finding of expropriation.[216] In *Suez v Argentina*, where Argentina invoked the necessity defence due to the crisis in which it fell, the tribunal denied the justification and held that, without the BIT containing a security exception, Argentina's human rights obligation to ensure its population with water does not trump BIT obligations, both having equal value.[217] And even if a BIT contains a security exception, it may still be construed narrowly in view of the customary defense of necessity, as happened in the first awards dealing with the crisis in Argentina 1999–2002.[218] In contrast, the arbitrators in *Continental Casualty* conceived the public order and security exception in Argentina's BIT broadly and interpreted the necessity requirement in reflection of pertinent WTO jurisdiction to the effect that Argentina enjoyed considerable legislative leeway to respond to its economic crisis.[219] Furthermore, even though most

[211] Behn and Langford (2017), p. 14.

[212] See *EDF and others v. Argentina*, ICSID Case No. ARB/03/23, Award, 11 June 2012.

[213] See *Methanex Corporation v. United States of America*, UNCITRAL, Final Award of the Tribunal on Jurisdiction and Merits, 3 August 2005.

[214] See *Parkerings v. Lithuania*, ICSID Case No. ARB/05/8, Award, 11 September 2007.

[215] See *Sempra Energy International v. Argentina*, ICSID Case No. ARB/02/16, Award, 28 September 2007.

[216] *Metalclad Corporation v. The United Mexican States*, ICSID Case No. ARB(AF)/97/1, Award, 30 August 2000, para. 111.

[217] *Suez I v. Argentina*, ICSID Case No. ARB/03/17, Decision on Liability, 30 July 2010, paras. 240, 243; *Suez II v. Argentina*, ICSID Case No. ARB/03/19, Decision on Liability, 30 July 2010, paras, 262, 265.

[218] See Stone Sweet and della Cananea (2014), pp. 926 ff.

[219] Continental Casualty v. Argentina, ICSID Case No. ARB/03/9, 5 September 2008, paras. 192 ff. This award caused considerable controversy about judicial law-making and the capacity of courts to receive jurisprudence from other international law regimes, see Stone Sweet and della Cananea (2014), pp. 914 ff and 934 ff.

cases are on older BITs that do not contain dedicated provisions on other policies, arbitrators have frequently read into investment protection disciplines the police power doctrine, which enshrines the states' right to regulate in matters of public interest.[220] Some tribunals even defined 'investment' in terms of its contribution to sustainable development.[221] In *Cortec*, despite the absence of explicit language to this effect in the BIT, the panel read an implicit requirement to comply with domestic environmental laws in order to be a protected investment.[222] Even when investors have won a dispute in which non-economic justifications were raised, this was usually because of suspicions related to states' intent and manner of application,[223] or because states did not sufficiently argue the pertinent justification.[224] Accordingly, it would be erroneous to assert that investment arbitrations have consistently disregarded non-economic values. In fact, recently, investment arbitral tribunals seemingly started considering non-economic values more and more often.[225]

With regard to standard of review, the arbitrators also apply a rather deferential control standard when assessing the appropriateness of measures for the objectives pursued,[226] admittedly though this is not a universal practice. Thus, one of the most notable recent cases is *Philip Morris v. Uruguay*, in which the arbitrators recognized the police power doctrine for the protection of public health as a self-standing defence by making reference to customary international law (even if measures did not amount to indirect expropriation in the first place), and found no violation of the FET standard because of reasonable measures taken to protect public health.[227] Recent developments with respect to allowing states to initiate their own counterclaims, especially based on non-economic issues, is another positive development. In *Urbaser* case, a tribunal interpreted for the first time Article 46 ICSID Convention and the BIT in question as allowing the state to bring a counterclaim based on human

[220] Mitchell (2023), pp. 462 f. For instance, *Saluka Investments BV (The Netherlands) v Czech Republic*, Partial Award, UNCITRAL, 17 March 2006, para. 264; *Methanex Corporation v United States*, Final Award on Jurisdiction and Merits, Part IV, Chapter D, paras. 7, 15; *Chemtura Corporation v Canada*, UNCITRAL, Award, 2 August 2010, para. 266. For more see Dooley (2022), p. 855.

[221] See *Salini v. Morocco*, ICSID Case No. ARB/00/4, Decision on Jurisdiction, July 23, 2001, para. 52.

[222] *Cortec v. Kenya*, ICSID Case No. arb/15/29, Award, 22 October 2018. For more see Rees-Evans (2020), pp. 366–371.

[223] Behn and Langford (2017), pp. 27–28. See, for example, *Crystallex v. Venezuela*, ICSID Case No. ARB(AF)/11/2, Award, 4 April 2016, paras. 581 ff; *S. D. Myers Inc. v. Canada*, UNCITRAL, Partial Award, 13 November 2000, para. 254.

[224] Choudhury (2020), p. 19. See *Azurix v. Argentina Republic*, ICSID Case No. ARB/01/12, Award, July 14, 2006, para. 261.

[225] Choudhury (2020), p. 32; Grierson et al. (2021), p. 338.

[226] Cheyne (2014), pp. 40 ff and 50 f.; Henckels (2014), pp. 130 f.

[227] *Philip Morris v. Uruguay*, ICSID Case No. ARB/10/7, 8 July 2016, paras. 287 ff, 307, 410, 420. In order to show the customary status of police powers doctrine, the arbitrators referred to international treaties, OECD documents, and investment jurisprudence and treaties.

right to water, albeit it failed.[228] States have subsequently brought successful environmental counterclaims in other disputes, investors being liable to pay damages to the host state.[229]

Thus, while regulatory chill may persist and the jurisprudence is still inconsistent, there are clear indications that the approach adopted in investment arbitration converges with that applied by the EU and the trend found in other multilateral and bilateral trade law. Thus, we can observe not only a development in BITs texts to use the same mechanisms as in FTAs to give greater leeway to non-economic policy objectives and values (as shown in Sect. 4.3), but also with regard to interpretive approaches and standards of reviewing domestic decision-making in the context of necessity tests/proportionality control, applying rather deferential standards and conceiving itemized justifications rather broadly.[230]

5 Conclusion

The present analysis could demonstrate a considerable convergence in the way how in trade and investment policy the endeavors to bring trade or investment disciplines into conformity with non-economic policy objectives have developed towards more coherence and providing better tools for a due balance. Even though this development is far from being concluded and does not represent a straightforward exercise but testifies a certain level of back and forth and shows many inconsistencies and contradictory movements, one can observe considerable parallel and far-spread, even globally simultaneous developments, both with regard to the textual means used in international trade and investment agreements to effectuate a better balance of trade/investment interests with non-economic policies, and with regard to jurisprudential interpretive approaches and control standards. With regard to the latter, however, arbiters' practice in investment treaty arbitration develops slowly as arbiters are able to roll back textual changes in BITs by reference to former decisions on other, older BITs, and indeed they do so.[231]

As regards the means used for a just balance of economic and non-economic policies, one could observe an ever more prevalence of confirming the states' right to regulate in treaty preambles and texts, including for specifically named policies such as human rights, sustainability or climate protection. Referencing the right to regulate or regulatory autonomy in newer BITs serves different legal functions, i.e. as a treaty objective in the preamble, as a limitation of the scope of application,

[228] *Urbaser v. Argentina*, ICSID Case No. ARB/07/26, Award, 8 December 2016.

[229] *Burlington v. Ecuador*, ICSID Case No. ARB/08/5, Decision on Counterclaims, 7 February 2017; *Perenco v. Ecuador*, ICSID Case No. ARB/08/6, Award, 27 September 2019. For more see Nedumpara and Laddha (2021), pp. 1831–1849.

[230] For examples for referencing pertinent WTO jurisprudence see Kurtz (2016), pp. 222 ff.

[231] See Alschner (2022), pp. 183 ff and 219 f.

as a more or less explicit exception to investor protection standards or as their interpretive context. Also general or specific exceptions increasingly find their way into treaty texts, as well as policy specific obligations and even chapters with sometimes more lenient language fostering domestic policy making by determining that measures pursuing (specific) legitimate policy objectives do not breach the treaty. Hence, exceptions in their most current shape significantly go beyond merely allowing for flexibility for the pursuit of public policies, but reflect a comprehensive convergence and a quite common set of principles required for an appropriate balance between economic and non-economic objectives taking into account the great importance of often superior public policy objectives, such as proportionality, consistency in the application of public policies, and a deferential control. Some agreements even provide for positive disciplines in which states agree on certain standards e.g. by consenting to implement international treaties on climate protection or certain labour rights. Treaties also employ stricter language and substantive determination with regard to traditionally rather indeterminate investment protection standards (FET, indirect expropriation) in order to guide the leeway of arbitrators.

With regard to the jurisprudential developments, one could observe that the states' right to regulate and the recognition of legitimate policies impact the interpretive conceptualisation both of rather general treatment standards such as non-discrimination, fair and equitable treatment or indirect expropriation, and of itemized justifications or legitimate policy objectives indicated in specific provisions. Whereas the former are interpreted in a way to consider other policy objectives already at the level of the commitment, the latter are interpreted rather broadly so as to enlarge the policy space of states and to allow for more legitimate reasons to introduce domestic measures despite the resulting negative effects on cross-border trade. This statement, admittedly, deserves some caution with regard to FTA dispute settlement as there currently are only few decisions so that a far-spread trend in dispute settlement in relation to 'trade and...' issues has not yet solidified, but WTO approaches on interpreting GATT/GATS exception provisions and dealing with their chapeau are followed. Also standards of reviewing domestic decision-making in the context of necessity tests or a proportionality control come closer as arbiters apply rather deferential standards.

Thus, the convergence in the mechanisms used for a proper balancing of trade and investment interests against non-economic policies and values can be welcomed as an endeavor of socio-economic constitutionalism in process and progress.

References

Abel P (2022) International investor obligations. Towards individual international responsibility for the public interest in international investment law. Nomos, Baden-Baden

Acconci P (2018) Sustainable development and investment: trends in law-making and arbitration. In: Gattini A, Tanzi A, Fontanelli F (eds) General principles of law and international investment arbitration. Brill Nijhoff, Leiden, pp 290–319

Alschner W (2022) Investment arbitration and state-driven reform. Oxford University Press, Oxford

Alvarez J (2010) Why are we “re-calibrating” our investment treaties? World Arbitr Mediation Rev 4(2):143–161

Arcuri A, Violi F (2021) Public interest and international investment law: a critical perspective on three mainstream narratives. In: Chaisse J, Choukroune L, Jusoh S (eds) Handbook of international investment law and policy. Springer Nature, Singapore, pp 2185–2210

Asteriti A (2017) Article 21 TEU and the EU’s common commercial policy: a test of coherence. In: Bungenberg M, Krajewski M, Tams C et al (eds) European yearbook of international economic law. Springer, Cham, pp 111–138

Bartels L (2014) The European Parliament’s role in relation to human rights in trade and investment agreements: study for policy department for external relations, European Parliament, 13 February 2014. https://www.europarl.europa.eu/RegData/etudes/etudes/join/2014/433751/EXPO-JOIN_ET(2014)433751_EN.pdf

Bartels L (2015) The Chapeau of the general exceptions in the WTO GATT and GATS agreements. AJIL 109:95–125

Behn D, Langford M (2017) Trumping the environment? An empirical perspective on investment treaty arbitration. JWIT 18:14–61

Beise M (2001) Die Welthandelsorganisation (WTO): Funktion, Status, Organisation. Nomos, Baden-Baden

Beke L, D’Hollander D, Hachez N et al (2014) Report on the integration of human rights in EU development and trade policies. https://www.europarl.europa.eu/cmsdata/86030/FP7%20report.pdf

Bhala R (2005) Modern GATT law: a treatise on the general agreement on tariffs and trade. Sweet & Maxwell, London

Bilal S, Hoekman B (2019) Introduction: EU trade and external policy in troubled waters. In: Bilal S, Hoekman B (eds) Perspectives on the soft power of EU trade policy. CEPR Press, London, pp 9–15

Boisson de Chazournes L, Lee J (2022) The European Union–Korea free trade agreement sustainable development proceeding: reflections on a ground-breaking dispute. JWIT 23:329–346

Bonne W (2022) Unresolved labor disputes under the USMCA’s rapid response mechanism: probing the applicability of the ATS in Light of Nestle v. Doe. N Y Univ J Law Bus 19(1): 189–235

Bronckers M, Gruni G (2021) Retooling the sustainability standards in EU free trade agreements. JIEL 24(1):25–51

Cannizarro E (2021) The value of the EU international values. In: Douma WT, Eckes C, Van Elsuwege P et al (eds) The evolving nature of EU external relations law. T.M.C Asser Press/ Springer, Berlin, pp 3–18

Cass DZ (2005) The constitutionalization of the World Trade Organization: legitimacy, democracy, and community in the international trading system. Oxford University Press, Oxford

Cheyne I (2014) Deference and the use of the public policy exception. In: Gruszczynski L, Werner W (eds) Deference in international courts and tribunals. Oxford University Press, Oxford, pp 38–57

Cho S, Kurtz J (2018) Convergence and divergence in international economic law and politics. EJIL 29(1):169–203

Choudhury B (2020) International investment law and noneconomic issues. Vanderbilt J Transnatl Law 53(1):1–77

Claussen K (2020) Reimagining trade-plus compliance: the labor story. JIEL 23(1):25–43

Côté C (2018) A chilling effect? Are international investment agreements hindering government’s regulatory autonomy in the areas of health, safety and environment? Int Trade Law Regul 24(2): 51–61

Cremona M (2011) Values in foreign policy. In: Evans M, Koutrakos P (eds) Beyond the established legal orders. Hart Publishing, Oxford, pp 277–315

Cremona M (2017) A quiet revolution – the changing nature of the EU's common commercial policy. In: Bungenberg M, Krajewski M, Tams C et al (eds) European yearbook of international economic law. Springer, Cham, pp 3–34
Cremona M (2018) Shaping EU trade policy post-Lisbon: opinion 2/15 of 16 May 2017. EUConst 14:231–259
Dimopoulos A (2010) The effects of the Lisbon Treaty on the principles and objectives of the common commercial policy. EFARev 15(2):153–170
Dooley J (2022) The co-existence of mitigation and international investment law. JWIT 23:849–846
Duggal K, Rangachari R, Gupta K (2021) Consequences of crisis and the great re-think: COVID-19's impact on energy investment, sustainability and the future of international investment agreements. J World Energy Law Bus 14:133–146
Dumberry P (2022) Art. 8.10. In: Bungenberg M, Reinisch A (eds) CETA investment law: article-by-article commentary. Nomos/Beck/Hart, Baden-Baden
Duval Y, Natnicha S (2023) Trade agreements in Asia and the Pacific: bigger, deeper, digital and more supportive of sustainable development? Asia-Pacific Trade and Investment Trends 2022/2023
Farber DA, Hudec RE (1994) Free trade and the regulatory state. Vanderbilt Law Rev 47(5): 1401–1440
Ferrari A, Fiorini M et al (2024) EU trade agreements and non-trade policy objectives. In: Manchin M, Puccio L et al (eds) Coherence of the European Union trade policy with the EU's non-trade objectives. Cambridge University Press, Cambridge
Furculiță C (2021) The WTO and the new generation EU FTA dispute settlement mechanisms: interacting in a fragmented and changing international trade law regime. Springer, Cham
Gehring M, Tokas M (2022) Synergies and approaches to climate change in international investment agreements. JWIT 23:778–812
Giest A (2017) Interpreting public interest provisions in international investment treaties. Chic J Int Law 18(1):321–352
Grierson J, Granier T, Karsenti S (2021) Is arbitration helping or hindering the protection of the environment and public health? J Int Arbitr 38(3):327–344
Han JS (2021) The EU-Korea Labour Dispute: a critical analysis of the EU's approach. EFARev 26(4):531–552
Harrison J, Barbu M, Campling L et al (2019) Labour standards provisions in EU free trade agreements: reflections on the European Commission's reform agenda. WTRev 18(4):635–657
Henckels C (2014) Deference in Investor-State Arbitration. In: Gruszczynski L, Werner W (eds) Deference in international courts and tribunals. Oxford University Press, Oxford
Hilf M (2001) Power, rules, and principles – which orientation for GATT/WTO law. JIEL 4(1): 111–130
Hoekman BM (2018) Behind-the-border regulatory policies and trade agreements. East Asian Econ Rev 22(3):243–273
Hoffmeister F (1998) Menschenrechts- und Demokratieklauseln in den vertraglichen Außenbeziehungen der Europäischen Gemeinschaft. Springer, Berlin
Horn H, Mavroidis PC, Sapir A (2010) Beyond the WTO? An anatomy of EU and US preferential trade agreements. World Econ 33:1565–1588
Howse R, Nicolaidis K (2001) Legitimacy and global governance: why constitutionalizing the WTO is a step too far. In: Porter RB, Sauvé P et al (eds) Efficiency, equity, and legitimacy: the multilateral trading system at the millennium. Brookings Institution Press, Washington, D.C., pp 227–252
Jackson JH (2006) Sovereignty, the WTO, and changing fundamentals of international law. Cambridge University Press, Cambridge
Jančić D (2017) TTIP and legislative-executive relations in EU trade policy. West Eur Polit 40(1): 202–221

Kassoti E, Wessel RA (2021) The conclusion of trade agreements and the EU's duty to respect human rights abroad. In: Cunha Rodrigues N (ed) Exterritoriality of EU economic law. The application of EU economic law outside the territory of the EU. Springer, Cham

Kassoti E, Wessel RA (2023) The normative effect of Article 3 (5) TEU. Observance and development of international law by the European Union. In: García Andrade A (ed) Interacciones entre el Derecho de la Union Europea y el Derecho Internacional Público. Valencia, Tirant lo Blanch, pp 19–46

Kettunen E (2023) Competing regionalisms in the Asia-Pacific? Versatile sustainable development issues in FTAs. Peace Rev J Soc Justice 35(4):672–682

Krajewski M (2012) The reform of the common commercial policy. In: Biondi A, Eeckhout P (eds) EU law after Lisbon. Oxford University Press, Oxford, pp 292–311

Kübek G (2022) Sustainable development chapters in EU FTAs and dispute settlement: lessons learned from *Ukraine – Wood Products* and *Korea – Labour Rights*. In: Fahey E, Mancini I (eds) Understanding the EU as a good global actor. Edward Elgar, Cheltenham, pp 277–293

Kurtz J (2016) The WTO and international investment law. Cambridge University Press, Cambridge

Lanovoy V (2022) Standards of review in the practice of international courts and tribunals. In: Gabor K, Çali B, Milanović M (eds) Secondary rules of primary importance: attribution, causality, standard of review and evidentiary rules in international law. Oxford University Press, Oxford, pp 42–64

Larik J (2016) Foreign policy objectives in European constitution. Oxford University Press, Oxford

Leal-Arcas R, Anderle M, Santos F et al (2020) The contribution of free trade agreements and bilateral investment treaties to a sustainable future. ZEuS 23(1):3–76

Lee C K, Lee J, Park H et al (2021) Linkages of trade, environment and labour in FTAs: trends and prospects. Korea Institute for International Economic Policy. World Economy Brief 11-16, pp 1–5

Lévesque C (2013) The inclusion of GATT Article XX exceptions in IIAs: a potentially risky policy. In: Echandi R, Sauve P (eds) Prospects in international investment law and policy—World Trade Forum. Cambridge University Press, Cambridge, pp 363–370

Low P (2013) The role of services in global value chains. In: Elms DK, Low P (eds) Global value chains in a changing world. World Trade Organization, Geneva

Lydgate DE (2017) Is it rational and consistent? JIEL 20(3):561–582

Manchin M, Puccio L et al (2024) Introduction. In: Manchin M, Puccio L et al (eds) Coherence of the European Union trade policy with the EU's non-trade objectives. Cambridge University Press, Cambridge

Marceau G (ed) (2015) A history of law and lawyers in the GATT/WTO: the development of the rule of law in the multilateral trading system. Cambridge University Press, Cambridge

Marín Durán G (2020) Sustainable development chapters in EU free trade agreements: emerging compliance issues. Common Mark Law Rev 57(4):1031–1068

Marisi F (2020) Environmental interests in investment arbitration: challenges and directions. Kluwer Law International, Alphen aan den Rijn

Mavroidis PC (2012) Trade in goods, 2nd edn. Oxford University Press, Oxford

Meissner KL, McKenzie L (2017) Human rights conditionality in European Union trade negotiations: the case of the EU–Singapore FTA. J Common Mark Stud 55(4):832–849

Milewicz K, Hollway J, Peacock C et al (2018) Beyond trade: the expanding scope of the nontrade agenda in trade agreements. J Confl Resolut 62(4):743–773

Ming Du M (2011) The rise of national regulatory autonomy in the GATT/WTO regime. JIEL 14(3):639–675

Ming Du M (2016) Treatment no less favourable and the future of national treatment. World Trade Rev 15(1):139–163

Mitchell AD (2023) The right to regulate and the interpretation of the WTO Agreement. JIEL 26(3): 462–482

Moore M, Scherrer C (2017) Conditional or promotional trade agreements - is enforcement possible? How international labour standards can be enforced through US and EU social chapters. Friedrich Ebert Stiftung, https://library.fes.de/pdf-files/bueros/singapur/13446.pdf
Morin J-F, Rochette M (2017) Transatlantic convergence of PTAs' environmental clauses. Bus Polit 19(4):621–658
Müller-Ibold T (2019) Die Externe Dimension der EU-Politiken. In: Hatje A, Müller-Graff P-C (eds) XXVIII. FIDE-Kongress vom 23. Mai bis 26. Mai 2018 in Estoril: Die Deutschen Landesberichte. Nomos, Baden-Baden, pp 79–180
Nedumpara JJ, Laddha A (2021) Human rights and environmental counterclaims in investment treaty arbitration. In: Chaisse J, Choukroune L, Jusoh S (eds) Handbook of international investment law and policy. Springer Nature, Singapore, pp 1831–1849
Newcombe A (2011) General exceptions in international investment agreements. In: Cordonnier Segger M-C, Gehring M, Newcombe A (eds) Sustainable development in world investment law. Kluwer Law, pp 355–365
Novitz T (2021) Enforceable social clauses in trade agreements with 'bite'? Implications of the EU–South Korea panel of experts report of 20 January 2021. 6 European Trade Union Institute Policy Brief. www.etui.org/publications/enforceable-social-clauses-trade-agreements-bite
Pacheco Restrepo YV (2019) Enforcement practice under preferential trade agreements: environmental consultations and submissions on environmental enforcement matters in the US-Peru TPA. LIEI 46(3):247–262
Petersmann E-U (2017) Democratic legitimacy of the CETA and TTIP agreements? In: Rensman T (ed) Mega-regional trade agreements and the future of international trade and investment law. Springer, Cham, pp 37–59
Postnikov E (2019) Unravelling the puzzle of social standards' design in EU and US trade agreements. New Polit Econ 24(2):181–196
Qureshi AH (2015) Interpreting WTO agreements: problems and perspectives, 2nd edn. Cambridge University Press, Cambridge
Ranjan P (2021) Essential security interests in international investment law: a tale of two ISDS claims against India. In: Chaisse J, Choukroune L, Jusoh S (eds) Handbook of international investment law and policy. Springer Nature, Singapore, pp 579–601
Rees-Evans L (2020) The protection of the environment in international investment agreements – recent developments and prospects for reform. Eur Investment Law Arbitr Rev 5:357–391
Rigod B (2015) Optimal regulation and the law of international trade: the interface between the right to regulate and WTO law. Cambridge University Press, Cambridge
Schill SW (2019) The EU's foreign direct investment screening paradox: tightening inward investment control to further external investment liberalization. Leg Issues Econ Integr 46(2): 105–128
Sheargold E, Mitchell AD (2021) Public health in international investment law and arbitration. In: Chaisse J, Choukroune L, Jusoh S (eds) Handbook of international investment law and policy. Springer Nature, Singapore, pp 1851–1876
Shell GR (1995) Trade legalism and international relations theory. Duke Law J 44:829–927
Sommermann K-P (2013) Art. 3. In: Blanke H-J, Mangiameli S (eds) The Treaty on European Union: a commentary. Springer, Berlin
Stone Sweet A (2004) The judicial construction of Europe. Oxford University Press, Oxford
Stone Sweet A, della Cananea G (2014) Proportionality, general principles of law, and Investor-State Arbitration: a response to José Alvarez. NYU J Int Law Polit 46:911–954
Stone Sweet A, Matthews J (2019) Proportionality balancing and constitutional governance: a comparative & global approach. Oxford University Press, Oxford
Tienhaara K (2018) Regulatory chill in a warming world: the threat to climate policy posed by investor-state dispute settlement. Transnatl Environ Law 7(2):229–250

Tietje C, Lang A (2021) Community interests in world trade law. In: Iovane M, Palombino FM, Amoroso D et al (eds) The protection of general interest in contemporary international law. Oxford University Press, Oxford, pp 264–292
Titi C (2014) The right to regulate in international investment law. Nomos, Baden-Baden
Trachtman JP (2009) Constitutional economics of the World Trade Organization. In: Dunoff JL, Trachtman JP (eds) Ruling the world? Cambridge University Press, Cambridge
Trapp P (2022) The European Union's trade defence modernisation package: a missed opportunity at reconciling trade and competition? Springer, Cham
van den Bossche P, Zdouc W (2022) The law and policy of the World Trade Organization, 5th edn. Cambridge University Press, Cambridge
Van Elsuwege P (2021) The nexus between common commercial policy and human rights. In: Van der Loo G, Hahn M (eds) The law and practice of common commercial policy: the first ten years after the Treaty of Lisbon. Brill Nijhoff, Leiden, pp 416–433
van Engen N, Steijn B et al (2019) Do consistent government policies lead to greater meaningfulness and legitimacy on the front line? Public Adm 97(1):97–115
Van Vaerenbergh P (2022) The EU's commitment to social and environmental standards in its modernised trade defence instruments. Zeitschrift für Europarechtliche Studien 25(4):843–858
Vandermerwe S, Rada J (1988) Servitization of business: adding value by adding services. Eur Manag J 6:314–324
Vandevelde K (2009) A comparison of the 2004 and 1994 US model BITs. Yearbook of International Investment Law and Policy (2008/9)
Velut J-B, Baeza-Breinbauer D, De Brujine M et al (2022) Comparative analysis of trade and sustainable development provisions in free trade agreements. London School of Economics and Political Science, Trade Policy Hub
Vidigal G (2022) Regional trade adjudication and the rise of sustainability disputes: Korea—Labor Commitments and Ukraine—Wood Export Bans. AJIL 116(3):567–578
Von Bogdandy A, Venzke I (2013) On the functions of international courts: an appraisal in light of their burgeoning public authority. Leiden J Int Law 26(1):49–72
Wasilczyk P (2023) Fragmentation of international trade law reassessed: analyzing the role of PTA-DSMs based on their adjudication of general exception clauses. Springer, Cham
Wei D, Rafael ÂP (2023) China's approach to sustainable development in free trade agreements. Law Dev Rev 16(2):367–384
Weiß W (2020) WTO law and domestic regulation. C.H. Beck/Hart/Nomos, Baden-Baden
Weiß W (2023) Enhancement of the European Parliament's monitoring for better coherence between trade policy and NTPOs. In: Manchin M, Puccio L, Yildirim AB (eds) Coherence of the European Union's trade policy with its non-trade objectives. Cambridge University Press, Cambridge, pp 236–262
Weiß W, Furculita C (2020) The EU in search for stronger enforcement rules: assessing the proposed amendments to trade enforcement regulation 654/2014. JIEL 23(4):865–884
Young AR, Peterson J (2006) The EU and the new trade politics. J Eur Public Policy 13(6):795–814
Zagel G (2021) Achieving sustainable development objectives in international investment law. In: Chaisse J, Choukroune L, Jusoh S (eds) Handbook of international investment law and policy. Springer Nature, Singapore, pp 1–55
Zhao C (2022) Implementing and enhancing labour standards through FTAs? A critical analysis of the panel report in the EU-Korea case. JWT 56(6):939–962

EU Merger Control and Climate Action: The Struggle for the Proper Framework

Jens-Uwe Franck

Contents

For insightful comments and suggestions, I am thankful to an anonymous reviewer, participants at the 19th ASCOLA Annual Conference in Würzburg (2024), the European Commission's Competition Summer School for officials from Asia at the College of Europe in Bruges (2023), and the 15th Speyerer Kartellrechtsforum at the Deutsche Universität für Verwaltungswissenschaften (Germany University of Administrative Sciences) in Speyer (2023). I gratefully acknowledge support from the Deutsche Forschungsgemeinschaft (DFG) through CRC TR 224 (Project B05).

J.-U. Franck (✉)
University of Mannheim, Department of Law, and Mannheim Centre for Competition and Innovation (MaCCI), Mannheim, Germany
e-mail: franck@uni-mannheim.de

S. Hindelang et al. (eds.), *YSEC Yearbook of Socio-Economic Constitutions 2024*, YSEC Yearbook of Socio-Economic Constitutions (2025) 2024: 247–282, https://doi.org/10.1007/16495_2024_78, Published online: 28 January 2025

Abstract The EU has set itself an ambitious agenda to tackle climate change. Competition policy, including merger review, is called upon to play its part. Based on an analysis of the Commission's practice, this chapter identifies the key framework issues for the consideration of climate change concerns in merger control and the parameters for addressing them under the EU Merger Regulation and in the light of the European Treaties. One focus will be on the implications of a differentiated allocation of regulatory powers across different policy areas. It is argued that a distinction must be made between scenarios in which the climate change argument is used to justify stricter or conceptually extended merger control and those in which it is argued that merger control should need to be relaxed for climate change reasons. With regard to the first scenario, shifts of a normative nature can be observed and are indeed called for, but these take place within the consumer welfare paradigm and it remains the case that the protection of competition is the sole overriding principle of the EU Merger Regulation. In contrast, in the second scenario, merger-specific 'green' efficiencies need to be considered even if they are not captured by the consumer welfare paradigm.

1 Introduction

Climate change has plunged humanity into an existential crisis. The survival of our civilization will depend on the action we take to respond. Humanity must not lose the chance to turn the tide in time because of petty, formalistic concerns and an unthinking adherence to the status quo. Under the European Green Deal,[1] every EU policy must contribute to the overall goal of making the EU climate-neutral by 2050. This call for climate action also applies to EU merger control, a cornerstone of EU competition law. The relevance of merger policy has been demonstrated, for example, by its impact on the circular economy, energy efficiency and innovation, which is crucial, for example, in the transition to a low-carbon economy and the protection of biodiversity.

[1] European Commission, The European Green Deal, COM(2019) 640 final, pp. 15–19 ('Mainstreaming sustainability in all EU policies').

The protection of consumer welfare in the markets affected by a proposed merger has become the most important guiding principle of merger control. The regulation of negative externalities has been relegated to other areas of regulation, notably environmental law. Looking at the EU Merger Regulation (EUMR),[2] however, there are several elements to which climate concerns may be relevant and into which this aspect could be integrated: the criteria for assessing mergers under the substantive impediment to effective competition (SIEC) test pursuant to Article 2(2) and (3) EUMR, including sub-elements of the test such as market definition and market power, or a possible efficiency defence. Furthermore, climate change concerns could be taken into account in the proposal of any commitments that support the Commission's decision to clear a merger.

The overall aim of this chapter is to identify the key framework issues for the consideration of climate change concerns in merger practice and the parameters for addressing them. The 'framework' with which I am concerned here is twofold: it refers both to the requirements of the EUMR, which governs the merger practice of the EU Commission, and to the EU constitutional requirements within which the EUMR must be applied. The following study is based on an analysis of the EU Commission's practice[3] with regard to whether and how climate protection aspects have been taken into account. Particular attention will be paid to whether the consideration of climate protection concerns can be understood as an expression of a normative shift. Roughly three approaches seem conceivable here:[4]

- First, it may be that the implementation of the consumer welfare paradigm has been adapted but the approach itself has not been questioned. This could include, for example, taking into account identified changes in consumer preferences, or changing the time horizon, the standard of evidence, etc. for identifying potential impacts on consumer welfare.
- Second, a change in the welfare standard could result from the inclusion of the creation or avoidance of negative externalities in the substantive assessment of mergers. The approach thus goes beyond the conventional consumer welfare framework for analysing the effects of a merger.
- Third, it is conceivable that merger control proceedings could be used to directly promote and implement climate protection measures. This would openly declare climate protection to be an objective of merger review in its own right, alongside the protection of competition. This would create scope for moving away from the welfare paradigm and for an open balancing of the objectives of protecting competition and climate protection based on qualitative criteria.

---

[2] Council Regulation (EC) No 139/2004 of 20 January 2004 on the control of concentrations between undertakings (the EC Merger Regulation), OJ 2004 L 24/1.

[3] An overview of relevant decision practice can be found, for example, in Badea et al. (2021), pp. 6–7, and in Lecchi (2023), pp. 74–79.

[4] For similar conceptual approaches and options, albeit with a focus on sustainability agreements, see Ackermann (2023), pp. 11–15; Monti (2020), pp. 128–130.

Below, I will outline my findings in five steps. First, I will analyse Commission practice on the role of climate protection and environmental sustainability in market definition, the identification of unilateral price effects and risks to innovation competition (Sect. 2). Second, I will show that the Commission refuses to consider climate protection an independent objective of merger control under the EUMR, and I will discuss what implications this has and does not have (Sect. 3). Third, I will examine an area where the Commission's practice is not yet clear: scenarios where climate change considerations might require a relaxation, rather than a tightening, of a (competition-only) merger standard (Sect. 4). Fourth, I will look at the scope for Member States to clear or block mergers on climate change grounds, alongside or on the basis of the EUMR (Sect. 5). Fifth, I will explain how these findings can be understood in the light of the EU's constitutional framework with its differentiated distribution of regulatory powers (Sect. 6). Section 7 concludes.

2 What We See in the Commission's Practice (1): Stricter Merger Control—Protecting the Climate Under the Consumer Welfare Paradigm

Through an analysis of the Commission's merger practice, this section will identify the different legal parameters used to take climate change and environmental sustainability into account in merger control. It is true that in individual scenarios there may be trade-offs between climate protection and other facets of environmental sustainability: the construction of wind turbines may harm bird populations or marine life. The extraction of mineral resources, which seems essential to the energy transition, can threaten biodiversity. For the purposes of this chapter, which focuses on the key normative (framework) question of the relationship between these 'green' objectives and the protection of competition based on a consumer welfare paradigm, these 'intra-green' trade-offs can be ignored. However, it should not be underestimated that in some cases these trade-offs may make the implementation of 'green' policy objectives more difficult.

2.1 Observable Consumer Preferences for Climate Action: Market Definition and Closeness of Competition

2.1.1 Market Definition as an Analytical Step for the Assessment of Market Power

The assessment of market power is an essential element of merger control. In EU practice, which at this stage is in line with many other jurisdictions, market definition appears to be a practically mandatory analytical step[5] to assess whether a concentration would (or would not) significantly impede effective competition in the common market or in a substantial part of it, in particular as a result of the creation or strengthening of a dominant position.[6]

In several decisions, the Commission has defined product markets in terms of sustainability as a parameter of competition. For example, the Commission considered that there were separate markets for conventional bananas on the one hand and organic and fair trade bananas on the other.[7] This assessment was based on surveys of retailers, who were asked to give their own views but also to estimate what end consumers preferred. According to the questionnaires analysed, conventional and non-conventional bananas are not seen as substitutes.[8] It was also found that retailers typically award supply contracts on a differentiated basis and that there are significant conversion costs on the producer side. Retailers organize separate tenders for fair trade bananas and for organic/double-label bananas, as opposed to conventional bananas.[9] A range of suppliers have specialized in organic and/or fair trade bananas[10] and the production and import of the different types of banana varies considerably. Switching to organic production requires a change in the production process, and switching to fair trade requires compliance with specific standards.[11] However, we do not find any evidence on the willingness of end consumers to pay.

The market definition substantially affected the market shares of the notifying parties in Germany.[12] As one of the parties (Chiquita) was not active in the supply of fair trade or organic bananas at the time, the parties' combined market share of conventional bananas in 2011 was in the range of 30 to 40 per cent in the public version of the decision, as opposed to 5 to 10 per cent in the fair trade or organic segment and 20 to 30 per cent for all types of banana.[13] Ultimately, however, this was not decisive for the assessment of the merger because the market power of the notifying parties was counterbalanced by the strong buying power on the part of

[5] See Case C-68/94, *France and Société commerciale des potasses and de l'azote and Entreprise minière and chimique v Commission*, ECLI:EU:C:1998:148, para. 143; Case T-342/99, *Airtours v Commission*, ECLI:EU:T:2004:192, para. 19; Case T-151/05, *NVV and Others v Commission*, ECLI:EU:T:2009:144, para. 51. See also European Commission, Guidelines on the assessment of horizontal mergers under the Council Regulation on the control of concentrations between undertakings, OJ 2004 C 31/5 ('Horizontal Merger Guidelines'), para. 10.

[6] See Article 2(2) and (3) EUMR.

[7] Case COMP/M.7220 (3 Oct 2014), *Chiquita Brands International/Fyffes ('Banana Industry')*, para. 73.

[8] Id., paras 67–68.

[9] Id., para. 66.

[10] Id., para. 69.

[11] Id., paras 70–71.

[12] See also Commission Notice on the Definition of the Relevant Market for the Purposes of Union Competition Law (C/2024/1645), paras 15 and 50.

[13] Id., para. 245 with Table 12.

retailers and the presence of three competitors with market shares above 10 per cent.[14]

In another decision, the Commission assumed that a distinction should be made between organic and conventional salmon production. This was based on different price levels and the consumer perception that organic salmon is healthier and perceived as a premium product. Unlike in bananas, the Commission left the final market definition open.[15] This is also the case for a decision on cocoa beans, even though the Commission found strong indications that separate markets should be defined for certified and/or traceable cocoa beans. The former refers to beans that have been certified by third-party organizations for good agricultural, environmental and social practices, while the latter refers to beans whose supply chain can be traced back to individual farmers. The Commission noted the higher investment costs and longer timeframes for setting up procurement operations for non-standard beans, that these beans tended to be supplied on the basis of long-term contracts (as opposed to spot trading) and that they were sold at a premium price, paid to farmers and cooperatives.[16]

In a merger involving salt slag recycling services, the Commission noted that the use of zero-waste technology is perceived as an advantage by many customers, but nevertheless concluded that the scope of the product market was salt slag recycling, irrespective of the technology used.[17]

As far as can be seen, this consideration of sustainability in the Commission's market definition has not yet been decisive in the assessment of a merger. However, an example can be found in France. In the *Carrefour France/Bio c'Bon* case, the Autorité de la concurrence examined effects on a separate upstream market for the supply of organic food[18] and a separate market for the retail distribution of (predominantly) organic food products, which is restricted to supermarkets and hypermarkets.[19] While the narrow market definition did not lead to the transaction being expected to cause harm to competition in the upstream supply markets,[20] it did require the parties to agree to the divestment of a number of stores in order to avoid an excessive concentration of the retail distribution of organic food products in 10 identified areas.[21]

---

[14] Id., paras 248–252.

[15] Case COMP/M.6850 (30 Sept 2013), *Marine Harvest/Morpol*, paras 61–62.

[16] Case COMP/M.7510 (10 June 2015), *OLAM/ADM Cocoa Business*, paras 15–19.

[17] Case COMP/M.10702 (19 Oct 2022), *KPS Capital Partners/Real Alloy Europe*, paras 59–61.

[18] Autorité de la Concurrence, Décision n° 21-DCC-161 du 10 septembre 2021 relative à la prise de contrôle exclusif de certaines activités du groupe Bio c' Bon par la société Carrefour France (Carrefour France/Bio c' Bon), paras 14–19 (https://www.autoritedelaconcurrence.fr/sites/default/files/integral_texts/2021-10/20-188_publique_decision_21dcc161_0.pdf).

[19] Id., paras 23–41.

[20] Id., para. 65.

[21] Id., paras 200–208.

Similar considerations can also lead to a narrow geographical market definition.[22] Consumers may prefer local or regional products because they see them as more climate-friendly, because of lower transport costs[23] or simply because they assume that local or regional producers are more environmentally aware.

A narrower market definition, driven by consumer preferences for more sustainable, climate-friendly products, will lead to a more rigorous assessment of potential competitive harm from mergers in relation to these products. How can this contribute to climate protection? If, because of competitive pressure, climate-friendly products are made available to consumers at more favourable conditions, they will be consumed on a larger scale. Protection of competition and climate action converge.

The consideration of climate change concerns in market definition is therefore an example of adjustments in merger control; however, they do not reflect normative shifts in the merger control framework. The fact that consumer preferences for climate-friendly products need to be taken into account in market definition is nothing that should surprise observers. However, it does require sensitivity to such changes in consumer preferences and the recognition of environmental sustainability as a non-price parameter of competition.[24]

It should therefore be noted that here, as elsewhere in competition practice, market definition analyses must be based on actual identifiable consumer behaviour. It is therefore crucial to establish that consumers have a clear demand for, and are willing to pay more for, products marketed as ‘organic’, ‘fair trade’, ‘green’ etc., without it being necessary or even appropriate, in the view of the competition authority, to determine whether such a label is ‘justified’ in each individual case on the basis of the way in which a product is produced or distributed. Market definition takes consumer preferences as it finds them; it is not the place to expose greenwashing.

2.1.2 Closeness of Competition and Unilateral (Price) Effects in Differentiated Products

Preferences for climate- and environment-friendly products may in some contexts not be strong enough to justify the delineation of a separate market but they may still

---

[22] Market Definition Notice (n 12), para. 72.

[23] See, for example, Case COMP/M.10047 (14 April 2021), *Schwarz Group/Suez Waste Management Companies*, para. 56 (‘The information available, notably calls for tenders and their specifications, shows that next to transport costs, the environmental cost of transport is also a factor taken into account by customers in awarding tenders. Sorters with more distant [lightweight packaging] sorting plants are sometimes penalised, through a correction of the price quoted or through negative points for quality, not only because of higher transport costs but also for environmental reasons related to the increased CO2 emissions associated with longer transport’).

[24] See Market Definition Notice (n 12), para. 3 (‘[C]ompetition policy … can complement the Union’s regulatory framework on environmental sustainability by taking into account sustainability factors to the extent relevant to the competition assessment, including as part of market definition’).

be strong enough to be relevant for assessing the possible unilateral effects of a merger. Such unilateral effects give merging parties scope to raise prices and, therefore, have to be considered when applying the SIEC test. This scope to raise prices is known to be a possible result of a merger because the positive effects on a firm's profits caused by a price increase by one of its competitors (which at the same time faces a reduction in volume) are internalized by their merger. A key parameter in predicting the extent of such unilateral effects is the closeness of the notifying parties: the stronger their ex ante rivalry (technically measured by the so-called diversion ratios), the more likely it is that significant unilateral effects will result from their merger.

In assessing the closeness of competition, climate-related factors may play an important role. This was the case in *Schwarz Group/Suez Waste Management Companies*, for example. Both companies were active in a number of countries along the entire waste management chain. The Commission was particularly concerned about the merger's impact on the market for sorting light packaging in the Netherlands. Without any divestment commitments, the merged entity would have become by far the largest provider. With regard to competitive pressure from providers located relatively far away from the municipalities where the waste is generated, the Commission stated that:

> plants located at greater distances from the collection points than the Parties' plants may also be seen as environmentally less efficient than the local ones … [D]istance is … a relevant factor for customers when assessing the environmental efficiency or transport sustainability of the different offers submitted in a tender. Longer transport distances imply more CO2 emissions and therefore higher long-term environmental costs. Customers accounting for close to half of demand openly admitted this preference, citing reasons linked to sustainability and environmental reasons and, expressly, the need to reduce CO2 emissions and to minimise environmental costs.[25]

This was essential to the Commission's view that the parties 'appear to be particularly close competitors, and possibly the closest to each other'.[26] The Commission's assessment ultimately led to significant remedies. The Schwarz Group had to sell its entire light packaging sorting business in the Netherlands.

The assessment of the closeness of competition must therefore take into account consumer preferences for climate-friendly and environmentally sustainable products. This should be based on consumers' preferences as reflected in their actual behaviour in the market. Normative shortcuts should be avoided: assuming that Dutch law requires municipalities to take climate change concerns into account when purchasing waste management services, this could at best be an indication of their actual behaviour. Therefore, as in the case of market definition, this is not a question of a normative shift in the assessment of competition. Protecting competition and protecting the climate go hand in hand: recognizing that municipalities are

---

[25] Case COMP/M.10047 (14 April 2021), *Schwarz Group/Suez Waste Management Companies*, para. 118.

[26] Id., para. 123.

interested in reducing CO_2 emissions and therefore want to avoid long distances between waste collection points and waste treatment plants, the Commission has ensured that sufficient competition is maintained between suppliers that meet these criteria, thereby satisfying customers' demand for the 'greenest' waste disposal at the best possible conditions. The Commission's intervention was able to prevent a merger from increasing the price of environmentally sustainable products through unilateral (price) effects.

2.2 *Sharpening of Tools Within the Consumer Welfare Paradigm: Protection of Competition for Green Innovation*

The Commission can block a merger if it reduces the potential for innovation in a market. This is not new and is indeed required by Article 2(1) EUMR,[27] but the Commission has used the protection of environmental sustainability as an impetus to strengthen the protection of competition in innovation. Of particular note are decisions in the agrochemicals sector, where risks to innovation competition have led to significant commitments. Moreover, the Commission has used the *Norsk Hydro/Alumetal* case to signal that it is prepared to protect innovation competition against so-called 'killer acquisitions'.

2.2.1 Elimination of Close Competition in 'Innovation Spaces' as a Stand-Alone Theory of Harm (Dow/Dupont and Bayer/Monsanto)

In two key merger decisions in the agrochemicals sector, the Commission recognised that innovation and environmental sustainability can be inextricably linked: if companies develop more effective active ingredients for pesticides, fungicides or herbicides, the same level of crop protection can be achieved with less toxicity. These more sustainable crop protection solutions help to protect biodiversity and the environment, and therefore justify a stronger focus on protecting the race for innovation:

> The Commission has, in particular, paid specific attention in its review to ensure that post-Transaction innovation in the agroindustry sector is preserved as the key for the emergence of more effective, healthier, safer and more environmentally-friendly products.[28]

[27] Article 2(1)(b) EUMR ('[T]he Commission shall take into account ... the development of technical and economic progress provided that it is to consumers' advantage and does not form an obstacle to competition').

[28] Case COMP/M.8084 (21 March 2018), *Bayer/Monsanto*, para. 3011. See also Case COMP/M.7932 (27 March 2017), *Dow/DuPont*, paras 1977, 1980.

The Commission took the opportunity to implement a more sophisticated and indeed sharper concept of how the elimination of close competition in innovation can lead to merger-induced harm to innovation. It identified 'innovation spaces' to explain how rivalry between firms is a driver of innovation. The basic idea is that, by measuring overlapping research efforts, incentives to eliminate or reduce research and development (R&D) investments after the merger can be identified.[29] The Commission used an approach that modelled the reduced incentives to innovate in a loose analogy to the analysis of unilateral price effects:[30] one driver of innovation is the ability to capture sales from competitors with new and improved products ('business stealing effect'). At the same time, a firm must also consider 'cannibalization effects', as sales of its existing products will also decline. However, when firms that compete closely in innovative products merge, they may internalize the negative externalities that the other merging party imposes on its profits through innovation efforts. In other words, after the merger, each merging party may gain little or nothing by capturing the other's sales by developing and marketing an innovative product. In more technical terms, the ability of the merging firms to internalize the business stealing effect will increase the opportunity cost of the cannibalization effect and reduce the merged firm's incentives to innovate.[31]

This effect could be expected to be larger the more likely it is that an innovation investment by one of the merging parties could lead to the capture of sales from the other merging party, i.e. the higher the 'innovation diversion ratio'. This in turn depends to a large extent on the degree of innovation competition between these companies, which is reflected in the R&D approaches, research lines, pipeline products etc. pursued.[32] In addition, there is the 'second-order effect' that, if the merged entity's incentives to innovate are reduced for the above reasons, the competitive pressure to innovate vis-à-vis the non-merging parties in the market will also be reduced and the market as a whole might be less inclined to innovate.[33]

In both cases, the Commission found that the merging parties are indeed close competitors for innovation in herbicides, pesticides and fungicides. After the merger, they would therefore have strong incentives to stop costly duplicative pipeline

[29] See for an overview of the Commissions line of reasoning Deutscher and Makris (2023), pp. 364–368.

[30] The Commission does not conceptualise 'innovation spaces' as 'markets'. This approach can be directly linked to the SIEC criterion and the protection of innovation competition. However, as laid down in the Commission's Market Definition Notice (n 12), at para. 92, 'it may still be relevant to identify the boundaries within which undertakings compete in such earlier innovation efforts, in order to assess whether there could be a loss of innovation competition due to a concentration or behaviour'. The 'innovation space' approach thus presupposes a demarcation similar to that used to define markets.

[31] Case COMP/M.7932 (27 March 2017), *Dow/DuPont*, paras 2002, 2043, 3017–3022; Case COMP/M.8084 (21 March 2018), *Bayer/Monsanto*, paras 281, 1041.

[32] Case COMP/M.7932 (27 March 2017), *Dow/DuPont*, paras 2000–19, 3287–89; Case COMP/M.8084 (21 March 2018), *Bayer/Monsanto*, paras 281, 1164–1170, 1088, 1093, 1113, 1124, 1164, 1685, 1979.

[33] Case COMP/M.7932 (27 March 2017), *Dow/DuPont*, paras 2005, 2044–2045, 3239, 3244, 3292.

projects and to reduce duplicative R&D infrastructure, so that the innovative capacity of the merged entity would be lower than the combined capacity of the merging parties before the merger.[34] The Commission did not see a sufficient counterbalance in terms of efficiency gains from innovation.

In the end, the Commission cleared both mergers, subject to strict remedies. In the *Dow/DuPont* case, for example, the Commission noted that the notifying parties were two of the five firms in the world active in the entire R&D process in the agrochemicals sector. The parties had to divest almost all of DuPont's global R&D organization and pipeline. This was intended to enable the purchaser to emerge as a new, fully integrated R&D competitor in the global agrochemicals market.

So, what is new and what is not new about the Commission's approach in these two landmark cases? And how does it relate to the protection of environmental sustainability and climate change? There are three aspects to consider.

First, the Commission has adopted a new theoretical basis for pursuing an innovation theory of harm.[35] On this basis, it has for the first time implemented reduced innovation competition as an independent theory of harm, i.e. without recourse to price effects. In doing so, the Commission referred to the normative weight of environmental sustainability concerns. It can be assumed that it would apply this approach to other industries in a similar way if it identified risks to innovation competition, for example in relation to climate-friendly technologies or products.

Second, in *Dow/DuPont* and *Bayer/Monsanto* the Commission focused on innovative capacity, effort and results. The novelties in protecting innovation competition thus lie within the traditional consumer welfare paradigm.[36] What is new, however, is that innovation is now subject to a more precise set of instruments. As a result, there is a prospect that the protection of innovation will be given greater weight than in the past, when the focus was on price and output effects, simply because there is a more straightforward way to implement these concerns.

Third, within the consumer welfare paradigm, we may therefore observe a considerable shift in the relevant time horizon. Traditionally, in the pharmaceutical and agrochemical sectors, for example, time horizons of typically two to three years and a maximum of five years have been used to analyse manufacturers' product

[34] Case COMP/M.7932 (27 March 2017), *Dow/DuPont*, paras 3284–3297; Case COMP/M.8084 (21 March 2018), *Bayer/Monsanto*, paras 878–888, 1263–1273.

[35] In its attempt to develop a concept of unilateral effects on innovation competition, the Commission relied on studies by Motta and Tarantino (2017) and by Federico et al. (2017, 2018). At the time of writing these articles, Valletti was the chief economist in the Directorate-General for Competition at the European Commission (2016–2019). Federico and Langus were members of the chief economist's team. Their model was contested, however, by Denicolò and Polo (2018, 2019). Federico et al.'s (2017) analysis and conclusions, however, were challenged by Denicolò and Polo (2018, 2019), who showed that a merger, even between close rivals in innovation competition, may have an overall positive effect on innovation through the elimination of duplication of R&D expenditure. See also Jullien and Lefouili (2018) (discussing the Federico et al. (2017)/ Denicolò and Polo (2018) debate on pp. 375–376).

[36] Deutscher and Makris (2023), pp. 368–376.

pipelines. By contrast, a focus on (short-term effects on) innovation capacity implicitly leads to a longer time horizon. This protects the interests of consumers who, in 10 or 15 years or more, will be buying products whose quality will be determined by innovation decisions taken now.[37]

2.2.2 Acquisition of Nascent Competitors: Eliminating Potentially Disruptive Innovations at an Early Stage

It is not a new finding that the acquisition of start-ups and small, emerging companies (often with no, or at least no significant, turnover) by established companies is a cause for concern, particularly in terms of competition for innovation. On the one hand, this can be detrimental if the R&D efforts of the target company are discontinued, thereby suppressing or preventing innovations that have been or can be achieved. On the other hand, the acquirer can integrate the R&D of the target company but terminate its own innovation projects in return (a scenario that is referred to as a 'reverse-killer acquisition'[38]). In both scenarios, the innovation potential available in the market or in the companies cannot be fully exploited.

With regard to climate protection and the promotion of environmental sustainability, a scenario was outlined in which a (particularly) innovative sustainable start-up company could be acquired in order to take this innovation off the market and continue production with 'dirty' technology ('green killer acquisitions'). In addition, there is certainly a weakening of competition for 'green innovation', where companies buy up emerging 'green' competitors in order to reduce or even discontinue their own innovation projects for sustainable technologies. Pierre Régibeau, then chief economist at the Directorate-General for Competition, was quoted as saying that the Commission would be 'particularly vigilant' against such 'green killer acquisitions'.[39]

Although there has not yet been a Commission decision discussing these aspects, the acquisition of Alumetal by Norsk Hydro has been analysed from the perspective of a possible 'green killer acquisition'. Norsk Hydro is a Norwegian company active in the entire aluminium value chain, from bauxite mining and aluminium production—and the generation of the (significant) amounts of energy required for this—to aluminium recycling. The firm has a leading position in the production of aluminium foundry alloys as an end product, which are mainly supplied to the automotive industry. Alumetal is a Polish company that also produces aluminium

[37] See Case COMP/M.7932 (27 March 2017), *Dow/DuPont*, paras 2032–2034.

[38] The term has originally been coined in the context of acquisitions by digital gatekeepers. See Crawford et al. (2020).

[39] See MLex, 'Green "killer acquisitions" to face EU vigilance', Régibeau says (24 Feb 2021) (https://mlexmarketinsight.com/news/insight/green-killer-acquisitions-to-face-eu-vigilance-r-gibeau-says).

foundry alloys but specializes in the production of aluminium master alloys (a precursor to aluminium foundry alloys) based on aluminium recycling.

The competitiveness of the aluminium foundry alloys market was central to the assessment of the acquisition. Commissioner Vestager had already given a 'green touch' to this aspect in the press release on the Phase II (in-depth) investigation, stressing that the availability of 'competitively priced green aluminium products' was essential to the fight against climate change. Indeed, the press release contained a reference to a suspected 'green killer acquisition':

> The Commission has preliminary concerns that, by acquiring Alumetal, Norsk Hydro … may eliminate a growing competitor able to bring cheaper and advanced recycled aluminium products to the market.[40]

In the Commission's view, it was therefore conceivable that Norsk Hydro might want to acquire a small competitor in order to slow down its emergence as a supplier of recycling-based and therefore more sustainable aluminium precursors. However, its investigation did not confirm any competition risks and it cleared the transaction without conditions.[41] Commissioner Vestager was quoted as saying:

> Green aluminium is a key lever to decarbonise industrial processes … Our in-depth investigation has shown that the proposed acquisition … will not have a negative impact on the competitive landscape for certain aluminium products. Especially green ones, which will remain widely available to customers at competitive prices.[42]

Both the statement by Régibeau quoted above and the statements made in connection with the opening of the Phase II investigation in *Norsk Hydro/Alumetal* show that the Commission has the acquisition of nascent and emerging competitors on its radar as a threat to innovation competition and is prepared to attach particular importance to this threat in the context of climate protection and the protection of environmental sustainability.

Tighter control over the acquisition of nascent and emerging competitors has the potential to protect a different facet of innovation competition from the *Dow/DuPont* or *Bayer/Monsanto* approach. While the latter is about identifiable and definable 'innovation spaces' and the established rivalry typically of larger incumbents, the former is about maintaining open access to new innovation pathways combined with the hope of disruptive innovation that can successfully challenge the incumbents.[43] In the context of climate change and the need to decarbonize industry, it is certainly plausible to attach particular importance to the protection of potentially disruptive, revolutionary technologies.

---

[40] European Commission, Press Release (6 October 2022), Mergers: Commission opens in-depth investigation into Hydro's proposed acquisition of Alumetal.

[41] European Commission, Press Release (4 May 2023), Mergers: Commission clears Hydro's acquisition of Alumetal.

[42] See https://ec.europa.eu/commission/presscorner/detail/en/IP_23_2566.

[43] Rubinfeld and Hoven (2001), p. 72.

However, implementation poses serious challenges. First of all, there is the question of whether the relevant acquisitions can be reviewed by the Commission. As the target companies in the relevant scenarios typically have low turnovers in the internal market, the thresholds of Article 1 EUMR will often not be exceeded. From the Commission's point of view, as expressed in the 'Article 22 Guidance' of 2021, the possibility of referrals under Article 22 EUMR should have ensured that these mergers find their way to Brussels for review.[44] However, with its *Illumina* judgment, the ECJ has blocked this route for cases in which the intended acquisition does not exceed the national thresholds.[45] Therefore, the effectiveness of this mechanism will depend, first, on the Member States casting a wide net under their national merger control laws to capture these cases and, second, on their willingness to cooperate and to refer relevant cases to the Commission. Moreover, undertakings will (permanently) face a higher degree of legal uncertainty. For the time being, it remains to be seen whether the Commission will seek to amend the EUMR by modifying its Article 22 or even to introduce the power to require ('call in') the notification of individual mergers where the Commission identifies competition risks.[46] However, if an amendment to the EUMR will be considered, it would seem to be preferable to introduce a transaction value threshold in Article 1 EUMR as this would provide a higher degree of legal certainty and ensure a workable and robust coverage of the relevant cases.[47]

What is more remarkable, however, is that, although it is in principle undisputed that it can be a rational and coherent business strategy to prevent potential competition by acquiring up-and-coming competitors,[48] it will usually be difficult for an authority to identify the truly problematic cases and to prove with sufficient certainty

[44] Communication from the Commission, Guidance on the application of the referral mechanism set out in Article 22 of the Merger Regulation to certain categories of cases (the 'Article 22 Guidance'), 2021/C 113/01, para. 19 ('[T]he categories of cases that will normally be appropriate for a referral under Article 22 of the Merger Regulation where the merger is not notifiable in the referring Member State(s) consist of transactions where the turnover of at least one of the undertakings concerned does not reflect its actual or future competitive potential. This would include, for example, cases where the undertaking: (1) is a start-up or recent entrant with significant competitive potential that has yet to develop or implement a business model generating significant revenues (or is still in the initial phase of implementing such business model); (2) is an important innovator or is conducting potentially important research'). See Badea et al. (2021), pp. 6–7; Deutscher and Makris (2023), pp. 392–393.

[45] Case C-611/22 P, *Illumina v Commission*, EU:C:2024:677. The case concerns the acquisition of Grail by Illumina. See Commission Decision C(2021) 2847 final of 19 April 2021; Commission Decisions of C(2021) 2848 final, C(2021) 2949 final, C(2021) 2851 final, C(2021) 2854 final, and C (2021) 2855 final of 19 April 2021. The General Court had initially upheld the Commission's broad interpretation of Article 22 EUMR. See Case T-227/21 *Illumina v Commission* EU:T:2022:447.

[46] See Speech by EVP M. Vestager at the 28th Annual Competition Conference of the International Bar Association (6 Sept 2024), https://ec.europa.eu/commission/presscorner/detail/en/speech_24_4582.

[47] See Franck et al. (2021), pp. 24–25.

[48] See Cunningham et al. (2021).

the harm to (future) competition.[49] Thus, while strengthened control of nascent competitor acquisitions to protect innovation competition is legitimate within the conventional consumer paradigm, a workable analytical framework may require certain normative adjustments:[50] on the one hand, this may concern the time horizon to be considered, which needs to be extended significantly. On the other hand, it may also be appropriate to lower the standard of proof and/or to shift the burden of proof to the notifying parties in certain situations.

3 What We See in the Commission's Practice (2): Climate Protection Is Not a Stand-Alone Merger Control Objective

In the *Bayer/Monsanto* case, the European Commission made it clear that the overriding objective of merger control is the protection of undistorted competition. Other public interest objectives—such as climate protection or environmental sustainability—can only be included indirectly or implicitly. This argument is first traced here, before exploring how much room for manoeuvre this might still leave for including negative externalities in the consumer welfare paradigm.

3.1 **Bayer/Monsanto***: Under EU Merger Rules, the Commission Can Only Intervene to Protect Competition*

Could the Commission prohibit a merger if and because it would have a negative impact on climate and environmental sustainability? In the *Bayer/Monsanto* case, the Commission found reason to take a position on this issue. In the run-up to the decision, stakeholders warned the Directorate-General for Competition that the merger would consolidate the chosen path of global industrialized agricultural production. This would further reduce biodiversity and damage the environment.[51] On the one hand, the Commission acknowledged that it was obliged to take other objectives enshrined in EU primary law into account when enforcing competition policy and, therefore, also in merger practice:

[49] See OECD (2020).

[50] Deutscher and Makris (2023), pp. 396–398.

[51] Case COMP/M.8084 (21 March 2018), *Bayer/Monsanto*, paras 3006–3007, 3009; Deutscher and Makris (2023), pp. 356–358.

> The TFEU requires the Commission to take into consideration a plurality of objectives including human health, environment and consumer protection.[52]

This follows from the horizontal clauses of the Treaty, in particular Articles 7, 9, 11 and 12 TFEU, and is also set out in recital 23 of the EUMR.[53] The Commission then goes on to say that it takes this into account by considering how a lessening of competition affects these wider objectives:

> [T]he Commission is mindful of the potential implications of a possibly reduction of competition caused by the Transaction on … environmental protection and climate.[54]

The way in which a merger is assessed from a competition perspective is thus also influenced by other public interest objectives such as climate protection and environmental sustainability. However, these other objectives, in addition to the protection of undistorted competition, may not (directly) influence whether a merger can be blocked:

> [T]he Merger Regulation does not empower the Commission to intervene against a merger on grounds other than the protection of competition.[55]

The EUMR therefore does not empower the Commission to balance the protection of undistorted competition against the achievement of other non-competitive objectives in the event of a conflict.

3.2 *Implications: Six Key Takeaways on Reduction of Competition, Consumer Welfare and Negative Externalities*

The above raises the question of the implications for merger analysis: which climate-related arguments will the Commission take into account, and which will it not? In my view, six key takeaways can be derived from this.

First, effects in climate and environmental sustainability can and, in fact, need to be taken into account when analysing, weighing, and balancing the potential effects of a merger on competition. The Commission itself set an example in the *Bayer/Monsanto* case by strengthening the protection of innovation competition, in particular because a high level of innovation in the market concerned was seen as serving a sustainable agricultural economy.[56] Tighter control of the acquisition of nascent

[52] Case COMP/M.8084 (21 March 2018), *Bayer/Monsanto*, para. 3010.

[53] Id., paras 3010–3011. Article 23 EUMR reads: '[T]he Commission must place its appraisal [of concentrations with a Community dimension] within the general framework of the achievement of the fundamental objectives referred to in Article 2 of the Treaty establishing the European Community and Article 2 of the Treaty on European Union.'

[54] Case COMP/M.8084 (21 March 2018), *Bayer/Monsanto*, para. 3011.

[55] Id., para. 3017.

[56] See above n 28 and accompanying text.

competitors[57] is also part of this. It is also linked to a more rigorous assessment of competition, through narrower market definitions[58] or taking into account preferences for climate- and environment-friendly products when estimating unilateral price effects.[59] In all of these scenarios, enhanced competition can benefit climate, environmental sustainability and biodiversity by making products that are improved in line with these objectives available to consumers at more favourable conditions.

Second, it is understood that the Commission will not take into account in its assessment whether a merger has adverse effects on the climate that are not related to a reduction of competition. This could be the case, for example, if a merger leads to production efficiencies and, consequently, to an increase in volume that results in an increase in CO_2 emissions.[60] This is consistent with the fact that in the *Bayer/Monsanto* case the Commission did not carry out detailed analyses of the climate and environmental impacts of the merger as such. It did not consider the argument that the merger (including the innovation spaces protected by the Commission for the development of less toxic pesticides, herbicides and fungicides) would consolidate the conventional paradigm of industrial agriculture at the expense of agricultural diversity and sustainability and would therefore be detrimental in the long term in terms of climate protection and environmental sustainability.[61]

Third, the Commission's statements stand in the way of attempts to include in the consumer welfare analysis negative externalities, such as climate and environmental damage, which are detrimental to the public at large or at least essentially detrimental to consumers outside the markets under consideration. To enable (and legitimize) such analyses, there are various approaches available that could be used to measure the value that consumers in the market affected by the merger would place on avoiding these externalities.[62] Such analyses and assessments could lead to a merger being challenged even though it is expected to lead to lower prices or innovative products in the affected market. However, this is ruled out by the Commission's statements in the *Bayer/Monsanto* case, as the 'reduction of competition' link would be missing: a negative external effect would then be cured, albeit measured in terms of the welfare of consumers in the market. However, the Commission's focus on the protection of undistorted competition as the (only) overriding guiding principle should be understood as an endorsement of the fact that merger control does not empower the Commission to address all forms of market failure that may be associated with a merger.

Fourth, the Commission is, however, taking the liberty of making quite significant normative shifts within the consumer welfare paradigm, which may in fact allow the avoidance of negative externalities to become implicitly a matter of merger

---

[57] See above Sect. 2.2.2.

[58] See above Sect. 2.1.1.

[59] See above Sect. 2.1.2.

[60] See the scenario outlined by Kar et al. (2021), p. 127.

[61] Deutscher and Makris (2023), pp. 370 and 376.

[62] For an overview, see van Dijk (2021), pp. 61–66; Haucap et al. (2023), pp. 238–259.

control. If we take, for example, the tighter control of restrictions on innovation competition in the *Bayer/Monsanto* case or the looming tighter control of acquisitions of nascent competitors, this consideration is based on a significantly extended time horizon. However, if the welfare of consumers in 10 or 15 years, or perhaps even longer, is taken as the yardstick for weighting possible restrictions on innovation competition, and if these effects can be normatively reinforced in the light of the horizontal clauses of the Treaty and recital 23 of the EUMR, then it becomes clear that this approach can potentially provide significant (indirect) protection against negative externalities.

Fifth, the Commission's approach of (indirectly) including climate protection or environmental concerns if they are associated with a restriction of competition in the assessment of mergers in fact allows negative externalities to be taken into account independently of consumer welfare effects. A good illustration of this is the Commission's investigation into *Aurubis/Metallo*, a merger of two companies that were, inter alia, market leaders in the smelting and refining of copper scrap in the European Economic Area. One reason for the Commission's in-depth investigation was that it saw the possibility that the merged entity could have greater buying power in the purchase of copper scrap, which would lead to lower purchase prices and thus reduce the incentive to collect copper scrap and return it to the circular copper economy.[63] This is notable because the Commission appears to have taken it as an independent theory of harm (i.e. without focusing on consumer welfare effects) that the functioning circular economy would be disrupted by buyer power and that this would be accompanied by sustainability losses as recycled copper would be substituted for primary copper in the supply chain. Commissioner Vestager was quoted as saying that:

> [a] well-functioning circular economy in copper is important to ensure a sustainable usage of resources in the context of the European Green Deal. This is why we carried out an in-depth investigation.[64]

Ultimately, however, this did not matter as the Commission concluded that the merger was unlikely to have a significant impact on incentives to invest and innovate in the treatment of copper scrap or to lead to a reduction in the collection of copper scrap.[65]

Sixth and finally, it should be noted that the Commission's statements in the *Bayer/Monsanto* case referred only to preventing negative effects on climate and

[63] European Commission, Press Release (19 Nov 2019), Mergers: Commission opens in-depth investigation into proposed acquisition of Metallo by Aurubis ('Therefore, at this stage, the Commission is concerned that, following the transaction, the merged entity could hold a dominant position in the procurement of copper scrap for refining, giving it increased buyer power to negotiate lower prices for the copper scarp it purchases. By preventing competition on price, the merger could thus disrupt the normal functioning of the copper recycling industry, lowering the incentives for recyclers to collect and sort copper scrap').

[64] European Commission, Press Release (4 May 2020), Mergers: Commission clears Aurubis' acquisition of Metallo.

[65] Case COMP/M.9409 (4 May 2020), *Aurubis/Metallo Group Holding*, para. 871.

environmental sustainability through a tendency towards stricter merger control. The question of whether and under which circumstances merger control should be relaxed in order to achieve these objectives was not addressed. This aspect will be analysed next.

4 What We Do Not (Yet) See in the Commission's Practice: Relaxed Merger Control

EU merger practice has often focused on the question of whether, in which contexts and under which conditions a stricter or a conceptually extended merger control is possible or necessary to protect the climate and environmental sustainability. However, contrary to what sometimes has been assumed,[66] these objectives have so far barely played a role in the European Commission's practice as a justification for clearing a merger and thus for a tendency to relax merger control.[67] Here, we will briefly outline three aspects that could lead to such a choice. Finally, we would like to point out that the Commission's option to clear a merger against commitments must not lead to an (implicit) lowering of the standard for the competitive control of mergers to achieve a practical balance with climate protection concerns.

4.1 (Green) Efficiency Gains (1): Scaling Up of Green Innovation

Efficiency gains from a merger may compensate for consumer welfare losses resulting from restrictions on competition. In its Merger Guidelines, the Commission requires that efficiencies be substantial, timely, merger-specific and verifiable.[68] As regards the significance of possible efficiencies, the guidelines state that 'the later the efficiencies are expected to materialize in the future, the less weight the Commission can assign to them'.[69] In analogy to the above-mentioned possible tightening of merger control for the protection of innovation,[70] a normative overlap must also be taken into account here: given the importance of climate protection and environmental sustainability emphasized in EU primary law, and recital 23 of the EUMR, 'green' innovations and their potentially significant future benefits for consumers must be given a high profile.

66 Holmes (2020), p. 391.

67 See Kar et al. (2021), pp. 128–132.

68 Horizontal Merger Guidelines (n 5), paras 76–88.

69 Horizontal Merger Guidelines (n 5), para. 83.

70 See above text accompanying n 37 and n 50.

In practice, this could be important if the acquisition of an emerging competitor with an innovative 'green' business idea can help to scale up the idea and thus make the innovation available more quickly. This might be particularly the case in markets where business models benefit from network effects and economies of scale and scope. It is not uncommon for simple barriers to the rapid diffusion of new approaches, such as lack of access to capital or lack of a European or global distribution network, to be overcome by an acquisition by a major player. If, thus, in an individual case concentration helps to accelerate green innovation, this must not be disregarded.[71]

4.2 (Green) Efficiency Gains (2): Direct Reduction of the Carbon Footprint

It is easy to see how a merger could lead to productivity gains and thus lower costs but at the same time reduce the overall carbon footprint, for example by reducing energy consumption or air pollution from production facilities or transport of inputs.[72] Given the reduction in negative externalities, shouldn't this second aspect be given particular weight? The Merger Guidelines state that 'efficiencies ... should, in principle, benefit consumers in those relevant markets where it is otherwise likely that competition concerns would occur'.[73] But, assuming that the notifying parties could demonstrate in a case that consumers in the market concerned attach a quantifiable value to the avoidance of negative externalities, should this not be taken into account in light of the primary law requirement to protect the climate and the environment?

On the question of tightening merger control, we have rejected this logic (as a follow-up to *Bayer/Monsanto*): merger control is designed to avoid distortions of competition caused by concentration, not to avoid negative externalities caused by concentration.[74] To be sure, the aspect of avoiding negative externalities as a defence was not at issue in the *Bayer/Monsanto* decision. Besides, the rationality of this decision does not apply (at least not necessarily) regarding this aspect. This can be seen from the fact that, for example, the climate-damaging effects of a merger owing to increased air pollution can, at least in principle, be directly addressed by alternative regulatory instruments, namely emission limits. In contrast, the merger-specific avoidance of negative externalities (air pollution etc.) cannot (or at least cannot easily) be achieved through alternative regulatory instruments. In fact, it is hard to imagine that climate or environmental legislation could force concentration to reduce air pollution etc.

---

[71] See Article 2(1)(b) EUMR.

[72] See Deutscher and Makris (2023), p. 5 note 22.

[73] Horizontal Merger Guidelines (n 5), para. 79.

[74] See above Sect. 3.2.

4.3 Vertical Upstream Integration and Compliance with Climate Standards

Companies operating in the EU often have an interest in ensuring that their upstream suppliers meet certain sustainability standards or at least provide sufficiently reliable information to identify and assess adverse impacts on climate and environmental sustainability. The incentive may be to protect the company's reputation, to meet voluntary commitments to customers, or to comply with legal requirements. The result can be a drive towards control of the entire supply chain through upstream integration. For example, the French luxury group LVMH has announced that '[t]o ensure responsible practices, LVMH will also continue vertical integration of farming and tanning, particularly for precious leathers'.[75]

Such a tendency can be accompanied by competitive risks in the form of input foreclosure at the expense of competing buyers.[76] Should the notifying parties be able to claim efficiency gains from increased climate protection by controlling the supply chain against competitive risks? I do not see why this should a priori be objectionable: indeed, upstream integration will usually be the surest way to achieve these objectives. It therefore follows from the argument in the previous section that 'green' efficiencies may also compensate for the harm that consumers suffer from restrictions on competition. Whether this is in fact the case should in principle depend on how consumers in the markets concerned value supply chain control and compliance with due diligence obligations along the supply chain.

When it comes to meeting legal requirements, it should be considered whether the legal requirement to meet a certain standard may obviate the need to measure how consumers value the enforcement of certain standards on suppliers. If the risk of non-compliance with certain regulatory standards due to merger-related market power can justify a prohibition,[77] then clearance should also be possible where market power through concentration can lead to compliance with regulatory standards.

4.4 Clearance of Mergers Based on Climate Commitments?

The European Commission will clear a merger subject to remedies if the remedies are sufficient to remove the competition concerns raised by the merger. The commitment to climate-friendly behaviour can therefore only be taken into account if it

[75] LVMH (22 April 2021), 'The alliance of nature and creativity for a new vision of luxury: LVMH announces new objectives of LIFE 360 Environmental Strategy' (https://www.lvmh.com/news-documents/news/the-alliance-of-nature-and-creativity-for-a-new-vision-of-luxury-lvmh-announces-new-objectives-of-life-360-environmental-strategy).

[76] Lecchi (2023), p. 75.

[77] Deutscher and Makris (2023), p. 361, Table 1, Scenario (B).

eliminates the potential for the merger to restrict competition. If the Commission recognizes the risk that concentration will reduce the potential for innovative products and technologies that protect the climate and the environment, then proposed commitments must precisely address this point. Examples include the *Dow/DuPont* case mentioned above[78] and General Electric's proposed acquisition of Alstom's energy business. The Commission was particularly critical of the latter because Alstom's heavy-duty gas turbines division was in the process of developing a new and highly efficient product that promised significant benefits in meeting the climate change targets. The authority therefore cleared the merger only after the notifying parties had committed to divesting central parts of Alstom's heavy-duty gas turbines business to Ansaldo.[79]

However, to the extent that merger-related negative effects on the climate and environment do not raise any relevant competition concerns, the question of remedial measures does not arise from the outset. If increased freight traffic, emissions and noise are not in themselves a potential reason to block a merger under the SIEC test,[80] then it does not matter what remedies might compensate for such climate and environmental damage.[81] Furthermore, the offer of 'climate remedies' by the notifying parties must not be considered to be possible compensation for unrelated competition concerns. In other words, the possibility of a merger being cleared on the basis of commitments must not lead to an (implicit) lowering of the standard for the competition assessment of mergers by allowing for a practical balance with climate protection concerns.[82] Lina Khan, chair of the Federal Trade Commission and not suspected of downplaying the climate crisis or being hostile to sustainability issues as such, took the same line:

> I've heard would-be merging parties make all sorts of commitments to be better corporate citizens if only we would back off from a lawsuit. If only we hold off on suing to block the merger, they promise they will reduce their carbon footprints, give back to the community and so on … Some in corporate America seem to think that the FTC won't challenge an otherwise illegal deal if we approve of its ESG impact. They are mistaken. The antitrust laws

---

[78] See above Sect. 2.2.1.

[79] Case COMP/M.7278 (8 Sept 2015), *General Electric/Alstom (Thermal Power – Renewable Poer & Grid Business).* Ansaldo successfully completed the development of this new turbine and subsequently won several tenders against the two market leaders, Siemens and GE. Badea et al. (2021), p. 7, note 24.

[80] See above n 55 and Sect. 2.2.1.

[81] Cf. Kar et al. (2021), p. 134 ('[I]f the Commission were to take into account the carbon "price" when assessing the competitive effect, then a remedy that would reduce emissions or counter any negative effects (e.g. carbon off-setting) could be appropriate'). See also Holmes (2020), pp. 393–394.

[82] See Kar et al. (2021), p. 134 ('What would be more controversial, and arguably outside the scope of the legal framework, would be for the Commission to accept a "green remedy" that overall makes a merger less damaging to the environment, but without articulating how this resolves an identified competition concern').

don't permit us to turn a blind eye to an illegal deal just because the parties commit to some unrelated social benefit.[83]

5 What Member States Can Do: Blocking and Clearing Mergers for Climate Protection

The Commission has ruled out *prohibiting* a merger under Article 2 of the EUMR because of its negative effects on the climate or environmental sustainability as such.[84] *Clearing* anticompetitive mergers based on their climate benefits has not yet been addressed by Commission practice. In any case, there is no explicit legal basis for this under the EUMR. However, both options are conceivable for Member States, albeit in different scenarios.

5.1 *Blocking Mergers: Protection of Legitimate Interests Other Than Undistorted Competition (Article 21(4) EUMR)*

Under Article 21(4) EUMR, Member States may block a merger that has been cleared by the Commission if they consider it necessary 'to protect legitimate interests other than those taken into consideration by this Regulation and compatible with the general principles and other provisions of Community law'. Of the interests explicitly legitimized in the provision, only 'public security' could be considered in the context of climate concerns. The Commission understands this not only as national security against external attacks but also as internal security. The understanding of the identical justification in various provisions of the EU's fundamental freedoms, such as Articles 36, 45(3), 52(1) and 65(1)(b) TFEU, can provide guidance in this respect.[85] According to this, protection must be directed towards the fundamental interests of a society or state, namely the protection of its 'economy … all its institutions, its essential public services and … the survival of its

[83] Khan (2022).

[84] See above Sect. 3.1.

[85] Notes on Council Regulation (EEC) 4064/89, re Article 21(3), para. 2 ('The Commission considers that the three specific categories of legitimate interests which any Member State may freely cite under this provision are to be interpreted as follows: … There may be wider considerations of public security, both in the sense of Article 224 [now Article 347 TFEU] and in that of Article 36 [now Article 36 TFEU], in addition to defence interests in the strict sense'). Reprinted in Commission of the European Communities, Bulletin of the European Communities, Supplement 2/90, Community Merger Control Law, p. 25.

inhabitants'.[86] In light of this, it seems conceivable that tangible and significant threats to environmental sustainability and the climate are included here because of the associated risks to the population.[87]

Furthermore, it is apparent that the Commission, if requested by a Member State, would have to recognize that the protection of climate and environmental sustainability is to be counted among the 'other public interest[s]' within the meaning of Article 21(4) EUMR.[88] This is supported by the Commission's reasoning in the *Bayer/Monsanto* case:[89] if, on the one hand, the consideration of climate concerns and environmental sustainability in all policy areas is required by EU primary law but, on the other hand, the Commission does not see itself legitimized to consider these independent objectives under the EUMR, then it follows that the Commission must at least—where necessary—grant the Member States regulatory freedom in this sense on the basis of Article 21(4) EUMR.

This is apparently also the view of the European Parliament, which has combined the statement that the EUMR allows the Member States to take appropriate measures to protect the climate and sustainability with a call for the Commission to be given the same powers when assessing the impact of mergers on the internal market.[90]

5.2 *Clearing Mergers for Reasons of General Interest Under Member States' Law*

The Commission's prohibition of a merger is the last word in a case (unless it is successfully challenged in the European courts): while under Article 21(4) EUMR Member States may block mergers that have been cleared by the Commission, they cannot clear mergers that have been blocked by the Commission. We need to understand and accept that this was a deliberate choice made by the EU legislature.[91]

To gain an understanding of such a scenario, we can turn to Member State law. The so-called 'ministerial authorization' under German law provides a good illustration, because here reasons of general interest other than the protection of competition can lead to the clearance of a merger in a separate procedure: if the Bundeskartellamt prohibits a merger, the federal minister for economic affairs can nevertheless authorize it, inter alia, 'if the concentration is justified by an overriding

86 Case C-72/83, *Campus Oil*, ECLI:EU:C:1984:256, para. 34. See also the judgments of the ECJ in various 'golden shares' cases, e.g. Case C-463/00, *Commission v. Spain*, ECLI:EU:C:2003:272, para. 72.

87 Cf. Kar et al. (2021), p. 135 ('rather a stretch').

88 See Burnside et al. (2021), pp. 147–148.

89 See above Sect. 3.1.

90 European Parliament, P9_TA(2024)0011, Competition Policy – Annual Report 2023, para. 26.

91 Burnside et al. (2021), p. 142.

public interest'.[92] Climate protection and environmental sustainability are recognized as an overriding public interest. In approving the *Miba/Zollern* merger, the minister referred to Article 20a of the Grundgesetz, the German Constitution, which states:

> Mindful also of its responsibility towards future generations, the state shall protect the natural foundations of life and animals … by executive … action.

The merger had been prohibited by the Bundeskartellamt[93] but was subsequently approved by the minister, who felt that combining the companies' R&D would be beneficial to innovation in the field of plain bearings. The latter are important components for wind turbines, gas turbines and gas-fuelled ship engines, for example. Securing and promoting the potential for innovation was therefore seen as essential for the energy transition and thus for climate protection and the sustainable use of resources.[94]

Similar to the German 'ministerial authorization', in Spain the Council of Ministers can authorize a merger for reasons of general interest (other than the protection of competition) if it has been prohibited or cleared only subject to commitments by the Council of the National Competition Commission.[95] The list of relevant criteria includes, inter alia, 'protection of the environment'.[96] However, as far as can be seen, this instrument has not yet been used to approve mergers on the basis of their positive impact on environmental sustainability.

6 The Commission's Merger Practice, Climate Action and the EU's Constitutional Framework

Merger control is an integral element of competition policy, which is particularly important at the Community level, where it has been regarded since the Treaty of Rome as an essential instrument for ensuring the integration of the common market. Therefore, even if merger control—unlike the prohibition of cartels and of abusive practices under Articles 101 and 102 TFEU—is not laid down as a specific[97] element

[92] Section 42(1) of the German Competition Act (Gesetz gegen Wettbewerbsbeschränkungen – Act against Restraints of Competition).

[93] Bundeskartellamt, 17 Jan 2019, B 5 – 29/18, *Miba/Zollern*.

[94] Der Bundesminister für Wirtschaft und Energie, 19 Aug 2019, I B 2 – 20302/14–02, *Miba/Zollern*, paras 167–201.

[95] Article 60 of the Spanish Competition Act (Ley 15/2007, de 3 julio, de Defensa de la Competencia). See Mora-Sanguinetti and Hernández De Cos (2011), p. 486.

[96] Article 10(4)(d) of the Spanish Competition Act.

[97] Acquisitions by dominant companies may also be subject to control on the basis of Article 102 TFEU. See Case C-6/72, *Europemballage and Continental Can v Commission*, ECLI:EU:C:1973:22.

of primary law, it nevertheless serves an objective enshrined in primary law. Recital 2 of the EUMR states that,

> [f]or the achievement of the aims of the Treaty, [ex-]Article 3(1)(g) [of the Treaty establishing the European Economic Community] gives the Community the objective of instituting a system ensuring that competition in the internal market is not distorted.

With the Lisbon Treaty (2007), the establishment of a system of undistorted competition is no longer listed as an activity[98] of the Union in the text of the Treaty but has been moved to Protocol (No. 27), 'On the Internal Market and Competition'. However, the legal significance, in particular the hierarchical position of competition protection under EU law, has not changed.[99] Furthermore, Article 119 TFEU states that that activities of the Union for the purposes set out in Article 3 TEU (including the establishment of the internal market) shall include 'an economic policy which is ... conducted in accordance with the principle of an open market economy with free competition'.[100]

However, the protection of the climate, environmental sustainability, and biodiversity also enjoy the status of EU primary law objectives.[101] Various horizontal clauses apply, in particular Article 11 TFEU, and recital 23 of the EUMR expressly requires that the Commission 'must place its appraisal within the general framework of the achievement of the fundamental objectives' referred to in (now) Article 3 TEU, which stipulates, inter alia, that the Union must aim at 'a high level of protection and improvement of the quality of the environment'. In light of all of this, would it not make sense for EU merger control to weigh climate protection as a potentially conflicting objective against the protection of competition? Would it not make sense to include climate risks or opportunities in the merger review as negative or positive externalities that ultimately affect consumers—albeit outside the market whose competitiveness is affected by the merger under review?

6.1 Recognition of and Respect for Differentiated Regulatory Competences as a Key Consideration

We have seen that in *Bayer/Monsanto* the Commission positioned the protection of competition as the sole overriding guiding principle for merger control. Accordingly, climate protection aspects should not be directly taken into account in merger control, either quantitatively by offsetting out-of-market effects against consumer welfare effects or by means of a qualitative balancing. Even if this is in line with the

---

[98] See Monti (2013), pp. 31, 38–44.

[99] See Case C-52/09, *Konkurrensverket v TeliaSonera Sverige AB*, ECLI :EU: C:2011:83, para. 20; BGH 10 Feb 2011, I ZR 136/09, BGHZ 188, 326; Juris, para. 33 – *Flughafen Frankfurt-Hahn*.

[100] Note that Articles 120 and 127 TFEU explicitly link this premise to the objective of 'efficient allocation of resources'.

[101] See Ackermann (2023), p. 3.

(original) EU legislature's ideas, shouldn't the above-mentioned superimposition of primary law values allow for a different approach?

The Commission opposes this, referring to the 'principle of conferral of powers':[102] where a measure of secondary law is based on a competence conferred upon the EU legislature for a specific policy area, concurring policy objectives, even if they are enshrined in EU primary law, should not be allowed to directly determine the regulatory level imposed by the implementation of that measure. Otherwise, institutional, substantive or procedural requirements for rule-making under the Treaties could be undermined.[103]

This may concern the horizontal distribution of regulatory power at EU level but also the vertical distribution between the EU and the Member States, which may take different forms depending on the policy area. The EUMR is based on (now) Articles 103 and 352 TFEU. In addition, Article 114 TFEU could be used as a basis for procompetitive legislative measures including merger control.[104]

For climate action, the EU legislature can rely primarily on Article 192 TFEU, the power to impose measures to achieve environmental objectives as laid down in Article 191 TFEU. This provision has been the basis for a wide range of pieces of legislation that are also in the interests of climate protection. These include measures to limit industrial emissions,[105] to protect air quality,[106] to create an EU-wide scheme for greenhouse gas emission allowance trading[107] and to limit emissions in particular contexts, for example by setting CO_2 emission performance standards for new passenger cars.[108] In addition, the legislature has relied on internal market competence under Article 114 TFEU, e.g. in the case of the Taxonomy Regulation[109] in the field of sustainable financing and investment. Moreover, other bases of competence may also be relevant, such as Article 39 TFEU (agriculture) or Article 168 TFEU (health protection).[110]

---

[102] See Article 5 TEU and Article 7 TFEU.

[103] Case COMP/M.8084 (21 March 2018), *Bayer/Monsanto*, paras 3014–3018.

[104] Franck et al. (2021), pp. 43–55.

[105] Directive 2010/75/EU of the European Parliament and of the Council of 24 November 2010 on industrial emissions (integrated pollution prevention and control) (recast), OJ L 334/17.

[106] Directive 2008/50/EC of the European Parliament and of the Council of 21 May 2008 on ambient air quality and cleaner air for Europe, OJ L 152/1.

[107] Directive 2003/87/EC of the European Parliament and of the Council of 13 October 2003 establishing a scheme for greenhouse gas emission allowance trading within the Community and amending Council Directive 96/61/EC, OJ 2003 L 275/32.

[108] Regulation (EU) 2019/631 of the European Parliament and of the Council of 17 April 2019 setting CO2 emission performance standards for new passenger cars and for new light commercial vehicles, and repealing Regulations (EC) No 443/2009 and (EU) No 510/2011 (recast), OJ 2019 L 111/13.

[109] Regulation (EU) 2020/852 of the European Parliament and of the Council of 18 June 2020 on the establishment of a framework to facilitate sustainable investment, and amending Regulation (EU) 2019/2088, OJ 2020 L 198/13.

[110] See Case COMP/M.8084 (21 March 2018), *Bayer/Monsanto*, para. 3015.

6.2 *Implication: Climate Protection Through Conceptually Extended Merger Control vs. Climate Protection Through Relaxed Merger Control*

If the key argument against a stronger consideration of climate action, environmental sustainability etc. in merger control is respect for the differentiated allocation of regulatory competences, then it follows that a distinction must be made between two scenarios: conceptually extended vs. relaxed merger control.

6.2.1 Conceptually Extended Merger Control Risks Undermining Differentiated Exercise of Regulatory Powers

If the Commission were to use merger control as a lever to (indirectly) impose certain requirements on companies in the interest of climate protection, for example on emissions, it could as a matter of fact undermine the ordinary legislative procedure provided for in Article 192(1) TFEU.[111] It could also undermine a deliberate decision by the EU legislature not to specify a particular climate-related aspect at Union level. Given the shared competence of the Union and the Member States in the field of environmental regulation,[112] and in accordance with the principle of subsidiarity,[113] it could be considered beneficial to maintain, depending on the circumstances, the scope for decentralized rule-making to take account of different regional conditions, specific ecological features etc. Such a regulatory choice would be undermined if the Commission effectively implemented certain (stricter) rules through merger control.

If it is indeed deemed necessary to address merger-specific challenges separately, this could be done through a second (regulatory) merger barrier, which could be implemented on the basis of the regulatory power to combat climate change. As we have seen,[114] this is provided for in Article 21(4) EUMR—namely through intervention at Member State level. Such a parallel barrier could also be set up at Union level—as proposed by the European Parliament[115]—within the framework of its competences. The EU Foreign Subsidies Regulation[116] provides an example of this.

Against this background, in order to respect the exercise of differentiated regulatory competences, climate protection should not be implemented by means of climate-related extended control under the EUMR. By 'extended' merger control, I

[111] In certain sensitive areas, Article 192(2) TFEU even requires unanimity in the Council.

[112] Article 4(1), (2)(e) TFEU

[113] Article 5(1) and (3) TEU.

[114] See above Sect. 5.1.

[115] See above note 90.

[116] Regulation (EU) 2022/2560 of the European Parliament and of the Council of 14 December 2022 on foreign subsidies distorting the internal market, OJ 2022 L 330/1.

mean a conceptual extension of the assessment beyond the normative framework provided by the EUMR. This would be the case, for example, if (possible) negative externalities caused by the merger (such as increased emissions, either directly or through increased energy consumption) were included in the consumer welfare analysis under the SIEC test, so that business activities that are not prohibited by, for example, current emissions legislation could be prevented by (extended) merger control.

However, 'stricter' merger control should not be seen as problematic in the sense mentioned above if the Commission readjusts certain parameters within the conceptual and normative framework of the EUMR and this leads to stricter practice. This would be the case, for example, if the Commission attached greater importance to innovation competition or the protection of future (potential) competition in light of the primary legal requirement of climate protection. If, for example, the analytical framework for assessing the competitive risks of a merger were adapted by considering a longer time horizon[117] and also accepting a higher risk of false positives, this would certainly still be within the normative framework of the EUMR and would not run the risk of undermining the differentiated allocation of regulatory competences. All of the Commission's efforts to take account of climate change, environmental sustainability etc. in merger control, as outlined above,[118] are therefore clearly within the scope of its competences as laid down in the Treaties and reflected in the EUMR.

6.2.2 The Need to Allow for Relaxed Merger Control in Order to Respect Differentiated Regulatory Competences

As we have seen, there are scenarios where protecting the climate and environmental sustainability may make it necessary to clear a merger that would under a purely competition-based test have been blocked or cleared with commitments only.[119] Looking at these scenarios from the perspective of respecting differentiated regulatory competences, the implications are different from those of the call for stricter or conceptually extended merger control discussed in the previous section: if the competence to regulate climate change (whether at EU or national level) is to be respected, the purely competition-based standard cannot simply be allowed to prevail. Otherwise, the objective of climate protection as laid down in the primary law of the EU would be marginalised.

This is because neither the EUMR nor any other provision allows mergers blocked by the Commission (or cleared only with commitments) to be cleared on climate change grounds (without commitments). To pursue public policy goals, Article 21(4) EUMR allows a second (Member State) barrier for mergers, but no

[117] See above notes 37 and 50 and accompanying text.

[118] See above Sect. 2.

[119] See above Sect. 4.

clearance by Member States (even if they have the power for climate action regulation).[120] At EU level, there is no equivalent to the German ministerial authorization or the Spanish Council of Ministers authorization that would allow a merger to be approved for climate protection purposes. But could the EU legislator not remedy this shortcoming?

First, it should be noted that such an instrument could not be based, certainly not solely, on EU environmental policy and thus on Article 193 TFEU, because this would ultimately give the Commission or another body the power to define (i.e. lower) the level of competition protection in mergers. Ultimately, this would amount to a trade-off between the interests of climate protection and the interests of competition protection, with no a priori priority given to one or the other. In contrast, such an instrument could be adopted on the basis of Articles 103 and 352 TFEU, the current legal basis of the EU Merger Regulation. This is because the horizontal clause in Article 11 TFEU in particular requires and allows environmental and climate protection concerns to be taken into account in merger control.[121] However, this represents a very high hurdle in practice owing to the unanimity required in the Council. The objective of effectively pursuing environmental policy, which can in principle be implemented in the ordinary legislative procedure, is thus (indirectly) only partially taken into account at best.

Second, the climate-friendly merger-specific ‘green’ efficiencies discussed here cannot simply be replicated by EU legislation: the possibility that two companies would be forced to merge because of climate regulations seems purely theoretical. Therefore, if the merger were prohibited on competition grounds on the basis that climate protection could be pursued in parallel on the basis of the existing competences for this purpose, this would in practice mean that the merger-specific climate benefits would be lost.

The question of relaxing merger control for climate protection and sustainability reasons is therefore different from the similar debate under Article 101 TFEU on whether agreements between undertakings for these purposes should be allowed (and thus the level of competition protection actually weakened): the standards agreed by companies could in principle also be set in the same way by the EU or national legislature. Those who, from a constitutional point of view, consider it conclusive or even imperative to refer undertakings and consumers to the possibility of legislative regulation on climate protection and sustainability in Article 101 TFEU[122] do not necessarily have to do the same in merger control cases.

---

[120] See above Sect. 5.2.

[121] For this reason, there would be no need to combine the competence for implementing competition policy with the competence for implementing environmental policy.

[122] This argument has been developed in detail by Loozen (2019). See, in contrast, Ackermann (2023), p. 12, who has argued that Member State or EU legislation may prove inadequate for sustainable environmental protection due to the global and centralised nature of the task. See also Monti (2020), p. 126, stating that ‘the role of private actors in complementing regulatory efforts is by now well-established’ (with reference to Scherer et al. (2014)).

Therefore, in order to avoid climate change considerations, which argue for a more lenient approach to a merger, being a priori rendered irrelevant by this framework, it must be possible to take them into account in the assessment of individual cases under the EUMR. Recognizing this does not contradict the Commission's findings in the *Bayer/Monsanto* case: the statement that only the protection of competition empowers the Commission to intervene under the EUMR,[123] which is placed at the centre of the reasoning in this case, is obviously only meant to imply that climate protection etc. cannot justify stricter merger control than would be required from a purely competition point of view. In this case, the Commission had no reason to decide how to deal with the situation in which climate protection or environmental sustainability might require more lenient merger control.

Notifying parties must therefore remain free to put forward climate benefits from a merger. It must be possible that these benefits, such as the avoidance of negative externalities that materialize for the benefit of individuals beyond the competitively affected markets, can be taken into account even beyond the standard consumer welfare analysis under the SIEC test. In the interest of effective and efficient climate protection, the fact that the companies themselves are best placed to identify the 'green efficiency gains' associated with a merger can thus be exploited. However, companies will have to demonstrate that these benefits are substantial, merger-specific and verifiable, and thus meet the requirements of a 'standard' efficiency defence.[124] With regard to the time horizon, a distinction has to be made: on the one hand, we can demand a timely effect in terms of reducing emissions, saving energy etc. On the other hand, when balancing these effects against possible anticompetitive effects, the long-term positive effects on the climate must be taken into account.

The approach proposed here is not to transform the EUMR into an instrument that serves to pursue objectives other than the protection of competition. It is to ensure that merger practice leaves room for the pursuit of potentially conflicting objectives on the basis of other regulatory powers (whether of the EU institutions or of Member States). This means that the Commission must be given a wide margin of manoeuvre in the necessary assessment of whether, for climate protection reasons, a somewhat 'weaker' merger control is appropriate in individual circumstances. Consequently, the Commission has a great deal of leeway in the technical implementation of such an assessment. It is not necessarily the case that climate issues, even if accurately substantiated by the notifying parties, will in fact influence the final decision.

Finally, it should be emphasized that there is no institutional overload in requiring the Commission to weigh up incommensurable interests in individual cases.[125] Certainly, there are administrative costs involved. Yet, ideally, institutional

[123] See above n 55.

[124] See above n 68.

[125] See Holmes (2020), pp. 397–401. The opposing view, according to which the balancing of different policy objectives in competition and merger cases would undermine the effectiveness of competition law enforcement and the 'rigour and uniform application of the EU competition rules', is elaborated by Peeperkorn (2021).

arrangements should be found that avoid or minimize the scope of such trade-offs or at least provide transparent and clear guidelines for dealing with them. In principle, however, a democratically legitimized competition authority such as the Commission, which is accountable to the European Parliament, must be able to do this. Another question, which we will leave for another time, is whether an independent procedure with the possibility to approve mergers for climate protection reasons etc. would actually be preferable and how such a procedure could be structured at EU level.[126]

7 Concluding Remarks

Given the huge delta between what is currently being done to combat climate change and the level of climate action needed to ensure the survival of our civilization, it is not surprising that all the regulatory mechanisms at the Union's disposal are being examined to see what contribution they can make. However, despite the urgency of the matter, it remains crucial to respect the constitutional framework for intervention. This will ensure the democratic legitimacy and accountability of climate change policies. As these measures can have a profound impact on civil liberties and have significant redistributive effects, this is crucial for their legitimacy and for maintaining social peace. Against this background, it is not surprising, and indeed entirely justified, that the differentiated allocation of regulatory competences is at the centre of the discussion on whether and how climate protection should be taken into account in the European Commission's merger control practice. This chapter makes four key points to help find the right framework.

First, there are developments in which competition protection and climate protection go hand in hand and which in principle do not require any normative adjustments. This applies, for example, to market definition and the assessment of closeness of competition with regard to possible unilateral price effects. All that is required is sensitivity and consideration of consumer preferences for climate-friendly products. If merger control is tightened in this respect, this may lead to more favourable market conditions for these products and thus to greater consumption.

Second, we see scenarios where competition protection and climate protection also converge within the conventional consumer welfare paradigm but where at the same time some shifts of a normative nature can be observed. This can be seen, for example, in the Commission's theory of harm of eliminating close competition in 'innovation spaces' in the *Dow/DuPont* and *Bayer/Monsanto* cases. The same applies to the Commission's willingness to monitor acquisitions of emerging

---

[126] The risk of lobbying and horse-trading by national representatives—whether in the European Parliament, the Council or any other institution empowered to do so—on the outcome of different merger cases should be avoided at all costs.

competitors more closely, in particular with regard to the protection of 'green' innovation and technology, as demonstrated in the *Norsk Hydro/Alumetal* case. While stricter merger control in this respect fits perfectly into the conventional consumer paradigm, a workable analytical framework may require certain normative adjustments. This may concern the time horizon to be considered, which needs to be significantly extended. It may also require a lowering of the standard of proof and/or shifting the burden of proof to the notifying parties in certain situations, thereby accepting a higher risk of false positives.

Third, the Commission's reasoning in the *Bayer/Monsanto* case rules out the possibility of tightening merger control by taking account of negative externalities such as climate damage, even if these are measured in terms of consumer welfare. In doing so, the Commission respects the differentiated distribution of regulatory competences through the EU constitutional framework. Climate concerns must therefore not be implemented through a conceptual extension of the assessment of mergers beyond the normative framework of the EUMR, which is in fact characterized by the protection of competition as the sole overriding normative principle and objective. However, this insight should not obscure the fact that, in practice, possible merger-specific negative externalities can also be taken into account to a considerable extent, namely by indirectly linking climate protection concerns to potential restrictions of competition. The theory of harm analysed by the Commission in the *Aurubis/Metallo* case is an illustrative example of this.

Fourth, under the current merger control framework at EU level, the Commission will have to take into account merger-specific positive effects on climate concerns, even if they are not captured by the consumer welfare paradigm. Otherwise, merger practice would not sufficiently safeguard the pursuit of (possibly) conflicting objectives such as climate protection. There is no viable alternative because, first, the option to clear mergers on climate change grounds could not be implemented (solely) based on environmental powers and, second, merger-specific 'green' efficiencies are not easily replicable through (environmental) legislation. This finding does not contradict the Commission's findings in the *Bayer/Monsanto* case, which concerned only stricter or conceptually broader merger control. The Commission has a wide margin of discretion as to the extent to which merger control should be relaxed in order to preserve concurrent objectives of equal normative importance, such as the fight against climate change.

Finally, it should be emphasised that, while similar questions to those addressed here may arise in relation to other policy objectives that may conflict with the protection of competition, the answers are not necessarily the same: on the one hand, this analysis was based on a (climate change) policy-specific analysis of the EU constitutional framework with its vertically and horizontally differentiated distribution of competences. On the other hand, the fight against climate change has an especially prominent normative weight, as the survival of humanity is at stake. It is therefore particularly the protection of fundamental rights that obliges the EU institutions to make use of any regulatory leeway for climate protection.[127]

References

Ackermann T (2023) Der Einfluss des Umweltschutzes auf das EU-Kartellrecht. In: Pechstein M et al (eds) Festschrift für Rudolf Streinz. C. H. Beck, pp 3–15

Badea A, Bankov M, Da Costa G, Cabrera JE, Marenz S, O'Connor K, Rousseva E, Theiss J, Usai A, Vasileiou S, Winterstein A, Zedler M (2021) Competition policy in support of Europe's green ambition. European Commission, Competition Policy Brief 2021-01

Burnside A, De Backer M, Strohl D (2021) Can environmental interests trump an EUMR decision? In: Holmes S, Middelschulte D, Snoep M (eds) Competition law, climate change & environmental sustainability. Concurrences, pp 139–152

Crawford G, Valletti T, Caffarra C (2020) How tech rolls: potential competition and 'reverse' killer acquisitions'. VoxEU. https://cepr.org/voxeu/blogs-and-reviews/how-tech-rolls-potential-competition-and-reverse-killer-acquisitions

Cunningham C, Ederer F, Ma S (2021) Killer acquisitions. J Polit Econ 129:649–702

Denicolò V, Polo M (2018) Duplicative research, mergers and innovation. Econ Lett 166:56–59

Denicolò V, Polo M (2019) The innovation theory of harm: an appraisal. Antitrust Law J 82:926–953

Deutscher E, Makris S (2023) Sustainability concerns in EU merger control: from output-maximising to polycentric innovation competition. J Antitrust Enforc 11:350–399

Federico G, Langus G, Valletti T (2017) A simple model of mergers and innovation. Econ Lett 157: 136–140

Federico G, Langus G, Valletti T (2018) Reprint of: horizontal mergers and product innovation. Int J Ind Organ 61:590–612

Franck J-U, Monti G, de Streel A (2021) Options to strengthen the control of acquisitions by digital gatekeepers in EU law. TILEC Discussion Paper, DP 2021-016

Haucap J, Podszun R, Hahn R, Kreuter-Kirchhof C, Rohner T, Rösner A, Offergeld P, May A (2023) Wettbewerb und Nachhaltigkeit in Deutschland und der EU. Studie im Auftrag des Bundesministeriums für Wirtschaft und Klimaschutz

Holmes S (2020) Climate change, sustainability, and competition law. J Antitrust Enforc 8:354–405

Jullien B, Lefouili Y (2018) Horizontal mergers and innovation. J Compet Law Econ 14:364–392

Kar N, Cochrane E, Spring B (2021) Environmental sustainability and EU merger control: EU competition policy's dark horse to support green investment. In: Holmes S, Middelschulte D, Snoep M (eds) Competition law, climate change & environmental sustainability. Concurrences, pp 117–138

Khan L (2022) ESG won't stop the FTC. Wall Street Journal, 21 December. https://www.wsj.com/articles/esg-wont-stop-the-ftc-competition-merger-lina-khan-social-economic-promises-court-11671637135#comments_sector

Lecchi E (2023) Sustainability and EU merger control. Eur Compet Law Rev 44:70–80

[127] In *KlimaSeniorinnen*, the European Court of Human Rights (ECtHR) relied on the right to respect for private and family life enshrined in Article 8 of the European Convention on Human Rights (ECHR) to justify the obligation to take adequate measures against climate change. ECtHR Grand Chamber (9 April 2024), *Case of Verein KlimaSeniorinnen Schweiz and Others v. Switzerland* (Application no. 53600/20). Although the EU is not a party to the ECHR, this concept can be applied *mutatis mutandis* under Articles 7 and 52(3) of the EU Charter of Fundamental Rights, which the EU institutions must respect (Article 6(1) TEU).

Loozen E (2019) Strict competition enforcement and welfare: a constitutional perspective based on Article 101 TFEU and sustainability. Common Mark Law Rev 56:1265–1302

Monti G (2013) EU competition law from Rome to Lisbon – social market economy. In: Heide-Jorgensen C, Bergquist C, Neergard U, Troels Poulsen S (eds) Aims and values in competition law. DJØF, pp 27–66

Monti G (2020) Four options for a greener competition law. J Eur Compet Law Pract 11:124–132

Mora-Sanguinetti JS, Hernández De Cos P (2011) An assessment of the reform of the Spanish competition framework. World Compet 34:477–493

Motta M, Tarantino E (2017) The effect of horizontal mergers, when firms compete in prices and investments. BSE Working Paper 987

OECD (2020) Start-ups, killer acquisitions and merger control – background note. DAF/COMP (2020)5. https://one.oecd.org/document/DAF/COMP(2020)5/en/pdf

Peeperkorn L (2021) European Union. In: Holmes S, Middelschulte D, Snoep M (eds) Competition law, climate change & environmental sustainability. Concurrences, pp 405–414

Rubinfeld DL, Hoven J (2001) Innovation and antitrust enforcement. In: Ellig J (ed) Dynamic competition and public policy: technology, innovation, and antitrust issues. Cambridge University Press, pp 65–94

Scherer AG, Palazzo G, Matten D (2014) The business firm as a political actor: a new theory of the firm for a globalized world. Bus Soc 53:143–156

van Dijk T (2021) A new approach to assess certain sustainability agreements under competition law. In: Holmes S, Middelschulte D, Snoep M (eds) Competition law, climate change & environmental sustainability. Concurrences, pp 55–68

Government Intervention in Geoeconomics Uncertain Times: Rebalancing Conflicting Interests in Foreign Investment Screening

Yao Yuan

Contents

Abstract As geopolitical tensions rise and de-globalization trends gain momentum, many governments frequently use foreign investment screening mechanisms to strengthen their competitiveness and reduce dependence on other nations. However, governments' screening decisions based on national security reasons are not always in line with the interests of the domestic target company. With more takeovers being blocked due to national security concerns, domestic businesses may face challenges securing the necessary funding, miss out on essential innovations or operational improvements, struggle to penetrate foreign markets and be indirectly hurt by trade or investment retaliation. This chapter focuses on the conflict between the host states and the domestic companies targeted to be purchased by foreign investors. In current geoeconomics uncertain times, the complexity of defining national security and the government's broad discretion in this issue increased the difficulty of achieving a

Y. Yuan (✉)
Leiden Law School, Leiden University, Leiden, The Netherlands
e-mail: y.yuan@law.leidenuniv.nl

S. Hindelang et al. (eds.), *YSEC Yearbook of Socio-Economic Constitutions 2024*, YSEC Yearbook of Socio-Economic Constitutions (2025) 2024: 283–308,
https://doi.org/10.1007/16495_2024_73, Published online: 26 February 2025

proper balance. It has been widely accepted that state intervention is necessary in the case of market failure. However, to what extent the government can intervene, and whether the government shall play a relatively restrained or active role in balancing the conflict between public and private interests is difficult to define. This chapter argues that efforts to readjust the balance of interests can be undertaken from both the corporate and government perspectives. It concludes with implications that policymakers should be aware of in foreign investment screening, particularly in balancing national security concerns with the autonomy of domestic companies in the cross-border takeover market.

1 Introduction

As geopolitical tensions rise and de-globalization trends gain momentum, major economies have introduced various tools to strengthen their competitiveness and reduce dependence on other nations, aiming to mitigate potential risks associated with deepening economic interdependence across a broad range of sectors. One key tool is the screening of foreign direct investment (FDI) to protect national security and safeguard strategic assets from foreign acquisition. Increasingly, governments are using this screening mechanism to block or influence foreign takeovers on the grounds of national security or public order.[1] While domestic companies must comply with such decisions in the interest of national security, these measures are not always in line with the commercial interests of the domestic business involved. When governments impose conditions or block foreign investments based on national security, domestic companies may face challenges such as limited access to capital, missed opportunities for innovation and operational improvements, difficulties entering foreign markets, and exposure to trade or investment retaliation. This creates a conflict between the public interest, represented by the host state's strategic priorities, and the private economic interest of the domestic companies targeted by foreign investors.

In addition, with the international economic order shifting from the post-Cold War 'Neoliberal Order' to a 'new Geoeconomic Order', the rationale behind the economic relations—formerly characterised by 'World Peace through World Trade'

[1] For example, in the EU, 26 out of 27 Member States already have an FDI screening mechanism or are in a consultative or legislative process expected to adopt one. In 2022, 1444 acquisition authorisation requests from foreign investors were processed. Of the cases formally screened, 9% were approved with conditions or mitigating measures, and 1% were ultimately blocked by national authorities, according to the European Commission's Third Annual Report on the Screening of Foreign Direct Investments into the Union in 2023; In the US, between 2014 and 2023, 1150 transactions were investigated out of the 2137 notifications. Since the US President gained the authority to block transactions in 1988, seven cases have been blocked, six of which occurred after 2012, as reported in the 2023 CFIUS annual report.

in the neoliberal era—is being reshaped.[2] Interdependence, while boosting economic efficiency, also introduces strategic vulnerabilities, such as reliance on foreign countries for critical technologies vital to economic and military strength.[3] The traditional distinction between economic and national security has become increasingly blurred, with both factors now intertwined in the FDI screening decision-making process on whether a foreign investment poses a national security risk. Governments now view economic statecraft as a key element of foreign policy, leveraging interdependencies created by globalisation to influence or pressure other states.[4] Recent FDI screening developments reflect a growing tendency among major economies to broaden the definition of national security, incorporating economic security considerations into their screening processes. When national security is narrowly defined and rarely invoked, compromises are more easily reached. However, when the concept becomes vague and expansive, more business sectors and transactions are scrutinised, heightening the potential for conflict between domestic companies and adverse government decisions, making it necessary to rebalance these competing interests. Furthermore, legal remedies available to foreign investors and domestic companies in response to government screening decisions are limited. In many jurisdictions, such as the United States and China, screening decisions are final and not subject to judicial review. Even in regions where legal recourse is theoretically possible, such as Europe, there is little judicial precedent or guidance. This leaves governments with broad discretion, which can significantly affect the involved parties—including domestic companies—yet provides limited legal recourse for those adversely affected by screening decisions. In light of these challenges, it is essential to consider how to safeguard company autonomy from excessive government intervention in uncertain geoeconomic times and to maintain a healthy cross-border investment environment and a balanced takeover market.[5]

While state intervention is widely accepted as necessary in cases of market failure, such as protecting national security in foreign investment screening, the extent of such intervention and whether governments should adopt a restrained or active role in balancing public and private interests remain difficult to define. In the context of FDI screening, the line between economic and national security becomes even more blurred. If governments freely use economic considerations to justify national security measures, it risks encouraging protectionism, which could ultimately harm domestic industries. Although international organisations have established general legal principles for safeguarding national security within the

[2]Roberts et al. (2019). This article has outlined the concept of the post-Cold War 'Neoliberal Order', the 'new Geoeconomic Order', and the transition between them. Following the Cold War (from 1991 onward), the neoliberal economic order became progressively more internationalised and institutionalised. However, since the 2008 financial crisis, the Neoliberal Order has faced growing pressures, leading to the rise of a new Geoeconomic Order.

[3]Ibid.

[4]Gertz and Evers (2020), p. 117.

[5]See Blackwill and Harris (2016). The author defines 'geoeconomics' as the 'use of economic instruments to promote and defend national interests, and to produce beneficial geopolitical results'.

context of globalisation,[6] whether these non-binding principles will be adhered to in uncertain geoeconomic times has received limited scholarly attention. This chapter seeks to explore new considerations for policymakers in balancing national security concerns with the autonomy of domestic companies in cross-border takeovers.

The chapter is structured as follows: Sect. 2 examines the evolving relationship between the public and private sectors, highlighting conflicts of interest in the current geoeconomic landscape. Section 3 explores three factors that exacerbate these conflicts: the expanding interpretation of 'national security', the broad discretion of governments, and the lack of sufficient legal remedies for the private sector, followed by a discussion of their implications. Sections 4 and 5 propose solutions to realign the balance of interests from both corporate and governmental perspectives. Finally, Sect. 6 summarises the key arguments and reflects on the implications of the emerging geoeconomic reality for governments and businesses.

2 Conflicting Interests Between Public and Private Sectors in Foreign Investment Screening

As part of international investment law, numerous studies explore the dynamics and conflicting interests between states and foreign investors.[7] The primary aim of international investment law is to address a foreign investor's need for protection when a host state jeopardises its unprejudiced profit expectations. However, in foreign investment screening, there is notably less research centring on the interaction between states and domestic target companies. Current literature does not adequately address how business actors perceive investment screening policies, or whether enterprises in the private sector contribute to serving public interests.[8] With the changing international geoeconomic landscape, domestic businesses are more susceptible to the gradually expanding influence of state intervention, heightening the prominence of conflicts of interest between them and governments.

Historically, conflicts between state and business interests have not always existed. There have also been times when the interests were aligned. In the era of after-Cold War neoliberal economics, foreign investments mutually benefited the host country and domestic companies, and both of them viewed FDI as a vital contributor to fostering an open, modern economy and ensuring welfare and

---

[6] Such as the guidelines set forth by the Organisation for Economic Co-operation and Development (OECD), the United Nations Conference on Trade and Development (UNCTAD), and other international instruments.

[7] E.g. Acconci (2023); Bian (2021); Gadocha (2020); Hatchondo and Martinez (2011); Giofré (2013); Accaoui Lorfing (2021).

[8] Nibe (2023), p. 142. Nibe's research provides a direction that shows that businesses shaped their investment screening policy preferences in uncertainty by the influence of government and local political elites.

economic growth.[9] Through regional integration and globalisation of the economy, states have agreed to limitations on their sovereign rights to facilitate trade and investment. For much of the past decades, many developed economies lacked dedicated national instruments for managing essential security risks linked to FDI and did not recognise the necessity of evaluating such risks. This was partly due to a large share of global FDI taking place among allies, and the developed economies, most of the time, acted as investment exporters.[10] In these countries, cross-border investments were viewed purely as economic activities between private sectors, not necessitating government intervention. At the international law level, national security considerations and exceptions for actions taken to safeguard security-related interests have been frequently expressly outlined in international trade and investment regimes.[11] Also, these national security exceptions were interpreted by international tribunals and commissions in a relatively narrow manner.[12] Under such open markets and an international, rules-based world trading system, domestic companies enjoy greater access to capital and have better prospects for achieving their value-maximizing goals. In this scenario, the drive for national security usually coincided with the stance of the private sector.

However, recent shifts and upheavals in the global economy, characterised by a move from liberalism to geo-economics, have strained the alignment between public strategic interests and private economic interests.[13] A significant factor in this shift is the intensifying strategic competition, particularly between the US and China. Following China's accession to the WTO, it was viewed as an economic competitor that could be managed through existing trade rules. However, as China's political, military, and economic influence expanded globally, this economic competition evolved into a broader strategic and security rivalry.[14] This shift was underscored by the US National Security Strategy of 2017, which identified China as a 'revisionist power,'[15] and by the EU labelling China as a 'systemic rival promoting alternative models of governance.'[16] Global disruptions such as COVID-19 and the Russia-Ukraine war further accelerated this trend, highlighting that the benefits of globalisation can no longer be taken for granted. While Chinese investment continues to be a significant focus in the West, the evolution of FDI regulations reflects growing concerns about foreign investments in general, particularly their implications for the security of domestic industries, technologies, data, and resources—

[9] Te Velde et al. (2006).

[10] OECD, The Relationship Between FDI Screening and Merger Control Reviews - Background Note, 2022, p. 7.

[11] OECD (2008).

[12] Ibid.

[13] Choer Moraes and Wigell (2022), p. 44.

[14] Henrique Choer Moraes (2024).

[15] White House (2017) National Security Strategy of the United States of America.

[16] European Commission et al., *Joint Communication to the European Parliament, the European Council and the Council: EU-China – A strategic outlook*, 12 March 2019.

extending well beyond a sole focus on China. Today, foreign investment regulations aim to pursue broader goals, such as to ensure economic growth and prosperity.[17]

Only recently have the risks of market-driven globalisation, which relies heavily on interdependent and fragmented production chains, received adequate attention.[18] In today's geoeconomic uncertainty, the boundaries between the economic and security spheres are increasingly blurred, with economic decisions often shaped by security concerns.[19] National security concerns, not only as grounds for FDI screening, indirectly affect private sectors, but also came up as a consideration of industrial policy to enhance the state's competitiveness, directly affecting domestic companies. The distinction between commercial policy and traditional security concerns is eroding, which redraws the boundary between the government and the market.

Advanced economies have started to employ national security measures, which in the past essentially or almost marked the policies of developing countries, to safeguard strategic interests against foreign investors. State sovereignty is not directly jeopardised in this emerging geoeconomics dynamic. Instead, the current increase in state economic interventionism is propelled by the pursuit of autonomy. Policymakers are concerned about potentially entering a situation of economic dependence on an external power, which could compromise the state's autonomy.[20] Occasionally, these measures taken by states to strengthen their independence may have adverse effects on the interests of local industries. The primary objectives of states—including boosting competitiveness, enhancing the securing supply chains, and broader foreign policy goals such as reducing dependencies or pursuing ideological agendas—can cause general antagonism between central decision-makers and private sector interests. Government undue intervention in foreign investment screening, in the short term, brings about tangible costs and imposes regulatory burdens; in the long term, these restrictions limit firms' access to alternative investment financing, heighten uncertainty, and are likely to influence business investment decisions negatively.[21]

---

[17] Horst Henschen, Martin Juhasz (2023) Foreign Investment Regulation: Widening the Focus on Both Sides of the Atlantic. https://globalcompetitionreview.com/guide/foreign-direct-investment-regulation-guide/third-edition/article/foreign-investment-regulation-widening-the-focus-both-sides-of-the-atlantic.

[18] Choer Moraes and Wigell (2022), p. 40.

[19] European Commission, 2023 Strategic Foresight Report, COM(2023) 376 final, 6 July 2023, p. 13.

[20] Choer Moraes and Wigell (2022).

[21] Nibe (2023), p. 141. See also Bauerle Danzman and Meunier (2021).

3 Potential Government Undue Intervention in Geoeconomics Uncertain Times

In the context of FDI screening, the complex and evolving concept of national security, coupled with the broad discretion given to the government, increased the difficulty of achieving a proper balance between the conflicting public and private interests. The blurred dividing line between traditional 'national security' and broadened 'economic security' grants states significant leeway, increasing the potential for undue intervention. This situation heightens the possibility of conflict between domestic companies and adverse government screening decisions, making the need to rebalance these interests in times of geoeconomic uncertainty more pressing.

3.1 Broader 'National Security' Concept

National security, as a ground, enables states to exercise exceptional powers.[22] States are recognised to have a certain measure of discretion when evaluating national security threats and deciding how to combat these. However, national security is a dynamic and evolving concept that has been gradually extended over time. It initially represented the military and defensive aspect of border protection.[23] By the end of the Cold War, there was still a clear distinction between security and economy in the post-war liberal order.[24] Then, this concept went beyond its traditional meaning, increasingly including the protection of community interests of other nature, such as public order, the environment, health, and the protection of critical sectors of the national economy. In today's evolving geoeconomic landscape, there is greater convergence between security and economic concerns, more attention to related economic benefits by their security implications, and a greater focus on security risks deriving from interdependence, which would weaken state control and its self-sufficiency and resilience.[25] Therefore, many states have departed from the market-oriented rationale of the neoliberal order, adopting more rigorous approaches towards foreign investments that incorporate economic security concerns into national security screening processes.[26] In the context of FDI screening, the inclusion of economic security allows the government to conceal its true objectives under the broad guise of national security, which may further intensify conflicts with the private sector.

[22] Eisenhut (2010).

[23] Kelsen (1948), pp. 783–796.

[24] Heath (2020), p. 1020.

[25] Roberts et al. (2018).

[26] Mauro and Pernazza (2023), pp. 24–25; Choer Moraes and Wigell (2022), p. 30.

The United States is one of the countries that started incorporating economic security considerations relatively early in national security reviews. During the US legislative process surrounding national security reviews, there were constant disputes between Congress and the government over how broadly national security should be defined.[27] For instance, during discussions on the Exon-Florio Amendment in 1988, the Reagan Administration maintained that foreign investment was beneficial to the US economy and was reluctant to expand the definition of national security beyond the traditional military and defence framework to include economic factors.[28] In the earlier years, such debates, to some extent, helped to prevent the overextension of the national security concept. However, the US stance began to shift around 2008, with a significant transformation emerging in the 2017–2018 US Economic and Security Strategy, when the Trump Administration explicitly declared that 'economic security is national security.'[29] Under Trump, new protectionist measures were introduced across various economic sectors, and the Biden Administration further advanced this approach by promoting US industrial development.[30] As a result, the concept of national security has significantly broadened in practice, with the national security review mechanism increasingly being used as a tool for achieving political objectives.[31]

Unlike the US, the EU has only recently started to contemplate economic security. The establishment of the EU was founded on the belief that great power competition was detrimental to global well-being and that increased economic cooperation and connections were guarantors of peace.[32] Economic security was, therefore, absent in the principles underpinning the birth of the European idea. For an extended period, the EU resisted embracing a geoeconomics approach, and refraining from using economic tools for geopolitical objectives. However, since 2017, the EU has increasingly prioritised identifying and addressing security vulnerabilities stemming from open markets. In recent years, the EU has rapidly developed innovative policy instruments that integrate trade and investment with economic security considerations.[33] The concept of security in the EU is now

[27] Yuan and Koster (2024), p. 12.

[28] Jackson (2013a), pp. 172–173.

[29] White House (2017) National Security Strategy of the United States of America.

[30] Bade G (2023) Joe Biden wants a 'new economic world order.' It's never looked more disordered. In: POLITICO. https://www.politico.com/news/2023/05/25/joe-bidens-economy-trade-china-00096781.

[31] For example, the proposed merger of the Japanese Nippon Steel and American industrial giant US Steel, which proponents say would benefit both countries, is trapped by political and labour opposition. President Biden signalled his opposition to foreign ownership of US Steel in mid-March 2024. About a week later, the United Steelworkers endorsed Biden's bid for re-election. For details, see Davis RA (2024) Why Nippon Steel's $15 Billion Takeover of U.-S. Steel Is in Peril. N. Y. Times.

[32] Nogués EC (2024) Economic security: a new age for the EU. https://www.realinstitutoelcano.org/en/commentaries/economic-security-a-new-age-for-the-eu/.

[33] Rosén and Meunier (2023), p. 123.

inseparable from the idea of Open Strategic Autonomy, wherein Brussels considers not only the immediate security implications of FDI but also the long-term consequences of increasing dependence.[34] This geoeconomics shift reached its peak with the unveiling of the European Commission's Economic Security Strategy in June 2023.[35] This new strategy reflects a similar approach to the US, focusing on minimising risks associated with specific economic flows amid heightened geopolitical tensions and accelerated technological shifts. In January 2024, the EU Commission adopted five initiatives to strengthen the EU's economic security at a time of growing geopolitical tensions and profound technological shifts.[36] In the field of foreign investment screening, the EU plans to further strengthen the protection of EU security and public order by proposing improved screening of foreign investment into the EU, identifying potential risks stemming from outbound investments in a narrow set of technologies, and extending EU screening to investments by EU investors that are ultimately controlled by individuals or businesses from a non-EU country.[37] While the European Union and the United States share many similarities, they also differ significantly in their preferences and levels of vulnerability.[38] Europe's challenge is not merely about 'shielding key technologies from Chinese influence' but rather about preserving economic policy autonomy and safeguarding the interests of European companies from the damage caused by the US's aggressive chip war.[39] The US government has been criticised for exploiting the notion of 'economic security' to pressure its allies into aligning with its strategic competition against China.[40] There are growing concerns that the EU's economic security strategy could fall under U.S. influence.[41]

[34]Ghiretti F, Gunter J (2022) COSCO's Hamburg Terminal Acquisition: Lessons For Europe. In: War Rocks. https://warontherocks.com/2022/11/coscos-hamburg-terminal-acquisition-and-the-lessons-europeans-should-take-away/.

[35]European Commission (2023) European Economic Security Strategy.

[36]European Commission (2024) Communication From the Commission to the European Parliament and the Council Advancing European economic security: an introduction to five new initiatives.

[37]Ibid.

[38]Lúcio Vinhas de Souza (2024) Developing an Economic Security Strategy: EU and U.-S. approaches. https://www.csis.org/blogs/geoeconomics-360/developing-economic-security-strategy-eu-and-us-approaches.

[39]Wang Y (2024) It's folly for EU to follow US chip war in its economic security strategy. Glob. Times.

[40]For example, Dutch government policies are sometimes influenced by the US, as seen in the case of ASML's export controls. Since 2019, the Dutch government has blocked ASML from selling its most advanced lithography machines to China. In October 2022, the US announced that any company using American tools or software to produce semiconductors would require a license to export to China, regardless of where the chips are made. The US has been pressuring the Netherlands to implement comparable restrictions on its technology exports. See BBC (2023) US-China chip war: Netherlands moves to restrict some tech exports. BBC News.

[41]Wang Y (2024) It's folly for EU to follow US chip war in its economic security strategy. Glob. Times.

Different rationales have been followed by the Chinese government. Economic security has been incorporated as the most important dimension of the national security concept in China for a long time.[42] Following the collapse of the Soviet Union in 1991, China became more convinced that national security relies on a robust economic foundation in addition to military strength.[43] In 2014, during the inaugural meeting of the National Security Commission, China officially introduced the concept of 'comprehensive national security,' framing economic security as its basis.[44] In recent years, China's approach to economic security has evolved from addressing vulnerabilities associated with globalisation to tackling new concerns shaped by political factors such as perceived U.S. containment and the intensifying U.S.-China rivalry.[45] As part of its response, China has sought to reduce risks and prioritise economic security, introducing a new national security review system for foreign investments in 2021.[46] However, since the implementation of this system, there has been little public information about its practical application, and no foreign transaction has been officially blocked by the Chinese government. Consequently, there is a lack of data to assess how economic security is evaluated in China's FDI screenings.

3.2 *State's Broad Discretion*

The expanded concept of national security grants screening authorities considerable discretion in their review process, allowing ample room for justifying their decisions. State intervention can be motivated by factors beyond pure national security concerns. An increasing number of measures have been implemented to safeguard economic security, which, in reality, constitutes a means of protecting the national economy.[47] In other cases, political considerations, such as those of specific political

[42] Huang (2021), p. 26.

[43] Yuan (2022a), pp. 118–119.

[44] The First Meeting of the Chinese Central National Security Commission in 2014, see https://www.gov.cn/xinwen/2014-04/15/content_2659641.htm. Article 2 of the National Security Law of the People's Republic of China in 2015 introduced a definition of national security, which refers to 'a status in which the regime, sovereignty, unity, territorial integrity, welfare of the people, sustainable economic and social development, and other major interests of the state are relatively not faced with any danger and not threatened internally or externally and the capability to maintain a sustained security status'.

[45] Wong (2024), p. 71.

[46] Foreign Investment Law of the People's Republic of China, which is issued on March 15, 2019, effective on January 1, 2020, provides a general clause about the establishment of national security review system. Further details and procedures of the new national security review mechanism has been regulated later in the Measures for the Security Review of Foreign Investment, which entered into force on 18 January 2021.

[47] Mauro and Pernazza (2023), p. 25.

parties, can also influence investment screening decisions. FDI screenings may even be leveraged as bargaining tools in political negotiations.

For example, in the case of COSCO's proposed acquisition of a stake in one of Hamburg's terminals, differing opinions within the German government were more influenced by concerns over the relationship with China than by the actual national security risks posed by the deal itself. The internal divisions within Germany's three-party coalition government have intensified the debate on China, adding further uncertainty for businesses.[48] This case involved COSCO Shipping Ports Limited (COSCO) acquiring a 35% share in one of the terminals operated by Hamburger Hafen und Logistik AG (HHLA) in the Port of Hamburg in 2022. The German Ministry of Economics initiated a screening process, resulting in a months-long debate. Eventually, with the backing of Chancellor Olaf Scholz's Social Democrat-led ministries, the cabinet approved a reduced 24.9% stake for COSCO, which did not grant the Chinese company any influence over management or strategic decision-making.[49]

Foreign investment in ports often raises public concerns, as there is a common perception that foreign control over critical infrastructure could jeopardise national logistics and supply chains, posing potential threats to national security. However, in this particular case, the situation is notably different. HHLA clarified the case details. Firstly, as part of the planned partnership, COSCO will not acquire any shares of the Port of Hamburg; the transaction only concerns a maximum of 35% of the shares in HHLA's operating subsidiary, CTT GmbH. Secondly, CTT GmbH is ultimately an operating subsidiary. HHLA retains sole control over all significant decisions. COSCO has no exclusive rights at CTT—the terminal remains open to container volumes from all customers. Thirdly, COSCO does not gain access to strategic know-how. The port infrastructure remains the property of the City of Hamburg. IT and sales data remain the sole responsibility of HHLA.[50] Ultimately, the approved investment is less than the originally proposed 35% stake that COSCO and HHLA had sought and does not grant COSCO any influence over management or strategic decision-making.

However, Germany's painful experience with over-reliance on Russian gas has shifted many politicians' attitudes toward strategic foreign investments. Initially, there were divergent views within the Federal Chancellery and several ministries about the proposed acquisition.[51] The primary backing for halting this deal has been

---

[48] Zenglein M (2023) Germany can ignore anxious CEOs while setting China policy. In: Nikkei Asia. https://asia.nikkei.com/Opinion/Germany-can-ignore-anxious-CEOs-while-setting-China-policy.

[49] Rinke A, Schwartz J (2022) German go-ahead for China's Cosco stake in Hamburg port unleashes protest. Reuters.

[50] Hamburger Hafen und Logistik AG (HHLA) (2022) Port of Hamburg will not be sold to China. In: HHLA Hambg. Hafen Logist. AG. https://hhla.de/en/media/news/detail-view/port-of-hamburg-will-not-be-sold-to-china.

[51] Hans von der Burchard (2023) Germany's Scholz overruled Habeck to approve China port deal. POLITICO.

voiced by the Green Party, notably by the head of the Ministry of Economic Affairs, Robert Habeck. He has garnered widespread support from various federal government ministers on this matter. The Chancellor's Office, however, holds a contrasting stance and advocates for proceeding with the sale of the shares.[52] In the end, with the support of Scholz's Social Democrat-led ministries, the cabinet approved a 24.9% stake investment, interestingly, one week before Chancellor Scholz's first visit to China as Chancellor.

This decision triggered unprecedented opposition within the coalition government. According to a Reuters report, the foreign ministry, dissatisfied with the approval, prepared a formal note at the cabinet meeting to document its objection.[53] The note expressed concerns that the investment 'disproportionately expands China's strategic influence on German and European transport infrastructure, as well as Germany's dependence on China.' It also highlighted risks associated with Chinese influence and control over elements of European transport infrastructure, while China does not permit Germany to participate in Chinese ports. The economy ministry, along with four ministries led by the liberal Free Democrats, also contributed to drafting the note. Scholz, a former mayor of Hamburg, once again imposed his stance against his coalition partners, the Greens and the Free Democrats.[54]

Geopolitical factors were in play, particularly addressing concerns about whether the sale would increase Germany's economic dependency on China and whether such a development would be inconsistent with German national interests, such as security and sovereignty.[55] The Greens and most of the Free Democratic Party are inclined to diminish their economic dependence on China and gradually broaden their collaboration with other global regions, particularly democratic countries. Conversely, the Social Democratic Party of Germany and its leadership approach this issue more cautiously.[56] The Social Democrats have recently emphasised more frequently that the German economy cannot afford an open conflict with China, and that Germany should maintain diplomatically correct relations with countries even when there are differences in values. These disagreements are currently under discussion as part of the ongoing efforts to draft a new government document outlining a revised strategy toward China.[57] The pressure exerted by Scholz to sell the shares in the Hamburg terminal will likely heighten the coalition partners'

---

[52] Ibid.

[53] Rinke A, Schwartz J (2022) German go-ahead for China's Cosco stake in Hamburg port unleashes protest. Reuters.

[54] Ibid.

[55] Ibid.

[56] Gibadło L (2022) A dangerous resemblance. Moves to revise Germany's China policy. In: OSW Cent. East. Stud. https://www.osw.waw.pl/en/publikacje/osw-commentary/2022-10-19/a-dangerous-resemblance-moves-to-revise-germanys-china-policy.

[57] Ibid.

caution and prolong the time it takes for them to reach a consensus on this crucial issue for Germany's future.[58]

Political considerations among different parties not only increase the uncertainty of screening decisions but also ultimately affect the interests of domestic enterprises and further exacerbate conflicts of interest between the public and private sectors. While the Federal Ministry of Economics justified the screening by citing risks to public order and security, HHLA, the target company, disputed this view. HHLA, which is majority-owned by the city of Hamburg and one of the main users of the port, welcomed the deal, arguing that partnering with COSCO would strengthen supply chains, secure jobs, and boost economic value in Germany. HHLA further emphasised that cooperation with COSCO would not create one-sided dependencies but enhance Germany's global trade competitiveness.[59] This case illustrates how the perceived national security threat posed by foreign investment can differ significantly between the government and the business sector. For businesses, governments' broad discretion in FDI screening allows for decisions influenced by political considerations rather than genuine security concerns. As a result, screening decisions can serve as leverage in political negotiations, intensifying conflicts and introducing greater uncertainty.

3.3 *Lack of Legal Remedies*

The expanded discretion in matters of national security provides the state with increased authority, tipping the balance in its favour during conflicts. In cases of more frequent adverse screening decisions or the imposition of conditions based on national security concerns, domestic target companies, as participants in cross-border transactions, are compelled to adhere to government directives. Making a bad situation worse, the legal remedies available to these domestic companies in response to screening decisions are often limited.

In certain jurisdictions, such as the United States and China, government screening decisions are conclusive and not open to judicial review. In the United States, the President's decisions and the accompanying findings cannot be reviewed by the judiciary.[60] This arises from the separation of powers outlined in the US Constitution, and specific political questions are meant for the President or Congress alone to decide.[61] US courts frequently invoke the 'political question doctrine' to abstain

---

[58] Płóciennik S (2022) Selling shares in the Hamburg terminal: Scholz does not want a clash with China. In: OSW Cent. East. Stud. https://www.osw.waw.pl/en/publikacje/analyses/2022-10-25/selling-shares-hamburg-terminal-scholz-does-not-want-a-clash-china.

[59] Hamburger Hafen und Logistik AG (HHLA) (2022) Port of Hamburg will not be sold to China. In: HHLA Hambg. Hafen Logist. AG. https://hhla.de/en/media/news/detail-view/port-of-hamburg-will-not-be-sold-to-china.

[60] Section 721 of the Defence Production Act of 1950, 50 U.S.C. App. 4565 (e)(1).

[61] Mercado, p. 601.

from delving into the substance of national security cases, choosing instead to defer to the decisions of the executive branch. In the *Ralls* case—the first lawsuit in the history of the Committee on Foreign Investment in the US, the Court of Appeals used the political question doctrine to affirm that the President's decisions are determinations that cannot be subjected to judicial review.[62] Similarly, under China's Foreign Investment Law, all security review decisions are deemed final, without explicitly mentioning whether these decisions are subject to administrative reconsideration or judicial review.[63] Consequently, if domestic target companies wish to contest security review decisions, how they can pursue legal remedies remains unclear.

In contrast, some regions allow for legal recourse, such as the European Union, where foreign investors and affected parties can challenge national authorities' screening decisions. This is one of the critical requirements regulated by the EU FDI Screening Regulation that all EU Member States need to follow to establish their own national screening mechanisms.[64] However, only a few cases have been filed at national courts in EU Member States until now.[65] Therefore, whether these national screening mechanisms provide domestic entities with adequate and effective protection remains uncertain.

In summary, the expanding interpretation of 'national security', the broad discretion afforded to governments, and the lack of sufficient legal remedies for the private sector may lead to unwarranted government intervention in the affairs of domestic companies. When considering these factors collectively, there is a risk of an imbalance between public and private interests. In geoeconomic uncertain times, characterised by an increased likelihood of undue state intervention, companies may find themselves in an increasingly disadvantaged position. Thus, the challenge lies in achieving a better equilibrium and exploring whether efforts to rebalance interests can be made from both corporate and governmental perspectives.

4 Private Sector Participation in the Screening Process

The conflicts between public and private interests fundamentally arise from corporations' pursuit of maximising economic benefits. Typically, business managers have fiduciary responsibilities to shareholders to optimise return on investment and enhance shareholder value. However, the goals of domestic target companies

[62] *Ralls Corp. v. Committee on Foreign Investment in the US*, 758 F.3d 296 (D.C. Cir. 2014). The Court of Appeals also held that Ralls, a Chinese-owned company, was subject to due process rights.

[63] Article 35 of the Chinese Foreign Investment Law.

[64] Preamble (15) and Article 3(5) of The European Parliament and the Council of the European Union (2019) Regulation (EU) 2019/452 establishing a framework for the screening of foreign direct investments into the Union. Official Journal of the European Union.

[65] Among these cases, the *Xella Magyarorszá* (Xella) case has been sent to the ECJ for a preliminary ruling.

may not always be profit-driven. The emergence of Environmental, Social, and Governance (ESG) criteria threatens to challenge the long-standing paradigm in corporate law, which asserts that the primary purpose of a corporation is to maximise shareholder value.[66] Under the stakeholder model, companies are accountable to a variety of stakeholders, including investors, employees, consumers, and the government.[67] Firms prioritising ESG initiatives are more likely to align their strategic interests with the government's. This raises the question of whether private sector enterprises can also contribute to public interests, potentially alleviating conflicts from the company's perspective.

4.1 *The Importance of Private Sector Participation*

As the distinction between economic and national security collapses, integrating economic statecraft into foreign policy has become increasingly prevalent.[68] However, without support from the private sector, the effective implementation of government policies and measures to safeguard national security may face challenges. Acknowledging this, the government recognises the importance of engaging with key social actors, particularly private sector managers and entrepreneurs, to influence the behaviour of the national business community.

It remains uncertain whether private enterprises are willing to prioritise public interests. The understanding of threats between government and business sectors is not easily fully aligned. This disparity is evident in the growing tensions surrounding technology transfer, where the business objective of serving clients may conflict with governmental interests in restricting competitors' access to specific technologies. Scholars Borchert, Moraes & Wigell have introduced a new concept of 'corporate geoeconomics', which seeks to explain how firms strive to maintain a degree of autonomy in an economic landscape characterised by increased state intervention and how market players attempt to shape, limit, and adapt to state actions.[69] This theory contented that companies not only have the power to use and shape economic interactions across different geoeconomics domains to advance their commercial interest, termed 'direct corporate geoeconomics power'; but also the power to support or oppose governments' geoeconomics intentions, referred to as 'indirect corporate geoeconomics power'.[70]

According to this framework, private sectors may adopt different strategies and reactions to the growing number of states' geoeconomic measures and

[66] Schoenmaker et al. (2023).

[67] Romoser (2023).

[68] Gertz and Evers (2020), p. 117.

[69] Borchert (2022), pp. 31–34; Choer Moraes and Wigell (2022), pp. 44–47.

[70] Borchert (2022), pp. 32–33.

interventions.[71] The first type of response is a resistant attitude, wherein companies attempt to restrict or resist state intervention in economic matters. The second type is an accommodating attitude, where companies recognise their inability to influence government strategic aims and thus strive to adjust their operations to meet the needs of both sides. The third type is a proactive assistance attitude, where companies actively support the implementation of geoeconomic measures as a means to enhance their country's strategic competitiveness.[72] For governments, it is crucial that private sectors are willing to share a similar awareness of potential risks and, in the end, implement measures that address the dependencies effectively. In the context of foreign investment screening, although public and private stakeholders have distinct sources of information, the evolving geoeconomic environment emphasises the necessity for a more organised exchange of information and collective awareness of potential risks associated with cross-border transactions.[73] Enhanced coordination and dialogue between national policymakers and the private sector are crucial for a comprehensive strategy to mitigate national security risks, particularly in specific cases that have not received adequate attention in the past.

4.2 *The Role of Business-Government Relationship*

In navigating the delicate balance between public and private interest and facilitating public-private cooperation, the nature of domestic business-government relations plays an important role.[74] When there is a close and robust relationship between government and business, the commercial interests of companies are more likely to align with the state substantially; it is also easier for states to cooperate with firms in pursuit of geopolitical goals.[75] Thus, the degree of alignment between commercial enterprises and the state is a critical variable in assessing the effectiveness of public policies.

Most Western countries maintain a more arms-length relationship with the private sector. In the United States, the government has limited means to enforce compliance from firms and few expectations that companies will independently pursue state interests.[76] The situation in the EU is more complicated. Unlike the US, China or any other sovereign states, the EU operates as a complex supranational organisation, relying on the principle of sincere cooperation among its member states. This

[71] Choer Moraes and Wigell (2022), pp. 44–47. The authors put forward three types of corporate geoeconomics strategies: (1) business as usual; (2) one company, two systems; (3) patriotic capitalism.

[72] Ibid.

[73] Strobl and Borchert (2022), p. 9.

[74] Choer Moraes and Wigell (2022); Gertz and Evers (2020).

[75] Gertz and Evers (2020), p. 119.

[76] Ibid., pp. 117–118.

principle mandates that the EU and its member states support one another in fulfilling treaty obligations.[77] Consequently, the EU's FDI screening policy operates on two fronts: economic competitiveness, dictated by Brussels, and national security, governed by the individual member states.[78] This duality complicates the ability of companies operating within the EU to balance national and collective union interests effectively.

In contrast, China is often perceived as having a close relationship between business and government. To some extent, these deep ties can help mitigate the conflicts between public and private interests, enabling the Chinese government to leverage interdependence more effectively. However, such close connections also pose challenges for Chinese companies seeking to establish influential positions in the global economy.[79] This, in essence, also cannot fundamentally resolve the issue of conflicting interests.

4.3 EU's Attempt of Public-Private Cooperation on Economic Security

The EU has made efforts to improve public-private cooperation on economic security, encouraging the private sector to adopt an expanded definition of 'national security' and associated risks. In June 2023, the European Commission unveiled the European Economic Security Strategy to deal with the economic risks arising from increasing geopolitical competition.[80] 'De-risking' is central to the EU's new economic security strategy. Identifying and reducing undesired economic dependencies is also a top priority for European governments. Likewise, translating de-risking into practical measures requires close collaboration between governments and the private sector. To achieve this, it is crucial to gain a deeper understanding of corporate perspectives on economic security and the risks to business continuity. Therefore, the European Economic Security Strategy proposes a methodology for risk assessment. The Commission and Member States need to assess cooperation with the High Representative, where appropriate, and with input from the private sector.[81] The EU Commission further outlines various new actions, including engaging in 'a structured dialogue with the private sector to develop a collective understanding of

---

[77] Tobler and Beglinger (2020), p. 16.

[78] Nogués EC (2024) Economic security: a new age for the EU. https://www.realinstitutoelcano.org/en/commentaries/economic-security-a-new-age-for-the-eu/.

[79] Gertz and Evers (2020), p. 131.

[80] European Commission (2023) European Economic Security Strategy.

[81] Clingendael Institute (2023) De-risking responsibly: how to come to better public-private cooperation on economic security? Clingendael.

economic security and encourage them to conduct due diligence and risk management in light of economic security concerns.'[82]

The EU's initiative regarding public-private collaboration on economic security is not baseless but is supported by tangible real-world examples. A case study by Nibe examines the legitimisation of FDI screening among Danish business stakeholders. This study illustrates how the policy preferences of Danish businesses can be gradually influenced by European and local political elites in times of uncertainty. Initially, there was a general alignment between Danish businesses and the state regarding FDI screening, with little enthusiasm for its implementation. However, external pressure from the European Commission to establish a comprehensive screening mechanism to address potential security risks posed by foreign investors, coupled with internal concerns about China and the 'Huawei Storm', along with vulnerabilities exposed by the Covid-19 pandemic, led to a shift in the Danish government's perception of threats.[83] Importantly, the smooth implementation of the Danish FDI screening mechanism relies on private sector participation in the assessment process. As Danish business groups, which lean towards liberal policies, are increasingly exposed to security discourses across various levels and networks, they are gradually accepting the new geopolitical reality where economic policies are intertwined with security considerations.[84] This collaboration between businesses and policymakers has significantly mitigated the conflicting interests between the two parties, allowing for smoother implementation of screening policies with reduced resistance from the business sector.

However, corporate cooperation does not imply that companies completely abandon the pursuit of profits. Instead, they are exploring ways to sustain profitability within a more politicised environment.[85] It means that the government's intervention should not be excessive to the extent that it hampers the normal operations of domestic enterprises. Otherwise, it could severely undermine the enthusiasm for corporate collaboration.

5 The Boundary of Government Intervention

5.1 The Risk of Government Failures

With perfect markets, there is a theoretical presumption favouring the minimalist state.[86] Adam Smith famously argued that society's best interests are served through

[82] European Commission (2023) European Economic Security Strategy, p. 14.

[83] Nibe (2023), pp. 145–149.

[84] Nibe (2023).

[85] Choer Moraes and Wigell (2022), p. 47.

[86] Brown (1993), p. 3.

individual self-interest and the freedom of production and consumption.[87] Extending Smith's view, some proponents of laissez-faire economics suggest that the government's optimal contribution is minimal or nonexistent, allowing market participants to thrive or fail based on their own choices. At its extreme, this view holds that governments should refrain entirely from involvement in private enterprises, leaving companies to grow, diminish, or perish based on market forces.[88]

The existence of market failures, however, reinforces the necessity for state intervention. Economist Joseph Stiglitz categorised various types of market failures, outlining the range of possible market imperfections and the areas where government intervention may be beneficial.[89] One such instance is 'the need for public goods, desirable goods, and services that could not be produced profitably under free markets.'[90] Due to these market failures, state involvement in specific, well-defined areas of economic management, such as infrastructure, education, and basic scientific research, is widely accepted. Additionally, the existence of market power supports the need for competition policy.[91] A fundamental principle of contemporary liberal democracies is the shared pursuit of enhancing economic growth and social welfare by government and private enterprises. The government is entrusted with managing the institutional framework and providing public goods to address market failures and social conflicts.[92] Companies can pursue their economic goals in a state's strategic interest in an environment with minimal political interference.[93] Under the social market economic system, the ideological foundation is formed by the understanding that neither purely market-based nor purely planned systems are ultimately convincing from a socio-political standpoint. Thus, state intervention, particularly in foreign investment screening on national security grounds, can be seen as legitimate when aimed at implementing socio-political standards in market activities.

However, markets are not the only systems that fail—governments, too, often struggle to correct market inefficiencies. It is crucial to understand that the existence of market failures does not automatically justify interventionism. Even though the necessity for state intervention in the case of market failure is widely accepted, there are also possibilities of 'government failures'.[94] Rather than rectifying market imperfections, the government may be accused of introducing distortions. Applying public choice theory to economic policymaking implies that state bureaucrats may

[87] Wells (2013).

[88] Srivastava et al. (2022).

[89] Stiglitz (1988).

[90] Brown (1993), p. 3.

[91] Ibid., p. 3.

[92] Srivastava et al. (2022).

[93] Choer Moraes and Wigell (2022), p. 44.

[94] Stiglitz and Rosengard (2015), p. 10.

prioritise their own interests over those of the broader society.[95] Restrictive policies have been used by policymakers to win voters or strengthen authorities.[96]

Furthermore, even well-intentioned government actions can lead to government failure, as political and economic constraints may limit a state's capacity to implement its desired policies.[97] Government undue intervention in foreign investment, for instance, can be seen as a form of 'government failure'. When States use FDI screening tools to achieve strategic goals, they may unintentionally distort markets, rather than effectively address genuine national security concerns. Therefore, the question remains: to what extent should the government intervene in the affairs of private enterprises? Shall the government play a relatively restrained or active role in balancing the conflict between public and private interests? How do we preserve company autonomy while preventing undue government interference, especially in times of geoeconomic uncertainty?

5.2 *Approach for a Desirable Extent of Intervention*

Recognising the limitations of government intervention further implies that governmental actions should focus on areas where market failures are most pronounced and where there is clear evidence that intervention can make a meaningful difference.[98] Irrespective of the chosen approach, a state's right to invoke national security interests must be subject to certain limits.

Various international initiatives have been undertaken concerning the fundamental principles of law that necessitate safeguarding national security within the context of globalisation, such as the guidelines set forth by the Organisation for Economic Co-operation and Development (OECD), the United Nations Conference on Trade and Development (UNCTAD), and other international instruments. These instruments, being recommendations, although non-binding, have served as guides for states in determining the limits of the national security approach and mitigating the impact on investment flows.[99] For example, the OECD Guidelines for Recipient Country Investment Policies relating to National Security set out four principles: (1) non-discrimination, (2) transparency of policies and predictability of outcome, (3) proportionality of measures, and (4) accountability of the implementing authorities.[100] Similarly, the G20 Guiding Principles for Global Investment Policymaking promote non-binding principles, including transparency and coherence, to guide

[95] Buchanan and Tullock (1965); See also, Brown (1993), p. 4.

[96] Nibe (2023), p. 142; Schill (2019).

[97] Brown (1993), p. 4.

[98] Stiglitz and Rosengard (2015), p. 10.

[99] Accaoui Lorfing (2021), p. 179.

[100] Guidelines for Recipient Country Investment Policies relating to National Security, Recommendation adopted by the OECD Council on 25 May 2009. The exact text is in the OECD

investment policymaking.[101] However, these guidelines and principles are based on states' shared consensus that globalisation benefits all market players, and economic interdependence would foster peace and cooperation by increasing the costs of interstate conflict.[102] It remains uncertain whether states will continue to adhere to these non-binding principles in the current geopolitical and geoeconomic uncertainty era. This raises the question of what new considerations policymakers should be aware of in FDI screening when balancing national security concerns with the autonomy of domestic companies in the cross-border takeover market.

It is exceedingly difficult to distinguish between justified and undue intervention by the state. The best approach might be to set up a procedure for weighing the benefits and costs of intervention. Jackson proposed a potential method involving a complex cost-benefit analysis that could assess the economic impact of more restrictive investment policies and facilitate the differentiation between absolute national security concerns and economic protectionism.[103] This analysis is centred on the concept of marginal cost and benefits to the nation associated with FDI screening policies, where the benefits include a combination of economic and non-economic advantages anticipated from the restrictions, while the costs encompass a set of actual costs expected to be borne by the economy due to these policies. Presumably, national policymakers would need to justify the economic costs by ensuring that the economic benefits are at least as substantial as the non-economic benefits. If the non-economic benefits constitute the majority of the expected advantages resulting from the policy action, adopting such a policy might resemble economic protectionism under the guise of national security. Policymakers might benefit the nation more by pursuing an alternative policy course that incurs fewer economic costs.[104] However, conducting such a cost-benefit analysis presents several challenges, particularly in peacetime when there is no immediate national security threat, and the complexity on a multilateral basis given that each nation has its own understanding. In most cases, government interventions to halt or limit foreign direct investment through mergers, acquisitions, or takeovers are primarily precautionary measures aimed at addressing potential future actions that a foreign investor might undertake, rather than addressing immediate threats. Since there is often no concrete data available for such assessment, making accurate cost-benefit calculations is difficult, if not impossible.[105]

When governments do intervene, a 'functional' rather than a 'selective' approach is advisable. Functional interventions address general market failures without

---

Recommendation of the Council on Guidelines for Recipient Country Investment Policies relating to National Security, OECD/LEGAL/0372.

[101] UNCTAD Investment Policy Hub (2016) UNCTAD facilitates G20 consensus on Guiding Principles for Global Investment Policymaking.

[102] Gartzke (2007).

[103] Jackson (2013b), pp. 18–22.

[104] Ibid., p. 22.

[105] Yuan (2022b), pp. 22–24.

favouring one activity over another. In contrast, selective interventions narrow their focus to specific activities.[106] Selectivity involves the challenging task of 'picking winners,' which increases the likelihood of government failure in this context. The US, for example, continues to perceive economic security through the lens of the Cold War, viewing it as a form of economic warfare against strategic rivals. While nuclear deterrence was the primary weapon in the past, today, economic deterrence takes the form of export restrictions, customs duties, and limitations on foreign investments.[107] There are concerns that the EU compromising to the US pressure will further undermine global economic cooperation. The EU's Economics Security Strategy mentions that the new instruments would be applied with proportionality and precision to limit any unintended adverse spill-over effects on the European and global economies.[108] It is hoped that EU policymakers will prioritise the concerns raised by the business community over the influence of US lobbying, as overly broad restrictions in the name of national security could harm domestic companies' competitiveness. The potential risks stemming from 'de-risking' may outweigh any associated benefits.[109]

Given the close interconnections among states, it is questionable whether a Cold War-style approach is viable in today's global economy. No country can secure economic security in isolation. States often find themselves trapped in a cycle of retaliatory actions, responding tit-for-tat out of fear of being left vulnerable. This tendency to mirror negative actions can escalate crises and erode trust. Rather than focusing on the actions of others, states should concentrate on defining their own interests and developing strategies accordingly. Today's concerns about economic interdependence go beyond straightforward legal issues and cannot be solved solely through legal frameworks. At its core, this is a matter of trust. The theme of the 2024 Davos World Economic Forum, 'Rebuilding Trust', offers a timely platform for fostering a new global order of trust.[110] The current geopolitical landscape is marked by tensions that could lead to heightened economic fragmentation driven by competition for technological leadership between the West and China, and fostering increased collaboration between the two sides of the Atlantic becomes more desirable. This collaboration aims to avoid protectionist impulses and seek alternatives for preserving globalisation through novel forms of 're-coupling' rather than 'decoupling.[111]

---

[106] Pack and Westphal (1986).

[107] Tentori D (2023) Towards an Atlantic 'Economic Security'? ISPI.

[108] European Commission (2023) European Economic Security Strategy, p. 3.

[109] Wang Y (2024) It's folly for EU to follow US chip war in its economic security strategy. Glob. Times.

[110] World Economic Forum (2024) Davos 2024: Why we must restore mutual trust in the world. In: World Econ. Forum. https://www.weforum.org/agenda/2024/01/rebuilding-trust-collaberation-future/.

[111] Tentori D (2023) Towards an Atlantic 'Economic Security'? ISPI.

6 Conclusion

The global shift from liberal to more restrictive foreign investment policies reflects growing concerns over national security in an era of increasing geoeconomic tension. Governments are increasingly using FDI screening mechanisms to intervene in foreign takeovers, driven by the erosion of the traditional separation between economic and national security concerns. However, while safeguarding national security is critical, these interventions can conflict with domestic companies' goals of maximising value and competing globally. The challenge lies in striking a balance between market failures and the risk of government overreach. Broad, unchecked government discretion complicates this balance, as national security remains ambiguously defined and is often used to justify restrictive economic measures. In these uncertain geoeconomic times, it is essential to rebalance the roles of the public and private sectors based on their respective strengths. Governments should work closely with businesses to mitigate genuine security risks while avoiding policies that stifle economic growth or global competitiveness.

The government and businesses can work together to mitigate potential security risks at the forefront of policy-making and corporate decision-making to ensure a prosperous future for all. States shall, on the one hand, strive for the cooperation of private firms and try to persuade private sectors to share a similar awareness of potential risks; on the other hand, limit their unrestricted expansionist interpretation of the concept of national security. In an interconnected world, reverting to the attitudes of the Cold War era is not a viable solution. The expansion of the concept of national security is more the result of the impulsive actions of countries in the current context of great power rivalry. States should exercise greater caution when wielding their public power. It is the rule of law, instead of rule by law, that can help us to get out of the dilemma of lose-lose. FDI screening mechanisms should be narrowly tailored to address specific national security risks, without being used as tools for broader economic protectionism or national prestige. A precise, principled framework for invoking the national security exception—rooted in good faith and transparency—can help preserve both state sovereignty and the rights of private enterprises. Ultimately, this balanced approach can help ensure a more equitable, stable relationship between national security imperatives and economic openness, benefiting both states and companies in the long term.

References

Accaoui Lorfing P (2021) Screening of foreign direct investment and the states' security interests in light of the OECD, UNCTAD and other international guidelines. In: Titi C (ed) Public actors in international investment law. Springer International Publishing, Cham, pp 179–199

Acconci P (2023) The relationship between a host state and a foreign corporate investor: a few remarks under international and the EU law. In: Mauro MR, Pernazza F (eds) State and enterprise. Springer International Publishing, Cham, pp 285–305

Bauerle Danzman S, Meunier S (2021) The big screen: mapping the diffusion of foreign investment screening mechanisms. SSRN Electron J. https://doi.org/10.2139/ssrn.3913248

Bian C (2021) Foreign direct investment screening and national security: reducing regulatory hurdles to investors through induced reciprocity. J World Invest Trade 22:561–595. https://doi.org/10.1163/22119000-12340218

Blackwill RD, Harris JM (2016) War by other means: geoeconomics and statecraft. Harvard University Press

Borchert H (2022) New geoeconomics: a primer. In: Storms ahead: the future geoeconomic world order

Brown J (1993) The role of the state in economic development: theory, the east Asian experience, and the Malaysian case

Buchanan JM, Tullock G (1965) The calculus of consent: logical foundations of constitutional democracy. University of Michigan Press

Choer Moraes H, Wigell M (2022) Balancing dependence: the quest for autonomy and the rise of corporate geoeconomics. In: The political economy of geoeconomics: Europe in a changing world. Springer, pp 29–55

Eisenhut D (2010) Sovereignty, national security and international treaty law. The standard of review of international courts and tribunals with regard to 'security exceptions'. Arch Völkerr 48:431–466

Gadocha PM (2020) Assessing the EU framework regulation for the screening of foreign direct investment—what is the effect on Chinese investors? Chin J Glob Gov 6:36–70. https://doi.org/10.1163/23525207-12340046

Gartzke E (2007) The capitalist peace. Am J Polit Sci 51:166–191. https://doi.org/10.1111/j.1540-5907.2007.00244.x

Gertz G, Evers MM (2020) Geoeconomic competition: will state capitalism win? Wash Q 43:117–136. https://doi.org/10.1080/0163660X.2020.1770962

Giofré M (2013) Investor protection rights and foreign investment. J Comp Econ 41:506–526

Hatchondo JC, Martinez L (2011) Legal protection to foreign investors. FRB Richmond Econ Q 97:175–187

Heath JB (2020) The new national security challenge to the economic order. Yale Law J 129:1020–1098

Henrique Choer Moraes (2024) Foreword: the dissemination of investment screening mechanisms - the vocabulary for a new logic driving global economic relations. In: Weaponising Investments

Huang C (2021) China's take on national security and its implications for the evolution of international economic law. Leg Issues Econ Integr 48

Jackson JK (2013a) The Exon-Florio National Security Test for Foreign Investment

Jackson JK (2013b) Foreign investment and national security: economic considerations

Kelsen H (1948) Collective security and collective self-defense under the Charter of the United Nations. Am J Int Law 42:783–796

Mauro MR, Pernazza F (2023) General introduction: state and enterprise in the global market. In: Mauro MR, Pernazza F (eds) State and enterprise. Springer International Publishing, Cham, pp 1–50

Mercado H Resolving national security questions: a comparative analysis of judicial review in the United States, Israel, and Europe. 51

Nibe AV (2023) Legitimisation of foreign direct investment screening among business actors: the Danish case. Polit Gov 11:140–153

OECD (2008) Essential security interests under international investment law. In: International Investment Perspectives 2007. OECD, pp 93–134

Pack H, Westphal LE (1986) Industrial strategy and technological change: theory versus reality. J Dev Econ 22:87–128

Roberts A, Choer Moraes H, Ferguson V (2018) Geoeconomics: the variable relationship between economics and security

Roberts A, Choer Moraes H, Ferguson V (2019) Toward a geoeconomic order in international trade and investment. J Int Econ Law 22:655–676. https://doi.org/10.1093/jiel/jgz036
Romoser K (2023) Corporate ESG initiatives: a complicating factor in national security policy
Rosén G, Meunier S (2023) Economic security and the politics of trade and investment policy in Europe. Polit Gov 11:122–128. https://doi.org/10.17645/pag.v11i4.7858
Schill SW (2019) The European Union's Foreign Direct Investment screening paradox: tightening inward investment control to further external investment liberalization. Leg Issues Econ Integr 46
Schoenmaker D, Schramade W, Winter J (2023) Corporate governance beyond the shareholder and stakeholder model. Erasmus Law Rev 16:27–35. https://doi.org/10.5553/ELR.000237
Srivastava A, Silva FBG, Ilyas H, Enache L (2022) Reassessing the boundaries of government. Calif Manag Rev Insights
Stiglitz JE (1988) Economics of the public sector
Stiglitz JE, Rosengard JK (2015) Economics of the public sector, Fourth edition, international student edition. W.W. Norton & Company, Inc, New York London
Strobl J, Borchert H (eds) (2022) Storms ahead: the future geoeconomic world order
Te Velde DW, Trade UNC on, Development (2006) Foreign direct investment and development: an historical perspective. Overseas Development Institute ODI London
Tobler C, Beglinger J (2020) Essential EU law in text. HVG-ORAC
Wells TR (2013) Adam Smith on morality and self-interest
Wong A (2024) China's Perspective on Economic Security
Yuan J (2022a) Chinese national security: new agendas and emerging challenges. In: Clarke M, Henschke A, Sussex M, Legrand T (eds) The Palgrave handbook of national security. Springer International Publishing, Cham, pp 117–138
Yuan Y (2022b) Economic security considerations in FDI screening. Law Econ Yrly Rev 11:64–93
Yuan Y, Koster H (2024) Tilted balance to security or economy? A comparative study of national security review mechanisms in the Netherlands and the United States. Eur Co Law 21

GPSR Compliance

The European Union's (EU) General Product Safety Regulation (GPSR) is a set of rules that requires consumer products to be safe and our obligations to ensure this.

If you have any concerns about our products, you can contact us on ProductSafety@springernature.com

In case Publisher is established outside the EU, the EU authorized representative is:

Springer Nature Customer Service Center GmbH
Europaplatz 3
69115 Heidelberg, Germany

Batch number: 08545060

Printed by Printforce, the Netherlands